AMERICAN FOREIGN POLICY
LATIN AMERICA IN THE 80s AND 90s

AMERICAN FOREIGN POLICY TOWARD LATIN AMERICA IN THE 80s AND 90s

Issues and Controversies from Reagan to Bush

Howard J. Wiarda

NEW YORK UNIVERSITY PRESS
New York and London

NEW YORK UNIVERSITY PRESS
New York and London

Copyright © 1992 by New York University
All rights reserved

Library of Congress Cataloging-in-Publication Data
Wiarda, Howard J., 1939-
American foreign policy toward Latin America in the 80s and 90s :
issues and controversies from Reagan to Bush / Howard J. Wiarda.
p. cm.
Includes bibliographical references and index.
ISBN 0-8147-9250-2
1. Latin America–Foreign relations–United States.   2. United
States–Foreign relations–Latin America.   3. Latin America–Foreign
relations–1948-   4. United States–Foreign relations–1981-1989.
5. United States–Foreign relations–1989-   I. Title.
F1418.W648   1992
327.7308–dc20   92-80
                                                                     CIP

New York University Press books are printed on acid-free paper,
and their binding materials are chosen for strength and durability.

Manufactured in the United States of America

c 10 9 8 7 6 5 4 3 2 1

Contents

Preface

It is always somewhat embarrassing to pull together one's earlier papers and articles and publish them in book form. To do so seems rather immodest. But in this case I am encouraged to complete the project by the facts that (1) friends, colleagues, and readers have urged me to do so; (2) many of these pieces were published in obscure places or were never published before; and (3) the subject matter of U.S. foreign policy in Latin America in the Reagan and Bush administrations is so important that a great variety of approaches to and perspectives on the policy deserve to see the light of publication.

This is actually the third in a trilogy of volumes on U.S.-Latin America policy in the 1980s and 1990s. The first, entitled *In Search of Policy: The United States and Latin America,* was published by the American Enterprise Institute in 1984. As the title implies, it reflected the skepticism I felt about early Reagan administration policy in Latin America, and was part of a process by which the Latin American studies program at AEI sought to encourage the administration in more centrist and responsible directions. The second, *Finding Our Way? Toward Maturity in U.S.-Latin American Relations,* was published in 1987 by AEI and the University Press of America. This volume, as reflected in the title, was more hopeful: it was a product of my work on the National Bipartisan (Kissinger) Commission on Central America and of the sense I had that U.S. policy in Latin America *was* becoming more sophisticated, balanced, and multifaceted.

The present volume takes up where the previous two left off, analyzing the transition from Reagan to Bush and the issues and policies of the contemporary period. Mr. Bush is a more sophisticated foreign policy practitioner than was Mr. Reagan, but that does not necessarily translate into better policy toward Latin America. Along with his skillful secretary of state (and campaign manager), James Baker, Mr. Bush has largely finessed Latin America, gotten it off our front pages and television screens, and, with the exception of the underfunded Enterprise for the Americas

Initiative, followed a policy of "benign neglect." Meanwhile Latin America, as the essays included here make clear, runs the danger of falling into a "black hole"—poor, neglected, marginalized, and of decreasing importance to U.S. policy.

I began this preface with an apology for the chutzpah of bringing out one's own essays in a collected volume, but actually I would like to make a plea for more of these kinds of collections. My experience in Washington during the 1980s taught me that many times the most important papers influencing policy never see the light of day and are completely unknown by scholars, who thus often make erroneous judgments about policy on the basis of incomplete facts. The papers that I have in mind, for example, are those prepared at AEI for the incoming Reagan administration, the background and briefing papers prepared for the Kissinger Commission, those prepared by Georges Fauriol and William Perry for the incoming Bush administration, and the papers of Peter Field that served as the basis for Bush's Enterprise for the Americas Initiative. All of these are crucial documents in shaping policy, but few of them have ever been published and they are all but completely unknown in the academic community.

So let's have more, not less, of these kinds of collections, uneven though they sometimes are. The papers collected are not always the most elegantly written and they are often overtaken by events; but they do represent policy in the making, often written while the policy was being made or to influence the policy, and they are invaluable both as primary sources and as secondary analyses by those close to power. Let's make these papers available and let scholars and practitioners, not just editorial boards and academic reviewers, decide what is worthwhile and what should be available in the public domain. I believe that would better serve the goals both of scholarship and of policy; and since I spent all those years at AEI, I suppose this could be justified as a plea for letting market forces decide!

During the 1980s and on into the 1990s four institutions have been particularly important in enabling me to carry out a rather large and ambitious research agenda. These are the department of Political Science at the University of Massachusetts/Amherst, where I have good colleagues, which has been "home" for many years, and which has been exceedingly generous with its leave policy; the Center for International Affairs at Harvard, which has long supported my work on Comparative Politics and Political Development and which has provided a research position for many years; AEI, where I spent many stimulating years in Washington and which continued generously to provide me with a Washington office; and the Foreign Policy Research Institute in Philadelphia, where I was the Thornton D. Hooper Fellow in National Security Affairs and with which I also maintain a continuing relationship. None of these institutions bear any direct responsibility for this work—that is mine alone—but over the years they have certainly been supportive, stimulating institutions with which to be associated.

I am fortunate to have a wonderful family that has also been supportive of my endeavors; above all, thanks go to Dr. Ieda Siqueira Wiarda, who has never allowed her own blossoming professional career to get in the way of what she believes to be even higher family obligations.

H.J.W

Introduction

During the course of the 1980s, President Ronald Reagan introduced some profound and very controversial changes into United States foreign policy toward Latin America. Now, several years after the end of his tenure and well into the 1990s and the Bush administration, things have calmed down and one wonders how much has really changed. We seem to have come full cycle, after the human rights activism of the Carter administration and the conservative policies of Reagan, back to a position under Bush of benign neglect, which is not unlike the policies of the administrations that predated Carter. Meanwhile, Latin America itself remains poor, neglected, and marginalized, still searching for an appropriate development strategy.

Actually, I believe that a great deal *has* changed in the interim, both in U.S. Latin America policy and in Latin America itself. But before returning to that analysis, let me say a few words about my own role in and perspectives on these issues. I do not intend to make this a memoir but some background information is useful to provide setting and context for the analyses that follow.

I had been a longtime Democrat who had been for John F. Kennedy in 1960, Lyndon Johnson in 1964, and Hubert Humphrey in 1968. But as a political scientist I was turned off by the sheer ineptness of the McGovern campaign in 1972 (run by future senator Gary Hart) and then by what I viewed as excessively romantic, amateurish, and heavily ideological influences creeping into the Democratic party's foreign policy in the 1970s. Nevertheless, I had served as a sometimes adviser and consultant to both the Ford and Carter administrations.

In December, 1980, I was invited by Jeane Kirkpatrick, a longtime academic friend, to serve with her as one of the deputy ambassadors at the United States United Nations mission in New York. This was an exciting and heady opportunity, a wonderful chance to see policy in action, and so the prerequisite background checks began. But it turned out that Jeane had offered more ambassadorships than there were am-

1

bassadorial positions available at the United Nations. So she asked if I might instead be interested in coming to the American Enterprise Institute for Public Policy Research, to serve as director of AEI's program in Latin American studies.

When I flew to Washington for the interview for an AEI Resident Scholar and Program Director position, I was not quite sure what to expect. I knew AEI as a conservative and business-oriented think tank, and I expected that the institution would have a conservative orthodoxy. That would have left me very uncomfortable. Instead what I found was a genuine commitment to "the competition of ideas in a free society" (AEI's motto), a political science group probably as good and as noni-deological as any political science department in the country (Austin Ranney, Howard Penniman, Thomas Mann, Norman Ornstein, Michael Malbin, Robert Pranger, Jeane Kirkpatrick, Evron Kirkpatrick, Richard Neustadt, Giovanni Sartori, Nelson Polsby), and an AEI administration without overriding ideological preconceptions. I consider myself a scholar first and foremost, and politically a moderate; so I remember during the interview asking AEI President William Baroody, Jr., about my concerns for serious scholarship. He assured me not only that I would be free to reach the conclusions to which my research led me, but also that no one would ever even tell me what projects to undertake. Under these conditions of absolutely free scholarship, I accepted the AEI position.

I spent the next three years, 1981–84, at AEI. During the following two years, 1984–86, I lived in Amherst and resumed my teaching obligations so as to retain my tenured professorship in a lovely part of the country, meanwhile commuting to Washington on weekends (Thursday night–Monday evening) to carry out AEI obligations. From 1986–88 I went back to AEI on another extended leave.

I consider those AEI years to be not only the most productive but also among the most intellectually stimulating of my life. The reason I describe them in some detail here is that being associated with AEI gave me access to institutions and levels of policy-making, often described in these pages, that I would never have had as a university-based academic. I served as a consultant to the State Department and the Department of the Army, lectured and consulted at the Department of Defense and the Central Intelligence Agency, taught in the Foreign Service's training program, hobnobbed with the CEOs of major U.S. corporations, got to know journalists and lobbyists, was called on by the National Security Council and the White House for advice, served as the lead consultant to the Kissinger Commission, and was appointed by President Reagan to a

White House task force. All this was rather heady stuff. I mention all these connections not to sound egotistical but to indicate the levels of access by which the papers in this collection are often informed. Being on the inside also gave me greater knowledge of the details and, I am sure, therefore also greater empathy for American policy than was true of most university-based academics. However, I did not become an ideologue—a posture that kept me from getting some high-level government positions for which I was nominated—and chose to retain my scholarly independence. One American ambassador and high-level Reagan official liked to describe me during the 1980s as "the last moderate left in Washington."

In another book,[1] I have described the role and increasing influence of the Washington think tanks on policy-making, including, now, in the area of foreign policy. There is no need to repeat all that analysis here, but some comments should be offered as a way of placing the papers collected in this volume in their proper policy context. Several issues need to be addressed. The first is, why do Washington think tank scholars have more influence on policy than university-based scholars who may be just as good? The first reason is sheer proximity: the think tank scholars are close to where policy is made, only a short walk or ride from the State Department or other policy-making agencies, close to the talk-show studios that enable them to reach a national audience and especially the audience of Washington policymakers, and therefore the think tank scholars are called on for advice far more often than university academics. A second reason is that the think tank scholars stay closely attuned to the bureaucratic, political, and personal rivalries and factions in Washington, and therefore know how, where, and when to plug their analyses into the policy-making process in ways that those outside of Washington cannot possibly know.

A third reason the think tanks are influential is that they host seemingly endless lunches, dinners, seminars, receptions, conferences, and now even breakfasts at which the research and writings of their scholars are highlighted and the audience consists of congressmen and their aides, executive agency personnel, journalists, and others who either make policy or are in a position to influence it. These functions help make think tank personnel part of the "in" group, make their ideas well known to important people, and put them on a first name basis with policy makers and policy influentials—all of which translates into access and influence. A rule of thumb that we observed at AEI was that if a desk officer, a congressional staffer, an assistant secretary, or a National Security Council (NSC) official had *your* book, paper, or article open and in front of him or her while writing a memo or options paper for the secretary, the congressman, or the president, then you had influence.

Think tanks provide some important services for the government, a number of which may even be deemed essential. First and foremost, we carried out our own research projects, put together anthologies of others' research and writing, and spoke virtually every day at conferences, symposia, seminars, and forums. I did books and anthologies on human rights policy, Central America, Brazil, Spain, trade policy, the Soviet presence in Latin America, and Latin America in general; in addition, I wrote a large number of papers, perhaps twenty–thirty of them per year, of varying length.[2] The chief purpose of these books and papers was to enlighten, not in a partisan way, but to teach policymakers, who had never paid much serious attention to Latin America before but now by force of circumstances were called upon to do so, what Latin America was all about, what its main institutions were, how it functioned. In the early 1980s policymakers were *hungry* for good, careful, balanced analyses of Latin America—as distinct from the usual partisan pleading, of which there was a great deal also. Essentially I did at AEI what I do in my classrooms: inform and instruct about Latin America but without imposing my own political biases on the subject. Sometimes I would be called on to provide a political message as well, but I never felt comfortable in that role; after being a scholar for so long, it's hard to change coats and function as a pure partisan. But whether it was a political or a more scholarly forum, the big difference between Amherst and Washington was that influential people were now listening and incorporating my ideas into their own policy recommendations.

Second, but related, our role at AEI was to provide, in the form of memos, letters, and telephone conversations as well as personal get-togethers, the ideas and arguments that congressmen or executive agency officials could use in their own speeches and statements. Because congressmen and White House or State Department officials are exceedingly busy and seldom have the time to do so, the think tanks often do their thinking for them. That is, the think tanks may prepare budgets for the departments, may prepare congressional testimony, may write speeches, may prepare policy options papers, or—most importantly—may provide the background, arguments, and rationales as to why an administration should follow such and such a policy, or why a congressman should vote in certain ways.

Third, the more partisan of the think tanks, such as the Heritage Foundation, may actually instruct a congressman on *how* he or she should vote or an administration on which policy it should pursue. The reason for this function, again, is that congressmen and executive agency personnel are very busy people; they do not have time to read all the literature on a given issue, and they may not know how their constituents or the voting public will react to a given vote. The think tanks can prepare the background materials and examine the constituency implications of a vote in detailed ways that not only congressmen but also often their aides cannot.

Fourth, think tanks provide important linkage, brokerage, and transmission belt functions. Congressmen and White House staffers do not have the time to get into the sometimes arcane arguments about corporatism, dependency theory, or bureaucratic authoritarianism. Nor do they often see the relevance of the highly abstract, theoretical, conceptual, methodological, and sometimes ideological analyses that scholars present. The congressman or policymaker may need to be aware of these intellectual currents and interpretations but he or she also needs to know how to vote or what actions to take *today*. Hence, one of the important functions that the think tanks perform is to take academic writings on an issue and put them in terms a congressman or policymaker can understand, deal with, and act upon. The academic literature needs to be rendered in terms that are relevant for the political and bureaucratic pressures and realities of Washington that the congressmen or policymakers must face in *their* jobs and on an everyday basis. So at AEI one of my roles was to organize conferences, convoke seminars, preside over forums, etc., bringing in outside academic experts, at which we would take the best of the academic literature and translate it into terms that policymakers could deal with, understand, and see the relevance of. These activities also necessitated that we write in a different style—clear, unburdened by "heavy" concepts, aimed at an informed but still general reader, about midway between journalism and the turgid prose of much academic writing. These intermediation and transmission belt roles are somewhat removed from traditional academic scholarship but I am convinced that in this modern age, when so many activities need to be brokered, such activities are essential if foreign policy is to be informed by the most enlightened thinking on the subject.[3]

Many academics are frustrated policymakers; the years at AEI gave me, as one of those academics, the possibility actually to influence policy. How was that done and what, if any, results could be observed? First, it must be said that measuring who has influence on what precise policies is always an imprecise science; such evaluation is even more hazardous if it is one's own influence that one seeks to assess. It is probably better to say what we did. The endless conferences, forums, seminars, etc., at AEI and elsewhere have already been mentioned; no one can be sure what impact these all had, but we had little doubt that they had some. Second, I was called on numerous occasions by the State Department, the CIA, the Defense Department, and the White House to brief their personnel on Central America and Latin America more generally. Third, I have to assume that someone read all those books and papers my division at AEI was producing because they were distributed widely and had to be reprinted numerous times; the language of these works also found their way into various government documents and policy position papers. Fourth, many U.S. ambassadors assigned to Latin America during this period came to see me for a briefing at AEI before heading for their posts: my message to them was to keep their eye on domestic politics in the United States *as well as* what was happening in El Salvador or Nicaragua.

Many Latin American ambassadors and delegations from the Latin American countries also stopped by at AEI, no doubt thinking—given the Institute's reputation for influence on policy at that time—that as soon as they left my office, I would surely call up Ron or Nancy or George or Jeane or Cap and tell them that we should support this or that faction of the Peronistas or other groups. Several times per week such delegations would seek an audience at AEI; Latin American presidential candidates also learned that it was de rigueur to stop at AEI on their visits to Washington. Naturally, since it enhanced my own importance, I didn't disabuse these visitors of the notion that AEI had such influence; and sometimes I did in fact pass recommendations on to the persons named.

I also hosted lunches several times a week at AEI where I would bring together friends, colleagues, and policymakers for an elegant meal, some white wine, and a couple of hours of conversation. Whenever I heard of anyone in Washington doing something interesting on Latin America, I would invite that person over for one of AEI's superb (and subsidized) lunches. As an aside, I note that it was striking to me how often a free lunch or an honorarium for speaking or writing for one of our projects served to break down whatever ideological qualms an individual might have about being involved with AEI. In any case, our table at AEI became a center where ambassadors, NSC staffers, congressmen, legislative assistants, assistant secretaries, bank officials, journalists, and others could all come together, unwind, eat, and discuss the latest policy. Not knowing quite what he was up to but hearing that he was doing interesting and important things, we invited Ollie North to grace our lunch gatherings on various occasions. My assessment then, as now, and as reflected in my *journal* entries for this period, was that this was a person whose energy and ambition outran his talents and abilities, who was in way over his head, and who could not possibly control all the projects he had launched.

Direct influence on policy was probably exercised most clearly through my position as Lead Consultant to the National Bipartisan (Kissinger) Commission on Central America in 1983–84. My functions for the Commission included lining up witnesses for the commissioners to hear, recruiting other consultants (one Democrat, one Republican for each of the main topics the Commission was investigating), and preparing position papers and chapter drafts for the Commission's report. We also spent a very nervous weekend lobbying heavily with the White House to ensure that a centrist and moderate report would not be repudiated by a very conservative administration (Edwin Meese was actually the first reader of the report). After all, this was a White House commission, appointed by President Reagan, so that if its report was repudiated by the president, it would have no impact at all on the larger policy process. Through this Commission and its report, I believe we succeeded in moving Reagan administration Central America policy a few degrees back toward the center and the mainstreams of American foreign policy. The broader context of those efforts as well as the setbacks are analyzed in more detail in chapter 1.

The Ronald Reagan that I observed during this period, several times up close and personally at the White House, other times at larger dinners and lunches, was not the Ronald Reagan that has been portrayed in several recent derogatory journalistic accounts. The Reagan I talked to during this period was sharp, informed, invariably courteous, and on top of the issues—not the "sleepy," detached, uninvolved person of recent interpretation. Moreover, it was our impression that the staff system, which consisted during the first term of the "troika" of Michael Deaver, Edwin Meese, and James Baker, somehow worked efficiently, smoothly, and rather well. These men not only complemented each other despite their vast differences but they were often also able to bring out the best in their president. Under Donald Regan the staff system worked far less well in the second term; in addition, by then Reagan was visibly older, had been shot, had been operated on several times, and was a lame duck president. The "detached, uninvolved" view of the president that now dominates the literature was probably a product of the last half of the second term; it certainly was not an accurate picture for the first term, when I saw Reagan most often.

In the sessions where I met with him, Reagan was very much concerned about Central America but not "obsessed" with it, as some of the critical accounts have alleged. He believed that in Central America the Cold War was coming awfully close to home, that the Soviet Union and Cuba were manipulating these conflicts for their own advantage and to embarrass the United States (undoubtedly true), and that it was his duty to stand up to and resist these aggressions. President Reagan never believed that the Contras were the "moral equivalent of the founding fathers" (that was a phrase Patrick Buchanan had inserted into one of his speeches) nor did he believe that the conflicts in Central America were the products of the East-West struggle alone. He understood that the basic causes were poverty, class differences, and injustice; but he also believed (correctly) that the Soviet Union was seeking to exacerbate these conditions for its own purposes. As president, he believed he had an obligation primarily to respond to these national security concerns.

I recall one particular session with Reagan where we discussed Nicaragua policy and laid out the options for him: (1) do nothing and try to live with the Sandinistas, (2) try to resolve our bilateral differences through diplomacy, (3) impose an economic embargo and political pressure, (4) break diplomatic relations and enforce a full blockade, (5) use CIA activities and support of the Contras, and (6) intervene militarily with U.S. troops to oust the regime. The pros and cons of each of these alternatives were carefully weighed. Reagan rejected the first option as not living up to his responsibilities as president, and the last option as politically unacceptable. After considerable discussion he also rejected option 4 because he felt on the one hand that a blockade was an act of war and at the same time he wanted to keep the diplomatic channels open for possible future discussion. That left options 2,3, and 5.

But among these three, Reagan refused to choose. He wanted to keep maximum pressure on the Sandinista regime but at the same time keep open the possibilities for future diplomacy. In fact, Reagan insisted on playing these cards so close to his chest that few if any people on his staff knew exactly where he stood. That, it seemed to me then, and now, was very clever and shrewd on his part, for he could simultaneously pressure the Sandinistas and at the same time remain open to a diplomatic solution. Now, one can still argue with the policy or the options chosen; but that is a far cry from saying Reagan was detached and uninvolved. In fact, in this and other meetings with the president, I found him to be not only always cordial at a surface level but also at other levels clever, manipulative, and even Machiavellian. As a political scientist I have to say that I admire this capacity in a politician to act simultaneously at several different levels; that is, after all, what sophisticated observers admire about Franklin Delano Roosevelt, whom Reagan not only also admired but also sought to imitate in various ways.

Both Jimmy Carter and Ronald Reagan, we know, were political outsiders, part of whose campaigns involved running against Washington, D.C. This is arguably acceptable as a campaign tactic but the realities are that one cannot govern effectively without utilizing the "movers and shakers," the experienced politicians and bureaucrats, of Washington. The trouble with Jimmy Carter was that he continued his anti–Washington stance even after he became president, and therefore never learned how effectively to operate in the Capital City. Reagan had also campaigned against Washington, but once in office he effectively socialized and schmoozed with congressmen, lobbyists, and think tank personnel. That is why, in terms of its accomplishments—and again, regardless of one's political proclivities—the Reagan administration is widely considered to have been more effective in terms of carrying out its legislative agenda than the Carter administration.

Both administrations went through learning processes, particularly about foreign affairs, while in office. I talk about this later in more detail in the book, but at least the rough outlines need to be provided here. Both President Carter and President Reagan came out of the more ideological wings of their respective parties. Carter came from the left wing of the Democratic party and his early policies and appointments reflected those proclivities. Reagan came from the right wing of the Republican party and his appointments and policies similarly reflected those ideological bases. But once in office, for a combination of political and bureaucratic reasons, both presidents gravitated increasingly toward the middle, Carter moving from the left and Reagan from the right. Approximately halfway into their terms both had moved to recapture the broad center of the political spectrum. Their foreign policies came more and more to resemble each other's—much to the consternation, incidentally, of the real ideologues in both parties.

That leads us to President Bush. After twelve years of highly ideological and often divisive politics, four under Carter and eight under Reagan, the electorate was apparently ready for a "safe," nonideological, centrist, almost nondescript president. George Bush fit that mold exactly, being a careful person, skilled in the ways of government, a manager and technician, with hardly an ideological bone in his body. On most issues Bush followed a moderate, middle-of-the-road policy; the intensely partisan and ideological debates of the past receded. But that has not necessarily meant a better or more constructive policy toward Latin America.

For in the meantime, since the 1980s, the world had changed enormously. I would identify at least four major trends of particular importance for the discussion in this book.

1. *The triumph of the democratic idea.* In Latin America in the last decade there were major transitions to democracy. It can be said at this stage that over 90 percent of the people of Latin America now live under a democratic regime (obviously with some mixed cases) or a regime aspiring toward democracy. The alternatives of corporatism and bureaucratic authoritarianism have been thoroughly discredited. The democratic ethos, of course, has by now triumphed not just in Latin America but almost globally.

2. *The discrediting of Marxism-Leninism.* Not only has the democratic idea triumphed but the other main alternative, Marxism-Leninism, has also been discredited. Almost no one wants to be a Marxist-Leninist nowadays, any more than one would want to be a bureaucratic authoritarian. The dismal economic, human rights, and ecological record of the Soviet Union and other Marxist-Leninist states (Eastern Europe, North Korea, China, Ethiopia, Angola, Mozambique, Cuba, and Nicaragua under the Sandinistas) has been the primary factor in the decline of attractiveness of Marxism-Leninism.

3. *The end of the Cold War.* With the decline and, seemingly, disintegration of the Soviet Union and a good part of its empire has come the winding down of the Cold War. I am not myself sure the Cold War is entirely "over" in such countries as Cuba, El Salvador, Nicaragua, and Peru; but throughout Latin America it has declined in intensity. The question for Latin America is whether this is good or bad. For while we may applaud the easing of Cold War frictions, the result for Latin America is likely to be decreased attention from *any* of the major world actors and therefore the increased isolation and marginalization of the area.

4. *More open economies alongside open polities.* Democracy has emerged ascendant in Latin America, and the sense is growing stronger that free, open economies are related to free, open political systems. I am not sure how much real privatization there will be in Latin America but I am impressed by the growing realization throughout the hemisphere that to "make it" and compete in the modern world means reducing inefficiency, cutting corruption, streamlining bloated bureaucracies, and opening markets to genuine competition. I am also encouraged by the dawning Latin American conclusion that only Latin

America can solve its own problems and that, if it does not, it will be left woefully behind and, furthermore, almost no one will care.

At the same time that these megatrends were occurring, a quite remarkable consensus was beginning to emerge on U.S. Latin America policy as well. For a long time this consensus was obscured, even buried, by the intense disagreements over Central America policy and the ideological and partisan squirmishes that marked the 1980s. But beginning with the Kissinger Commission report in 1984 and gradually emerging triumphant with bipartisan support in later years, this consensus included the following elements:

1. *An emphasis on democracy and human rights.* The United States, it was concluded, could not have an effective foreign policy without an emphasis on democracy and human rights. Democracy triumphed as a foreign policy goal not just on ethical and moral grounds but also on eminently pragmatic ones: democracies do not destabilize other countries, do not cause endless grief for U.S. policy, etc.[4]
2. *A better balance of military/strategic and socioeconomic aid.* After an earlier stronger emphasis on military solutions, the traditional balance of two socioeconomic aid dollars for every one of military aid was restored.
3. *A multifaceted program.* This would encompass democratization, human rights, development, debt relief, immigration, drugs, trade, strategic concerns, etc. No one single facet (human rights under Carter, strategic concerns in the early Reagan term) would be sufficient; rather, a complex, multipronged strategy would be followed that assisted Latin America on multiple levels.
4. *Emphasis on the new issues.* With the winding down of the Cold War, a number of the older strategic concerns about Latin America have declined in importance and a number of new ones have risen to take their place: pollution, water resources, immigration, trade, drugs, ecology, etc. What makes these new issues so complex and difficult is that they are, at one and the same time, domestic *and* international issues. Hence our domestic politics and our foreign policy come together in often confusing, overlapping, conflictual ways.

President Bush has been following this new, more balanced, more multifaceted agenda—although obviously with his own priorities. But while we may welcome the more centrist Latin America policy of the administration, we must also recognize that Latin America is currently off the front pages, off the front burners, maybe off the agenda altogether. While the policy may be "balanced," it also is a policy based largely on rhetorical flourishes (the Enterprise for the Americas Initiative) and benign neglect. But we know from earlier experiences that benign neglect is seldom very benign and that it often allows small problems that go unattended to fester into larger and more dangerous ones later on. So the verdict is still out on Bush's Latin America policy: we have some strong indications of the directions of policy, as the essays collected here make clear, but the final results are by no means yet in.

A PREVIEW

The book is divided into five sections. The first contains two essays, one a retrospective as the author saw it of Reagan administration policy in Latin America, the second an early assessment of the Bush administration.

The book's second section deals with policy issues. The first essay in this section deals with the vexing question of how the U.S. should deal with "friendly tyrants"—the Batistas, Trujillos, Somozas, Pinochets, and Marcoses of this world. The second essay explores the role of the armed forces in Latin America and urges an approach that deals realistically with the place of the military in society, as distinct from the efforts simply to wish it away. The third essay examines the new European presence in Latin America, showing the rise in European interest in the 1970s and early 1980s but the declining European interest today. The next essay focuses on the politics of the Latin American debt, showing how all parties to the issue have engaged in hypocrisies that may yet enable them to edge their way out of the crisis. Finally, the last essay in this section wrestles with the issue of superpower relations in Latin America in a time of declining Soviet interest.

The third section contains a number of essays on theoretical issues. The first is a statement about the relations between the state and the society of Latin America; closely related to my earlier work on corporatism, it sets forth an approach and a way of thinking about the structures and processes of Latin American politics. The second examines the literature on political development: the critics as well as the advocates, the alternative approaches (dependency theory, political economy, etc.) that emerged in the last two decades, as well as the recent resurrection of the political development approach. The third essay focuses on political culture and the "renaissance" that has recently occurred in political culture studies.

Part IV provides country and regional case studies. The first essay, written at the time of the February 1990 election in Nicaragua, wrestles with the prospects for change and stabilization in that strife-torn nation. The second focuses on reform or, alternatively, breakdown in Mexico, the country that, since it lies right on our southern border and is politically volatile, may be the most important country in the world for U.S. foreign policy. There follows a detailed examination of democracy in the Dominican Republic and how incomplete and insecure the democratic transition is there. Next is an essay on Cuba, based on my two recent trips to the island, which shows the profound systemic crisis that Marxist-Leninist state is facing. This section closes with a chapter on South America and the increasingly disparate agendas that the U.S. and the nations of South America bring to their relations.

In the final section we explore Latin America's cloudy future. There are hopeful signs, signs of change, but also so many problems that one wonders if Latin America will ever escape from them.

Part I

UNITED STATES FOREIGN POLICY IN LATIN AMERICA

1

United States Policy toward Central America: A Retrospective of the Reagan Years

During my seven years at AEI, 1981–88, I was both a close observer of and a sometimes participant in U.S. foreign policy-making with regard to Latin America. At AEI we had remarkable access to the highest levels of the United States government and to all the agencies involved in foreign policy decision-making. Access of course means influence, and on some issues and during some periods our team at AEI was able to influence U.S. Latin American policy—hopefully for the better.[1]

I had spent many years working in Latin America and writing about it. My books and policy writings had been both scholarly *and* policy-oriented, but they had been written largely from a Latin American point of view. That is, they had been written to try to explain Latin America to a U.S. audience and to U.S. policymakers. But in Washington I learned that very few people are interested in Latin America; and if they are interested, it is almost always from a U.S. point of view. I concluded in one of my books that roughly 80 percent of foreign policy with regard to Latin America derives from *U.S.* political and domestic considerations and probably only 20 percent from what actually occurs in Latin America. Under Secretary of State James Baker, who was also President Bush's chief campaign manager, the domestic considerations in shaping foreign policy may be as high as 90 percent.

Being in Washington, D.C., for this extended period was an eye-opener for me. For during these seven years I learned or relearned a great deal about American foreign policy-making especially as it affects Latin America—not all of which will sit comfortably with all readers. Among other things I learned or had reinforced were: (1) that scholars and academics, particularly those outside Washington, have almost zero influence on U.S. policy-making; (2) that Latin America, even with all the attention

Reprinted from James M. Malloy and Eduardo A. Gamarra (eds.), *Latin America and Caribbean Contemporary Record* (New York: Holmes and Meier, 1990).

devoted to it in recent years, remains among the lowest of U.S. foreign policy priorities; (3) that the debate over Central America is driven almost exclusively by U.S. domestic political (reelection) considerations and very little by what actually occurs in Central America; (4) that the partisan character of the debate simply overwhelms oftentimes the development of a more prudent and centrist policy; (5) that "rational actor" models of what the U.S. should do in Central America are frequently simply submerged under the weight of political and bureaucratic requirements;[2] (6) that Central America is never considered in isolation but is always a part of some bigger (East-West, North-South, Cold War, domestic politics) considerations; (7) that the administration seldom spoke with one voice on Central America but consisted of shifting factions with differing perspectives and differing constituencies that rose and fell over time; and (8) that good policy on Central America (prudent, sensible, moderate) is almost always a by-product—sometimes accidental—of the larger framework (conceptual, policy, or political) in which it is considered. If we understand these forces, which of course were present in past administrations both Democratic and Republican, will be present in future ones, and were also present under Reagan, then we may begin to understand the administration's Central America policies.

It should be said that the focus of this chapter is on the domestic sources of U.S. foreign policy-making, and not so much on the situation in Central America or the effects of U.S. policy there. I have written extensively on how things look from the other, or receiving end of U.S. policy,[3] but here the focus is almost exclusively on the U.S.-based processes of policy and not on Latin America per se.

THE SETTING

In order to comprehend Reagan administration policy on Central America, it is necessary to understand the context in which the administration came to power.[4]

First, there was the previous Carter administration and what were widely viewed as its failed policies—in Iran, Central America, Afghanistan, and southern Africa, among other places.[5] Carter was perceived as well-meaning but naive and ineffective. His emphasis on human rights was applauded, but not to the exclusion of other (political, economic, diplomatic, strategic) considerations. Hence there was a consensus among Reagan and his advisers that the Carter policies would have to be changed and, in some policy areas, reversed.

Second, there was the situation of the Soviet Union. By the late 1970s, while the United States remained traumatized by Vietnam and Watergate, the Soviet Union had massively built up its military capacities. While the United States withdrew into isolationism and self-flagellation, the Soviets were making impressive gains in Southeast Asia, the Middle East, Africa, and Central America. While the United States was mesmerized and lulled into inaction by détente, the Soviets were taking advantage of the era of good feeling that then prevailed to advance their strategic interests in various areas of the globe, especially the Third World. The notion was widespread in the foreign policy community—and not just among Reagan supporters—that this new Soviet aggression and expansionism had to be resisted and that lines needed to be drawn.

Third, the United States and its economy appeared to be running downhill. The United States had stood idly by while OPEC imposed the two great oil "shocks" of the 1970s; the U.S. economy was producing a smaller share of the world's GNP relative to other nations. Inflation was up, unemployment was up, and interest rates were up. Worse, the then president seemed unable to do anything about these problems except wring his righteous hands and talk of "malaise." There were many discussions of U.S. slippage, of creating a society of "limited goods," even of returning to individual self-sufficiency and "feudalism." But most Americans preferred not to accept that fate and wanted a government that did something to reverse the sad course of the 1970s.

Fourth was the situation in Central America. The Marxist revolutions in Grenada and Nicaragua had just triumphed, Michael Manley in Jamaica was flirting with Castro, Guyana and Suriname were turning into Marxist states, El Salvador seemed about to fall and Guatemala was shaky. The Carter administration had been deeply divided over how to respond to these developments, retreated into a disastrous temporizing and paralysis, and talked lamely of "ideological pluralism."[6] Meanwhile, opinion surveys indicated that while Americans did not want U.S. fighting forces involved in Central America, 80 percent of them wanted no "second Cubas" either.[7]

A fifth factor was the evolution of the Democratic Party. Many moderate Democrats and independents had been appalled and angered by the Eugene McCarthy-led antiwar movement of 1968, which probably cost Hubert Humphrey the presidency (and thus brought on Nixon), by the naiveté and amateurism of the McGovern campaign of 1972, by McGovern himself and his program, by the capture of the party machinery in 1972 and 1976 by its most liberal and left-wing elements, by the monopolization under Carter of assistant secretary positions (where policy is really made) in the Department of State by the party's liberal and even radical wing, and by the perceived incompetence of Mr. Carter himself. Hence the formation in the 1970s within the party of such organizations as the Henry Jackson-led Coalition for a Democratic Majority and, later, the Committee on the Present Danger, which met with President Carter and tried to impress on him the dangers of Soviet expansionism and the need for the United States to devote greater resources to military preparedness, and whose only response from Carter was a lecture on the need to support his policies. When that happened, many party influentials either left the Democratic Party, became independent, or joined what came to be called the "neoconservatives." Evidently a large share of the general public, the so-called Reagan Democrats, followed a similar course.

On the other side of the political aisle, sixth, important developments were also occurring. The conservative or Goldwater wing of the Republican Party had been shut out of power since the landslide victory of Lyndon Johnson in 1964. Richard Nixon and Gerry Ford had both come out of the more moderate and pragmatic wing of the Party, though both had paid homage to the conservative wing. By the late 1970s, however, the conservatives were staging a comeback and in Ronald Reagan they had found an attractive candidate. The conservatives rallied to the Reagan message of free markets, anticommunism, and American renewal. In November 1980, their candidate triumphed overwhelmingly and they now stood on the threshold of power, determined not just to reverse the Carter policies but to purge moderate Republicans as well and keep them from acquiring positions of influence in the new government. The size of Reagan's landslide made them even surer of their positions.

THE POLITICS OF THE TRANSITION

As in all modern campaigns, candidate Reagan had put together prior to his election a team of foreign policy advisers. These advisers prepared position papers, helped draft the party platform, answered media requests for information, prepared op-ed articles designed to sway public opinion, helped prepare answers to the questions Reagan might face in the presidential debates, and spoke on behalf of the candidate before various groups and forums. Some moderate Republicans were present on the list but the majority of the 40–50 names, approximately three-quarters, came from the conservative wing. As the election campaign drew to an end and it became apparent that Reagan would win, this core group of advisers began planning for the new administration. It split up into various more specialized groups, one for each geographic and functional area of foreign policy, took on additional staff, and began preparation for the transition from Carter to Reagan. That meant, from November 1980 to January 20, 1981, the preparation of new policy position papers, decisions about the future priorities among these policies, and decisions about who would be kept and who fired from the outgoing administration, and who would take their place.[8]

The Reagan team already had in its hands a number of documents that served as a partial basis for its Latin America policy. These included a chapter entitled "The Soft Underbelly" from Richard Nixon's book *The Real War;* the chapter on Latin America from the Heritage Foundation's now-quadrennial *Mandate for Leadership;* a document by the Committee of Santa Fe (L. Francis Bouchey, Roger Fontaine, David C. Jordan, Lt. General Gordon Sumner, and Lewis Tambs) of the conservative Council for Inter-American Security; and the writings of Jeane Kirkpatrick, most particularly her famous *Commentary* article on "Dictatorship and Double Standards."[9]

While these documents all undoubtedly had an influence on the Reagan transition team and ultimately on administration policy, they were not the only influences. Scholars tend to cite them often, precisely because they are written documents and in the public domain. But it is also important to emphasize that right from the beginning other influences were also present. Within the White House presidential assistants James Baker and Michael Deaver were not enamored of the conservatives' agenda or of certain conservative persons in the administration.[10] Vice-President Bush was not a conservative true believer; there were other, more moderate position papers coming from AEI and other sources that influenced policy that were privately prepared and delivered and never made public; Secretary of State Alexander Haig had his own priorities; and the State Department itself was already planning how it could take the sharp edges off (and eventually change) the more ideological conservatives' agenda. Thus the administration was never so monolithic as some of its critics have represented—or as the hard-core Reaganites believed and hoped.

As it operated in Latin American affairs, nonetheless, the Reagan transition team seemed quite brutal. At the Department of State, the deputy assistant secretaries of state in the Bureau of Inter-American Affairs were invited in for interviews, treated cordially, and then curtly dismissed after their backs were turned. The process and experience left a deep feeling of betrayal and bitterness all around. Later on, the State Department would wreak its revenge on the Reagan administration by trying to ignore, sabotage or go around its policies and by following its own course.

Although less brutal, similar purges occurred in other agencies and across the board at the top levels of the government.[11]

At the National Security Council, the incoming administration enforced greater ideological conformity than had any previous administration. In this regard the administration was reacting to the lack of discipline in the Carter administration's foreign policy, the fact that it had so many loose cannons who had highly romantic views of the world, and the fact that the Carter foreign policy was the most fragmented of any in the post-World War II era. The Reagan administration therefore sought to avoid these problems by appointing only "true believers" in the Reagan agenda to NSC and other foreign policy positions. Later on, foreign policy under Reagan would prove to be just as fragmented as it had been under Carter. Moreover, the emphasis on consistency and cohesion at the NSC, while laudable, resulted in some arguably mediocre appointments to that agency. Ideological orthodoxy came at the cost in some cases of preparedness and foreign policy skills.

Among some members of the incoming Reagan administration foreign policy team, another disturbing characteristic was the arrogant sense that now "it's our turn." Deprived of power for so long (at least since Nixon; but in the case of most of the Reaganites they had *never* been in power before), their sense was strong that this was finally their chance. Not only did they believe that their turn was long overdue but also that their people should have a monopoly of the positions available. More moderate elements were thus excluded, at the cost of diversity and pluralism in the points of view that would be presented to the president.

Competence and experience were, in some cases, also sacrificed. This was true not only in terms of the ideological orthodoxy enforced but also in the fact that the Reagan foreign policy team had not gone through the same winnowing that other foreign policy teams had.[12] Reagan, like Carter, had run *against* Washington during the campaign; his foreign policy advisers, for the most part, had not been recruited from the usual foreign policy establishment. Neither they nor their ideas had been tested and filtered in the endless forums, conferences, and dinner meetings of the Carnegie Endowment, the Wilson Center, or the Council on Foreign Relations (CFR). These more establishment agencies were in fact reviled by the Reaganites as too liberal; then-Vice-President George Bush was even forced to resign his position in the CFR. The sentiments were mutual, of course: the establishment did not think much of the Reagan appointees either. Inexperience was thus coupled with bitterness and simmering resentments; and when the factor of "it's our turn" was added to this simmering brew, the possibilities for heated exchanges or even an explosion increased that much more.

THE HARD LINE, 1981–83

In the first two or two and a half years of the Reagan presidency, the hard line appeared to be triumphant. The National Security Council staff was dominated by Richard Allen appointees, the more ideological advisers who had accompanied Reagan during the campaign now followed him into office, the hated State Department appeared to have been routed, and Reagan himself was basking in the accolades of his very impressive first-year legislative accomplishments. Whatever one's political views about these programs, the agenda accomplished was a stupendous one, especially given the fact the House of Representatives was not controlled by the Republican Party. The legislative agenda carried out was comparable to the first-year accomplishments of Lyndon Johnson and maybe even the first hundred days of Franklin D. Roosevelt.[13]

The policies affecting Latin America during this early period are familiar to us: they represented a mixture of continuities from previous administrations as well as some new, and occasionally unfortunate, departures. The latter included Secretary of State Alexander Haig's threatening comments to the effect that the U.S. might "go to the source" (meaning Cuba) and that El Salvador was where the United States was drawing the line in the East-West struggle; Ernest Le Fever's position that he would abolish the Human Rights office in the State Department if he were confirmed as assistant secretary for that position; and the U.S. posture (widely seen as anti-Argentine and anti-Latin American) in the Falklands/Malvinas war. The litany of other "early sins" committed by the Reagan administration includes the sending of aid to the Salvadoran military, the cutting off of assistance to Nicaragua's Sandinista revolution, the deep-freeze into which the prospects for a U.S.—Cuban normalization sank, and finally (and perhaps marking the end point of this first phase) the invasion of Grenada in November 1983.

Jeane Kirkpatrick also put many liberals' teeth on edge during this period with her arguments that from the point of view of fundamental U.S. national interest considerations, totalitarian leftists who allied themselves with Cuba and the Soviet Union were worse than authoritarian rightists; that authoritarian regimes (Argentina, Brazil, several others in Central and South America, even Chile by the late–1980s) were easier to reform or even replace than were those of the totalitarian type; and that even from the point of view of their own people the totalitarian regimes were worse because they provided no opportunity to their populations to alter their internal systems. In authoritarian regimes, in contrast, the hope and possibility for changing the system—an argument apparently borne out by the many transitions to democracy in Latin America from the late-1970s into the 1980s—remained continuously present, even in the darkest days of dictatorship. On the strength of these arguments, Dr. Kirkpatrick was then named ambassador to the United Nations by president-elect Reagan.

While these events and policy positions are by now the "stuff" of lore, they do not present a full picture; moreover, considerable change had occurred since the early foreign policy "set" of the Reagan administration was established.

First, it should be noted that the main priorities of the administration in its first year were reform of the domestic economy and the defense build-up, *not* Latin America. In fact, the White House seldom wanted to hear about Latin America at all in this early period and resented Secretary Haig's and others' efforts to force it onto the White House agenda. The White House dealt with Latin America reluctantly when it dealt with it at all. This was not an administration with a clear and coherent, top-level and agreed-upon plan eager to leap into Latin American affairs; indeed the preference of the political advisers in the White House was to avoid Latin America so far as possible, rather like a plague, fearing the political damage that it would probably suffer once it got involved in what was widely regarded as a murky and potentially dangerous "swamp." This was not a White House, as some have alleged, with an "obsession" with Central America or, specifically, Nicaragua. In the absence of very much White House attention, however, power and policy on Latin America issues tended to drain off in the direction of the more ideological activists who did have a plan and a program, the program laid out in the Santa Fe Report.

A second issue involves divisions within the administration that had already—even in this first and "hard-line" period—begun to surface. These included the unhappiness within the State Department over the direction of administration policy (and the fact that State had been excluded from the process), fear on the part of such top-level White House aides as James Baker and Michael Deaver that the ideologues were running rampant and needed to be reigned in before they did damage to Reagan's reputation and reelection possibilities, dissent on the part of such moderates as Vice-President Bush and Secretary of State Haig (who on some issues was an ideologue and on others a pragmatist) over some of the directions of policy, and (now we know) unhappiness on the part of Nancy Reagan who, in alliance with Baker and Deaver, also disliked the more ideologically inclined of Reagan's advisers, was above all protective of her husband's image and place in history, and herself became involved in some of the plots and counterplots to oust the hard-liners and bring more moderate voices to prominence.[14]

A third factor was change in the administration itself, even within this hard-line period, toward greater emphasis on human rights, in favor of foreign aid, and toward a more moderate overall position. These trends do not become fully visible until the next period, analyzed below, but they were present by 1982–83 and beginning to bubble to the surface. Many academic analyses, however, ignored these other trends toward change, focused on the early hard-line positions, and assumed that position was the dominant or *only* one all through the administration. That same misreading affected political events, as the losing Democratic presidential candidates in 1984 and 1988 both fought the 1980 campaign all over again and campaigned as though the Reagan policy of 1981–82 were still in effect in those later years. But it was not, as the following section makes clear. Both academics and Democratic politicians missed the boat on the significant evolution through which administration policy went.

TOWARD MODERATION, 1983–85

During 1983–85 the administration moved steadily toward moderation: it emphasized human rights, and put strong pressure on the El Salvadoran military to clean up its act. It supported the movement toward democratization in Latin America, and in some countries actually *led* the push. It recognized that the problems of Central America stemmed from both North–South (poverty, underdevelopment) problems as well as East–West ones; hence it incorporated a major socioeconomic assistance program. It saw the need to emphasize public foreign aid as well as private investment.

The administration also began to incorporate a broader conception of U.S. security in Latin America, one that emphasized development and not just military solutions. It toned down the decibel level and began to speak with greater sensitivity and moderation. Overall, there was in the Caribbean Basin Initiative, the Kissinger Commission Report, and other reports prepared for and by the administration, a trend toward greater pragmatism and centrism in policy, back toward the mainstream.

What were the causes of these trends? Here the author can only summarize his earlier published arguments and provide some new twists.[15] First, the administration determined that for electoral reasons, to help diminish the criticism that had been leveled against it, and to pass its legislative agenda, it needed to have public opinion, the media, and the Congress on its side—or at least neutralized. Hence it needed to soften the rhetoric and enact a positive program for Latin America, not just react with simplistic slogans and strictly military solutions that proved quite unpopular. Second, the administration recognized that to defuse the criticisms and to mobilize our European allies on other issues (cruise missiles, NATO, etc.), it also needed to set forth a more moderate position on Latin America. Third, the administration went through a learning process—part of which included the growing realization that difficult countries like El Salvador and Nicaragua were not as easily manipulable or subject to U.S. blandishments and pressures as the administration had thought.

Another set of factors were bureaucratic. These included the substitution of George Shultz for Alexander Haig as secretary of state, which caused most of political Washington to breathe a sigh of relief, and a considerable turnover of personnel at the National Security Council, which resulted in the departure of many of the original Richard Allen staff and the appointment of more moderate, often State Department personnel. At the NSC as well as in other foreign policy-making agencies (State, Defense, CIA), this was the period when the more pragmatic foreign policy professionals and their area and functional expertise began recapturing foreign policy influence from the more ideologically inclined advisers who had accompanied President Reagan into office and had largely dominated policy-making in the first two years. This transition was of course incomplete and partial, and there were still fights over many foreign policy appointments as well as policies; but of the fact that the shift was underway there could be no doubt.

A major influence in helping shift Latin America policy back toward the center was the published work of such moderately conservative think tanks as the American Enterprise Institute for Public Policy Research (AEI) and the Georgetown Center for Strategic and International Studies (CSIS). Both of these research institutes had developed centers for Latin American research in the late–1970s–early–1980s, had recruited well-known scholars to staff them, built up their programs, and by the early 1980s were producing large numbers of in-depth, scholarly analyses on a wide range of subjects: Brazil, Chile, Central America, Cuba, Puerto Rico, Mexico, debt, trade, political development, energy.[16] It is to be emphasized that these were serious and scholarly studies, strongly policy-oriented, and centrist in orientation. They emphasized, for example, the complex roots of the Central American crises, the multiple forces operating there, and the difficulties of implementing a successful U.S. policy.[17]

These studies were disseminated widely through the administration; more than that, they were actually *read*. The impact of all these studies in pulling administration policy back toward the center was considerable.[18] The movement in a more moderate direction was so strong that it evoked the wrath of the real conservatives who tried, for the most part unsuccessfully, to block the trend toward the center and began accusing the Reagan administration of following a Jimmy Carter-type foreign policy.

Probably the most important influence during this period was the *Report of the National Bipartisan [Kissinger] Commission on Central America*.[19] The Kissinger Commission Report has been criticized in some academic circles for various sins of omission and commission, some of which are valid and others not. The criticisms often ignore the following facts: (1) The report was produced by a commission of seven Republicans and seven Democrats and had to be acceptable to *all* of them. (2) The report was the product of a *presidential* commission and therefore first of all had to be acceptable to the White House; if it was repudiated by the White House; it would have no impact at all and would not even see the light of day. (3) Hence the staff spent long hours discussing how it could get as many centrist proposals into the report as possible and still get the White House to give it its stamp of approval. (4) The report, thus, must of necessity be seen as a political document with political purposes as well as a semischolarly one, designed to push administration policy back toward a more reasonable and balanced approach, but recognizing there were severe limits beyond which it could not go. The lack of understanding of these preeminently political purposes of the report in the academic community and their strong criticisms of it make one wonder whether some academics really wanted a more balanced policy or whether their purpose was the grander political one of trying to undermine the administration entirely, polarize the issue, and thus help perpetuate the Central American crisis rather than resolve it in reasonable ways.

It was, after all, the Kissinger Commission Report that led to the consolidation of all those trends noted earlier: the emphasis on democracy and human rights as well as U.S. strategic interest, a better balance between socioeconomic aid and military assistance, an emphasis on political and economic development as the only long-term solution to Central America's ills as distinct from short-term military solutions, and the emphasis on a multifaceted approach (aid, trade, education, development, democratization, human rights) that bore a striking resemblance to John F. Kennedy's Alliance for Progress. These goals were incorporated in the Kissinger Commission Report as well as subsequent legislation, and—even while not entirely funded by the Congress—they became the basis for a more nuanced and multi-faceted administration Latin America policy from this point on.

SLIPPAGE, 1985–87

It appeared during the 1983–85 period that the administration was returning to the moderate mainstream of American foreign policy. But that transition was never so complete as it sometimes appeared—or as most persons in the foreign policy establishment hoped. On virtually every appointment and on every slight shift in policy, there was a tremendous battle. Jesse Helms in the Senate could still block policy changes or hold up appointments—sometimes for years—of persons that he and the arch-conservatives considered unacceptable. At the White House, the high-level combination of CIA Director William Casey, UN Ambassador Jeane Kirkpatrick, and Defense Secretary Casper Weinberger sometimes teamed up to block the influence and initiatives of the moderates led by George Shultz, the State Department, and National Security Council Director Robert McFarlane.[20] Moreover, the conservatives often had a sympathetic ear in Ronald Reagan—when they could get to him. Hence while there was considerable movement toward a more centrist policy, that evolution was always sporadic, partial, and by fits and starts. For every two steps forward, there was always at least one step back.

The absence of a clear direction in policy may be accounted for by several factors. First, President Reagan after one shooting and several operations, to say nothing of age, was not the same vigorous leader in his second term as he had been in the first. Second, from the time of his reelection in 1984, Reagan was a lame duck president; and once the glow of the large electoral victory over Walter Mondale had worn off, Reagan's effectiveness quickly faded. Third, Congress sensed this weakness and soon became more assertive, standing up to the president and rejecting his initiatives in ways it would not have done in the first term. After 1986, in addition, *both* houses of Congress were in the hands of the Democratic opposition; many of the Congressional Democrats had presidential ambitions and were disinclined to go along with a Republican White House, and when Jim Wright replaced Tip O'Neil as speaker of the House, there was definitely a hardening of partisan lines.

Fourth, there was a staff change at the White House; and the fact is Donald Regan was both more hard line and less effective than the troika of Baker, Deaver, and Meese had been in the first term. Another factor—related to these others—was the failure of the Congress to implement fully the recommendations of the Kissinger Commission and of the White House to push harder for them. A sixth factor—again related to the foregoing—was the paralysis and gridlock that increasingly affected foreign policy and that prevented U.S. policy from going in any clear directions.[21] And finally came the Iran/contra scandal, which poisoned the political atmosphere, destroyed the credibility of the administration and its foreign policy, and left in its wake a crippled and sclerotic presidency and administration that persisted to the end of Reagan's term.

The reading of most foreign policy experts is that while the trends toward moderation continued in most areas of foreign policy—Soviet relations, NATO, nuclear disarmament, southern Africa—Latin America was different. Again there are several factors involved. The first is that while George Shultz, unlike Haig, emerged as the true vicar of American foreign policy, he was not at all interested in Latin America; he saw Central America as a morass of problems to which there were no happy solutions, and determined to avoid the potential political damage this might cause by letting the Bureau of Inter-American Affairs at the State Department run its own, quite autonomous policy. Second, that bureau, which had earlier been headed by foreign policy professionals (Thomas Enders) or political appointees co-opted by the State Department (Tony Motley), was now headed by Elliott Abrams, a tough-minded political appointee with strong ambitions and close ties to the neoconservatives (he is *Commentary* editor Norman Podhoretz's son-in-law). The neoconservatives strongly supported U.S. aid to the Nicaraguan contras and made that issue virtually the only one that received high-level attention in the field of inter-American relations. Among other things, that focus detracted from the more complex and multipronged emphasis that the Kissinger Commission had outlined and doomed its recommendations to a lower-order priority.

A third important difference was at the NSC. By 1985–87, most of the old Richard Allen appointees had been rotated out of the NSC, replaced by less ideological professionals and technocrats recruited from State and other agencies. Robert McFarlane and John Poindexter are the prototypes. But while this shift was *generally* true at the NSC, it did not at all occur with regard to Latin America. If anything, the position of the officials responsible for Latin America at the NSC was even "harder" now than it had been in the early 1980s. These officials included Jeane

Kirkpatrick's lieutenant, Jacqueline Tillman, Georgetown professor (and also Kirkpatrick protégé) José Sorzano, and former William Casey assistant at the CIA Constantine Menges. Hence while the overall direction of U.S. policy during this period was back toward the center, Latin America policy—especially as regards Central America—was more complicated.

THE TRIUMPH OF "MODERATION," 1987–88

The fourth and final phase of the Reagan presidency began in the aftermath of the Iran/contra controversy. By this point the president himself was visibly older, more tired, less vigorous, less involved. With the exception of Soviet relations and the signing of the historic arms reduction treaty, he took less and less interest in everyday policy-making, especially on peripheral areas like Latin America. The president could still be aroused to vigorous action from time to time (such as on the contra issue), but less and less frequently.

The White House staff also seemed to be asleep at the wheel. No new initiatives were forthcoming all through 1988. Easy-going, everything-is-compromisable Howard Baker replaced the flinty Donald Regan as chief of staff. Frank Carlucci, a political moderate and a consummate professional bureaucrat, took over at the NSC and then moved to Defense when Weinberger resigned. Colin Powell, another able professional bureaucrat but hardly a Reaganaut, then moved up to the number one position at the NSC. The Jeane Kirkpatrick team at the NSC, Menges and Sorzano, was either forced out or resigned. William Casey died and Shultz emerged, by default as much as by his own considerable bureaucratic skills, as the administration's single voice on foreign policy. Abrams stayed on, although more and more isolated and ignored. The power of the leading conservatives—Kirkpatrick, Casey, Weinberger—had by now been definitively broken; their lieutenants had similarly been routed and replaced in all the crucial foreign policy-making agencies.

With Reagan increasingly detached from and uninvolved in critical policy decisions and with a staff no longer committed to the original administration program, the White House floundered. It was no longer willing to assert itself *vis-à-vis* Congress to achieve its agenda (if it still had an agenda), and its public relations efforts to educate the public concerning the strategic issues involved in Central America all but completely died. The White House largely abandoned the policy battleground to the religious groups and the opposition, and, after a few unhappy mutterings, accommodated itself to the unprecedented foreign policy leadership role—analyzed in more detail below—of House Speaker Jim Wright.

The key planks in the conservatives' foreign policy program were also removed. After five years of controversy and thorough tiredness with the trouble and divisiveness of the issue, Congress voted in 1987 to cut off assistance to the contras. The Resistance, which the U.S. had created, armed, and sustained, was abandoned. With Reagan exercising less vigorous leadership, in addition, the Central American Peace Plan launched by Costa Rican President Oscar Arias became the main focus of attention and slowly came to represent a substitute for an energetic U.S. policy in the area. The State Department became entirely dominant at the NSC as well as in Foggy Bottom.

And finally, in what amounted to a congressional coup d'état, Democratic House Speaker Wright took over U.S. Central America policy for himself, bypassing the White House and the president (who, the last time any of us looked at the Constitution, was still supposed to be in charge of foreign policy, not the Speaker) and throwing his weight behind the Arias-Wright-Reagan plan! This was an enormous flip-flop, indicating a complete rout and reversal of administration policy. It also left conservatives, true Reaganites, thoroughly disillusioned: Jeane Kirkpatrick told the author that she was so angry over these turns of events that she no longer followed Central American affairs as closely as she once had.

In this battle between the conservatives and the so-called moderates, it is plain on which side most Latin America experts would stand. And most reasonable people want the United States to have a good, decent, moderate, and mainstream foreign policy, on Latin America and elsewhere. But it is also plain that the triumph of the State Department in U.S. foreign policy should not be viewed as an unmixed blessing. First, State has its own problems, often immense ones, including elitism, arrogance, lack of analytical skills, inability to conceptualize, and many others.[22] Second, State has never been known for its expertise in or serious attention to Latin America, so Latin Americanists should be careful before they put all their eggs in the State Department basket. And third, while many of us applaud the evolution toward greater pragmatism, moderation, and restraint in U.S. foreign policy, we should not forget either that Reagan received huge, 60 percent mandates in both 1980 and 1984. If we value democracy, those figures are awfully impressive. Hence whatever our political and policy preferences, we still need to give serious attention to the need to achieve a proper balance between the popular mandate a president may receive as expressed through the democratic preferences of the voters, *and* the need to utilize effectively the foreign policy expertise found in the professional bureaucracies.

CONCLUSIONS

Several conclusions emerge from this analysis of Reagan Administration Latin America policy which may offer some lessons for the future.

The first is how difficult it is at any one time to think of a single, monolithic "administration" policy. When Washington-based policy-makers read or hear analysts say that "The administration did this" or "The administration did that," their eyes tend to glaze over. In fact, the process is far more complex: as illustrated here, administration policy is constantly changing, relating to changing balances of power in Washington, shifting personnel, rival cliques and policy positions, and so on. In fact, the administration—any administration—speaks with many voices on foreign policy and it is incumbent upon scholars, albeit very difficult, to know which is the dominant voice or voices and which are rising or falling at any one time.

The second conclusion is to point to the several stages of policy. Here we have identified four (five if one counts the campaign and the transition) quite distinct phases: a "hard-line" phase (1981–83), a movement toward moderation (1983–85), a period of "slippage" (1985–87), and the triumph of "moderation" (1987–89). Policy was clearly not the same in each phase; there were nuances and shifting personnel, changes of emphases and priorities, and some actually quite dramatic turnabouts.

And this gets us to the third conclusion: that these changes in U.S. policy toward Latin America were almost always related to larger forces extraneous to the region. These included presidential and Congressional reelection considerations, the president's vigor as well as the quality of his staff, the changing balance of forces within the administration and its competing bands of stalwarts, the relations between the president and Congress, Iran/contra, etc. These domestic forces had perhaps more to do with the ups and downs and changes in administration policy than anything occurring on the ground in Central America.

Fourth, these changes provide considerable room to maneuver and to change the policy. New people come and go, a nuance is introduced, the nature of the competition and the relative power of the president's advisers change, an opening is provided, the political winds shift. All these shifts, which are sometimes subtle, hard to predict, and very difficult especially for outsiders to fathom or penetrate, offer opportunities to alter the policy or to move the process along.

Fifth, the analysis points to the conclusion that policy on Latin America, as well as on some other areas, tends to be derivative. It is derivative not just of overriding Cold War considerations but also of forces operating in the U.S. domestic politics context. These domestic forces, rightly or wrongly, are often more important than the realities of the situation in the countries that are the objects of U.S. policy. Overwhelmingly, one is forced to conclude, what happens in Washington, D.C., is far more important in terms of U.S. policy than anything happening in Managua, Tegucigalpa, or San Salvador.

Sixth and finally, what emerges from the discussion is how fragmented and politicized our foreign policy process has become.[23] One wonders how, in this context, the United States can ever fashion a rational, sustained, coherent, long-term foreign policy. Behind the politicization and the partisan posturing, there is in fact a consensus waiting to emerge on Central America policy; but under Reagan there was such division and the partisanship was so intense that the consensus position never was able to establish its dominance.

The consensus lies, even with their many false starts and sometimes questionable assumptions, in an updated version of the Alliance for Progress or in a revival of the Kissinger Commission recommendations. Such programs will not be acceptable to some purists but given present political realities they are about as much as we can expect. Such a program would involve strong emphasis on democracy and human rights as well as on U.S. strategic considerations, a balance of socioeconomic and military assistance, emphasis on economic and political development as well as on U.S. security concerns narrowly defined, some gradual and incremental relief for Latin American debtors but not in ways that pass all the costs onto U.S. taxpayers. President Bush is certainly committed to this mainstream approach. But his mandate is weak, the Democratic majorities in the Congress will play politics with the issues, the true conservatives will try to force him to follow their line, and liberals and radicals will be suspicious and perhaps hostile. The battle will go on, as much in Washington as in Central America.

2

United States Policy in Latin America: The Bush Agenda

With the inauguration of George Bush as the forty-first President of the United States on January 20, 1989, policy toward Latin America moved toward the center, toward the mainstream. That process had begun earlier under President Ronald Reagan, particularly under the foreign policy team of Secretary George Shultz at the Department of State, Secretary Frank Carlucci at the Department of Defense, William Webster at the Central Intelligence Agency (CIA) and General Colin Powell at the National Security Council (NSC). But the changes had been incomplete, especially with regard to Latin American affairs.[1] However, under President Bush a far more pragmatic policy was put into place and consolidated.

George Bush is more experienced in foreign affairs than any American President since Richard Nixon, perhaps since Dwight Eisenhower. As a congressman, businessman, member of the Council on Foreign Relations, member of the Trilateral Commission, director of the CIA and ambassador to China, President Bush has had far more experience in foreign policy than his three immediate predecessors. In addition (and unusual among American Presidents), George Bush has lived abroad for an extended period; he is personally interested in foreign policy issues and draws heavily on his own considerable knowledge and experience when making foreign policy decisions.

At the highest levels, the foreign policy team that President Bush has recruited for his administration reflects the same prudent, centrist and pragmatic approach. With James Baker as secretary of state, Richard Cheney as secretary of defense, Webster at the CIA, and Brent Scowcroft at the NSC, Bush has a politically shrewd, experienced and technocratic team. They all come from the pragmatic, centrist wing of the Republican party.

Reprinted from *Current History* 89 (January 1990).

In fact, while both Presidents Jimmy Carter and Ronald Reagan recruited officials for their administrations from the more ideological Washington-based think tanks, President Bush's recruits came mainly from the mainstream Council on Foreign Relations (CFR). In the Bush administration, the CFR is back in power after a 20-year hiatus; it is significant that, in sharp contrast to President Reagan's administration, the Bush administration has not recruited a single person for a foreign policy position from the conservative think tanks, either the Heritage Foundation or the moderately conservative American Enterprise Institute for Public Policy Research (AEI).

On Latin American affairs, however, other criteria came into play. At the State Department, for example, there were several experienced and qualified candidates for the position of assistant secretary of state for inter-American affairs; but Secretary of State James Baker chose Bernard Aronson, a liberal Democrat who had been a Walter Mondale supporter, who knew little Spanish and had little experience in Latin America, but who once wrote part of a speech for President Reagan urging congressional support for the contras in Nicaragua. Conservatives grumbled that if they had wanted a liberal Democrat as the chief official on Latin America, they could have voted for Democratic presidential candidate Michael Dukakis.

To appease the conservatives, a conservative had to be appointed to the NSC, the other key position in the administration on Latin America. The choice was Ellis (Ted) Briggs, former United States ambassador to Panama and a career foreign service officer—not a conservative ideologue but a man who favored continuing United States pressure on the Sandinista regime in Nicaragua and could provide conservative access to the White House. But in the meantime, in an effort to downplay the importance of the area, the number of Latin America specialists on the NSC staff was reduced from three to one.

If political objectives were the primary motivation in filling the State Department positions, what precisely were those objectives? Four may be identified, all interrelated.

First, Secretary of State Baker wanted to appease the congressional Democrats and defuse the partisan conflict over Central America that had all but paralyzed foreign policy in the Reagan administration. That is why he appointed a liberal Democrat as assistant secretary for inter-American affairs. By defusing the Central American issue, Baker could gain the goodwill of the Democrat-controlled Congress on issues he considered more important.

Second, Baker saw Central America as a can of worms for his President, a no-win situation, a "black hole" into which the United States pours billions of dollars and receives nothing but grief.

Third, Secretary Baker wanted to concentrate all his attention on what he viewed as more pressing foreign policy matters: the President's trip to Europe for the NATO (North Atlantic Treaty Organization) summit and a projected summit with Soviet President Mikhail Gorbachev later. These larger goals were not to be diminished by the ugly divisive issues of Central America; thus Central America and the congressional critics had to be finessed and removed from the front pages in favor of the pageantry, drama and favorable headlines of summitry.

Fourth, Secretary Baker, who was also President Bush's 1988 chief campaign strategist, was already planning the presidential campaign of 1992. To that end, once again, Central America had to be defused as a hot issue and the congressional Democrats and the press given less ground for criticism of President Bush. Baker wanted favorable and positive news coming out of the White House, not the negatives that seem to go with Central American policy.

Baker's strategy succeeded masterfully, at least in the short run. The congressional Democrats were quieted; Central America was relegated to the back pages; criticism was muted; the President had a successful NATO summit and will have a summit meeting soon with Gorbachev; and, preparing for the 1992 campaign, the President's popularity had remained at a record high. In 1989, domestic political considerations were initially far more important in shaping Latin American policy and appointments than anything actually happening in the region.

Despite Baker's well-laid plans, however, Latin America could not be shunted aside. The simmering Nicaraguan issue could not be counted on to die down so readily, particularly with the call for disbanding the contras in the Central American peace accords and with presidential elections in Nicaragua scheduled for February, 1990. The question of what to do about Panamanian dictator General Manuel Antonio Noriega, the drug issue, the Latin American debt and the question of the survival of democracy in Latin America were all issues that could be expected to surface again. Eventually, Baker's political strategy was overtaken by events, as the realities of Latin America and the complex United States interrelations with it once again flared into focus.

The Baker strategy and the preeminence of politics over policy might lead one to be cynical about United States policy toward Latin America. The good news is that there is more than mere domestic politics in the Bush administration's Latin America policy. The administration has a plan, rather close to the recommendations made by former Secretary of

State Henry Kissinger's commission, for a comprehensive program in Latin America, including social and economic assistance, trade, debt relief, human rights, democracy, a drug policy, as well as the furtherance of United States strategic interests. The bad news is that there is no money to pay for any of these plans.

Until the funds are available, therefore, Latin America policy will be dominated by politics and rhetorical flourishes, with relatively limited substance. As usual, Latin America is a low priority and "benign neglect" is popular; but benign neglect as a basis for policy can be maintained only for a limited time, while the problems of Latin America continue to fester. If the past is any guide to the future, the seemingly endemic problems of the area will almost certainly force events in Latin America once again onto the front pages and the television screens.

PANAMA AND NORIEGA

Panama's General Manuel Noriega had for some time been a major thorn in the side of United States policy—almost as sharp a thorn as Libya's Colonel Muammar Qaddafi or Iran's Ayatollah Ruhollah Khomeini. Noriega was one of the last remaining right-wing dictators in Latin America, a drug profiteer, a repressive thug, a former CIA informer and (at the same time) a new-found buddy of Cuba's strongman Fidel Castro and the potential chief beneficiary of the United States-Panama Canal treaties. Overall, he was a major embarrassment for United States foreign policy.

The United States had tried every trick in the book to get rid of Noriega—and many that were not previously in the book—including cajolery, diplomacy, bribery and arm twisting.[2] The United States had used a prestigious private Washington law firm to orchestrate the economic strangulation of Panama; it had tried to use the Organization of American States (OAS) to put pressure on Noriega; and it sent United States troops to rattle their sabers in the Canal Zone and to exchange gunfire with Noriega's forces. The Bush administration had tried to persuade Noriega to resign peacefully, to share power, to go into exile along with his treasury or to hold democratic elections. But when Noriega's candidate lost, he promptly annulled the election, beat up the opposition and installed another puppet President.

An October, 1989, coup attempt directed against Noriega failed; the Bush administration was strongly criticized for its inept performance during the coup. Playing on nationalist sentiments, mobilizing his not inconsiderable supporters and cleverly dodging and ducking, Noriega had apparently outsmarted the United States at every turn. Ironically,

Noriega's ability to outwit the United States had turned him into something of a folk hero in Panama and elsewhere in Latin America.

The key was patience—not a commodity for which United States foreign policy or United States public opinion is famous. The pressures and sanctions were all in place; it would take time for them to take effect and time for the Panamanian political process to reassert itself. That process, aided and supported by the United States, would eventually result in Noriega's removal, if not through the democratic process, then perhaps through action by the Defense Forces in Panama, or most likely a combination of the two. But United States efforts to act precipitously or unilaterally, or to remove Noriega through military action, would almost certainly evoke a cry of protest in Latin America and prove counterproductive. Nevertheless, in December, 1989, its patience exhausted and despairing of the Panamanians doing the job by themselves, the Bush administration sent in U.S. military forces to oust Noriega and restore democracy.

CENTRAL AMERICA

There was a major breakthrough in August, 1989, with regard to Central America when the five Central American Presidents signed an accord whose essential quid pro quo was the disarming and disbanding of the Nicaraguan rebels (contras) in return for Nicaragua's promise to hold democratic elections in February, 1990.

The issue was complicated in terms of United States domestic politics. Conservatives criticized the Bush administration for "selling out" and "abandoning" the contras. But the administration already knew that it could not persuade Congress to approve a new contra aid package. So in response to conservative pressure it issued a rather meek criticism of the Central American Presidents and called for some renewed aid to the contras. The administration eventually compromised and Congress approved some "humanitarian" aid, which was to be used chiefly to resettle the contras. Resettlement, however, meant an end to the contras as a fighting force and to their ability to exert pressure on the Nicaraguan government.

For the Sandinistas, in contrast, this agreement was a major triumph: they would have to suffer the inconvenience of holding an election but they would rid themselves once and for all of the hated contras—not a bad bargain in Sandinista eyes since they had no intention of losing the election they were obliged to hold.

The United States reaction to the Central American accords was a product of Secretary Baker's domestic political calculations. He knew he would be criticized by conservatives on this issue but he gambled—correctly, as it turned out—that this reaction would be mild and short-lived. On the other hand, the gains in terms of defusing congressional criticism and ensuring high political popularity ratings for President Bush outweighed the disadvantages. The negative consequences of the Baker-Bush strategy—if the Sandinistas cancelled or blatantly rigged their elections, if the contras proved a disruptive force in Honduras or in the United States, if another Central American country fell to a Marxist-Leninist guerrilla challenge—could have still returned to haunt the administration; but at this writing the domestic aspects of the Bush policy seem to have succeeded brilliantly. In February, 1990, the Sandinistas were voted out of office, thus defusing the issue still further.

DEBT

It has been obvious for a long time that the countries of Latin America could not pay back their massive international debts (which at the end of 1988 totaled $426 billion), and that the debts were essentially uncollectible. But if that were so, then the main question became political—how to handle or manage this debt. Over the past several years managing the issue involved some considerable dissembling.[3] The debt was both unpaid and unpayable, but no one could say so publicly for fear that the private commercial banks, some Latin American governments and maybe even the international financial system would collapse.

By 1989, the situation had changed. Many United States banks had rolled up record profits in the preceding years and were therefore able to absorb losses on their Latin American loans. The international financial system was no longer threatened by collapse. For the most part, the Latin American countries had managed austerity well for several years, but austerity could not be sustained indefinitely. And within the United States government, a consensus began to emerge on how to relieve the debt burden without telling American taxpayers that they would ultimately pay the bill. Meanwhile, several Latin American democracies seemed to be on the verge of collapse.

To avert major problems for President Bush, Secretary of the Treasury Nicholas Brady introduced a corollary to the "Baker Plan" (named for his predecessor at the Treasury Department, James Baker, now secretary of state). Known as the "Brady Plan," it tried to offer the private banks incentives to forgive a portion of their outstanding Latin American loans. In return for forgiving some loans, the banks would receive guarantees for their remaining loans while the Latin American countries would receive new credits to pay these loans from the multinational lending agencies (the World Bank, the International Monetary Fund, and the Inter-American Development Bank).

Meanwhile, the United States agreed to support stronger funding for these lending agencies. In short, the United States taxpayer would help guarantee Latin America's outstanding debts indirectly and in disguised form through enhanced United States support of the multinational banks. Meanwhile, the private banks were to have the option of choosing between debt reduction, reducing the interest rate charges or providing new loans with guarantees.

While the Brady Plan was probably one step toward a realistic resolution of the debt issue, its negative consequences should not be forgotten. First, United States taxpayers must pay for Latin America's debts; second, it removes the stringent requirements that forced Latin America's often inefficient public agencies to reform themselves in return for new loans; and third, it gives the private banks the opportunity to stop making any new loans to Latin America. Thus, while the Brady Plan offers some short-term solutions, its long-term implications may turn out to be negative.

DRUGS

United States drug policy has gone through three stages. In the first phase in the early 1980's, the United States determined to crack down on domestic consumption. But that made little impression because drugs were often seen as a "lifestyle" issue and thus a matter of choice, and because tactics like mass arrests of suspected drug users and mass testing of employees ran afoul of concerns for civil liberties.

In the mid-1980's the government turned to cutting off drugs on the production or supply side, by sending United States Drug Enforcement Agency (DEA) officials to Latin America and United States troops to Bolivia. But the DEA, which had little foreign affairs experience and which sees the issue mainly as a law enforcement problem, found itself in conflict with the State Department, which seeks to maintain good relations with the governments whose officials DEA often wanted to arrest.

In addition, the DEA underestimated the immensity of drug production in Latin America, the inaccessibility of the drug "factories" and the simple and low-level technology needed to set them up and, hence, the difficulties of eradication. The DEA also failed to understand the reasons for drug production in Latin America. Drug production adds to exports, increases the gross national product (GNP), pays for government social programs, and raises per capita income. It allows farmers to increase their incomes many times over, enables government workers and military officers to supplement their meager incomes and even helps pay Latin America's foreign debts. Herbicide sprays cannot be used because of popular fears of cancer or, in Colombia, fear of tainting the coffee crop. Furthermore, extradition of the drug kingpins to the United States often provokes strong nationalistic reactions.

President Bush's program, the third phase, suggests a more comprehensive approach. It seeks to curb consumption through education, rehabilitation and arrests; it tries at the same time to limit production by providing support, including equipment and military advisers, for Latin American armed forces and police agencies. In addition, the Bush program attempts to stop the flow of funds through interdiction and prosecution of those who help "launder" the money; and it aims at intermediaries like couriers and delivery networks. So far the plan has been concentrated in Colombia, where the power and numbing violence of the drug cartels threaten the civil society and the government, and in Peru and Bolivia, where production is also large-scale.

DEMOCRACY

President Bush has continued President Reagan's strategy of support for Latin America's democracies. That means ongoing support for the democratic opening in Chile, efforts to shore up weak democracies in Central America and in South America, continued pressure on Nicaragua to democratize its regime, and ongoing worries about democracy in Mexico and some of the larger South American countries.

Without democracy (or even with it), Mexico could become an unstable neighbor on the United States southern border. Peru's democracy is chaotic and very fragile. Fears for Colombia's democracy partly motivated President Bush's drug campaign, and riots in Venezuela and the potential destabilization of that democracy gave impetus to the Brady Plan to alleviate Latin America's debt problem.

The two greatest worries for the United States in South America are Argentina and Brazil. Argentina has a populist Peronist President, Carlos Saúl Menem, and it is feared that he may mismanage the economy, thus precipitating a military coup d'état in two or three years. But so far President Menem's policies have been prudent, sensible and encouraging. Brazil, the proverbial "sleeping giant" of the continent, is no longer sleeping, but these days it is a shaky giant. Skyrocketing crime, widespread social and political discontent, galloping inflation, and a sense of malaise and of impending national collapse have shaken Brazil's traditional optimism and have frightened United States policy-makers.

THE FUTURE

The per capita income for Latin America as a whole fell by 1.5 percent in 1988; it has fallen by 7 percent between 1980 and 1988. There has also been a sharp decline in capital inflows and investment rates; foreign exchange reserves are down; and private banks no longer wish to lend to the area. Unemployment and inflation are rampant.[4] Because of its own budgetary restraints, the United States is not in a position to provide a new Marshall Plan or a new Alliance for Progress for Latin America; and, after showing some interest in the area in the early 1980's, Europe is not now very much involved in Latin America either.

Rhetoric aside, the cold war is the reason the United States pays attention to Latin America. As the cold war recedes, the United States will not entirely abandon the area, and the new issues—drugs, debt, immigration, instability—will force the administration to remain involved. But Latin America will almost certainly become more like Africa; an assistant secretary will deal with its problems, but few people will care.

In the abstract, Latin America's needs are obvious: a serious, sustained, multifaceted United States program; mature and normal relations; a policy that emphasizes democracy, human rights, socioeconomic assistance and development as well as more narrowly defined United States security concerns. But the United States is now following a policy of benign neglect. And as the cold war winds down and as United States investment and attention are turned in other directions, its indifference to Latin America will probably increase.

Earlier periods of benign neglect, however, led to the Cuban revolution at the end of the 1950's and to the Central American revolutions at the end of the 1970's. One hopes that the United States has absorbed the lessons of these events, and that the administration will realize that neglect of the area leads to deeper crises for United States policy later. But there are few signs at present that the lesson has been learned.

Part II

POLICY ISSUES

3

"Friendly Tyrants": Gauging When to Change U.S. Policy

What to do about nondemocratic regimes that are friendly to the United States, but that are abusive of human rights, that may be faced with serious guerrilla/communist insurgencies, and yet are unable or unwilling to reach an accommodation with moderate and democratic forces in order to avoid the polarization and breakdown that leads to crisis and, in some cases, a communist takeover? This is one of the most important, persistent, and thorny foreign policy dilemmas facing the United States today.

The problem has already been encountered in virulent and dramatic form in, among other places, Cuba (Batista), the Dominican Republic (Trujillo), Nicaragua (Somoza), Haiti (Duvalier), Iran (the Shah), and the Philippines (Marcos). More limited or more nuanced cases include the government of South Vietnam during its entire brief life, Greece under the colonels, Turkey under periods of military rule, and Argentina under its junta. We have experience, too, with other cases that might have generated serious crises and dilemmas—notably Spain and Portugal under Franco and Salazar, respectively—but for various reasons did not.

Yet these experiences, many of them quite prominent chapters in postwar U.S. foreign policy, have not raised the issue to the level of visibility that it deserves. Each successive case is treated as if it had no precedent whatsoever. This bespeaks a lack of historical interest and vision; policymakers do not seem to have tried very hard to learn lessons from these earlier experiences, lessons that might be of use to us in dealing with such more recent difficult cases as Chile, Paraguay, South Africa, Pakistan, and others. In academia, too, we still lack the monographic and comparative literature on which to base sound policy judgments. Comparative studies of transitions to democracy out of authoritarianism are

Reprinted from Adam Garfinkle and Daniel Pipes (eds.), *Friendly Tyrants* (New York: St. Martin's Press, 1991).

emerging,[1] and that is all to the good, but of policy-oriented studies of the U.S. legacy in dealing with "friendly tyrants" whilst they were still tyrants, there are none.

Our quandaries are multiplied if we allow ourselves to think not just about right-wing authoritarian regimes but also about left-wing dictatorship—"unfriendly tyrannies"—such as Cuba and Nicaragua. How are they the same, how are they different? How do our interest in and obligations toward them differ? Is there any justification for pressing human rights issues upon regimes that like or need or use us, but ignoring even more egregious situations in anti-American regimes solely because we lack leverage over them?

Dealing with "friendly tyrants" may be seen as a twofold problem, one part analytic and one part prescriptive. The first revolves largely around the question of how we gauge when an authoritarian regime may be susceptible to an overthrow that will damage U.S. interests. Such a judgment turns on a definition of what "damage" to U.S. interests really means, of course, and since that itself is often a contentious issue, it goes to the heart of the U.S. foreign policy debate. Thus, a further and unavoidable analytic question is how dealing with this or that "friendly tyranny" resonates in U.S. domestic politics.

Moreover, should we judge a friendly tyranny to be faltering, we have a choice as to whether to try to force its reform, disengage our interests, or facilitate its removal. This is where the second problem, the prescriptive one, comes into play: What exactly do we do by way of policy responses about authoritarian regimes whose continuation or whose clattering and ungainly collapse may be damaging to U.S. interests.[2] This essay concentrates on the first set of questions seen historically, and then suggests a more systematic way to evaluate policy choices made in years past that may also be relevant to current and future troubles.

THE GENERAL PROBLEM

Two polar positions have been advanced as to how the United States should respond to authoritarian regimes, an issue closely related to earlier debates over the place of human rights and democracy in U.S. foreign policy that have pitted "idealists" against the apostles of realpolitik. The idealist school would have the United States sever its relations with all such authoritarian regimes.[3] The argument is that the United States, as a special nation, a paragon of democracy, should not be associated with authoritarian regimes that violate our standards of acceptable political behavior. They are viewed as repressors of their own people and should be punished for their abuses, not coddled or rewarded. To the argument that alliances with such regimes sometimes enhance U.S. security and that we must accept the allies we can get, the counterargument is offered that repressive regimes detract from American security more than they advance it, that dictatorships, instead of serving as the bulwarks against communism, actually prepare the soil in which communism may one day thrive.[4]

The "realist" school takes the opposite tack, suggesting that the United States should only pay attention to the internal politics of any regime when it impinges on the pragmatic defense of the U.S. national interest. If a regime is friendly to us and, during the time of the Cold War, opposed to the Soviet Union, we should not undermine it no matter how unpleasant it may be. Cutting ourselves off from such regimes may salve our moral conscience, but it leaves the United States without any way to influence that regime, reduces our ability to guide the regime in a more democratic direction, and gives us no means to control any post-authoritarian transition. Thus, a policy of disengagement (as was adopted at times toward Cuba, Argentina, and Nicaragua) may lead to an even worse situation from the point of view of both U.S. strategic interests and political morality than existed under the old regime.

The issue surfaces in a variety of vital areas.[5] South Korea has had a long-standing authoritarian regime but it has served as a bulwark holding the line against communist expansion from the north. Saudi Arabia is not a democracy but it has vital oil supplies and a strategic location. Pakistan was a dictatorship but it helped supply the rebels in Afghanistan to resist the Soviet occupation. Mexico is an authoritarian-corporate state but it lies right on the southern border of the United States and is the last country in the world we would want to destabilize. Taiwan may not be a pure democracy but it is a strategic outpost and an economic wonder. The South African regime represses blacks but it has vital strategic minerals and commands major sea lanes. Jordan is a narrowly based monarchy but all the practicable alternatives—especially PLO control—seem far worse. Iran and Brazil in years past were not democracies but they were major regional powers who helped protect U.S. interest. Somoza was an SOB but, as Franklin Roosevelt's famous aphorism supposedly put it, at least he was "our SOB." Kuwait is nondemocratic but the world requires its petroleum.

How do we reconcile the dilemmas in all these cases and arrive at a sensible foreign policy position? Do we emphasize our security interests above all else or do we stress human rights and morality? Which of these better serves U.S. interests? Do we see authoritarian regimes primarily as allies in the struggle to contain the Soviet Union or as oppressors of their own people? Do we reward such authoritarian regimes for their helpfulness in keeping the lid on potential guerrilla uprisings or do we punish them for their violation of human rights? Do we accept such regimes as friends and collaborators regardless of the nature of their internal policies or do we ostracize them, treat them as pariahs, and cast them out from the community of civilized states? These are very difficult questions and it is hard to strike a balance between the contending arguments. Nonetheless, such authoritarian regimes that are also pro-American force both the American public and their officials to make such choices, and there is hardly any foreign policy issue that is as difficult and that presents itself so often.

In sum, there are two strains in American foreign policy. We want to preserve the nation's security, defend its borders, protect its vital interests, resist Soviet expansionism, preserve and augment our economic well-being, and enhance our own influence. We also wish to spread our domestic moral and political values internationally: to support democracy, human rights, freedom, and the rule of law with whatever nations we have relations. And clearly, while our dealings with other democracies pose no problem in this regard (supportive), and while our attitude toward totalitarian regimes is equally unproblematic (opposition), the same does not hold true for allied authoritarian regimes. Here is where geostrategic and moral congruence, whether positive or negative, disappears and our choices become truly difficult.

Whenever theory or ideology confronts reality, something has to give. It seems to me that both the pure idealist position and the pure realpolitik position are too extreme. If we sever our relations with all the world's authoritarian regimes, we would cut ourselves off from fully two-thirds of the nations of the globe. We cannot give up all our ties to all authoritarian regimes, despite our distaste for their nondemocratic character and human rights abuses, because too many vital interests are involved. We simply cannot have a foreign policy that focuses *only* on the human rights/democracy agenda and expect to remain a great power for very long. The American people want a foreign policy that *both* protects our security interests (including oil) *and* works in favor of democracy and human rights. The fact that both desires are strong, and that they are at times contradictory, implies that compromises must be made and balances struck. To the extent that we cut off relations and contacts with governments of which we disapprove—such as the Carter administration did toward the Argentine junta—we reduce our capacity to influence that government for the better or to help shape what happens when that government falls—as it inevitably will.

But pure realpolitik arguments seem as problematic as idealist ones. The United States cannot be indifferent to the nature of the more nefarious regimes with which we must deal or to the plight of those who live under them. The realist school, if its arguments were taken to their logical conclusions, would hold that we must be indifferent to the plight of the Soviet Jews who wish to emigrate and to Christians and others in the Soviet Union who wish only to practice their religion, that we must not be concerned with the situation of South African blacks, that we should ignore the pleas of harassed and often intimidated democratic oppositions trying to operate in authoritarian regimes, or that we should be deaf to the cries of nuns or peasants in Central America who are brutalized or caught in the cross fires of conflict there. But in the United States of America it is simply not possible to conduct foreign policy without a strong pro–human rights and democracy component. In the American context, and perhaps only in the American context, pure realism is not realistic. Even the foremost apostles of realpolitik have come to recognize this. Nowhere was this clearer than in the policies of the second Reagan administration toward the Philippines, Haiti, Paraguay, Chile, South Korea, and South Africa.

We must proceed carefully, draw distinctions, and blend idealism with realism. Clearly, one reason that forces upon us judgments of degree rather than kind is the obvious fact that authoritarian regimes are not all the same. Some are of such overwhelming strategic importance (Saudi Arabia) that we are probably best advised not to tamper with their internal political structure; others (Paraguay) have rather limited strategic importance. Some authoritarian regimes are fresh and full of vigor; others are wobbly and on their last legs, which is characteristically when such regimes become major concerns of U.S. foreign policy. Some authoritarian regimes, particularly if they are also wobbly, may be faced with strong communist or guerrilla challenges while others are not; and it is plainly the former that will be of most concern to U.S. policymakers.

Authoritarian regimes also vary greatly in their character and degree of popular support. Some authoritarian regimes are populist and enjoy widespread public backing at least during certain stages of their tenure. Perón's Argentina and Vargas's Brazil come quickly to mind but many other examples exist as well. It is probably not appropriate, no matter how pure our democratic motives, for the United States to try to unseat such populist-authoritarian regimes if to do so would be contrary to the wishes of the people living under that regime. The fact is, difficult though it is for many Americans to believe, that many authoritarian regimes enjoy genuine popularity. Cultural attitudes toward authority and its practice also vary widely in different parts of the world. Many authoritarian regimes are welcomed and admired because they provide order, coherence, and stability in countries that have long been chronically and pitifully unstable. Such regimes are often at once nationalistic and paternalistic. They may not be our cup of tea but in their own cultural context such regimes are often admired, even revered. A rational and effective foreign policy toward authoritarian regimes must recognize these differences and distinguish wisely between different types of authoritarianism. U.S. judgment on this score has been inconsistent.

The making of such distinctions must start from measures derived, for the most part, from local standards. We must judge authoritarian regimes and their policies in their own cultural contexts, not simply through criteria reflective of American or West European preferences. Some regimes—a Hitler or a Pol Pot or a Bokassa or an Idi Amin—are so far beyond the pale that they deserve condemnation from any point of view, even if they are apparently locally popular. But, in general, with less extreme authoritarian regimes that constitute the vast majority of cases, indigenous standards must be carefully considered as well as universal ones. It clearly will not do for us in a policy sense simply to issue a standard and blanket condemnation of all authoritarian regimes as unacceptable to the United States. Degrees of unacceptability must be recognized as well as such criteria as the age of the regime, its wobbliness and potential for losing power, levels of popular support, strategic location, and possibilities for post-authoritarian democracy or, alternatively, a communist takeover.

Moreover, some authoritarian conditions are aptly described as authoritarian episodes within a generally democratic experience—as with the case of the Greek colonels and Turkish interludes of military intervention. And finally, as with the Republic of Vietnam, some regimes may want to be authoritarian but cannot accumulate enough real authority to pull it off.

Authoritarian regimes change and evolve. Most get old, ossified, and out of touch. As they do, they also tend to develop ever more repressive methods of control to keep themselves in power. The trick is to recognize when an authoritarian regime that has been in power for a long time and early on enjoyed considerable popularity becomes increasingly wobbly, slips over the line toward greater repression, becomes increasingly unpopular, and is therefore no longer acceptable not only by our standards of human rights but by the standards of its own people.

That is the evolution of the most notorious of recent authoritarian regimes: Batista, Trujillo, Somoza, Salazar, the Shah, Duvalier, Marcos, and perhaps Pinochet. All started as authoritarian figures with considerable popular support, often as populists, or as "saviors" of their country. A few were even elected to power. But they all, similarly, gravitated toward such levels of repression, corruption, and brutality that they became either full-fledged or quasi-totalitarians, controlling more and more areas of their countries' and peoples' existence. As they became more brutal, more totalitarian, and stayed in power too long, they became less and less acceptable to their own populations. And as their base of support dwindled to, typically, a few handfuls of cronies and military officers, the question inevitably arose of how long the United States could continue to support such unpopular regimes, now often challenged by a serious left-wing insurgency, and in a strategically important country.

This is, in a sense, a new twist on the older, political science distinction between authoritarianism and totalitarianism,[6] elevated to foreign policy significance through the writings of Jeane Kirkpatrick.[7] Ambassador Kirkpatrick rightly distinguished between traditional authoritarianism and communist totalitarianism. She argued that from a foreign policy viewpoint—though not from the point of view of the domestic victims of such regimes—authoritarian regimes are to be preferred over totalitarian ones because they tend to be less permanent; they may be reformable and may even be amenable to transitions to democracy; and they tend to do less harm to broader U.S. interests. Nevertheless, traditional, limited authoritarianism may also evolve in the opposite direction, not toward democracy but toward full-scale, right-wing totalitarianism—with disastrous consequences both for the country affected and for U.S. policy.[8] That is the route taken by all the most notorious and difficult cases with which we have had lately—and still have—to deal.

Fulgencia Batista was a populist and a nationalist when he first came to power in the 1930s. Even his second coup d'etat in 1952 was welcomed by most Cubans as a harbinger of order and stability after the corruption and chaos of the previous eight years. But as Batista became more bloody and repressive from the mid-1950s on, he lost virtually all support. And the United States was unable to control or even influence the post-Batista transition that produced the Marxist-Leninist regime of Fidel Castro.[9]

The Dominican Republic's Rafael Trujillo also began with considerable popular support in the 1930s as the "savior" and "benefactor" of his nation. But by the late 1950s his was such a cruel and terroristic regime that it had alienated all of its support. Although on several occasions the situation nearly got out of hand, this time the United States did manage to shape and guide the post-Trujillo transition.[10]

The elder Anastasio Somoza, who founded the family dynasty in Nicaragua, was an authoritarian and a dictator, but not an excessively brutal one by the standards of his own society. His elder son Luis even accommodated the regime somewhat to the requirements of the Alliance for Progress. It was his second son, Anastasio Jr., who became so corrupt and repressive that he brought the whole house of cards down on his head and, like Batista, paved the way for a Marxist-Leninist takeover.[11]

The Shah of Iran, Mohammed Reza Pahlavi, was similarly popular in his early days. But we failed to recognize in time how all-pervasive and technologically proficient (a hallmark of rising totalitarianism) his secret police became and how he had squandered his popularity through corruption and ostentatious displays of wealth.[12]

The elder Francoise Duvalier had been a country physician who built up a political base by helping his clients, but in office he proved dictatorial and his son and heir, Jean-Claude, or "Baby Doc" (not a trained physician like his father), was even worse. Ferdinand Marcos also enjoyed considerable initial popularity by bringing order and coherence to the chaotic Philippine polity and, let it not be forgotten, he was *elected* to his office. But he became corrupt and increasingly brutal, lost his popular support, and eventually had to flee. Even Pinochet was welcomed by many Chileans as providing order and stability after the upheavals of the Allende years, but the mass killings after the coup shocked the country and led to an erosion of his support and to Chile being widely viewed as a pariah state.

The pattern in all these regimes is clear. A chaotic, corrupt, and disorganized moderate or democratic regime is initially replaced by an authoritarian one that, because it stands for peace and stability, is at first welcomed by the population. As that regime persists in power, however, it gradually loses support and eventually turns to totalitarian tactics to keep itself in power, and thus loses whatever freely given support it had left. In the most difficult cases, the wobbly and unpopular dictator is faced not just by rising democratic opposition but also by a military insurgency, sometimes a communist or a communist-influenced one. The question then becomes, should the United States continue to support and prop up a regime that once was popular and that also served as a bastion against communism? Or should we then begin to disassociate ourselves from that regime (and when and how), with all the attendent possibilities for alienating the existing government and other dependent allies, and for losing control of the situation (and the country) that is implied in such a serious step?

THE UNITED STATES AND "WOBBLY AUTHORITARIANS": WHEN TO CUT THE TIES

To systematize the patterns of the past in order to better understand the present and plan for the future, a scale has been devised to help gauge the logical point when the United States should disassociate itself from tired and wobbly authoritarians.[13] This measure is based on the premise that the United States cannot act against all the world's authoritarian regimes; if we tried to do that we would find ourselves in official opposition to some 60 percent of the governments of the world.[14] The problem for U.S. policy is not authoritarianism per se but rather when an essentially unreformable authoritarian regime begins to wobble, verges toward totalitarianism and thus loses virtually all support, runs the risk of being superseded by a Marxist-Leninist regime allied with the Soviet Union, and thus becomes a palpable security concern for the United States. When that happens or threatens to happen, it is time for the United States to skillfully abandon the sinking ship, and to begin moving toward an alternative or even, if necessary, shaping that alternative.

The United States had done precisely that, or tried to, in a number of cases for avowedly realpolitik purposes. However, even with the best intentions, intelligence, and insight, sometimes things still do not work out well. The scale that follows, therefore, must be seen foremost as an aid to general analysis, not as a policy blueprint.

The following factors help us gauge when more or less tolerable (though not necessarily desirable) authoritarianism passes over that often indistinct line to become not only intolerable to the population of the country but also dangerous from a U.S. foreign policy viewpoint. Since variables are posed as ordinal and not dichotomous functions, the scale can measure not only authoritarian "slippage" toward totalitarianism but also movement in the opposite direction, toward democracy.

- When graft, traditionally in the range of 5–7 percent and constituting more or less acceptable patronage, soars to an unacceptable 25–30 percent and becomes little more than outright institutionalized bribery.
- When opportunities for legal opposition are increasingly snuffed out. Authoritarian regimes typically permit some opposition, but totalitarian regimes permit none.

- When institutional checks and balances are increasingly eliminated. Authoritarian regimes typically allow some limited institutional checks through the congress or the courts; totalitarian regimes do not.
- When freedom of speech, press, and assembly, always repressed in an authoritarian regime, are increasingly wiped out.
- When self-government at local levels is increasingly subordinated to the all-powerful central state.
- When social and political pluralism, always limited in an authoritarian regime, is increasingly limited.[15]
- When terror and technologically proficient torture (as distinct from the traditional techniques of jailings and exile) become institutionalized as state policy and encompass the broader population.
- When economical development and social justice are ever more sacrificed to dictatorial megalomania and the regime's self-enrichment.
- When virtually all human rights are systematically abrogated.
- When a government that was paternalistic and beneficent turns increasingly mean-spirited and selfish.
- When freedom from arbitrary and capricious authority is increasingly sacrificed.
- When the regime increasingly loses its representative and participatory character (this may involve systems of formal or informal ethnic, functional, or corporative representation very different from that in the United States).
- When the regime gets old and starts to wobble.
- When the country is important strategically to the United States.
- When the threat exists of a potential communist or Marxist-Leninist takeover of the country once the dictator falls.

To demonstrate the heuristic utility of the scale, a test has been devised involving Latin American countries, where there is sufficient cultural and historical commonality to make comparisons particularly vivid and compelling. The exercise was carried out in April 1987. First we employ an ordinal numerical scale, let us say from one to ten, for each of the criteria listed above—with ten indicating the degree to which the assertion applies to the country under consideration, a score of one indicating that it does not apply. If we then ask a panel of experts to provide their best judgment about the countries they know,[16] add up the totals for all the criteria, and then examine the clustering or groupings or countries that emerge, some interesting findings emerge. Such an exercise is illustrated in table 3.1. From the data, a rank ordering emerges from most authoritative and dictatorial, verging on totalitarianism, to least authoritarian or demo-

Table 3.1
Scale of Unacceptable Authoritarianism

Criteria	Arg	Bol	Bra	Chi	Col	CRi	Cub	DRp	Ecua	ElSa	Gua	Hai	Hon	Mex	Nic	Pan	Par	Per	Uru	Ven
Graft	3	7	3	5	4	2	4	4	5	5	6	5	5	7	5	6	6	5	2	4
No legal position	1	3	1	8	2	1	9	1	1	2	3	4	5	5	8	5	7	3	1	1
No checks & balances	1	1	1	8	2	1	9	2	1	3	3	4	3	5	8	4	8	3	2	1
No free speech	1	3	1	8	1	1	9	1	1	3	3	2	3	3	8	2	8	3	1	1
No self-government	2	3	2	6	2	2	8	2	2	3	3	4	3	5	8	3	7	3	2	2
No pluralism	1	1	1	7	2	1	9	2	2	3	4	3	3	3	7	3	7	3	1	1
Terror and torture	2	3	2	9	2	1	7	2	2	4	4	3	4	3	7	3	7	3	1	2
No development	2	5	1	2	2	3	5	2	2	5	4	5	4	4	5	3	3	4	2	3
No human rights	1	3	2	8	2	1	8	2	2	4	4	4	3	4	8	4	8	3	1	2
Mean-spirited and selfish	1	2	1	8	2	1	7	2	2	4	4	3	4	4	7	3	8	4	1	2
No freedom	1	2	1	8	1	1	9	1	1	2	3	4	4	4	7	3	8	4	1	1
No representation	2	2	2	8	2	1	9	2	2	3	4	4	3	3	5	4	8	4	1	1
Old, passé	1	3	1	7	2	2	8	3	3	4	3	4	4	4	5	4	8	3	2	3
Strategic importance	7	4	9	7	6	5	6	5	4	5	5	3	5	9	5	6	4	5	4	6
Threat of communist takeover	2	3	2	4	2	1	10	2	3	5	5	3	3	4	10	4	3	4	3	3
Total	28	45	30	103	34	24	117	33	33	55	58	55	55	67	103	57	100	54	25	33
Rank Order	3	9	4	18	8	1	20	5	5	11	15	11	11	16	18	14	17	10	2	5

Table 3.2
Rank Ordering of Latin American
Countries: From Authoritarian
to Democracy

Rank	Country	Score
1	Cuba	117
2	Nicaragua	103
3	Chile	103
4	Paraguay	100
5	Mexico	67
6	Guatemala	58
7	Panama	57
8	El Salvador	55
9	Haiti	55
10	Honduras	55
11	Peru	54
12	Bolivia	45
13	Colombia	34
14	Dominican Republic	33
15	Ecuador	33
16	Venezuala	33
17	Brazil	30
18	Argentina	28
19	Uruguay	25
20	Costa Rica	24

cratic, as indicated in table 3.2. By clustering those countries whose scores were close together, we can suggest the following classification:

1. Fully Democratic: Costa Rica, Uruguay, Argentina, Brazil, Venezuela, Ecuator, Dominican Republic, Colombia.
2. Mixed and Marginal, or en route to Democracy: Bolivia, Peru, Haiti, Honduras, El Salvador, Panama, Guatemala, Mexico.
3. Marxist-Leninist: Cuba, Nicaragua.
4. Traditional Authoritarian: Paraguay.
5. Pariah State: Chile.

It thus appeared that only one country in Latin America—Paraguay—was still an old-fashioned, traditional, caudillo-dominated, authoritarian dictatorship. Chile, on the other hand, was the single real pariah state, a regime that had alienated even its earlier supporters, rested on an exceedingly narrow base, and verged toward totalitarianism. This suggests that Paraguay is not likely to become a serious problem for U.S. policy, but that Chile could. This accords with common sense and much expert judgment, but that does not mean the scale is always marginal. Its advantage is that it can protect against "bad intuition"—sometimes the data is counterintuitive—and that it provides a more detailed taxonomy, albeit an impressionistic one, to help explain why the numbers turn out as they do.

Finally, the scale can serve as a post hoc means of judging past U.S. policy performance. The criteria suggested can, with some effort, be transported back to any year we like and, in retrospect, some supplementary data that always elude us in the present time (e.g., measures of capital flight, arrests, personnel shifts, and so forth) are easier to establish after the fact. Did the United States act too late against Somoza, Ferdinand Marcos, and Mohammed Reza Pahlavi? Too soon against Diem and the Argentine generals? Perhaps the scale can help.

"FRIENDLY TYRANTS": THE DOMESTIC DIMENSION

The preceding analysis is based largely on a "rational-actor model" of foreign policy-making; that is, it discusses in its several dimensions a discrete foreign policy issue, it suggests a range of options that policymakers are presumed to consider in analogous circumstances, weighing the pros and cons of each, and it assumes that policy has been, is, and will be generally dominated by "rational" evaluations in given circumstances. But as the cases of various "friendly tyrants" make clear, and as anyone who has ever served in the U.S. foreign policy bureaucracy knows, the "rational-actor model" is a very incomplete analytical approach.

There are other ways of looking at problem solving and collective decision making that must also be taken into account. These include a "bureaucratic model," an approach that focuses on the differences that may exist on a particular issue between several foreign policy-making agencies of the U.S. government (State versus Defense, etc.), and whose resolution on that basis may lack clarity and coherence. There is also an "organizational model," an approach that focuses on the organizational plans and procedures that foreign policy-making departments use in carrying out their activities that deeply affect policy outcomes—for example, the contingency plans that the Department of Defense has for various military operations that can be implemented more quickly than State Department decision making can usually proceed.[17] There is also a "political process model," which suggests that foreign policy decision making is not a simple matter of choosing rationally among competing options and then carrying out the chosen policy, but also involves a complex process of interaction with U.S. *domestic* political considerations.[18]

Both the bureaucratic politics and organizational process models, by focusing on decision processes and outcomes rather than intentions and individual judgments, help explain why some problems that logically ought to be seen together are instead compartmentalized. They can also help explain the pitfalls of bureaucratic clientelism, and how it is that the right intelligence rarely seems to reach the right people. The political process model helps explain how issues that ought logically to be defined as discrete are instead thrown together with various and sundry other matters. The latter is of some special interest in the matter of dealing with friendly tyrants.

Foreign policy and domestic policy have always been interwined but, since the war in Vietnam, the connections have become more numerous and more complex.[19] In the early cases briefly discussed here—those of Batista and Trujillo—it was not just a rational-actor model that played itself out. Bureaucratic dynamics aside, domestic politics also played a role, albeit a relatively minor one. There were interests and individuals within the United States who had a strong interest in the outcome of Cuban and Dominican events and who tried to make their influence felt accordingly. But these private interests could not often dominate the foreign policy-making process or determine its outcome—as is sometimes the situation now—nor did these earlier cases generate the "stuff" of public debate and mass political mobilization in the United States as some later cases (the Philippines, South Africa, Nicaragua) clearly have. Indeed, in these later cases domestic political considerations threaten to overwhelm and even submerge what (little) there is of a rational ordering of options and of a careful choosing between them. What has happened to U.S. foreign policy between "Batista" and "Marcos"?

Clearly, in the last twenty-five years domestic political considerations in the making of U.S. foreign policy have achieved a new and much greater importance. Not only are domestic considerations more significant, but they have also fed other factors leading to the increasing disarray, impotence, paralysis, *immobilisme,* and even sclerosis of U.S. foreign policy.[20] The matter is especially important, even crucial, for the future of American foreign policy-making because it goes beyond the issue of dealing with friendly tyrants. It may have already become a permanent and particularly debilitating feature of our foreign policy-making system; witness the intense and virtually constant debate in the 1980s over what the United States should do vis-à-vis Nicaragua.

Several factors are important in explaining this transformation and its impact on the question of how the United States should deal with "friendly tyrants." The first and most important is probably Vietnam and the persistent fear in the United States that our identification with and support for right-wing regimes in a context of revolution and civil war may again result in our being dragged into a bloody conflict in some far corner of the globe that will tear the country apart, result in the death of fifty thousand young Americans, and do irreparable damage to our foreign policy.

A second factor is Congress and the increasing politicalization of U.S. foreign policy. Politics no longer "stop at the water's edge"; foreign policy is now politicized in much the same way that domestic issues are. Congress plays a far greater role in foreign policy-making; when Congressman Stephen Solarz (Dem.-N.Y.) went to the Philippines to negotiate with both the Marcos regime and its opposition, he was acting in effect as a congressional secretary of state. Then there is the War Powers Act, the Boland Amendment(s), the requirements of human rights certifications of progress in difficult countries like Guatemala and El Salvador, the far closer congressional scrutiny of presidential appointments in the foreign policy area, and virtual nonstop and highly polemicized congressional hearings on difficult foreign policy issues. The White House, no matter who occupies it, tends to look upon these congressional initiatives as unwanted and unwarranted interferences in presidential foreign policy-making prerogative; the Congress, in the wake of Vietnam, Watergate, and Iranamok, feels that it cannot trust the executive branch to carry out a foreign policy that is in the best interests of the United States and that, therefore, the Congress must play a stronger role. The result is that seemingly every congressman has become his or her own secretary of state.[21]

The third new force is television, on which all those congressional "secretaries of state" appear. Many congressmen have become masters of the thirty-second instant analysis, designed to get them on the evening news, which is roughly the simplistic level that passes for foreign policy discussion in the United States these days. Moreover, television is itself covering—and hence popularizing—these issues of U.S. relations with right-wing dictators far more extensively than in the past, and is frequently asserting its editorial views on these matters into the newscasts, thus "hyping" the issue and sometimes leading the news and events rather than just covering them. One can make the case, for example, that television coverage of Marcos stealing the Philippine election or the revelation about Imelda's three hundred pairs of shoes had more impact in shaping

U.S. attitudes and hence policy toward the Philippines than did Philippine public opinion itself. Television's coverage of events in South Africa and South Korea has similarly not been mere reportage of events, but has constituted a precipitating factor in moving history—and U.S. policy with it—along, whether for good or ill we do not at this point know. And that is precisely the issue: the problem transcends that of the biases and oversimplified reportage of that particular medium[22] but also involves television's capacity to take a particular controversy out of the hands of presumably rational foreign policymakers, who approach it from the viewpoint of U.S. national interests, and "into the streets," where virtually any outcome is possible on virtually any grounds.[23]

Fourth, the domestication and politicization of foreign policy issues has been aided and abetted by the emergence of a variety of new interest groups playing a highly visible and activist role. These new groups—religious groups, human rights lobbies, associations of writers and actors, and others—have received almost no attention thus far in the foreign policy literature.[24] but their role is important and it is growing. In the Carter administration, these groups had access primarily through the executive agencies of government; under Reagan they have been particularly effective in working through the Congress. Through constant lobbying in the corridors of Congress, op-ed pieces in the major newspapers, testimony before congressional committees, and presentation of first-hand "witnesses" from Latin America, these groups have succeeded in bringing home to the American public the abuses of various Latin American governments. Really for the first time, the human rights abuses of the Chilean or Paraguayan regimes, or of continuing human rights problems in El Salvador or Guatemala, have been brought into the living rooms of the American people and made a matter of our domestic politics. There is no doubt that U.S. policy toward the two right-wing dictatorships then remaining in Latin America, Paraguay and Chile—these groups were unevenhandedly quiet about human rights abuses in such left-wing regimes as Cuba or Nicaragua—has been strongly influenced by the activities of these organizations.[25]

A fifth factor has been public opinion. Here, two stages must be distinguished. In the early stage of the discussion about what to do with a "friendly tyrant" who seems to be wobbling, the debate between those who advance the national security interest argument and those who advance humanitarian concerns argument is usually fairly even, with the national security interest argument usually prevailing, if for no other reason than that it represents the status quo and obviates the need to take any risks. But once the particular case—be it South Africa, the

Philippines, or South Korea—becomes a matter of intense public scrutiny (i.e., it is on the evening news every night), human rights considerations tend to predominate. The shift may be ascribed to the biases in the media noted earlier or simply to the fact that riots and bloody corpses make "good television." The issue is particularly joined if there is some epic crisis that occurs in the midst of the coverage—the killing of Benigno Aquino on the tarmac in Manila practically in front of the television cameras, electoral fraud that is so obvious that all can see the ballot boxes being carried away, the murder and permanent disfiguration of young Chilean leftists on the streets of Santiago, tear gas wafting through the air and nightly beatings on the streets of Seoul, and so on. When such crises happen, foreign policy decision making regarding authoritarian regimes is taken out of the hands of the professionals where, presumably, the "rational-actor model" and the forceful, measured scenarios discussed earlier most typically apply. The chain of events is then accelerated, control over the rapidly unfolding situation is often lost, and U.S. policy must scramble to catch up to and stay even with events, exercising as much (now very limited) control over them as possible in the dramatic and rapidly changing circumstances and, in effect, being left with a policy of responding to events and hoping for the best. That was, essentially, what happened in the Philippines: Marcos left and Corazon Aquino took power at least in part because of the events on U.S. television and the shift in U.S. public opinion. But whether this transition, which we helped facilitate but could not really control, will in the longer run also serve U.S. foreign policy interests remains to be seen.[26]

The final factor, related to all the others, is the overall shift in the *context* of U.S. foreign policy-making since the 1960s. We are now, as a result of Vietnam, Watergate, and Iran/Contra, to say nothing of our various racial, political, social, and economic crises of the 1960s through the 1980s, a much more divided, more fragmented, more ideological, more politicized nation than we used to be. These divisions and polarizations have by now also been reflected in—or perhaps they were led by—conflicts over foreign policy issues. The result is, unlike the earlier foreign policy context where partisan politics and divisions really did for the most part stop at the water's edge, a foreign policy regarding dictators as well as other issues that is much more fragmented, polarized, and politicized than before. It is at the root of U.S. foreign policy sclerosis, and it is the source of the temptation to circumvent the system that was so much at the heart of the Iran/Contragate hearings in 1987. This is why, it seems to me, it is quite unfair for critics to speak of the "Reagan Junta" and the "imperial" uses of the National Security Council system.

There would be little temptation to circumvent constitutional strictures on the part of the executive branch had those strictures not already been attacked and altered in effect by the legislative branch and by other forces in American society.

If there ever was a time when a rational-actor model of foreign policy-making applied in dealing with "friendly tyrants" or other issues, that time has now, and perhaps irrevocably, passed. Each succeeding crisis leading to Nicaragua, South Africa, and El Salvador owes ever more to domestic political considerations for its essential character.

CONCLUSIONS

Because of their extreme differences of age, character and "wobbliness," because some authoritarian regimes are genuinely popular, because there are simply too many of them, because there are important security stakes involved, and because the alternatives may be far worse, it is not prudent or wise for the United States to divorce itself from all "friendly tyrants." We may wish to put some distance between ourselves and them—the cool handshake as distinct from the warm *abrazo*—but a divorce should come only under the most extreme circumstances: when the dictator starts to totter, when there is a viable alternative, when the security situation is still relaxed enough to allow room for maneuver, when the United States has the means and capacity to influence, if not control, the post-authoritarian transition. Too many other factors need to be considered for the United States to follow a pure and idealistic policy of having no relations at all with the globe's numerous tyrannical regimes left and right. On the other hand, some dictators are so offensive to us that we may wish for both moral and sound political reasons to have nothing to do with them.

A centrist position that lies between the pure idealist and the pure realpolitik positions is the most sensible and realistic general U.S. foreign policy toward "friendly tyrants." We cannot and should not seek to unseat all the world's authoritarian governments—neither we nor they would be well served by such a bull-in-the-china-shop approach—but we do need to know when such regimes cross that fine line that separates more or less tolerable authoritarianism by their own country's standards, and unacceptable totalitarianism that not only damages them but also may represent a danger to U.S. interests as well. It is at this crucial point that the U.S. government may not only wish to get off that dictatorial government's bandwagon but may also wish to facilitate its ouster, both as a way of promoting democracy and as a means of moderating and exercising some control over the post-dictatorial transition.

But policy questions also arise, or should arise, not only toward the end of an authoritarian regime, but before. There are occasions when "timely daring," as Theodore Friend describes it, is called for. In other words, there are different U.S. policy responses that ought to be advanced at different stages in the life cycle of "friendly" authoritarian regimes.[27] It is better for the United States to find a way to get an authoritarian regime to reform itself than it is to have to preside over its burial. But this is an exceedingly difficult issue, first, because it is the tendency of foreign policy-making to attend to nagging issues, not to create them, and, second, because it is never simple or clear that friendly authoritarians are entering a downward spiral. The last thing we should ever want to do is undermine a foreign policy asset on the basis of false pessimism about its future.

Nevertheless, there are some general parameters of policy that amount not to timely daring but to a constant watch over friendly tyrants. First, the United States should let it be known loud and clear that we stand unequivocally for democracy and human rights, both because that is the moral and right stance to take and because we have learned that democratic regimes, if we can have them, best serve U.S. policy interests. They are less bellicose, tend to interfere less in the internal affairs of their neighbors, are more pragmatic and centrist and, with a few exceptions, have proven to be much easier to get along with. In general, they cause us less grief, both in themselves and in an administration's dealing with the Congress, our allies, or domestic public opinion and interest groups.

Second, there is what we might call the "pre-tottering stage" where the United States may take limited actions to urge movement toward democracy, or to put some distance between itself and the dictatorship. Policy toward Paraguay in the late 1980s provides a good example of this.

Third, there is the "tottering stage"; here the scale presented above may be of particular use. Complacency seems to be a major danger at this stage, an unwillingness to recognize that the risks of doing nothing can outweigh the risks of acting.

Fourth is the crisis stage when the regime actually collapses, which calls forth a variety of possibly quite forceful policy responses to help manage and if possible control the post-authoritarian decompression and transition that are different from those employed at earlier stages.[28] Here, the Haitian case of Duvalier provides dramatic examples.

The new factor, the "joker," in all these considerations is the changed domestic political situation in the United States. For the reasons discussed above, the domestic context and domestic political considerations may overwhelm the generally rational foreign policy responses analyzed here. Indeed, the domestic context in the United States may be so fragmented, polarized, and divided that nothing can be decided until the situation in the foreign country under review gets entirely out of hand—timely daring may become impossible. Neither of these two possibilities need necessarily happen, but certainly the changed foreign policy context in the United States now as compared with twenty-five years ago makes it far more difficult at present to carry out a rational, coherent, and long-term policy toward authoritarian regimes, as on other issues, and has produced a situation in which paralysis, disarray, and incoherence are likely to result rather than a decent and sensible policy.

A wide array of policy instruments and sanctions exist for the United States to deal with "friendly tyrants" and help manage the period after the dictator has gone. These include, in rough ascending order of severity, diplomatic overtures, special missions, presidential jawboning, economic pressures, breaking relations, international sanctions, CIA machinations, or military interventions—all (or most of them) strategies that were tried at one time or another with Batista, Trujillo, the Shah, Marcos, and Noriega. But even a cursory review of the main cases does not offer great reason for optimism concerning U.S. efforts to deal with "friendly tyrants" or to control the post-dictatorial transition. Of eleven major cases considered as part of this research (Iran, Cuba, Nicaragua, Haiti, South Vietnam, the Philippines, Spain, Portugal, Turkey, Argentina, Greece), seven worked out more or less satisfactorily for the United States while four did not, namely South Vietnam, Cuba, Iran, and Nicaragua. In the seven cases that worked out tolerably well, only three (Portugal, Haiti, the Philippines) were due, in part at least, to what the United States did in a policy sense; while four (Greece, Spain, Turkey, and Argentina) worked out because of their own efforts and initiatives and largely regardless of or despite what the United States did or did not do.

The failures and the outcomes that had little to do with U.S. policy initiatives add up to two-thirds of our cases. This should give us pause about our rushing in pell-mell to unseat very many of the world's authoritarian regimes. Our capacities, to say nothing of our comprehension of all these different countries and their societies, cultures, and political processes, are often quite limited. We need a cautious, prudent, careful, and above all realistic approach in dealing with "friendly tyrants." There are things that we can do to influence such regimes in their various stages and even in their wakes, but there are many other actions that we should not even attempt. The cases considered here illustrate what comes of doing too little and of doing too much, of being too late and of being too early, and, very occasionally, what comes of getting it right.

4

The Military and Democracy

Our understanding of the social and political role of the Latin American armed forces has increased significantly over the last quarter-century. Since Edwin Lieuwen published his path-breaking study for the Council on Foreign Relations, *Arms and Politics in Latin America,* in 1960,[1] the literature on the causes of armed forces' intervention in politics, on the place of the military in society, and on the overall processes of change in Latin America has grown considerably.

Yet today we run the risk of losing sight of all the nuance, the sophistication of interpretation, and the detailed case study information built up over these years. In our enthusiasm for the democratic openings dramatically occurring in Latin America, we are again relying too often on simplistic formulas. We tend to picture the choices in Latin America as either military or civilian government, dictatorship versus democracy, as though those were the only choices available. The popular literature and the media encourage a wholesale condemnation of the military and its role in Latin America political life, a sometimes romantic and exaggerated view of the possibilities of civilian government, a desire to shunt the military aside and forget about it, and a great deal of wishful and ethnocentric thinking that we can create in Latin America political societies that look just like our own, including the firm subordination of the military to civilian authority.

Some cautionary warnings need to be introduced into these hopeful scenarios. The military in Latin America cannot be wished away. An appropriate role for the armed forces must be found, and it is unlikely that the United States can serve as a relevant model in this regard. In addition, it is quite probable that once the present euphoria for democracy in Latin America passes, once the past excesses of the military's last round of experiences in power fade from memory, and once Latin America overcomes its present economic and structural crisis, the severe dimen-

Reprinted from *Harvard International Review* 8 (May/June 1986).

sions of which helped drive the armed forces from power in the first place—and then when the next crisis comes and the armed forces feel obliged, or are called upon, to rescue again their countries from some new disaster—it is possible at that point to envision a new turning of the historical clock and the reentry of the military back into a more direct political role.

We are not saying that such an evolution is inevitable, let alone desirable, but it is certainly possible and, some would say, quite likely—at least in some countries. Should it occur, we may well regret having lost sight of the more sophisticated understandings of the Latin American military that had come to characterize the recent literature.

The argument has policy implications as well as scholarly ones. Even in the present, increasingly democratic context of Latin America, we need to find an appropriate position and function for the armed forces—if for no other reason than to keep them busy and preoccupied with activities other than domestic politics. Plus, we need to be prepared in a policy sense for the possibility of a new wave of future military regimes. For, should such regimes come to power, let us say for example, in El Salvador, it may still be necessary for the United States to support them, because our interests are affected and the alternatives may be even worse. In our current enthusiasm for Latin America's democratic transitions, I have so far seen no thought given to, let alone contingency planning for, the possibility that these transitions may be halted or even reversed. Lamentably, we need to be prepared for that eventuality in both a scholarly and a policy sense.

HISTORICAL BACKGROUND

The original Latin American armies emerged from the independence struggles of the early nineteenth century as unprofessional *caudillo-*dominated armies. With a severe legitimacy crisis occasioned by the withdrawal of the Spanish crown, and in the absence at that time of viable civilian institutions, praetorianism prevailed.

After mid-century, some greater regularity and even professionalism were brought to the military institution. The trend was accelerated in the bigger countries—Argentina, Brazil, Chile—by the presence of foreign military missions, chiefly Prussian. New military academies and training programs were established. From 1850 to 1890, in the larger and better institutionalized South American countries, praetorianism and caudilloism diminished, but by no means disappeared.

By the 1890's, a greater degree of stability had been brought out of the prevailing disorder in virtually all the countries of the region. In some countries, "liberal" oligarchic regimes provided stability and economic development over several decades; in others, "order and progress" men-on-horseback, such as Porfirio Díaz in Mexico, presided over national consolidation. In still others, United States military occupations enforced stability and established the infrastructure for future development. For forty years, under one or another of these three formulas, Latin America was comparatively stable, prosperous, even "developing." For the most part, the military stayed out of a direct role in politics.

The world market crash of 1929–30 changed all that. The bottom dropped out of the Latin American economies, and the region's political systems disintegrated shortly thereafter. Between 1930 and 1935, fifteen of the twenty Latin American countries experienced major politico-military transformations.[2] These were not just the usual barracks revolts or *pronunciamientos,* but implied profound alterations in the national social and political life. The military was back in power, and in quite a number of countries, was in for a long stay.

The causes of this new wave of military interventions were various and complex. They deserve especially close attention because many of these causative factors are still with us today. If these factors prompted widespread military interventions in the 1930's, and if the same precipitating factors are still present today, we may well expect that in the future—to the degree these conditions remain the same—they may well lead to a new or renewed period of military rule.

A number of factors help explain military interventions in the 1930's:

History and political culture. Not only did Latin America have a long and rather hallowed history of military interventionism, but the position of the military in society was special—the military was almost a fourth branch of government, with certain special rights *(fueros)* and position in the Hispanic tradition, and an obligation to intervene in the political order under conditions of instability and breakdown.

Absence of viable alternative institutions. In 1930, Latin America was still lamenting its *falta de civilización*—its lack of institutions and an associational infrastructure capable of holding society together. In the absence of such institutions, it was the military's duty to fill the void. In part, therefore, the importance of the armed forces derived from the weakness or absence of other political institutions such as political parties.

Military unity. Unlike the civilian institutions, the military institution in the 1930's remained unified, non-factionalized, and whole. The military "caste" was still intact; moreover, with its multiclass makeup, it could claim to be at least as representative of the nation as the splintered civilian factions.

Economic crisis. Latin American export economies were suffering severe setbacks. In times of such severe economic crises, the historical record shows, the tendency has been for larger numbers of military coups.

Class changes. The old order in Latin America had been oligarchic, but a rising middle class was clamoring for change. The military officer corps in Latin America, itself made up increasingly of middle class officers, was a reflection of and a response to both the bankruptcy of oligarchic rule and the desire of the new *mestizo* /mulatto middle classes for a share in power.

Class challenges. The lower classes and the nascent trade unions also clamored for change. In part, the military interventions of the 1930's may be looked on as a way to hold the lower classes in check and to prevent a class revolution from below. Fear of Bolshevism or of a Mexico-style revolution was pervasive.

Social escalator. In the closed, hierarchical, immobilist, semi-feudal societies of Latin America, a military career was one of few avenues of social advancement open to ambitious poor and middle class youth. In turn, a military career offered the opportunity for status and power on an even grander scale—the presidency of the republic.

Rapaciousness. It was not just power and status that some of these officers were after, but sheer money. High political office, in a patrimonialist and quasi-mercantilist state, offered abundant opportunity for self-enrichment at the public watering trough. Coup-mongers like Trujillo, Somoza, Batista, and later Perón and Pérez Jiménez used their official positions to garner immense riches, cars, houses, and land; they amassed some of the world's largest fortunes.

The forms of political organization. Military interventionism from the 1930's on seems also to have stemmed in part from the system of familial politics then prevailing, a system dominated by patron-client relationships and the existence of a small, still relatively unprofessional military—itself caught up in the same system of family-based and intra-elite politics.

If these factors help explain the coming to power of the military in the 1930's, they also help explain the longevity of military rule. Continuously in some countries and alternating with civilian rule in others, the military was a principal actor, if not the principal actor, in almost all the Latin American countries through the 1950's—and in some cases right through the 1970's. The military was often more unified, more effective, and more powerful than the civilian groups. Chile, Costa Rica, and Uruguay (all with strong civilian institutions) constituted the major exceptions during this earlier period—and even in these countries the army was a major presence. But by the 1950's this particular generation of military elites was passing from the scene; a popular book written at the time prematurely proclaimed that period the "twilight of the tyrants."[3]

In the late-1950's and early-1960's, a brief democratic interlude occurred in Latin America, stimulated both by changes within the region and by a change in administrations in the United States which seemed to augur well for Latin America's democratic openings. But as early as 1962 a new wave of coups began to occur, in part stimulated by the very changes the Kennedy Administration and the Alliance for Progress had introduced. In retrospect it is no longer clear if the Kennedy era was really a turning point in Latin American history or only a brief interruption in a general pattern that included repeated and often long-term military rule. By the end of the decade and into the early-1970's, twelve of the twenty Latin American republics were again under military rule; and in five of the remaining countries the military was so close to the surface of power as to make the usual civil/military distinction all but meaningless. We need to take account of the reasons for this new round of military intervention, thereby adding to the list of casual factors already enumerated and reinforcing some of those previously listed.

The anti-communist phobia. The Cuban revolution had a profound impact on the Latin American officer corps. Interviews at the time revealed that to the officers, communism meant more than just some alternative ideological or economic system but rather, with the example of what happened to the former Batista officer corps, a regime where they were summarily tried and shot. That stark image of communism helped "focus the mind," and it led the Latin American militaries to be suspicious of all new social and political movements that even hinted at Marxism or socialism.[4]

Mass mobilization. Encouraging the military were the local middle classes, who felt threatened by the Alliance-inspired mobilization of the lower classes. It was the Latin American civilian middle classes that often pushed, prodded, and manipulated their own militaries into power so as to head off and check the presumed revolution from below.[5]

Weakness of civilian institutions. While the Kennedy Administration had often pushed hard for democracy in Latin America, the new civilian governments that emerged were often weak, inept, ineffectual, and inefficient. Part of the blame for the new wave of military regimes may be ascribed to the failures of democratic leaders.

US machinations. In a number of notorious cases (Brazil, Dominican

Republic, Chile), the military took power in part because US advisers had urged them to, or because these advisers had said the US would not object overly if they wished to take over. Usually, this factor became important only after civilian institutions had already been discredited, and the armed forces were already inclined to intervene.

Military role expansion. The Latin American militaries were now far larger, more diversified and specialized in their functions, with wider responsibilities than they had had in the 1930's. Such a vast range of roles provided another reason for the military to exercise expanded political responsibilities.

Professionalization. Professionalization in Latin America led the military to become better trained, better educated, and more capable of running a government. Professionalization, unlike in other countries, led to greater intervention in politics, not less.[6]

National security doctrines and developmentalism. The curriculum followed in the leading Latin American military academies and advanced war colleges in the 1960's stressed public administration, central planning, management, international trade, and national development as means to enhance security. These were also the skills needed to run a country, which the armed forces soon discovered they were better trained and equipped to do than most of the civilian regimes they replaced.

All these factors provided added inducements or reinforced a proclivity and set of habits already present for the Latin American militaries in the 1960's to reenter the political arena to the extent of taking and holding power. These were not just barracks revolts where the military seizes power temporarily, holds elections, and then gets out; rather, the armed forces were determined to stay in power until their entire national political systems could be transformed. Additionally, these new Latin American militaries were no longer just *caudillo*-dominated as the old ones (Somoza, Batista, Trujillo) had been; rather they were more broadly institutionalized military regimes or combined civil/military regimes, described by some scholars as "bureaucratic-authoritarians."[7]

But by the late–1970's and accelerating in the early–1980's, the glow was long gone from the bureaucratic-authoritarian model. The Latin American militaries proved no more capable of governing than had the civilians. In addition, the armed forces had been discredited by corruption, incompetence, and in some cases the use of torture, violations of human rights, and wasteful foreign wars. Furthermore, the domestic problems of these countries proved intractable; economic disaster set in; the pressures for democracy arose anew; new social and political forces clamoring for change emerged; and the United States, for both ideological reasons and strategic purposes, began pushing for democracy and human rights. By the mid-1980's the situation had been entirely reversed from what it had been a decade earlier, with the vast majority of the Latin American countries and peoples again under civilian democratic rule and with the armed forces confined to the barracks.

LITERATURE ON THE MILITARY

The earliest body of literature on the Latin American armed forces was overwhelmingly condemning. The military was viewed as usurpers of power, perpetrators of corruption, violators of the constitution, and destroyers of democracy and civil liberties.[8] While there is a considerable degree of validity in this perspective, the approach is exceedingly ethnocentric and fails to take into account the special role and position of the armed forces in Iberian and Latin American history.

A second body of literature, popularized in the early-1960's (and thus corresponding to the heyday of the Alliance for Progress) viewed the military in a much more favorable light.[9] The military officer corps was becoming more middle class, better educated, more professionalized, more oriented toward constructive civic action, and even more democratic, the argument ran. This vision of the armed forces as "good guys" was at least as mistaken as the view that saw them entirely as "bad guys," but it did serve to provide rationalization for an immense US military assistance program in the 1960's.

During the course of the 1960's, some richer, deeper, and more sophisticated interpretations of the armed forces began to appear. Writing in the *Journal of Inter-American Studies* in 1961, Lyle McAlister urged that the Latin American militaries be understood in their own corporate, historical, social and institutional contexts and not from the point of view of either knee-jerk condemnation or approbation.[10] Elizabeth Hyman of the State Department's Office of Intelligence and Research published a superb article in the *Political Science Quarterly* (1972) that rejected the opposing arguments on whether the military was purely reactionary or wholly progressive and suggested instead, that the armed forces in Latin America be viewed neutrally and in their own context.[11] The author's earlier work in this area, in a monograph entitled *Critical Coups and Critical Elections* (Ohio University), similarly examined the place and role of the military in Latin American politics and treated violence, the coup process, and alternations between civilian and military regimes as normal, recurring features of the area's political systems.

By the 1970's, the monographic literature had begun to expand greatly, both as new case studies of individual countries appeared and as the interpretations became more sophisticated. The case study literature included Robert Potash's masterful study of the military in Argentina,[12] Samuel Fitch on Ecuador,[13] Luigi Einaudi on Peru,[14] Frederick Nunn on Chile,[15] Alfred Stepan on Brazil,[16] and Ronald McDonald on Central America.[17] These case studies emphasized the distinct patterns of civil-military relations in each country and hence the need for an approach that recognized these country differences and that was less sweeping and generalized than the earlier studies.

It was not just that the detailed case study materials were now richer, but that the interpretations available offered a variety of fresh perspectives. José Nun wrote a fascinating article on "The Middle Class Military Coup," showing how in the 1960's, the threatened and unstable middle classes of Latin America had joined forces with the military to turn back the threat of leftist and/or lower class revolutions. Stepan's work showed that military professionalism in Latin America, as contrasted with some other areas, led to greater military interventionism in politics rather than less. Einaudi's studies emphasized the new training programs in the military academies, while Charles Corbett focused on the military career system.[18] Corbett also suggested strongly that we pay attention to what the Latin American officers themselves say and write about their role, as Jack Child has recently done in a book on Latin American security doctrines and geopolitical thinking.[19] A number of scholars have written on the revolutionary or "Nasserist" military regimes that come to power—albeit temporarily, as it turned out—in such countries as Ecuador, Peru, and Panama.[20] Many of these newer approaches have been incorporated in a volume edited by Abraham Lowenthal.[21]

This literature and the insights it provides have added immensely to our knowledge and understanding of the Latin American militaries, civil-military relations, and the place of the Latin American militaries in the broader social and political systems of the area. It is precisely this nuance and greater comprehension that is threatened by the often simplistic notions now being bandied about that seek to portray Latin America as engaged in a dichotomous, either-or struggle pitting democracy against dictatorship. In fact, Latin America is infinitely more complex and variegated than that, and one hopes that these greater complexities can be kept in mind.

MILITARY ROLE EXPANSION IN THE INTERNATIONAL ARENA

Though Latin America is known to be characterized at the domestic level by a considerable degree of political violence, including that stemming from the military, to this point the area has been marked by the almost complete absence of violence at the international level. Latin America's record in this respect is far better than that of Western Europe or the United States over the last 160 years. In the entire history of the continent, among twenty or more countries, there have only been two or three serious wars, plus a number of other skirmishes of short duration. Given our image of Latin America as a chaotic, violent region, the absence of international conflict there is quite remarkable.

But that may be changing now. Irredentism, realpolitik, and international conflict, as Mark Falcoff points out,[22] have come to Latin America. There are both immense arms build-ups in Latin America generally as well as numerous regional arms races: Brazil and Argentina, Peru and Chile, Ecuador and Peru, Haiti and the Dominican Republic, El Salvador and Honduras, Nicaragua and Costa Rica, and so on. It is striking that such international conflict may be increasing at a time when domestic violence is decreasing. One could even state these relations in the form of a set of provocative propositions: where violence and conflict are strong, as in Latin America's past, the level of international violence is low. But when the level of domestic violence diminishes, including the military's withdrawal from direct political involvement, the possibilities for international conflict increase.

Latin America today is something of an international powder keg. The potential for future conflict is high, and the cases generally correspond to the arms races previously listed. Brazil has imperial designs on most of its smaller neighbors—not the crude kind but more subtle, in the form of strongly influencing and partially absorbing the satellites lying on its borders. Argentina rivals Brazil for influence in Bolivia, Paraguay, and Uruguay. Argentina and Chile are also poised for potential conflict in the Beagle Channel, in Antarctica, and along the towering Andes.

Bolivia is still seeking the outlet to the sea from which Chile deprived it in the War of the Pacific (1879–83). Such an outlet could only be achieved by taking from Chile the northernmost provinces, and those differences carry with them the potential for war. Bolivia would also like to recover from Paraguay the lands lost in the Chaco War of the 1930's. Peru also lays claim to Chile's northern provinces but has to worry about conflict on its northern border—a dispute with Ecuador over territory in

the Amazon rain forest. Ecuador and Colombia have similarly longstand-
ing territorial disputes; Colombia and Venezuela do not get along very
well either. And Venezuela still claims about two-thirds of the national
territory of Guyana, to a point in the jungle where it starts bumping up
against Brazil's interests. Virtually every border on the South American
continent is a potential flashpoint.

It hardly needs saying that the situation in Central America and the
Caribbean is even more explosive. With their immense military buildups
and capacity for subversion, Cuba and Nicaragua are viewed as threats
by all their neighbors. Costa Ricans and Nicaraguans have long hated
each other, and the present generation is no exception. Haiti and the
Dominican Republic are divided by racial as well as economic, cultural,
and political differences that have frequently resulted in armed clashes.
Guatemala still has designs on Belize; El Salvador and Honduras went
to war in 1969 and may well do so again. Mexico's military buildup
along its southern frontier has been immense, and the US-Mexican border
is not entirely peaceful either. The British Caribbean was long thought
of as more peaceful, but it is also wracked by violence, black power
movements, and revolutionary aspirations. US and Soviet navies and
warplanes now face each other in the Caribbean, and the US-supported
contras have been fighting the Nicaraguans from Honduran territory.
From this roster of troubles actual and potential, it is entirely possible
to envison an expanded, maybe even general, conflagration in the region.
That seems unlikely to me but the possibility cannot be ruled out entirely.
South America seems, at least temporarily, more peaceful in this sense,
but maybe only because in the United States we have not been paying
that area such close attention.

Seen in the light of these numerous potentials for inter-state, to say
nothing of intra-state conflicts, Latin America could well be an area of
significant future conflict. If violence, irredentism, realpolitik, and the
balance of power are all as close to the surface as presented here, and if
our earlier hypothesis concerning the possibility for external violence to
increase as the internal levels diminish is correct, then Latin America may
be in for some difficult times. These potential conflicts carry strong implications for United States foreign policy and for the internal stability
of the nations in the region.

DISCUSSION

Is there a long-term secular trend in Latin America toward greater subordination of the military to civilian control? Are the armed forces less

powerful as an actor now than previously, and will there be fewer *coups d'état* in the region? There have been numerous scholarly efforts to measure such trends, but the findings remain ambiguous. There is probably a trend in these directions, particularly now with the recent transitions to democracy in so many countries, but the empirical evidence is mixed, and one should not draw any hard and fast conclusions from it as to the permanence or continuity of present democratic developments.

Is the current change merely cyclical, therefore? Is Latin America destined to repeat once more the pattern of the past, where unstable or incompetent civilian-democratic governments were replaced by military regimes once the crisis became severe enough? Will the current economic hardships through which all the countries of the region are going, once again trigger the spiral of widespread social protests and breakdowns that leads to military takeovers? The answer is perhaps, at least in some countries—though that is not the whole story either.

A number of new conditions in Latin America make it unlikely that we will again see the kind of militarism and caudilloism of the past. The middle class is larger now, and it tends to see democracy as providing the stability it wants, not the military. Latin America is more affluent, and the wealth is distributed more broadly. Levels of literacy and education are higher than they were in the early 1960's, when the last great experiment with democracy was tried. The leadership is more mature and prudent and has a more solid base. In addition, Latin America is now far more institutionalized: political parties are better organized, the civic and associational life is now far richer and "thicker," and the level of institutionalization is considerably greater. Latin America (particularly the larger countries of South America) no longer suffers so acutely from the *falta de civilización* that has been its historical plague; the organizational void is being filled, albeit slowly in some countries. These conditions make it more difficult—more problematic—for the armed forces to seize power arbitrarily than in the past.

On the other hand, a number of other conditions that catapulted the military into power in the 1930's and then again in the 1960's and 1970's are still very much present. The political culture still affords a special role to the military. There is a new economic crisis of severe dimensions, which may lead to the familiar cycle of disorder, social unraveling, threatened instability, and military takeover. Revolutionary elements are still a threat in some countries, and the perceived challenge to the military by mass mobilization is still present. The armed forces remain one of the few avenues of upward social mobility open in the stratified societies of Latin America, including the possibilities for power and wealth on a grand scale that can only come from high political office. Civilian institutions are still weak in some countries, which may prompt military interventions, and in most countries the armed forces remain the ultimate arbiters of national political affairs. Professionalization, military role expansion, and new national security doctrines may all stimulate greater, rather than less armed forces involvement in politics. Finally, the threat of greater international conflict among the nations of the area may also give rise to greater armed forces demands on the political system or alternatively, if those demands are not met, to its takeover.

POLICY IMPLICATIONS

In the new democratic era on which Latin America has recently embarked, it will still be important to find an appropriate place for the military. The past dies hard; the Latin American armed forces cannot be wished away. They are important actors with which civilian groups interact in complex, interdependent ways, and to which the nation as a whole may, under certain conditions, look for salvation. In post-Franco Spain the armed forces were dealt with in part by enveloping them in NATO's myriad committees and exercises, thereby giving the military something to do and keeping it out of domestic politics. Some sort of functional equivalent must be found for the Latin American militaries: they cannot be ignored, they are unlikely to be disbanded, and therefore structures and means must be created to channel the military's behavior toward a proper set of functions. It is unlikely that talking simply about civic action or "professionalization" will do, for in fact a strong case can be made that professionalization and civic action were just steps leading to full military intervention in civilian affairs. As we think about and plan what the alternative appropriate roles for the military might be, we need to bear in mind the far more sophisticated understandings of the area that the literature of the last quarter-century has provided.

Second, we must be prepared to deal, conceptually and in a policy sense, with various mixed civil-military forms. Many scholars of Latin America find the usual distinction between civilian and military spheres not very useful. In fact there is considerable overlap and interchange between these two spheres, with most political movements consisting of factions of military officers allied with factions from various civilian spheres. In addition, we have mixed civilian-military juntas, gentlemanly understandings about alternating between civilian and military rule, and civilians in the cabinets of military governments and military officers in administrative positions in civilian governments. In many countries the civilian and military institutions coexist as competing, overlapping power structures reflecting the realities of these countries. These realities are not always well served by our usual civil-military distinctions or even by the democracy-dictatorship dichotomy. Conceptually, we need to work on a typology of these mixed forms; in a policy sense, we also need to be prepared for the infinite variety of forms to which this can give rise.

Third, we must be prepared to deal with the armed forces if they do again intervene to overthrow a civilian democratic government. The experience of the 1960's taught us that economic and/or diplomatic sanctions were insufficient to deter a military bent on intervening, or to reverse a coup that had already taken place. The United States government is so enthused about the transition to democracy in Latin America (and one understands why this is so: in addition to our intrinsic preference for democracy, support helps to turn the Congress, the media, public opinion, and our allies toward support of US policy) that it has not thought through the contingencies of a policy response should this process be reversed. The fact is that the new democratic openings in Latin America are both an opportunity and a potential trap: an opportunity if we are wise and perceptive, but a trap if the policy is not thoroughly thought through. For in difficult countries like El Salvador, should the present democratic government be overthrown, the US may still have to support a successor military regime, however distasteful that may be politically, because we will still have a fundamental interest in preventing the guerrilla left from coming to power. Similar contingencies and hard decisions may have to be faced in Bolivia, Ecuador, Guatemala, Haiti, Honduras, Panama, Peru, and the Dominican Republic. We need to be supportive of democratic rule in a policy sense, therefore, but we also need to be prepared if democracy does not work out.

5

Europe's Ambiguous Relations with Latin America: Blowing Hot and Cold in the Western Hemisphere

In The 1970s and early 1980s, the European presence and influence in Latin America seemed to be growing. The European influence was ambiguous and uncertain right from the beginning, however, because Europe's interest in Latin America rather consistently has been more rhetorical than concrete. There was a great deal of talk in both Europe and Latin America about the decline in Latin America of U.S. hegemony, of Latin America diversifying its dependence by loosening its ties to the United States and drawing closer to Europe, of tolerance for ideological pluralism that included Marxist-Leninist regimes in Cuba and Nicaragua, and of a new partnership or trilateral relationship that included firmer ties between Latin America and both Western and Eastern Europe and the United States.[1]

Stronger and more romantic expressions of these views hinted of Europe countering U.S. hegemony in the Western Hemisphere, allowing Latin America to "break" its dependence. Some Latin Americans spoke of emulating the European political models of parliamentary government, socialism, and social democracy, rather then taking any more political or economic cues from the United States. In turn, the Socialist International (SI) and some European socialist governments sought to use Central America as a means to castigate the United States and to satisfy their domestic Lefts, which were generally unhappy with the United States, especially regarding the deployment of Pershing missiles in Western Europe. Many Latin American intellectuals of the *izquierda festiva*, or the festive Left, which although small in number is, nevertheless, influential, began saying that they did not need the United States anymore, either economically or politically. Because, if they were to fall into trouble, the SI, European socialist governments, or maybe Eastern Europe and the Soviet Union surely would bail them out.[2]

Reprinted from *The Washington Quarterly* (Spring 1990).

Such loose talk seldom is heard any more. Cuba and Nicaragua are not thought of as models, but as depressing, ruinous regimes; and, correspondingly, European interest has waned. Secretary of State James Baker III has finessed problems facing Central America, removing them from the front pages through U.S. acquiescence in the revamped peace plan that was drafted by the Central American presidents and through assisting in the disarming and resettling of the contras, the latter of which has greatly reduced European condemnation of the United States regarding Central America. Although Europeans also had promised increased aid, criticizing the sparing U.S. levels, European aid and trade have not been overly forthcoming, and what has materialized, according to Latin Americans, has been just as restricted as aid from the United States, or more so. In recent years, European interest in Latin America has flagged, and the extent and range of European influence may have hit a plateau, if it is not already on a downward slope.[3]

Whether Latin American intellectuals like it or not, the region has been thrown back into the arms of the United States. The pragmatic ruling politicians of Latin America have seen that, regardless of their occasional preference for the European connection, foreign aid, debt, drugs, trade, and security matters require accommodation with the United States. The trouble is that, excepting drugs and, maybe, Mexico, the United States appears to be not interested in Latin America anymore. The U.S. Congress sees Latin America as a black hole into which it pours billions of dollars and gets nothing in return; Latin America's reputation with the U.S. public never has been worse; and the notion that the United States still would send combat troops to the area in order to defend U.S. interests almost is laughable and preposterous. The purported end of the Cold War has removed the single reason for U.S. interest in Latin America. With Europe preoccupied with the further integration in 1992 of the European Community (EC–92), as well as the incredible changes in Eastern Europe, the Cold War winding down, and U.S. policy again characterized by benign neglect, Latin America has been left as the odd continent out. Neither the United States, the Soviet Union, nor Europe is interested in Latin America. Among some thoughtful Latin Americans, this lack of interest has given rise to new soul searching, but whether it will result in every Latin American country scrambling to protect its own self interests, through bilateral relations or through greater and renewed efforts at regional integration, remains to been seen.[4]

HISTORICAL BACKGROUND

Throughout the nineteenth century and well into the twentieth, Great Britain was the major foreign presence in most Latin American countries. British money helped build the railroads in Argentina; British banks served as the primary houses of exchange in the Southern Cone; British investment stimulated modernization in Brazil; and British capital built the dock facilities, roads, and rail lines necessary for the export of primary products from Central America. In the nineteenth century, it was largely the British fleet that protected Latin American security, despite the injunctions of the Monroe Doctrine. The United States had issued the Doctrine in 1823 as a moral imperative, but lacked until the end of the nineteenth century the military or economic might to back up the extraordinary claims that were put forth in Monroe's famous piece of paper. Following the independence of Brazil from Portugal and other Latin American countries from Spain, Great Britain stepped in to fill the trade and security vacuum. In the absence of an alternative, the United States long had acquiesced in and even encouraged this strong British presence.[5]

Great Britain was not, however, the only strong European presence in Latin America during the nineteenth century. Latin America often imitated French culture, which France used in order to enhance its influence. In the 1860s, France tried to expand its empire to Mexico, but failed with the debacle of Napoleon III's agent, Archduke Maximillian, being killed, the Empress Carlotta spending the next 60 years in an insane asylum, and the French troops being driven out. Spain, too, played an active role, by retaining until 1898 its colonies in Cuba and Puerto Rico, and by seeking to recapture for the motherland some of its lost colonies, such as Santo Domingo in the 1860s. Late in the nineteenth century, having been invited to do so, Germany sent military missions in order to revamp Latin American military academies, providing the Prussian model for military training. In addition, significant German presence in Argentina, Bolivia, Mexico, Cuba, Chile, and Colombia was a cause for U.S. concern during both World War I and World War II.

The United States gradually began to supplant the European powers as the dominant influence in the hemisphere. In 1896, during a showdown with Great Britain over the boundary between Venezuela and British Guyana, the United States forced Britain to yield, with U.S. Secretary of State Richard Olney proclaiming that the United States was "practically sovereign" in the Western Hemisphere. In the War of 1898, the United States took Puerto Rico and the Philippines from Spain and attached the

Platt Amendment to the constitution of Cuba as a condition of that country's independence, which gave the United States virtual carte blanche to intervene at any time in the internal affairs of Cuba. By 1902, the United States had bought out the French rights to build the canal through Panama.

Some of the most interesting and, as yet, largely unexplored activities took place in the sphere of economics during this same period. The years in which the United States displaced Great Britain as the dominant trading partner and, thus, the dominant foreign economic presence in Central America and the Caribbean were the 1880s in Cuba and the Dominican Republic, the 1890s in Guatemala and Honduras, and by 1910 in the rest of Central America. By World War I, the United States was the major economic power in the Caribbean region; U.S. revenue agents were administering the collection of customs receipts in several countries; and U.S. Marines soon were being dispatched to protect U.S. customs agents and to preserve stability during the war. Meanwhile, during the era of so-called dollar diplomacy, U.S. investment, which was backed by U.S. military might, continued to flow into the region.[6]

This process of displacement took longer in the South American countries. The Caribbean Basin constituted the soft underbelly of the United States, where U.S. investments largely were directed, where U.S. strategic interests, such as protecting the Panama Canal, preserving stability, and keeping out hostile foreign powers were most important, and, hence, where U.S. foreign policy was concentrated. In South America, French, British, and German interests lingered on. Through World War II, French culture, British banks and capital, and German presence and imperial activities persisted as influences that were often more important than those of the United States. During the 1920s and 1930s, Britain continued to be seen as a rival to the United States in South America, and the German influence was viewed as downright threatening. Germany used its fifth columns in South America in order to stir up anti-American sentiment and even tried to foment a South American bloc of nations, led by Argentina, that would serve as a counterbalance to U.S. influence in the area.[7]

World War II fundamentally altered these alignments. The European nations were either exhausted, defeated, or both. The United States was now supreme. French culture continued to stir the hearts of Latin American elites. French cultural centers continued to be active, but politically, diplomatically, and strategically, French influence was almost nil. A German presence remained, but the influence in Latin America of a devastated and divided Germany had shrunk to next to nothing. Exhausted, poor, and withdrawn into itself and its commonwealth, Great Britain similarly ceased to be a major presence. From the 1940s until the 1970s, U.S. power, resources, investments, and hegemony reigned virtually alone in Latin America. For some 30 years, the United States in effect had Latin America all to itself.

In this context, the efforts of one other European "power," the mother country, Spain, deserve mention.[8] For a long time, Spain had sought to revive diplomatic and cultural ties to Latin America, emphasizing their common traditions of language, law, religion, history, and, arguably, sociopolitical organization. Under General Francisco Franco's concept of *hispanismo* or *hispanidad,* Spain's vague longings were given some concrete reality. Franco empowered an Institute for Hispanic Culture, began a flurry of diplomatic activity in Latin America, suggested strongly that his conceptions of Catholicism and authority were the foundations of all the societies shaped by Spain, and tried to offer his Falangist-corporatist regime as a model for Latin American nations.

The Spanish model resonated variously in Latin America. Liberals did not want to follow the Franco system; conservatives were often more sympathetic, but remained nationalistic in their own way; Mexico refused to have any formal relations with what it viewed as counterrevolutionary Spain; and Latin American military generals who were then in power saw in Spain an attractive example of how to achieve modernization without sacrificing authoritarian controls. Gradually, as the Franco regime grew old and ran out of gas, Spaniards themselves increasingly began to operate as if Franco were no longer in power; and the attractiveness of the Spanish model correspondingly waned in Latin America. In the post-Franco democratic era, a new formulation of *hispanismo* was to be offered.

RENEWED EUROPEAN PRESENCE

There are two stages in the early resurgence of European interests in Latin America. The first, a generally docile and peaceful phase, lasted from the early 1960s to the late 1970s. The second, far more acrimonious, dates from 1979, with the revolutions in Nicaragua, Grenada, and El Salvador, until the mid-1980s. A third stage recently has begun.

Since the 1960s and accelerating in the 1970s, there has been gradual renewal of European interest in Latin America. This new, or renewed, interest grew from the postwar European recovery and increasing prosperity, and the accompanying desire to play a greater international role, including in Latin America. European interest in Latin America actually emerged from several motives: the desire for Latin American resources; the potential for markets in the region; an interest in Third World development born of the 1960s splash of new nations onto the world stage; a recognition that within the larger Third World category Latin America was the most Western and, therefore, the area where European policy initiatives would have the best chance of success; and a perceived and, perhaps, real affinity between European parties and movements, such as socialist, Social Democratic, and Christian Democratic, and the newer Latin American ones.

From the beginning, the renewed European presence in Latin America was selective. West Europeans recognized that the Caribbean and Central America were part of what the United States considered its sphere of influence. Wishing neither to offend the United States and cause problems, nor to enter a market that was virtually a U.S. monopoly, West Europeans largely stayed away from that area. Instead, they concentrated on South America—Venezuela, Brazil, Argentina, and Chile—where not only were the markets larger and more open, but where there was less chance of running afoul of the United States. The Europeans did not ignore entirely the Caribbean and Central America, but, for the most part, their efforts were concentrated further south.

West Germans led the parade. Because the Christian Democrats were in power for so long in Germany, the Konrad Adenauer Foundation that was associated with the Christian Democratic Party (CDU), CDU trade unionists, and other affiliated agencies were able to undertake some of the early initiatives. With CDU support, a variety of Christian Democratic political parties, peasant associations, and labor federations were organized and assisted in Latin America. The German Social Democrats (SPD) had the Friedrich Ebert Foundation, and SPD trade unionists and peasant organizers were playing active roles in Latin America, either directly or through the Socialist International. Although the French had focused their efforts in the Third World on francophone Africa, their interest in Latin America was increasing as well. Both the French and British concentrated on the quieter arenas of expanded diplomatic and commercial relations and generally eschewed the manifestly political activities in which the Germans were engaged. During this period of the 1960s, most Europeans, including the Germans, not only felt that Latin America was a U.S. strategic sphere of influence in which they did not need to get engaged, but that any efforts on their part to do so would antagonize the United States, divide the Western alliance, and damage their own security position, that was based on the North Atlantic Treaty Organization (NATO).

Along with diplomatic and commercial activity, Europeans for the first time began to view Latin America as an area of serious research and scholarly interest.[9] Following the Parry report in 1964 (named for historian John H. Parry), Great Britain established a string of Latin American centers at its major universities, with a smattering of historians, sociologists, and political scientists, but concentrated its national interests on trade and economics. West Germany also established several prestigious Latin America research centers and attracted some leading young Latin American scholars to them. France preferred to treat Latin America not as a distinct region deserving separate research centers, but as part of Third World studies. Spain also lagged behind, in terms of establishing serious Latin American research institutes, and strongly suggested that it intuitively knew about Latin America because of the common history, language, and colonial past the region shared with Spain.

U.S. reaction to the rising range of European activities in what has been considered since World War II our lake or our backyard was ambiguous from the start. On the one hand, the United States welcomed European economic commitment to the area because it relieved some of the financial and foreign aid burden the United States bore in Latin America, and because, in keeping with the dominant Rostovian development theory of the time, such investment, presumably, would help create the happy, bourgeois, egalitarian, socially progressive, and democratic societies that mirrored those of the United States and Western Europe,[10] which provided the leading examples for Rostow's model. To this end, the United States welcomed West European membership into such agencies as the Inter-American Development Bank (IDB), a regional development agency that required infusions of new capital. Extracontinental membership also would help make the IDB appear to be more genuinely multilateral.

The United States was suspicious of European political motives, especially those of the European socialists and Social Democrats. The United States welcomed European aid and investment in Latin America, but it wanted minimal or no political activities. Throughout the course of the 1960s and 1970s, the United States enjoyed having European investment in Latin America with some limited economic aid, but without much political interference. Even in this early stage, U.S. officials often were suspicious and hostile toward the efforts of not only European socialists but also the Christian Democrats, who were further to the left than most U.S. officials or trade unionists, and were competing with the United States in organizing, providing scholarships for, and recruiting to their cause young Latin American party leaders, mayors, peasant organizers, youth leaders, labor officials, and others.

There were several causes for the newer and tenser relationship among the United States, Western Europe, and Latin America. The first cause was changes in the United States itself. Beginning with Vietnam, Watergate, and following the social and economic crises of the 1970s, or the "malaise" during the Jimmy Carter administration, the United States increasingly was perceived in Europe and Latin America as a declining power, unable to make effective presentation or implementation of its policies, either to or on behalf of its allies. In addition, both Presidents Jimmy Carter and Ronald Reagan from abroad were viewed as incompetent, especially in the field of foreign affairs. It appeared that the United States could not be trusted anymore, either to keep national and foreign secrets, or to act rationally and coherently in the execution of foreign policy. If the United States could not be trusted, another actor would have to fill the void.

Second, with a stronger and more confident Europe, the foreign policies of European countries became more aggressive and independent from the United States. In the face of a weakly coordinated U.S. foreign policy, Europe would have to take the lead. In addition, European public opinion increasingly was becoming convinced that U.S. policy in Latin America was just plain wrong. The Europeans often accepted, incorrectly, the notion that the U.S. approach to Central America was from a perspective of purely East-West conflict, highlighting Soviet and Cuban subversion, when the real causes of the problems were social and economic. That rendering, of course, was an echo of the criticism often put forth by the opposition in the United States. The views of both Europeans and those in the United States who were opposed to U.S. Central America policy frequently reinforced and fed off each other. The author's reading was that U.S. policy during this period[11] was much more complex and multifaceted than the above criticism implies; such simplistic renderings were issued mainly for polemical and political purposes. Nevertheless, in Europe, this simplistic view was believed widely, prompting the response that Europe should do something to correct so-called mistaken U.S. policy.

Third, changes were occurring in Latin America during the 1970s, when the region started to pursue a more assertive and independent foreign policy. In this context, independence came to mean independent of, and frequently contrary to, the United States. Under the banner of diversifying its dependence, Latin America began to draw closer to Europe. Latin American intellectuals always had closer ties to Europe than to the United States, preferring Europe to what they viewed as the crass and materialistic United States. Furthermore, there emerged a great burst of generally romantic talk about breaking or renegotiating the ties of dependence to the United States and entering into a new relationship with Europe. This was the height of popularity of the dependency theory, which conveniently blamed all of Latin America's problems on its dependence on the United States, suggesting as remedy the sundering of all such ties. Such talk was limited primarily to Latin American socialist and Social Democratic salons, but precisely because Latin American intellectuals were doing the talking, the theory received a great deal of publicity. More pragmatic politicians and business people knew that politically, strategically, and economically, Latin America could not break so easily with the United States, even if some intellectuals wished to do so. Latin American public opinion, characterized by a love-hate relationship with the United States, did not want to cut itself off from North American influences and opportunities.

The result of these three currents was, for a time, a considerable movement away from the United States by Latin America, a flurry of European activity in Latin America, and a burst of Latin American energies aimed at establishing new ties—not only with Western Europe, but also with Eastern Europe, the Soviet Union, and the People's Republic of China. European trade delegations began to scour Latin America looking for new deals; there were new cultural exchanges with Europe; and hopes were sky-high in Latin America that Europe conveniently would fill the gap left by diminished U.S. aid. Shrewd Europeans, however, were not concerned with the intellectual romance about diversifying dependence; rather, they saw an opportunity to sign trade and commercial contracts that were excluding the United States. Beneath the rhetorical flourishes were many opportunities for Europeans to make a buck.

On the political level, criticism was centered chiefly on U.S. policy toward Central America. European intellectuals and policymakers criticized the United States for, in their view, seeking military solutions to the civil war in El Salvador and for being opposed to what they perceived as a Robin Hood-like and ideologically pluralist revolution in Nicaragua. Ironically, such European criticism was launched precisely when Marxist-Leninist elements within the Sandinista government were cementing their control and pushing others out. The election during the 1980s of socialist governments in Germany, France, Spain, and Greece resulted in even stronger criticism being directed at the United States. The anti-American bandwagon was joined across Europe: in Spain, by Prime Minister Felipe González and his first foreign Minister Fernando Morán; in France, by Culture Minister Regis Debray, who had written fawningly of Che Guevara and was the author of a widely read guerrilla handbook;[12] in Germany, by Prime Ministers Willy Brandt and Helmut Schmidt; in Greece, by Prime Minister Andreas Papandreou; and by the Socialist International. The criticism was so harsh that it began to affect the other areas of U.S.–European relations, including NATO and the Atlantic alliance. When the full implications for Europe of a split in the alliance over an area as far removed from Europe's more fundamental interests as Central America became clear, the stridency and confrontational politics gave way to quieter and more reasoned discourse; but, meanwhile, a great deal of damage had been done.

The major European actors were no longer just Britain, France, and West Germany. With the death of Franco, Spain had begun to play a large role in Latin America and to modify its older concept of *hispanidad* into a new version that emphasized human rights and transitions to democracy—and socialist democracy, once Felipe González came to power. Interest in the region was not limited primarily to the larger European states. The Netherlands and the Scandinavian countries had begun to establish Latin America research centers in their major universities, were convening parliamentary hearings on Central America, were redirecting their foreign aid toward the Sandinistas or the guerrillas of the Farabundo Martí National Liberation Army (FMLN) in El Salvador, and were issuing broadsides directed against U.S. policy.

The result was a steady parade of European journalists, scholars, parliamentarians, and party and government officials through Washington, on their way to Central America. They stopped in Washington to lecture U.S. officials before going on to Nicaragua, where they were given very carefully guided tours. The American Enterprise Institute for Public Policy Research (AEI) widely was thought to be the think tank for Reagan administration policy; hence a visit to AEI, it was believed, would result in that research-*cum*-policy institute immediately contacting the president or the secretary of state in order to convey the message of visiting European delegations. Accordingly, AEI was the center to which such visitors most often came, and many of them could not contain their rage. It was AEI's experience that most of the European delegations did not want to be pleasant, did not want to have an intellectual exchange, and did not want to hear a rational argument about why U.S. policy was what it was. The same delegations appeared to have the answers already, wanting to lecture, not to exchange ideas.

Much of the new European fascination with Latin America was at the rhetorical and intellectual levels only, often having little to do with the real world. European intellectuals, such as Gunter Grass, invented an argument that because Latin America had made no progress at all since independence, the only solution for the region was to install Stalinist regimes, such as that of Fidel Castro. Similarly, many European intellectuals who never had been to Latin America received their understanding of the area from the booming and fantastic fiction of Latin American writers such as Gabriél García Márquez, Julio Cortázar, Isabel Allende, Alejo Carpentier, and Carlos Fuentes, who tend to paint cyclical, often stagnant, hopeless, and comic-opera pictures of the region. Such portraits have almost nothing to do with Latin America's modern dynamism, but many Europeans nonetheless believed the image that the fiction conveyed. In short, many European misconceptions derived not from any real experience in Latin America, which few Europeans had, but from fiction, or from the fertile imagination of the Europeans.

While debate and controversy at the European intellectual and policy levels were causing a great deal of noise and ferment, the real substance of European–Latin American relations—trade, commerce, and investment—was growing far more slowly. Eventually, this reality forced a corrective at the policy level.

A SECTORAL ANALYSIS

European trade, development assistance, investment, and political and strategic interests in Latin America always have been quite limited.[13] The rhetoric has increased without more concrete manifestations of interest. Latin America and Europe have talked a great deal about forging a new relationship, but the economic and financial base on which such a new relationship could be constructed simply is lacking. Moreover, current indications are for declining, rather than increasing, European interest.

European trade with Latin America, as a percentage of European total trade, never has been very significant. In the early 1980s, West Germany led the way, with about 3 percent of its trade going to Latin America. In 1981, Latin America accounted for only 2.6 percent of France's total exports; and in 1980, only 2.0 percent of Great Britain's exports went to Latin America. Similarly, imports from Latin America hovered around 2 percent of total imports for each European country. Significantly, for all these countries, the percentage of total trade going to Latin America is declining, falling below 2 percent of total exports. Spain's commerce with Latin America was about 10 percent of its total, before Spain joined the European Community (EC), which resulted in a significant drop of its trade with Latin America.

When one looks at European trade as a whole, the picture is very similar. In 1981, for example, the EC's overall share of trade with Brazil was only 13.6 percent, having fallen from 30 percent in 1972. Over the same time period, there had been a parallel decline in trade with Mexico, from 19.6 percent to 12.5 percent. More recent figures show that the percentages are continuing to fall. Superficially, it would appear that the European and Latin American economies are complementary: Europe exports the capital goods needed by Latin America, and Latin America traditionally exports the raw materials needed by Europe. Nevertheless, this appearance of complementarity on paper has not materialized in practice. Europe still acquires most of its raw materials from other areas, such as Africa and Asia, while an overwhelming share of Latin America's trade is with the United States. Furthermore, as European integration increases and deepens, the current trend of decreasing European trade with Latin America likely will continue. Meanwhile, the U.S. share of Latin America's trade has been increasing, not the opposite. The only area where there has been a significant shift away from the United States toward Europe is in the arms trade. In all other trade areas, Latin America is now more dependent on the United States than it was previously.

European development assistance to Latin America also appears to be stagnant, if not declining. Among Third World regions, Latin America is the area of highest per capita income. From about the mid-1970s, however, the criteria used by the European countries in providing aid has been to attack absolute poverty and to satisfy basic human needs. Because Latin America is a comparatively prosperous area, it has not been a high priority for Europe, nor a recipient of much European aid. Moreover, Latin Americans have discovered that European aid is every bit as tied as U.S. aid, and often more so. That is, European aid must be used to buy goods from European producers, which must be shipped in European vessels, etc. The Europeans have been providing some aid to Nicaragua. Because it is controversial, such aid, although it is a declining amount, has gotten newspaper headlines, making it appear that the Europeans are doing much more than they actually are doing. Over the last decade, despite considerable talk, there has been little European aid to Latin America.

The foreign direct investment that Latin America expected to receive from Europe, which it sorely needs, has not materialized. With the formation of the Andean Pact in 1969, Latin America became more restrictive with regard to foreign investment. In the 1970s, a wave of nationalizations coupled with the popular dependency theory scared off foreign investors. In the 1980s, Latin America's unpaid and unpayable foreign debt, the general grief accruing from corruption, inefficiency, and unwieldy bureaucracies that are associated with the business climate in

Latin America, and the widespread sense among chief executive officers that greater profits could be made elsewhere produced a crisis situation regarding the lack of new investment in Latin America. Not only was there very little new capital, but existing capital often attempted to pull out.

Like U.S. capital, European investment in Latin America was concentrated in a very few countries, among them Argentina, Brazil, Chile, Mexico, and Venezuela. The rest of the countries received almost no investments at all. With food riots in Venezuela, potential instability in Mexico, uncertainty over Chile's future, and economic mismanagement and increasing populist pressures in both Argentina and Brazil, there is no country in Latin America that at present looks attractive to new foreign investors, be they European or American. Brazil, which continues "to develop at night" while the government sleeps, may be the single exception.

The debt issue similarly has been problematic for Europeans. With publicity concerning the ongoing debt crisis focused primarily on U.S. banks, it has been forgotten that many European banks also are exposed. European banks, however, long ago wrote off as uncollectible most of their Latin American loans and built up their reserves as a hedge against default, the latter of which allowed them greater flexibility. Moreover, unlike U.S. financial institutions, European banks do not have the U.S. Department of the Treasury constantly monitoring them, urging that more loans be made available to Latin America for larger policy and political purposes. European bankers are hardheaded and even Calvinistic about their belief that Latin America should pay its debts, viewing countries that do not meet their financial obligations as untrustworthy. European bankers do not want to pay the bribes and play the patronage games that operating in Latin America, at times, requires. Therefore, they have little desire to remain in the Latin American market, and almost none to extend new credit to the region.

Europe also appears to have lost its political and strategic interests in Latin America. El Salvador had become less troublesome, out of European and U.S. headlines, while Nicaragua has proved to be just another failed and miserable Third World Marxist–Leninist regime. With the end of the Reagan administration, Europeans are no longer as worried with U.S. policy toward Latin America as before. Moreover, with the Cold War apparently winding down and with moderate, Europe-focused officials, such as President George Bush, Secretary of State James Baker III, and Assistant to the President for National Security Affairs Brent Scowcroft in charge of U.S. foreign policy, Europeans again are content to allow the United States to handle the major Central American security issues. For the Europeans, Latin America seems far away and without European strategic or security importance.

In the terrains of trade, aid, investment, debt, and political and security matters, European involvement in Latin America has been minimal. With these trends, the declining European interest in Latin America has major implications for the region and for U.S. foreign policy.

BILATERAL VS. EC RELATIONS

Do bilateral relations or the broader multilateral relations of the EC drive European policy toward Latin America? Therein lies not only a tale, but considerable conflict, requiring a country-by-country analysis and the examination of the newly created pan-European organization, the Institute for European–Latin American Relations (IRELA).

The influence of France in Latin America has been declining steadily since the nineteenth century. Except in its West Indian territories of Martinique and Guadeloupe, and the South American department of French Guiana, French influence in the region was primarily cultural. Following World War II, even French culture was eclipsed by the United States. France has concentrated its main political, economic, and strategic interests in francophone Africa, not in Latin America.

Whereas traditional French policy has favored relations with moderate regimes, recognizing states but not paying particular attention to types of governments, the Socialist government of François Mitterrand has come out in favor of change and has been sympathetic, at least verbally, to left-wing governments. Mitterrand has insisted that Latin America's basic problems are socioeconomic and not amenable to military solutions, a point that was aimed at the Reagan administration, and which found little disagreement among administration officials. Accordingly, the United States viewed such French pronouncements as gratuitous, and eventually they died away. The French commitment à la Debray and Culture Minister Jack Lang, to a radical policy in Latin America became more moderate. Latin America is only of tertiary importance to France. Because of the intensifying, internal economic and political problems it had to face during the 1980s, France was forced to accord even less attention to the region. In addition, France decided that Central America was too small an issue to risk antagonizing the United States.

Latin America may be an even lower priority for Great Britain than it is for France. Like the French Left, the opposition Labour Party in Great Britain recently has had considerable rhetorical and emotional interest in Central America. At concrete levels, very little has happened, and Britain's interests in Latin America, like those of France, generally are determined by its present or former colonial enclaves, among them Belize, the Falkland Islands, and the countries of the Commonwealth Caribbean. Great Britain has little interest in the remaining countries of the area. Although some investment remains in the Southern Cone, British aid and trade are small and not overall areas of high priority. British Prime Minister Margaret Thatcher may have been miffed at the U.S. invasion of the former British colony of Grenada, but, generally, she has been supportive of U.S. policy, or quiet about it. Still, there are persistent reports that Britain wants to negotiate an end to its modest remaining colonial presence in Belize and the Falklands. As a further indicator of declining British interest, the number of academic research centers on Latin America has been reduced sharply.

More than either France or Great Britain, West Germany has attached considerable importance to Latin America. Germany considers Latin America to have political groups and institutions akin to its own, and sees greater economic potential there than in other areas of the Third World. German political activities in the region operate through non-governmental organizations, such as political parties, labor unions, party foundations, and churches, that enable Germany to have a considerable presence in Latin America without risking a government-to-government conflict with the United States. Each of Germany's major political parties has its own foundation, or *stiftung*, which operates in Latin America to further the interests of both the party and nation.

Of the three countries thus far surveyed, Germany has been the most politically and economically involved in Latin America. Working through the various *stiftungen*, Germany has built an expertise on Latin America that is unmatched by France or Britain. Under SPD leaders Schmidt and Brandt, the latter of whom helped direct the Socialist International toward involvement in Latin America, German–U.S. differences sometimes have been sharp, although the Germans also have understood that the stakes were too low to risk a rupture with the United States. Under CDU Chancellor Helmut Kohl, the relations have been far less tense.

For reasons of history, culture, language, and tradition, Spain long has had a major interest in Latin America. Under Franco and ensuing democratic governments, Spain, nevertheless, has lacked the necessary resources to implement substantively its policy of *hispanismo*, in whatever incarnation.

Prime Minister González earlier had been critical of U.S. policy in Central America. The left wing of the ruling *Partido Socialista Obrero*

Español (PSOE) and former Foreign Minister Morán were scathingly denouncing U.S. policy. Morán, in arguing that Latin America's problems over the course of the last 200 years were the fault of the United States, seemingly had ignored Spain's own previous 300 years of colonial rule.[14] Morán since has been fired, González has modified his views, Nicaragua has turned sour, and Spain has focused its interests on the integration of the European Community in 1992.

With Spain now an active member of the EC, its ties, culture, economy, alliances, and psychology are oriented toward Europe, not Latin America. For a time, Spain had sought to condition its entry into the EC by retaining a special relationship with Latin America, using market-access arrangements of a mini-Lomé type. Moreover, many Latin Americans admire Spain, particularly its successful transition to democracy. As Spain becomes more integrated into Europe, however, its ties with Latin America will weaken further, with EC–92 only accelerating this trend.

To help coordinate European programs and efforts in Latin America, and to provide a channel for the members of the EC who have some interests but not significant representation in Latin America, the European Parliament in 1984 created IRELA. A private, nonprofit organization supported by the EC, in the amount of about 900,000 European Currency Units (ECUs) annually, with its office in Madrid. IRELA was established in order to promote and strengthen the relations between Europe and Latin America on an interregional level. IRELA serves as a forum for dialogue and contact between the two regions, supporting research, collecting information, issuing publications, advising governments and private groups in EC member countries on Latin America affairs, and holding conferences, seminars, and colloquia.[15]

IRELA has not lived up to its early promise. In addition to the general reasons for declining European interest in Latin America, IRELA has had to cope with specific problems. France and Britain have not been strongly supportive of IRELA, preferring bilateral relations. Other members of the EC perceive IRELA, begun at German initiative and with a German director, as an agency to advance German foreign policy, and not necessarily their own. In addition, the host country, Spain, is suspicious of IRELA, believing that it is interfering with Spanish foreign policy objectives. In fact, IRELA generally reflects declining European interest in Latin America.

CONCLUSION

Europe will remain a presence in Latin America. The pre-1960 days, when the United States was virtually the only outside actor in the continent, are over. With regard to U.S. relations with Latin America, the United States at times will view such presence as a nuisance, although on many other matters the United States and Western Europe will complement each other and be able to cooperate on Latin America. It is clear that Europe is in Latin America to stay, and that the U.S. monopoly in the region has been breached.

On the other hand, Latin America has been and remains a very low priority for Europe. Europe still has limited ties with no vital interests in the area, explaining why European policy toward Latin America in the past two decades has been so erratic and often diluted. None of the European countries have a medium-term or long-term policy for Latin America. Politically, economically, and strategically, the region is just not of much importance to Europe. Moreover, all the trends herein surveyed indicate that Europe's interest in Latin America is decreasing, not increasing. Once Central America faded from the headlines, Europe went back to its usual priorities, and once the administration changed in Washington, European interest in Latin America began to wane. That interest is likely to remain at a low ebb.

Western Europe's declining interest in the region, the economic doldrums of the Soviet Union and Eastern Europe, China's internal preoccupations, and Japan's narrow and highly selective interest in only certain countries of the region mean that Latin America will not be able to diversify its dependence, as was once thought. The further expansion of the EC in the 1980s that brought in Greece, Spain, and Portugal, with the move toward greater Community integration in 1992, likely will accelerate the trend toward greater European attention to its internal markets and less attention to Latin America. The openings in and toward Eastern Europe reinforce these trends. For trade and other purposes, Latin America increasingly will be shifted back into the orbit of the United States. Ironically, with the winding down of the Cold War, the debt crisis that has discouraged further U.S. private lending and investment in Latin America, Gramm–Rudman–Hollings and other U.S. budgetary restraints, and doubtless other factors as well,[16] the United States also appears to have diminished interest in Latin America. Although the recent decline of the competitive position of the Soviet Union may leave the United States the dominant world power until well into the twenty-first century, it seems unlikely that U.S. dominance will translate into real benefits for Latin America.

These trends would appear to leave Latin America almost completely isolated, unprotected by any of the major regional trade blocs, unable to make it on its own, and with no one interested in its fate. All the indices of trade and aid point downward, and Europe is just not very interested. The United States will continue to give the region some limited attention because many of the problems in Latin America, such as drugs, debt, emigration, human rights, and democracy, affect and resonate in U.S. domestic politics. Fundamental interest in and commitment to Latin America by the United States, however, comparable to the Kennedy-era Alliance for Progress or to a Marshall plan for Latin America as recommended by the Kissinger Commission, seems unlikely.[17] Given the present disintegrative forces that are at work, many Latin American countries likely will find themselves in grave circumstances in the coming years. It appears that they will have to face these problems on their own, with little help from either the United States, Europe, or anyone else. It is unlikely that in the future Latin America would be able to play off against each other any such external actors for its own benefit. The sad fact is that no one is interested anymore.

6

The Politics of Latin American Debt

The international debt of Third World countries may be approached from a variety of perspectives. There are moral perspectives on the debt, humanistic perspectives, and of course economic or financial perspectives. So far, the economists have largely dominated the discussion for obvious reasons. The debt has to do with money, finances, payments, international transfers, etc.; and we—or at least Washington, D.C.—assume that economists know about those matters. Most of the books written and congressional testimony offered have come from economists.[1]

But most analysts agree by now that the debt cannot and will not ever be paid. It is too big for the Third World to pay back in full. The debt then becomes preeminently a political issue. If the debt cannot and will not be paid back, the main questions become how to manage it, how to control politically its potentially devastating effects, who will pay if the Third World cannot, and how to exercise damage control given the fact that the American taxpayer will, ultimately, bear the burden of unpaid and unpayable Third World debt—in a time of powerful U.S. budget constraints and when politicians have told us to read their lips concerning "no new taxes." The political issues have been the predominant ones since the Third World debt first emerged as a major issue in 1982, but the *fact* that the Third World couldn't or wouldn't pay had to be covered over with the blue smoke, mirrors, and hypocrisy of "serious" economic analysis until a suitable political formula could be found. Although the Third World debt continues to linger on as an issue, political Washington now believes it has found the formula for dealing with it—not by solving the problem but by defusing its potential political damage.

THE DEBT ISSUE: BACKGROUND AND CAUSES

Latin America, as well as other Third World areas, during the 1980s went through the worst economic depression since the world depression

Reprinted from *PS (Political Science)* 23 *(September 1990)*.

of the 1930s. Compounded by the international debt situation, the economic downturn has major implications not only for the Third World countries affected but also for United States domestic and foreign policy. The debt the Third World owes, especially the Latin American part of the Third World, carries the possibilities of ruining just about everyone. Many Latin American countries are bankrupt, have no reserves, and have experienced deteriorating social and economic conditions; their political systems characteristically also fall when the bottom drops out of the economy. Many banks, the big New York money lenders especially, have faced (and may still face) financial disaster if the debt is not paid. The international financial system is also threatened by the unpaid Third World debt, although that threat has receded in the past few years. Finally the U.S. government, which may have to face the politically unpalatable prospect of bailing out all the others—Latin American governments, banks, the international finance system—has for years opted not to face the debt issue head on.

The sheer size of the Latin American debt is staggering: about $450 billion, larger than the Pentagon budget by another 50%! About $45 billion is added to the debt each year in the form of new interest and loans, although with the recent steps toward "debt forgiveness" the figures now appear not quite so bad. Brazil owes about $120 billion, Mexico about $100 billion, Argentina $70 billion, and Venezuela $50 billion. Approximations have to be used in setting forth these figures because many state-run corporations in Latin America have the fiscal autonomy to contract their own loans without necessarily letting their central banks know. Costa Rica's debt is far smaller than these "biggies" but on a per capita basis it is the continent's heaviest.

The causes of the debt are various but there is plenty of responsibility to go around. The private commercial banks in the 1970s were flush with petrodollars, eager to lend, and not too particular about the creditworthiness of their customers. Plus they were convinced—rightly, as it turned out—that, like the savings and loan banks, the U.S. government would ultimately help them out and guarantee the loans. The Latin American governments were similarly eager to borrow: for military hardware, advanced social programs that made some of them look like tropical Scandinavias, war in the Falklands (the Argentine case), subsidies for costly consumer goods for the middle class, more subsidies for the lower classes to buy their votes and prevent upheaval, bloated bureaucracies, vast patronage and sinecure networks, and even outright corruption. They too assumed the U.S. government would bail them out if they got in trouble, but didn't count on the banks being the first in line. Finally, the U.S. government encouraged the banks to make these loans to Latin America, and informally and in part guaranteed them, as a way of substituting for public foreign aid, which had been decreasing since the late-1960s, and as a means of serving the preeminent U.S. foreign policy goals of countering communism by preserving stability and promoting economic growth.

If the situation weren't so tragic for some countries and for some people, the international debt would be a *wonderful* issue for political scientists. It has everything: hypocrisy, double-dealing, high stakes, international posturing and intrigue, blue smoke and mirrors, Congress, the White House, the State Department, the Treasury Department, Think Tanks, reelection calculations, a rematch of the 1980 electoral campaign, and lots of emperors with no clothes on. Hence before proceeding further, it is necessary to clear up a number of myths about the debt.

The first myth is that the debt will ever be paid back. It cannot and will not. It is so large that it is inconceivable that Latin America could ever pay it back. In addition, not a single Latin American government has any intention of ever repaying the full debt back. In this sense the major agenda item in the so-called North-South dialogue—the massive transfer of resources from North to South—has to a large extent already occurred, albeit under a different name. In the same way the demand by some writers and Think Tanks that the debt be forgiven harks back to the Jimmy Carter agenda of a New International Economic Order (NIEO); debt forgiveness is simply a new means to achieve that goal. Meanwhile the early Reagan Administration's insistence that the debt be treated as a series of normal commercial transactions and be resolved by the parties affected—the banks and the Latin American governments—represents a similar transfer of a domestic debate (free markets versus statism) to the international arena.

Second, even though everyone knows Latin America cannot and will not pay, that fact can never be admitted publicly. Latin America cannot be allowed to "default," even though most of the countries of the area are already in *de facto* default. Actually to default would stigmatize the area as untrustworthy and "uncivilized," make it ineligible for new loans, result in the seizure of many of Latin America's assets, set back developmental prospects for many years, subject the area to a broad range of penalties, and likely destabilize the region's political systems. The costs of default to Latin America would be severe. In addition, the banks would then have to admit they made bad loans, would be unable to collect the significant interest they have had coming in, and would no longer be eligible for Treasury guarantees and tax write-offs on these loans. Default would also mean the U.S. government would have to come to Latin America's rescue to prevent the area from entirely destabilizing.

Third, therefore, even though the banks know they will never recover the principal from all these loans, they cannot completely write them off. If they did, their stock would plummet, bank management would come under severe criticism from the stockholders, and some of the banks, especially the large New York money-lender banks with an especially high exposure of Latin American debt relative to their assets, might have to fold. Actually that threat was greater six or seven years ago than it is now, as we see below.

Fourth, the U.S. government must maintain the mythology that the Latin American debts are payable. The reason is that in the age of Gramm-Rudman budget restraints, the alternatives are unthinkable. To admit the Latin American debts were unpayable would mean the U.S. would have to bail out the insolvent banks, come to the rescue of battered and broke Latin American governments, and bail out the international financial system as well. The U.S. taxpayer would have to shoulder the burden of such bailouts, a particularly unhappy prospect in this era of economic belt-tightening at home when many of our own needed social and economic programs are underfunded. Bailing out more banks, more Latin American governments who will undoubtedly be portrayed as "corrupt" and "inefficient," and international financiers is not exactly what congressmen or the White House wish to hear these days.

Hence the need in dealing with the debt issue for charades, smoke-screens, fig leaves, and dissembling. Things are not always what they seem on the matter of the debt, and the parties involved have a strong interest in keeping various fictions in place. These comments are not meant, of course, to obscure the seriousness of the debt or to minimize its crisis character. But they are to show how political and politicized the debt issue is and how agendas and outcomes other than the ones raised in the public debate may be operating.

MANAGING THE CRISIS

If the debt cannot be paid and if at the same time default cannot be acknowledged, then the only possible solution—the one that has in fact been followed for the last eight years—is to *manage* the debt crisis. The question then becomes what "managing" the crisis means to the various parties.

To the banks "managing" the debt means keeping the bad Latin American loans on the books as potentially collectible even though only the interest—and from some countries not even that—may be coming in. It means continuously rolling over the debt, foregoing fees, lowering interest charges, ignoring due dates, making new loans available, and even forgiving some debts—anything to avoid admitting that these loans are not good. It means allowing the small countries to go into default without saying so publicly for fear of starting a panic among stockholders and a chain reaction among the larger debtors. The banks will do almost anything within reason except admit they made bad loans on which they cannot collect.

To the Latin American governments, managing the crisis means some belt-tightening, some compliance with International Monetary Fund (IMF)-imposed austerity, continuous promises to repay the loans, and constant renegotiations over debt "restructuring"—i.e., how to avoid repaying while giving off the appearance of being willing. In this way Latin America can remain "credit-worthy" to the banks and international lending institutions but without ever having to pay very much. The debt burden has evoked some hardship in some countries; but contrary to the fears of some, it has not resulted in a single *coup d'etat* or a single overthrow of democracy. Meanwhile the Latin American governments have found a convenient way to blame all their own incompetence and mismanagement on outside scapegoats: the banks, the IMF, and the U.S.

For the United States, "managing" the debt means almost any concession to avoid having to face the unpalatable task of dealing with the issue squarely or bailing out either banks or Latin America with taxpayers' money. To this end the Treasury has put enormous pressure on understandably reluctant U.S. banks to make more loans available to Latin America, and on Latin American governments to avoid default even while not paying. Moreover, in this way the U.S. can continue the further fiction that the debt is purely a financial matter between debtors and creditors and not a "political" issue. Admitting the debt is a political issue is to admit that it is both uncollectible and negotiable, which means that ultimately the U.S. will pay, thus letting off the hook some Latin American regimes that are badly in need of structural reforms to encourage greater probity and efficiency. That is essentially what first the Baker Plan (named after then Treasury Secretary James Baker) and then the Brady Plan (after later Treasury Secretary Nicholas Brady) were all about. Not much new money was involved for Latin America in either plan but what was involved for the first time was the U.S. taking *political* responsibility for the debt. Clever Latin American politicians of course recognized those implications and now hope that they are home free: the Third World debt is now essentially a U.S. responsibility and no longer a Latin American one. All the parties to the debt, therefore, have a strong interest in maintaining the idea that it is "manageable."

The strategy on the part of all the participants in the debt crisis has hence been to play for time, keep postponing the day of reckoning, hope for the best, and meanwhile take a series of small steps that will make the debt not disappear (it cannot and will not) but reduce it to smaller, manageable, less damaging dimensions. This is not a "great and glorious" solution to the debt crisis, but we must recognize that there are no entirely happy outcomes on this issue. Meanwhile the strategy followed may not be an inappropriate one, it may well cause the debt issue to atrophy over time, and it is probably preferable to the alternative solutions that have been proposed.

The hope is that the world economic recovery that began in the United States in 1983 and then spread to other areas, including some parts of Latin America, will, when accompanied by suitable internal reforms, enable the Latin American countries to *grow* out of the crisis. Since foreign aid and public assistance for Latin America will always be meager, economic growth is the only long-term answer. In Latin America the 1980s are referred to as the "lost decade" but actually, beginning in 1986, most countries of the area began a considerable economic recovery. The recovery has been uneven since then and some countries have clearly recovered more than others. Meanwhile, under the impact of the crisis as well as now the example of the East Asian success stories, Latin America has begun to expand and diversify its exports, reform its finances and bureaucracies, and make the structural changes the U.S. and the banks have been calling on it to make. Latin America is still not exhibiting "miracle" growth rates like the East Asian Newly Industrialized Countries (NICs) but the image we have of the area as entirely mired in poverty and stagnation is not very accurate either.

The private banks have, at the same time, been similarly edging their way out of the crisis. They have been converting their Latin American debt holdings to negotiable paper, selling it off at discount rates, and thus getting out from under the burden of these vast, uncollectible loans. It may seem surprising that there are buyers for this risky Latin American loan paper, but it turns out that at the right price there are many purchasers. The buyers include the in-country subsidiaries of U.S. firms who may wish to expand and therefore can use large amounts of local currencies at discounted prices; Latin American governments who are using new loans to buy down their older loans at new rates; speculators who can make a buck on almost any kind of day-to-day transactions; and wealthy individuals in Latin America who may have a strong political interest in having their own countries in debt to them. Meanwhile the banks had also been rolling up immense profits in other areas to make up for the losses that they must eventually take, and are taking, on their uncollectible Latin American loans. Taking a 30 or even 50% loss by selling the debt paper at discount rates is obviously still better than getting zero back from some bankrupt countries later on.

The banks have been negotiating with the Treasury Department over the years to get the Treasury either to bail them out or to guarantee their existing loans. That is at the heart of the Brady and Bush Plan: the banks will forgive some Latin American loans in return for Treasury guarantees on their remaining loans. The banks have also been working out tax deals so that they can write off the losses from their Latin American loan ventures. At the same time the banks do quite often still collect the interest from the larger debtors, which at the rates of the late-1970s when these loans were first contracted, are quite substantial. A prominent banker told me five years ago (this would not apply to some of the overextended money-lender banks) that if he had five years to work it out, he would be all but completely out from under the burden of the unpaid Latin American debts. Well, he has had his five years and he is in fact out from under. In short, the strategy from the banks' point of view was to wait the crisis out, meanwhile doing a whole series of things that cumulatively would attenuate the crisis and make it go into what Albert Hirschman once called a "quasi-vanishing act."[2]

The United States government also had (and in many respects still does have) a problem on its hands with the debt. It did not want to bail out all the other parties (banks, Latin American governments, international financial system), but it could not allow them to go down the tubes either. Plus there was an ideological component: U.S. officials wanted to use the debt to *force* Latin America to become more efficient by reducing the size of its bureaucracies, eliminate corruption, and introducing open, free, capitalistic markets. In addition, the U.S. needed time to figure out a formula to disguise from the American taxpayers that they would pay a good share of the Latin American debt and not Latin America. Through the massive replenishment of such international lending agencies as the World Bank, the IMF, and the Interamerican Development Bank, as well as through the creation (with Japan and others) of an offshore clearing-house that would buy up some Latin American debt at subsidized prices and guarantee other loans, we have now arrived at such a formula; but all this took immense time to plan, to reach a consensus on, to grease the political tracks, and to coordinate in terms both of the separate bureaucratic agencies of the U.S. government involved and other governments.

How has the strategy been managed? The key components by now are familiar. They include ignoring the *de facto* defaults of such comparatively small debtors as Bolivia, Ecuador and Peru; periodically postponing or "rolling over" the due dates of payments; and renegotiating constantly over new packages of loan assistance and their repayment schedules. At the same time, austerity has to be carried out by the debtor nations. Meanwhile, the U.S. put pressure on the private banks and the international lending agencies to make more loans available, and on the Latin American governments to carry out more reforms. Through these methods the U.S. kept Latin America from defaulting and the banks continued to make new loans available, even though the banks' arms often had to be twisted to get them to stay in the new loans "game."

One should not underestimate the impact that austerity has had, on the poor and the middle class, in such countries as Argentina, Brazil, the Dominican Republic, Peru, and Venezuela. There have been food riots, protests, strikes, looting, and violent demonstrations. In some countries public sector wages and employment—an unheard of trend—are actually down. On the other hand, the effects of austerity have not been so bad as are sometimes portrayed, not a single government has fallen as a result of administering the IMF's medicine (thus negating the old saw that under austerity not only does the patient usually remain sick but the doctor handing out the medicine usually succumbs as well), and quite a number of Latin American governments have become quite adept at managing austerity just as they have managed the debt itself.

The IMF has not been nearly so draconian in the implementation of its austerity measures as its popular image, largely shaped by experiences of the 1960s and a literature reflecting that earlier time, would lead one to believe. The last time I checked the IMF had no political scientists on its staff (its charter forbids it, like the World Bank, from taking political criteria into account), but even economists and financial experts are capable of learning from experience and weighing political objectives against economic ones. The IMF measures often sound fierce and mean on paper but in fact the IMF's bark is much worse than its bite. It has learned how far it can go and when in pushing austerity, as well as when it should back off lest the government that it is advising actually fall. Recently the private bankers have been more critical of the IMF than the Latin American governments for not coming down harder on the Latin Americans.

The governments of Argentina, Brazil, and Mexico, who are among the better players at this game, have been clever in imposing austerity at one time, then relaxing the rules when the protests mounted or an election was upcoming, and then reimposing austerity once the election returns were in. The questions of which middle class and which lower class goods and services should be subsidized has been carefully calibrated by these same governments for maximum political advantage. Under the gun of a visiting IMF mission, for example, Mexico in 1985 fired 50,000 public employees, but then rehired 35,000 of them in the next few weeks when it thought no one was looking, and by the end of the year had found ways to put the rest—and more patronage persons besides—back on the public payroll. President Raúl Alfonsin of Argentina even discovered that he could get political mileage out of administering austerity—provided he did it in the right way.

A similar process may be observed with regard to the issue of privatization, upon which both the U.S. government and the lending agencies have been insisting. A handful of state-owned firms that form part of the bloated public sector in Latin America have actually been sold back into private hands. But in most cases "privatization" has meant the "sale" of a state-owned enterprise from one public sector corporation to another, or to the state-dominated labor federation as in Mexico, or to a group of well-connected government employees. In other cases Latin American governments have taken six state-owned enterprises and consolidated them into one large one, and then presented to the IMF statistics that they had reduced the number of state-owned enterprises by five. There has generally been less accomplished in the privatization campaign than meets the eye, and in addition even such privatization ideologues as Jack Kemp recognize that if privatization and the gutting of all those patronage and sinecure positions mean the destabilization of Mexico or Brazil, it isn't worth it from a U.S. foreign policy/security perspective.

Thus far, not a single Latin American government has taken Fidel Castro's advice to repudiate its foreign debts. Cuba itself has not done so. The Latin Americans recognize the severe consequences to them that would follow from such an act, and over a period of time they have learned they can get most of the advantages of repudiating their debts by not actually repudiating their debts. But they have appreciated having Castro or Peru's Alan García out there as "point men" saying demagogic things about the debt because it takes the heat off them and gives them more room to maneuver.

The Latin American countries are not without their own considerable manipulative capacities in dealing with the debt issue. Brazilians like to say, only partially in jest, that while a little debt is a bad thing, a big debt is good. Brazil's debt is so large that the country has literally make-or-break power over several of the commercial banks and maybe the entire global financial system. If Brazil goes under, everyone goes under; and since that cannot be permitted to happen, it gives Brazil added leverage and forces its creditors to in effect take out insurance policies on Brazil's longevity and continued good health.

Mexico has as its ace-in-the-hole a 2,000 mile border with the United States and the sure knowledge that Mexico is the last country in the world we would want to see destabilized. If we think little El Salvador and Nicaragua have been divisive foreign policy issues in the last decade, imagine what a destabilized, left-leaning, anti-American *large* country like Mexico, with millions (not just hundreds of thousands) of its people fleeing the chaos by crossing the U.S. border, would be like. Even a small country like Costa Rica has been very clever in saying to the U.S.: "We are the only true democracy in Central America, we can be a model for all these other unhappy countries, and besides we are the only country between that large Sandinista army and the Panama Canal—so you had *better* come to our aid." Most of the other Latin American countries also know that in the last analysis the U.S. would not allow them to disappear down the drain, that our own foreign policy and security interests dictate that we will step in with a rescue package before we would allow Latin America to become unstable and thus susceptible to upheaval from which only the Soviet Union would benefit. Of course the winding down of the Cold War may change that given as well, but so far the Latin American countries have not been entirely without their own resources in dealing with the debt issue.[3]

Seen in these lights, the debt crisis is not at all the one-way affair that it is often pictured. The Latin American countries have finely honed skills, considerable resources, and a strong bargaining position that they can utilize in dealing with the banks, the IMF, and the U.S. Cleverly employing the security and stability arguments, the Latin American countries have also at times been able to play off the U.S. government against the banks or the IMF, or to mobilize the State and Defense Departments, which are interested primarily in the foreign policy and strategic aspects, against the Treasury Department. Hence this is not simply the case of the "colossus of the north" (the U.S.) and its banks keeping Latin America "in chains" for their own private purposes. Though there are of course asymmetries, dependency, and injustice issues involved in the debt situation, by themselves explanations that flow from such perspectives are too simple, one-sided, and inadequate for a complete explanation. They do not take account of the nuance, cynicism, sophistication, and capacity for maneuver that *all* parties to the issue have demonstrated. Nor do they adequately deal with the preeminently *political* features of the debt crisis and the political bargaining and evolution that have brought the crisis, if not to resolution, then certainly to the point of being less troublesome.

TOWARD RESOLUTION?

To begin, one must distinguish between the near- and longer-term facets of the debt crisis. In the near term the Latin American governments and the U.S. have managed not altogether badly. Some Latin American governments and their peoples have faced hardship, but that has often been ameliorated through the avoidance of payments or the relaxation of austerity. Bankruptcy has been avoided, no governments have fallen, and the crisis has not precipitated financial or political collapse. Meanwhile the banks have gotten out from under the worst aspects of the crisis and they, the U.S., and Latin America have all learned some valuable lessons. So far, the debt has been *managed* and even austerity has proved survivable, though the debt problem has stubbornly refused to go away.

But all the small steps that have been taken, while useful in the short run, probably cannot be sustained indefinitely. It is estimated, for example, that it will likely take Mexico at least until the year 2000 to recover from debt-induced depression. It is inconceivable that Mexico or any other country in the region could maintain austerity—even on the on-again, off-again basis here described—for that long a period without something fundamental giving way. The other "biggies" like Argentina and Brazil are in similar straits, able to scramble and survive ok in the short run but facing systemic crisis a little farther down the road.

Nor can the facades and smokescreens be kept in place forever. Eventually someone will surely say, "But the emperor has no clothes on," and all the myths about the debt issue will be stripped away. The issue is politically volatile, with a variety of demagogic politicians waiting in the wings to take over from the present moderates, as well as economically precarious and hanging by slender threads. If the world economic recovery of the late-1980s proves short-lived, if more protectionist measures are passed in the U.S., if the banks' stockholders demand an honest accounting, if at once several of the big debtors refuse to pay, if the American taxpayers sense that they will be left holding the bag, if these or any number of other possibilities should come to fruition, then the entire edifice of managing the debt in the manner used so far could come tumbling down.

That is why many experts have agreed that while the cautious, prudent approach to the debt problem pursued at first may have been appropriate, a broader, more comprehensive approach is needed to deal with the longer-term effects of the debt. That is precisely the trajectory that U.S. policy has followed. It took some time to arrive at a formula for dealing with the debt and there are still differences—largely political—over where the emphasis should lie; but beneath the partisan wrangling there is now considerable consensus on how to deal with the debt crisis.

From the U.S. perspective, there are three ways to approach the debt issue. The first is to treat it as a private matter, between creditors and debtors, and follow an essentially hands-off or *laissez faire* policy. Before the full severity and all the ramifications, political as well as economic, of the debt crisis were recognized, that is how some officials were inclined to view it in the early days. The second method is to deal with debt problems on an *ad hoc* basis, responding to genuine crises as they arise; that is how the U.S. treated Mexico in 1982 when the debt crisis first exploded as a major issue, and Brazil on several occasions. The third is a general or comprehensive approach, most often advocated by Think Tank economists and some members of Congress, believers in central planning, a managed economy, and the capacity of experts and technocrats to "solve" the crisis. This last position has often been the basis of the partisan debate and of the lively op-ed discussion among scholars.

The administration of President Ronald Reagan was often accused of following a *laissez faire* approach toward the Latin American debt, but that is surely too simple a reading. The Reagan Administration, for quite understandable political and economic reasons, would have much preferred to have this matter remain in the hands of private banks and the Latin American governments, and not itself have to get involved except for jawboning about the virtues of the marketplace. But the Administration, or at least some elements in it, particularly at the State and Treasury Departments, recognized immediately that a hands-off policy was inadequate and did not hesitate to step in with major U.S. government-assisted relief packages for Mexico in 1982 and 1987, for Brazil in 1985, for Venezuela and other countries. Treasury Secretary Baker in particular recognized that when the threat of disaster loomed, the *laissez faire* approach was inadequate.

Two political processes were at work here. One was between the Administration and its critics, who urged that more be done and began using the debt issue—rather like Central America was used—as a political issue to gain partisan advantage. The second occurred within the Administration and involved some classic "bureaucratic politics" battles: State vs. Treasury, Treasury vs. White House, pragmatists *within* Treasury vs. the ideological true believers in *laissez faire* also within the Treasury and throughout the Administration. The outcome of this process was the so-called Baker Plan, which did not involve a great deal of new financial assistance to Latin America on the part of the Administration, but did involve a recognition of U.S. *governmental* responsibility on this issue and that it was a political as well as an economic matter. That was the true significance of the Baker Plan and, given the earlier debate, it represented a major breakthrough paving the way for later, more elaborate policy steps.

The Reagan Administration thus combined elements of solutions #1 and #2: hands-off in the early days and when no imminent crisis loomed, but strong involvement in times of genuine emergency. Moreover the Administration felt that it had very good reasons for not opting for a more comprehensive solution, fearing that the issues were so complex, the debtor countries so varied in their debt situations, and the possibilities for economic and political fallout so grave that a general plan could well make things worse rather than better. Plus, a comprehensive solution would immediately absolve Latin America of ever having to make any structural changes at all, a fact which the Latin Americans understood immediately of course and explains why they all favored a comprehensive plan. It would also leave the banks—and ultimately the U.S. government and its taxpayers—holding the bag—another powerful reason for the Latin Americans to favor the comprehensive approach. For whatever legerdemain we go through with the debt issue, it still remains a fact that *someone* must pay; and if Latin America cannot or will not, it does not require much imagination to figure out who eventually will.

The Bush Administration pragmatically respects the majesty of facts even more than the Reagan Administration. That is why Bush's Treasury Department began in 1989 to inch its way toward a more general debt formula. It had a good base to build on, in the form of the Baker Plan. Without ever saying publicly he was moving toward a more comprehensive plan, without admitting that he was edging his way toward a political solution, and still proceeding in a piecemeal fashion, Baker had taken a series of political steps to resolve the issue. He arm-twisted the commercial banks to make new loan funds available, helped redirect the international lending agencies toward providing debt relief, assured the Latin American countries that the U.S. would not allow them to go under, offered a "menu" of options to Latin America short of full repayment, and prepared the ground politically for greater official U.S. responsibility regarding the debt.

In 1989 new Treasury Secretary Nicholas Brady carried his predecessor's plan several steps farther. Under the Brady Plan the international lending agencies received a massive influx of U.S. Treasury and some other countries' currency, and an international clearinghouse was established with Japanese as well as U.S. money to buy up some Latin American debt at discount prices in return for guarantees on other debts. In addition, the commercial banks were given the option of forgiving some of their Latin American debts in return for making new loans available which the Treasury would guarantee. In this way the U.S. government began to pick up the tab for the Latin American debt but in indirect ways that disguised from U.S. taxpayers the fact that they would end up paying most of it, either through inflation, increased taxes, or, most likely, both.

It is too early to tell if the Brady Plan will succeed or fail—and maybe that is the wrong question. Obviously the debt problem has not been "solved" and indications are the banks would rather take their money and run, even at discount rates, rather than pour more—even with guarantees—into the "black hole" of Latin America. In addition, very few countries have qualified for the Brady Plan's debt reduction features. Nevertheless, what may be more significant in long-range terms is the political process involved by which the U.S. government, first under Baker and now Brady, has gradually, cautiously, and incrementally begun to assume responsibility for Latin America's debt *and* its future growth.

CONCLUSION

A fascinating educational and political process has gone on with regard to the Latin American debt. We have learned that the debt is not just a private matter between banks and debtor countries, that it is not just an economic issue, that agencies besides Treasury need to be involved, that it has far-reaching political as well as financial implications, and that it therefore requires—and has received—high-level political and strategic attention in the White House and at the National Security Council. We have also learned how complex the negotiations are over the debt, that there are many players with different interests, that the ground has to be prepared carefully before proceeding with new initiatives, and that it is often necessary to say one thing about the debt while doing another. On all these fronts there has been considerable movement since the debt problem first surfaced in 1982 and considerable progress toward, if not a resolution of the problem, then certainly its easing. The debt is now less of a "crisis" than it was in the early-to-mid-1980s.

Since the Third, World international debt is unprecedented in its scope as well as its immense financial and political implications, the several parties involved have had to proceed cautiously, feeling their way, moving patiently and prudently. But all the actors now know their roles quite well, and there is considerable consensus on what needs to be done. There is still posturing on all sides and an occasional monkey wrench thrown in to jam up the works. The debt cannot, perhaps ever, be "resolved" in some final sense but it can be *managed,* which in fact is what has been the strategy so far and a quite successful one at that.

The emerging consensus suggests that the only solution in the long run is for Latin America to *grow* out of its debt. That requires new loan and investment capital as well as foreign markets staying open. The strategy is to avoid both capitulation before the debt and demagogic appeals that will make the situation worse—although everyone recognizes that for nationalistic and political reasons some loose talk about repudiating the debt is permissible. The U.S. will continue to help provide for limited debt relief but the Latin American countries must continue their reform efforts. All parties need to be prepared to accept some losses—though how much and by whom remains contentious. The banks will absorb some losses by selling their Latin American debt holdings at discount prices and by writing off some of the loans altogether. The Latin American governments will have to absorb some pain through austerity and economic restructuring. And the U.S. government will probably absorb most of the agony through taxes, printing more money, forgiving part of the debt, and by providing tax relief to the banks and looking the other way when Latin America's reforms prove insufficient.

Meanwhile, the *problem* of the debt will be—and already has been—reduced to more manageable proportions. The U.S. will generally maintain a hands-off attitude at the level of public discourse knowing as State Department Secretary Baker does that anything having to do with Latin America is "poison" from a domestic politics viewpoint; meanwhile the U.S. will continue to pressure the banks, help replenish the lending agencies, step into genuine emergency situations, prepare the tracks for the taxpayers, and nudge all the other parties toward long-term adjustments and change. The banks have reduced and will continue to reduce their debt exposure over time to the point where it is no longer so threatening. Latin America will also continue to adjust, change, modernize, and grow, even if this occurs on a stop-and-go basis and through some crazy-quilt solutions. It will continue to lobby internationally for debt relief and it will achieve some successes. Meanwhile, through debt-for-equity swaps, debt-for-environment exchanges, bartering, sales at discount rates, relief, and a host of other small steps, the size of the debt—or at least its damage potential—will be whittled down to less harmful dimensions.

The debt is similar to fighting a counter-guerrilla war: it can never be completely defeated or "resolved," but it may become less severe, atrophy, and begin to exhaust its potential to provoke complete collapse. If this scenario proves correct, then we—all the parties—may over the long term begin to get out from under this mammoth debt burden. Latin America will still face immense social, economic, and political problems; and usually, when their economic systems have gone under, the Latin American political systems have been quick to collapse as well. But there is evidence that gradually, by fits and starts, quite a number of the Latin American countries are moving toward recovery and renewed economic growth and that the area's new and still struggling democracies may be strengthened in this process as well.

All this offers—without being Pollyannaish about it—considerable hope for the area. None of the worst case scenarios have happened: Latin America hasn't defaulted, democracy hasn't collapsed, political systems haven't been destabilized, and guerrilla and Marxist-Leninist movements have not been strengthened. In addition, the U.S. has not lost its influence in Latin America because of the debt—in fact, quite the contrary—and it may even be that through aid and debt forgiveness the U.S. has proved more generous than expected. In fact a good case could be made that the banks, Latin America, and the U.S. have all muddled through this crisis in quite successful ways. Moreover, a powerful, Lindblomian[4] argument can be advanced that such muddling through, ad hocism, gradualism, and incrementalism have actually strengthened the democratic process as well as, at the international level, the relations between the states and actors involved. All in all, not a bad outcome—probably better than most of us foresaw at the beginning and perhaps about as much as we could hope for.

We know that it is always a delicate juggling act in Latin America between collapse, and survival and change. But in the long run as well as the shorter term, by following the prudent and evolutionary course here described, both Latin America as well as U.S.-Latin American interrelations might just "make it," be better economically and politically. However—to throw my own final monkey wrench into this otherwise hopeful scenario—if the Cold War is truly over and the Soviets aren't really interested in Latin America, then the U.S. will probably not be much interested either; and if we're already, as many suspect, into a new era of "benign neglect" (which usually turns out to be anything but benign), then all bets are off.[5]

7

Opportunities and Obstacles to Superpower Conflict Resolution: Soviet-American Cooperation in Central America

In various parts of the globe, auspicious signs exist of superpower cooperation in seeking resolution of regional conflicts.[1] Under U.S. and *mujahedin* pressure, the Soviets have pulled their troops out of Afghanistan; in southern Africa, the U.S. brokered and the Soviets helped influence the Cubans to agree to a new arrangement in Angola; in Southeast Asia there have been meaningful discussions, a pullback of Vietnamese forces, and a torrent of diplomatic activity regarding the future of Cambodia; in the volatile Middle East the U.S. and the Soviet Union have been in agreement about some steps in the peace process; and in Eastern Europe the superpower understanding was that the Soviets would allow liberalization there to go forward without interference provided the United States refrained from manipulating that process to gain strategic advantage. For a long time the main exception in this trend toward superpower cooperation had been Central America, but even there some early steps were taken to resolve sensitive issues; what really accelerated that process and changed the whole equation were events "on the ground": the unraveling of the Soviet Union and the defeat of the Sandinistas in the election of February 1990.[2]

Both the United States and the Soviet Union had called for the peaceful resolution of the two main conflicts in Central America: El Salvador and Nicaragua. A number of earlier attempts were made to stop the fighting and reach a negotiated settlement. Some of the more prominent attempts, such as the Contadora process (involving the intermediation of Colombia, Mexico, Panama, and Venezuela) and the Arias Peace Plan (named for

This chapter was prepared for the Seminar Series on "Opportunities and Obstacles to Soviet-American Conflict Resolution," United States Institute of Peace, Washington, DC, 29 November 1989; revised and updated 30 March 1990. The questions that provide the framework for the paper were given to the participants by the conference organizers.

former president Oscar Arias of Costa Rica) were initiated not by the superpowers but by the parties to the conflict or by closely neighboring nations. Contadora was not successful, however, because it was perceived as biased, not satisfying U.S. interests, and even excluding the U.S. from the process, an unrealistic strategy that could not work. The Arias Peace Plan achieved some partial successes but in its earliest manifestations it could not resolve the more difficult issues of satisfying U.S. interests in the area or dealing with continued Soviet and Cuban arms shipments to the Sandinista government and to the guerrillas in El Salvador. The Arias Plan, as later modified at Esquipulas, provided a useful regional framework; but it was not until the superpowers directly negotiated some working agreements that the issue could be resolved.

This paper explores the opportunities as well as obstacles to past and future superpower conflict resolution in Central America. The questions the paper focuses on are as follows:

1. Why was it more difficult and why did it take longer to achieve superpower cooperation in Central America than in some other regions of conflict?
2. What are the motivations, interests, and expectations of the Soviet Union and the United States as regards a peaceful settlement of the Central American conflict?
3. What are and have been the motivations of the other main actors involved (Cuba, the Sandinistas, the Contras, the Salvadoran government, the Salvadoran rebels, other governments in the area)?
4. What are the opportunities and obstacles to peaceful resolution of the several conflicts in Central America?
5. If one or more of the parties seek to disrupt a peaceful resolution of the Central American conflicts, how will this action affect Soviet and United States motivations to press for continuing the peace process? Would they be willing to pressure other parties to reach a solution, and could the superpowers actually do this?
6. What is the prognosis as regards the final outcome of the Central American peace process, and how will this affect both the future of Latin America and U.S. policy there?
7. How will the experience of Soviet–United States conflict resolution in Central America affect Soviet-American conflict resolution elsewhere?

IS THE COLD WAR OVER? ALTERNATIVE ANSWERS

Before we discuss Central America specifically and the actions of the superpowers there, we need to locate the Central American issue within the larger context of U.S.-Soviet relations. Do the Soviets and the United States really intend to cooperate, and where specifically and to what extent, on these regional and other issues? What is the basis for their cooperation and/or conflict? What are the agendas, real or hidden, involved? And are we really entering a new era in superpower relations based more on seeking resolution to long-simmering regional problems than on trying to exacerbate them (the historic Soviet goal) for narrower foreign policy purposes? The larger question we are asking, in short, is, is the Cold War really over?

Two basic answers, or models, have been provided to try to answer that question. The first, which is currently receiving the most public attention, suggests that since the Soviet Union is in severe economic crisis, unable to compete technologically, oriented toward internal reform, with a flagging agriculture and outmoded industry, and facing a severe domestic political crisis as well as the possibility of even greater national unraveling, it will hence turn inward, concentrate on reforming its domestic economy, cease its adventurism in far-flung areas of the globe, and reduce its foreign policy commitments, especially in the Third World where the Soviet Union has few vital interests at stake. In this hopeful and optimistic scenario, not only is the Cold War over but we (capitalism, democracy, the free world) have won![3] In the future, therefore, it is argued, the Soviet Union will cease to be a challenge to the United States in Latin America and other Third World areas; the superpowers can hence work closely together toward the resolution of regional conflicts. Since the U.S. is unlikely to be challenged anymore by the Soviets in the Third World, the argument runs, it can therefore relax, not pay great attention to Third World Marxist movements (such as the FMLN in El Salvador), reduce its military budgets and preparedness, and turn its swords into plowshares.

Evidence for this scenario comes from the following factors:[4] (1) the Soviet Union apparently no longer sees the Third World as an important revolutionary force and, in recent Soviet literature on the subject, there is less enthusiasm for the Third World as an area for future Soviet involvement; (2) the personnel in the Soviet Union who deal with Third World problems are no longer orthodox Marxists in the traditional sense but pragmatists and realists; (3) rather than believing that socialism will soon "bury" capitalism, the Soviet Union now recognizes the efficiencies of some capitalist mechanisms and countries (such as the East Asian NICs) and the need for economic interdependence; (4) at the political level the Soviets are reassessing their priorities and asking what, exactly, they have gained, if anything, from such Third world problem areas as

Vietnam, Afghanistan, Ethiopia, Angola, Mozambique, Cuba, or Nicaragua; (5) Marxian categories and imperatives are being abandoned in Soviet analyses of foreign affairs in favor of a less ideological and doctrinaire approach; (6) the Brezhnev Doctrine, which called for the Soviet Union to intervene anywhere in defense of its interests or those of Marxism-Leninism, is currently being abandoned; (7) the Soviet economy is in such deep trouble that the country cannot *afford* to maintain its far-flung global commitments; (8) Soviet priorities are changing, toward needed internal reforms and problem areas and away from extensive commitments in distant places where Soviet vital interests are not affected; and (9) the Soviet Union is disintegrating internally and therefore is no longer a serious threat. Hence, the logic of this overall argument suggests, since the Soviet economy has so many problems, since its society is straining and maybe even cracking, since the Marxist-Leninist ideology has lost its appeal and legitimacy, and since its institutions and priorities are undergoing transformation, the Soviet Union will be *obliged* to reduce its international commitments and aggressions, and particularly so in the Third World, and is in fact already doing so.[5]

From the United States's point of view, this is obviously a hopeful and optimistic logic; we will call it the "rosy scenario." But there is a second and alternative logic as well, more pessimistic and at the same time more suspicious of Soviet motives and of the possibilities for backsliding.[6] This second logic was stronger a couple of years ago; it seems less convincing today. The alternative argument runs like this: yes, the Soviet Union is facing serious domestic problems but (1) in the past the Soviets have been very successful in passing the costs of their empire onto their allies in the form of obligatory subsidies, import requirements, etc., and it may be that they can and will continue to do so, at least partially; (2) the Soviet Union still has considerable resources, and it can continue to run its foreign policy on a lower cost basis or even on automatic pilot for a while; (3) while the Soviet economy is not robust, the Soviet Union has a vast military apparatus and has no trouble supplying ample military equipment to allies and guerrilla groups; (4) even in the absence of much expansionist activity on its part, the Soviet Union can continue to rely on its Cuban or may be other allies to help advance its interests; and (5) even with a weakened economy, the Soviets still have other things going for them: the Marxist ideology, which remains attractive in some quarters, still-active fifth columns in many countries, local communist parties and labor organizations, intellectual networks, the Leninist formula for seizing and holding power, active guerrilla groups often acting quite independently of Soviet support, and so forth.

In addition, (6) while the Soviet Union may not undertake very many new offensive actions in the present circumstances, it will not turn down new plums that fall into its lap and will likely do everything possible to avoid new strategic retreats; (7) the Soviets' allies (Cuba) do not at this time appear to be overtly threatened, are continuing their hold on power, and may be continuing their efforts to aid guerrilla movements elsewhere, such as in El Salvador; (8) while the Soviet Union seems to be in considerable trouble socially, economically, and politically, its military apparatus is still formidable, and militarily, the Soviet Union is still a superpower; (9) while the Soviets may shift their priorities (toward less financial or perhaps military aid to their allies), that may simply represent their assessment that these allies are no longer susceptible to an armed attack by the Reagan administration and therefore that they are currently less in need of Soviet help; and (10) the Soviets, because of their current economic troubles, may have determined on a temporary strategic retreat, but there is no certainty their basic ideological goals have altered in their fundamentals and that, if their economy recovers—hopefully, from their viewpoint, with U.S. aid, trade, and technology—they may come back once again with a vigorous foreign policy.

In short, according to the logic of this second position, the prognosis that sees the Cold War as over—especially the one that loudly proclaims "We Won!"—may well be premature. Worse than that, it could be dangerous for the United States because it results in the U.S. compromising its preparedness, forces premature reductions in the defense budget, and weakens our strategic position while allowing the Soviets to recover. Hence this logic suggests that for policy purposes, until we are absolutely certain about the Soviet Union's intentions and future, until we are sure that an authoritarian, aggressive dictatorship will not reassert its power, the U.S. should follow a cautious and prudent approach, maintain its strong defense posture, watch to see that the Soviets follow up their reformist words with deeds, and continue to maintain a posture of peace through strength.

The truth probably lies somewhere between these two scenarios—now closer to the first than the second. The trouble with the first one, the rosy scenario, is that American and global public opinion, to say nothing of most of the political leadership, so much *wants* the Cold War to be over with that wishful thinking may begin to drive policy rather than a cooler analysis of Soviet—and our own—capacities and strategies. The trouble with the second, more pessimistic logic is that it is *so*—perhaps excessively—skeptical of Soviet intentions and the new conditions that it may miss the real changes that are in fact occurring in the Soviet Union and the foreign policy opportunities these may provide for the U.S.

It is unlikely that the Soviets will soon withdraw entirely from Latin America, abandon the access and relations they have built up over the years, or give up entirely on such clients as Cuba. For a long time—until 1989—the Soviets had been increasing their military aid to Nicaragua, a matter that had been of considerable concern to the United States and was a main topic of U.S.-Soviet discussions. Nor is there evidence that the Soviets are reducing their commercial ties to Argentina, their programs in Peru, or their recently expanded political and diplomatic relations with most of the other Latin American countries.[7] Meanwhile, Cuba has been successfully breaking out of its diplomatic isolation as well, reestablishing relations with a variety of Latin American countries from which it has been estranged since the early 1960s.[8] Moreover, in such poor and unstable countries as El Salvador, Guatemala, and Peru, the possibilities for the Soviet Union, by relying on local and largely self-sufficient guerilla groups, to expand its network of Marxist-Leninist client states, or to woo them and others away from the United States, are—even after having been deprived of a guerrilla base and conduit in Nicaragua and without significant expenditures of funds—quite promising. So the scenario of the Soviet Union, precipitously or over the long term, abandoning entirely its empire without a struggle may be premature at best, dangerous at worst, and perhaps unlikely to happen.

On the other hand, the view that sees the Soviet Union as entirely unchanged, positively aggressive, warlike, and as expansionist as before is certainly inaccurate too. That view seems to come from persons who can't believe what is occurring in the Soviet Union, think the unraveling occurring there must be a hoax, or are nostalgic for the Cold War and don't want it to be over. But the fact is the Soviet Union is changing very rapidly and not all of the changes may be controllable.[9] As the intellectual, ethnic, and nationalistic ferment in the Soviet Union attests, the changes run the risk to the leadership of going too far, of getting out of hand. Like other incompletely developed countries faced with hard times and new pressures, or where cultural and social transformations outpaced the capacity of the economy or the political system to handle all the changes, the Soviet Union could well become disorganized, disoriented—could come apart at the seams or, if not unravel, then likely fragment. None of these trends augur well for the kind of aggressive, expansionist, even cocky foreign policy that the Soviets carried out in Latin America in the 1970s and early 1980s when one could almost "feel" the Soviets advance while the United States seemed to be in steady retreat.[10]

These are the two main scenarios or theories of future Soviet political behavior in Latin America. Now let us see how they have worked out in actual practice in terms of the changing balance of United States and Soviet power and interests in Latin America.

SOME BASIC QUESTIONS

In the last section we have talked about the two alternative logics of the Soviet role in Latin America and of the possible implications of these for U.S. policy. We now turn to the analysis of specific policies, by asking some basic questions relating to the potential for as well as obstacles to Soviet-American conflict resolution in Latin America.

Why Was Central America for So Long Such an Intractable Superpower Problem?

The Soviet Union has by now withdrawn its military forces from Afghanistan, to considerable U.S. applause. In southern Africa a deal was worked out between the Angolan government, Cuba, and South Africa, with the U.S. presiding over the proceedings and pressuring South Africa while the Soviets pressed the Cubans and the Angolan government. In Southeast Asia Vietnamese troops have been pulling out of Cambodia, even though the internal situation in that country is still very troubled. In the Middle East and the Horn of Africa there have been greater resistance and barriers to conflict resolution; but even in these troubled areas limited movement toward compromise by the superpowers and the local actors has occurred.

In a few of these regional conflicts (Afghanistan, southern Africa) some backsliding occurred after the initial, hopeful agreements. But nevertheless in all these areas a new spirit of U.S.-Soviet cooperation to resolve regional conflicts involving both the local actors and their superpower sponsors has been building. Only in Central America for a long time was there very little movement toward a resolution of the conflict. Until 1989, Central America had proved more intractable than the other regional conflicts. Why was Central America an exception?

The answer seems to be that the Soviet Union was mainly interested in changing its policy only in those regional conflicts where the costs had come to exceed the benefits.[11] The Soviet Union does not alter its foreign policy course for romantic reasons, because it wants to be a "good guy," or to help the U.S. solve its divisive domestic political debate over Central America. Rather, the Soviets change policy when it is in their interests to do so, when they have little choice, when pressures force them to change course, when the costs of staying exceed the costs of getting out, or when a beneficial deal is offered to them.

In Afghanistan the Soviets were facing a perpetual financial drain on their already troubled economy; the commitment of one hundred thousand troops and the loss of several thousands of these; the danger, by fighting the Afghans, of stimulating even greater resentment than already exists among the USSR's own large Muslim population; and a severe cost in international public opinion for its brutal invasion and occupation. In Angola also, although Soviet troops were not involved, the Angolan government was near collapse and the USSR faced the prospect of getting more deeply committed to shore up the wobbly government and its Cuban gendarmes in the face of considerable territorial gains made by the opposition UNITA.

But in Nicaragua, after the U.S. Congress cut off the funding for the Contras, there was no longer an armed threat to challenge the Sandinista regime or to further encourage a Soviet agreement with the U.S. There, except for modest financial aid and the steady flow of arms, the Soviet policy and position was virtually cost-free. The Soviets were able to score gains in an area they had seldom paid much attention to before, upset U.S. policy in the entire region, divert U.S. attention from other important regions and problems, and sow immense discord in the U.S. domestic political debate—all at very low expenditure. With these advantages and almost no costs, there was, for a period, no incentive for the Soviets to get out or reach a settlement with the U.S. Without an effective armed (Contra) threat to Nicaraguan bridges, fuel depots, and Soviet-supplied helicopters, the Soviets saw no reason to pull back and many reasons to continue their presence there. The arms and economic assistance that the Soviets gave Nicaragua were small compared with the advantages accruing from having it as a thorn in the U.S. side. Later, as the Soviets' domestic problems deepened, this position on Nicaragua began to change.

Hence the evidence from Central America, at least until 1989, suggests that *glasnost, perestroika,* and the Soviet "new thinking" on foreign policy do not necessarily require the abandonment of "old thinking." Soviet policy toward such countries as Syria, Libya, Iran, Cuba, and Nicaragua was still dominated largely by Brezhnevian concepts and doctrines, and not by much in the way of new ideas. New thinking prevailed in those countries (Eastern Europe, Angola, Afghanistan) where Moscow had no other choices, where the old thinking no longer worked. But old thinking persisted where and until the benefits were outweighed by the costs. This is a matter for the Soviets of *interests,* not of some headlong rush to embrace a new set of ideas before it is absolutely necessary. With few costs and almost no incentives for the Soviets to agree to a formula for resolution, there was no reason for them quickly to reach a resolution on Central America and to reduce their commitments to their Central American ally.

These givens changed in 1989–90. First, the Soviet domestic situation became dramatically worse, leading to increased internal questioning of Soviet interests and commitments in such a nonstrategic area as Central America. Second, the U.S. stepped up the pressure, threatening to withhold trade advantages, to go ahead with the Strategic Defense Initiative, and to curtail superpower collaborative efforts in other areas unless the Soviets agreed to end their arms shipments to Nicaragua. Third, there was most likely a deal: the quid pro quo may have concerned Afghanistan, Angola, or trade policy with the Soviet Union itself, but it probably involved an agreement for U.S. assistance in one of the areas mentioned in return for the Soviets stopping their military aid to Nicaragua. The defeat of the Sandinistas in the 1990 election in a sense completed a process of superpower negotiations that had been underway for a year before that.

What Are the Basic Interests of the Soviet Union and the United States in Central America?

The United States would clearly like to see a stable, prosperous, and democratic Central America.[12] These elements go hand in hand: that is, the United States believes a prosperous and democratic Central America will also be a stable Central America, which is one of the fundamental or bedrock interests of the U.S. in the region. Stable and prosperous countries do not become prey to outside interference, nor do they cause problems for U.S. foreign policy. The United States would like to see the defeat or, more likely, the atrophy of the guerrilla forces in El Salvador, so that fractured country can also enjoy stability, prosperity, and democracy. The United States would also like to see a stable, prosperous, and democratic Nicaragua, but that had been predicated upon the replacement of the Marxist-Leninist Sandinista regime and the end of Soviet influence in the area. Democracy is thus the means to achieve a strategic end, and with the election of Violeta Chamorro in 1990 U.S. foreign policy achieved a major goal.

Nicaragua had been a divisive issue in United States domestic politics and a fractious one internationally. By achieving a resolution of the Nicaragua issue through the opening to a democratic political process not only could the U.S. solve a foreign policy problem but it could also eliminate a contentious domestic problem, one that had caused difficulties with our allies, that had been a drain on our resources, and that detracted from other issues that were deemed more important—for example, harmony among the NATO allies and continued constructive relations with the Soviet Union. The United States, rhetoric to the contrary aside, would much prefer in a time of Gramm-Rudman to practice a policy of "benign neglect" in Central America but could not as long as the Sandinistas were in power.

By contrast, the interests of the Soviet Union in Central America seem minimal. Central America is far from the Soviet Union and of no vital strategic importance; but for the United States Central America is "close to home," in "our back yard." For the Soviet Union for a time, Nicaragua was both proof of the ultimate validity of the Marxist-Leninist principles, and a nice peach that fell fortuitously into its hands. Most importantly, Sandinista Nicaragua provided to the Soviets a means to tweak the United States, an issue by which to sow dissension in the United States, a drain on U.S. prestige, resources, and power. It also served as an example, a kind of demonstration effect: if the United States could not maintain control in its own back yard, couldn't keep its own regional house in order, couldn't control even its own client states, then the U.S. is shown to be an unworthy ally and patron. Like Cuba or, in an earlier era, Berlin, Nicaragua gave the Soviet Union a kind of panic button in Central America that it could push and evoke a predictable response for the United States.

United States policy was based on the hope that the pressure applied would result in the Nicaraguan regime being overthrown, but there were positions short of that for which the U.S. was willing to settle. If Nicaragua earlier had not sent arms to the guerrillas in El Salvador, had not attempted to destabilize its neighbors, had ceased trying to export its revolution, had sent home its Cuban, Libyan, and Eastern bloc advisers, and had curbed its heavy imports of sophisticated military equipment that threatened its neighbors and upset the regional military balance, the U.S. would have found a way of compromising on its insistence on full democracy in Nicaragua. Meanwhile, with the Contra war largely terminated, the U.S. had developed plans to so envelop Nicaragua in regional and global processes (for democracy, human rights, trade, markets, pluralism) that the Sandinista regime would eventually have had to modify itself or give away. The unexpected electoral victory by the opposition, however, rendered this policy option moot.[13]

The Soviets had gained considerable mileage from their Central American client, benefits that were almost cost-free. The Soviet Union gave ample arms to Nicaragua but only modest economic aid, and for that relatively small investment the Soviets got in return a friendly Marxist-Leninist regime on the Central American mainland, a regime that created havoc among the other countries of the area and that added a further divisive element to an already deeply fragmented U.S. foreign policy process.[14] But there were also costs to the Soviets in terms of their desire for good relations with the U.S. At numerous international meetings in 1988–89 the U.S. kept raising the Nicaragua issue until it became a major bone of contention. The U.S. had voted to cut off arms to the Contras and it expected the Soviets to do the same to their Nicaraguan clients. When they did not, or seemed to be stalling, the U.S. increased the pressure and let it be known that further steps in the U.S.-Soviet rapprochement would be dependent on the Soviets cutting off future arms transfers to Nicaragua and pushing for a more open, democratic political process in that country.

It remained uncertain, however, how strongly this concept of linkage would be applied. For one thing, the U.S. even admitted under political pressure that it would not allow Nicaragua to stand in the way of U.S.-Soviet arms agreements. At the same time, while the Soviets had pulled out of Afghanistan because they faced the threat of losing and agreed to a settlement in Angola as a way of allowing the Marxist-Leninist government there to survive, in Central America Moscow had fewer strong interests and, seemingly, fewer reasons to resolve the dispute.[15] The gains from its Nicaraguan venture were significant and the costs modest; plus, the Soviets were not sure the U.S. was serious about linkage of Nicaragua to other, larger issues. Nicaragua had not served as a barrier to a Bush-Gorbachev summit (although the issue was discussed in Malta and elsewhere), to new arms agreement, or to mutual conventional weapons reductions in Europe. Nevertheless, in these forums the U.S. kept insisting on the Nicaraguan issue, it threatened holdups in trade and other concessions to the Soviets, and it urged the Soviets to pressure the Sandinistas into holding democratic elections. Thinking that the Sandinistas would surely win, the Soviets eventually did that; but they, like everyone else, had the election figured incorrectly and when their clients lost, they had no choice but to go along with the electoral outcome.

The United States, most fundamentally, wanted the Soviet Union to forego any challenge to the U.S.'s historic sphere of influence in Central America. That is why the U.S. pressured the Soviets to stop the arms flow to Nicaragua. But the precise reasons for the Soviets actually doing so remain obscure. Linkage on weapons agreements may have had something to do with it. Or perhaps the Soviet domestic situation had grown so bad that the leadership determined to cut its international commitments. Maybe Nicaragua was a bigger drain on the Soviet economy than we had thought. Or perhaps the Soviets simply miscalculated. The final possibility is that a deal was cut: the Soviets agreed to stop arms shipments to Nicaragua in return for the U.S. agreeing to stop supporting one of its armed proxies or to continue sorely needed trade and technology transfers. It seems hard to believe the Soviets would agree to stop aiding their Nicaraguan client unless a quid pro quo were involved.

What Are the Motivations and Expectations of Other Actors?

The trouble with the modern world (or at least one of its troubles) is that the so-called hegemonic powers (the United States and the Soviet Union) have had a hard time keeping their own "client states" in line. The clients have become more assertive and independent, and it is no longer the case (if it ever was) that the superpowers can wholly control them and tell them what to do.

Let us take the case of Cuba and the Soviet Union. This is not the place to rehearse again the old argument about whether Cuba follows an independent foreign policy or whether it acts only at the behest of the Soviet Union. In fact, both are true: in some respects Cuba acts independently, in others it follows Soviet directions.[16]

With regard to Central America and the Caribbean, it is clear that Cuba has acted as a kind of revolutionary tour guide and mentor for the Soviet Union. In the Grenadian and Nicaraguan revolutions, it was Cuba that took the lead and not the Soviets.[17] Cuba in effect *introduced* the Soviet Union, which did not know the are well and had few missions there, to the circum-Caribbean. Cuba provided the training, the theory and ideology, the advisers and personnel, the political direction, and the intelligence for most of the Marxist-Leninist movements in the Caribbean. The Soviets provided the money, some of the arms, and the overall oversight; but the Cubans were the true leaders.

Nor should one underestimate the enormous importance of Fidel Castro's megalomania. Castro sees himself as a world leader and, after thirty years in power, as an elder statesman. Cuba is too small a stage for him. He *loves* playing a world role. And, despite its population of only nine million, with Cuban troops and advisers at one point in perhaps twenty-five to thirty-five countries, Cuba acts like a great power. At home the revolution has not been successful but abroad Castro remained a commanding presence. He would be loath to give up such an elevated position and so far has been unwilling to do so. Hence, even with some limited U.S.-Soviet agreement over Nicaragua, there was no absolute assurance the Cubans would go along. The Soviets have leverage and have put pressure on Castro, but the Cubans have retained their revolutionary, expansionist ideology and may continue to supply arms to guerrilla movements in Central America regardless of any U.S.-Soviet accord.[18]

The electoral ouster of the Sandinistas from power in Nicaragua in 1990 significantly changed the regional equation, but we will have to see how much. There is no doubt that revolutionary groups in Guatemala and El Salvador used Nicaragua as a source of arms, a guerrilla training base, a source of inspiration, and a base for rest and recreation. Depriving them of that base will undoubtedly hurt the guerrillas. But the Peruvian Tupac Amarú and Sendero Luminoso groups are capable of sowing immense destruction entirely on their own; and the Guatemalan and Salvadoran guerrillas have been fighting for some twenty years by now and are capable of continuing the struggle even if the Nicaraguan depot no longer exists. The pressures on the Salvadoran FMLN to reach an agreement with the government are greater now and there may well be an accord, but the larger struggle will undoubtedly go on.

The United States has not been much more successful in controlling its clients than the Soviets have theirs. Costa Rica is a longtime ally, a fellow democracy, a recipient of generous U.S. aid, and is in many ways strongly dependent on the United States; yet it was Costa Rica that initially launched the peace plan that for a considerable period seemed to undermine U.S. policy toward Nicaragua by forcing a cutoff of aid to the Contras and enabling the Sandinista regime to consolidate its hold on power. Both Honduras and Guatemala, nominal U.S. allies in the region and, like Costa Rica, heavily dependent economically on the U.S., have nevertheless often been highly critical of the U.S., joined forces with Costa Rica's former president Oscar Arias as well as Nicaraguan president Daniel Ortega in signing the Central American peace plan, and were therefore parties to an agreement that may have reduced U.S. leverage in the region and often was at odds with U.S. policy. El Salvador is a small country, again allied to the U.S. and dependent on it; and still, it has taken an immense U.S. effort over twelve years and an essentially proconsular role by the American Embassy, and even then it cannot be said that El Salvador today, with its ARENA government and continuing civil strife, violence, guerrilla offenses, and human rights abuses, is quite in the place that the United States would like it to be. Even the Contras, which were largely a U.S. creation at first and were paid for by the United States, were not always subject to U.S. blandishments and directions.

The trouble for U.S. policy is that all these nations and groups, hardly unexpectedly, see their interests differently than does the United States, or with different priorities, or from a different regional perspective; and they have become increasingly bold and skillful in asserting their independent views. Costa Rica is a nation without an army; as a defenseless nation military, it has therefore favored a policy that ends the military buildup in the region, dampens the potential for armed conflict in which it might be drawn, and looks for peaceful solutions to the region's conflicts. Costa Rica believed it was strong enough socially and politically to withstand any efforts at Sandinista subversion, it thought that over time it could help domesticate and calm down the Nicaraguan revolution, and it believed that if it were attacked by Nicaragua in some worst case scenario, the U.S. would certainly come to its defense.[19]

Honduras was more susceptible to and therefore more worried about subversion emanating from Sandinista Nicaragua. But it also had the Contras lodged within its territory, whom it saw as a potential destabilizing force domestically and which invited armed Nicaraguan incursions across its borders. The Honduran armed forces were always uncomfortable with the Contra presence as well as with the threat of a Nicaraguan invasion, and Honduran nationalists of various stripes had long been displeased with the U.S. using Honduras as a base for its military operations in Central America. In Honduras no less than in other countries, domestic political considerations often drive foreign policy decisions.

Guatemala, unlike Honduras and Costa Rica, does not share a border with Nicaragua; it, therefore, was one country removed from the potential for a direct clash. But Guatemala also has had a long history of left and nationalist guerrilla groups, the military had often expressed impatience with the Vinicio Cerezo government, and powerful drug lords and others would like to see a reduction of the U.S. presence in the region. In strife-torn El Salvador, there has long been both left-wing and right-wing anti-Americanism, impatience and resentment concerning the long U.S. proconsular role, and a deep desire to achieve domestic and international peace even if its form falls short of what the U.S. would like to see in the region.

Each country, in short, has its own interests and domestic pressures; each country insists more and more on going its own way; and it has often been difficult for either of the two superpowers to control its own clients.

Opportunities and Obstacles

It is plain that both sides in the Cold War are tired of the Third World. They may still get some advantages from their Third World involvements but for both sides these are becoming less obvious. Both superpowers are tired of the obligations that their Third World commitments place upon them, tired of the drain that Third World countries place on their resources, tired of the conflicts into which their Third World allies and clients drag them, and tired of propping up shaky and uncertain Third World regimes when the benefits of doing so seem more and more dubious. Hence both the U.S. and the USSR in the last few years have begun a retreat from the Third World, a process of disengagement aimed at distancing themselves from Third World obligations and conflicts.[20] This retreat from the Third World, coupled with the momentum of superpower or superpower-cum-client agreements in southern Africa, Afghanistan, the Middle East, and Southeast Asia, also made the climate increasingly propitious for superpower cooperation in Central America.

The United States had been angling and pressuring for such cooperation for some time. The U.S. had cut off aid to the Contras and eventually agreed to support the Central American peace plan. The U.S. had suggested strongly that since it had cut off aid to its clients (the Contras), the Soviets should do the same to the Sandinistas. The U.S. argued that *it* had lived up to the Central American peace plan and now it was the Soviets' turn to comply. That message was delivered strongly on several occasions to Soviet Foreign Minister Edward Shevardnadze and to Gorbachev personally, and it was the subject of secret, high-level State Department meetings with Soviet officials in both Moscow and London in the summer of 1989. For a time, despite these entreaties, the flow of Soviet and Eastern Bloc arms aid to Nicaragua continued; the U.S. expressed displeasure, saying that the level of military equipment far exceeded Nicaragua's legitimate defense needs.[21]

The Soviet response to these overtures was clear: we will end our arms aid to Nicaragua if the U.S. also ends its military assistance to the region. While in Havana in April 1989, Gorbachev also proposed a "zone of peace" to encompass all of Central America. He called for an end to military supplies to Central America from any quarter, reiterating that the USSR would end its military aid to Nicaragua if the U.S. cut off its arms assistance not just to the Contras but also to El Salvador, Guatemala, and other countries in the area.[22]

Later, the Soviets announced they would *suspend* military shipments to Nicaragua until after the February 1990 election. Then they said they would cut off arms aid *permanently* to Nicaragua and to other leftist rebels elsewhere in Central America if the United States would agree to a joint U.S.-USSR mechanism to guarantee peace in the region. The Soviets were saying that the USSR was a superpower with legitimate interests in Latin America that the U.S. should now recognize. Their proposal represented nothing less than a sharing of influence with the U.S. in the region. This was of course contrary to U.S. interests and to the Monroe Doctrine.[23]

The U.S. saw many problems with these features of the Soviet proposal. First, the Soviet statement made no mention of ending Soviet military help to Cuba, which in fact, more than the Soviet Union, had been the chief instigator of insurrection, guerrilla warfare, and general trouble in Latin America. Second, the U.S. had in fact already cut off military aid to the Contras; the U.S. position was that that should be both the incentive and the quid pro quo for the Soviets to end aid to Nicaragua. Third, since Central America and the Caribbean lie within what the United States considers its sphere of influence, it was unrealistic for the Soviets to expect that in return for their cutting off aid to Nicaragua, the U.S. should cut off aid to numerous of its allies in the region. Fourth, it was similarly unrealistic—and the Soviets knew this—for the U.S. in effect to grant the Soviet Union equal status to the U.S. in Latin America. There are strong U.S. security and diplomatic interests involved, the Monroe Doctrine could not be easily ignored, and the fact is that the Soviet Union's power and interests are not equal to those of the U.S. in Latin America. The Soviets wrapped their proposal in an attractive public relations package—establishing a "zone of peace," "guaranteeing peace and security"—but the overall proposal was unacceptable to the United States, a nonstarter, and in addition the Soviets themselves understood that this proposal was not a basis for serious discussion.[24]

By the fall of 1989, reflecting the earlier U.S. pressure, the Soviets had in fact cut off their arms shipments to Nicaragua. But some shipments from Eastern Europe nevertheless continued, Cuba remained as a supplier, and meanwhile such "intermediaries" as Syria and Libya continued to supply arms. In January 1990, just before the Nicaraguan elections, the CIA discovered that four large Soviet HI-17 helicopters were being unloaded at the Nicaraguan port of Corinto. When the U.S. expressed consternation over these new (or renewed) shipments, the Soviets replied that the helicopters were for civilian rather than military purposes. The U.S. remained skeptical of that response; hence the impasse over Central

America on the part of both the superpowers and the regional actors seemed to continue. Meanwhile, other forces were at work that would fundamentally alter the regional balance of power.

We pause here to ask, what was the Soviet Union really after in Central America? The Soviets have long regarded Nicaragua as a useful political windfall, a ripe apple that fell into its basket; but it was also thought of as a strategic luxury, not of vital importance, and certainly not worth a conflict with the United States or even very much coin in terms of a global negotiating strategy. Nicaragua is to the Soviet Union a bargaining chip, useful but expendable. It wanted to use Nicaragua as a means to pry some concessions out of the United States. But the Soviets had no primary interests there. Hence the Soviets dangled the prospect of a cutoff of arms to Nicaragua before the U.S. in the hope of winning some favors on other issues. Thinking like its Nicaraguan clients that the Sandinistas would surely win, the Soviets pressured the Sandinistas into going ahead with the election, respecting the ballot count, and allowing the elected government to take power. The Soviets, like the Sandinistas, were clearly surprised by the outcome. But they were trapped by their earlier commitment to respecting the democratic process, Nicaragua was in any case expendable, and the Soviets had already achieved their desired goal of getting U.S. favors—trade, technology, aid, perhaps others still unknown—in return for their arms cutoff and political position on Nicaragua.[25]

What to Do about Disaffected Parties

If there are additional moves on the part of the superpowers toward peace in the Caribbean and Central America, will all the parties go along? Might the superpowers then have to pressure them into compliance? Would and could they do so?

On the United States's side, this problem seems to be largely resolved—at least at the most obvious levels. The Contras had their military supplies and most of their funding cut off. For a long time there was still sensitivity on this issue, in the first instance from the Contras and in the second on the part of U.S. conservatives. Many Contras had promised to continue the struggle even after the United States had cut them off. There would also be problems with resettling and disarming the Contras, but over a longer period of time the issue will likely become less contentious and will probably be resolved. In El Salvador, if there is an agreement, some right-wing military and civilian groups will express disaffection, but under U.S. and international pressures they will probably have to go along.

Similarly with the domestic political situation. While Secretary James Baker's strategy was from the beginning to stop military aid to the Contras and agree to the Central American peace accords, thus appeasing the congressional Democrats, getting Central America off the front pages, and buying him and his president political space for other issues they deemed more important,[26] he was sensitive to conservative supporters of the Contras' goals. To this end he sought and obtained continued "humanitarian" aid for the Contras and made some half-hearted statements about seeking military aid. That kept the conservatives at least from seeing red; and while there were some expressions of conservative disenchantment with the Baker strategy, it was muted and in any case the conservatives have nowhere to go except to support a Bush-Quayle administration. Meanwhile, the election of Chamorro enabled the conservatives to claim that their policy position was right all along.

Within the region it was the U.S. allies that took the lead in agreeing to the Arias peace accords. Little opposition to the movement toward peace, therefore, should be expected from that quarter. Not only did they support and help push the peace process but none of them will be sorry to see the Sandinistas go. None of the small Central American countries had any use for the Sandinistas. They all feared destabilization, subversion, or perhaps even an invasion by that mammoth Sandinista army. Both the peace process and the electoral victory of Chamorro enormously cheered them. Several of these countries may still want to pursue independent foreign policies, but from their perspective the main threat in the region, the Sandinistas, has now been removed.

We do not know at this moment what precisely the Soviets can or will do about their allies and clients in the region. It seems likely that the outcome of the Nicaraguan election will increase the possibility that the Salvadoran guerrillas will either atrophy over the long term or try to reach a negotiated settlement with the government in the short term. The effects on Cuba, however, are uncertain. On the one hand, the Nicaraguan outcome has increased the pressure on Cuba, which is already feeling internal tensions, and has made it more isolated. On the other hand, Gorbachev's visit to Cuba in the spring of 1989 provided little cause for optimism concerning the Soviet Union's willingness or capacity to force changes in Cuban foreign policy. Cuba is very dependent on Moscow financially and militarily, but also very independent. Cuba continues to insist on following its own foreign policy, including a policy of assisting revolutionary movements in Latin America. Hence while the Soviets seem inclined to pull back from some of their commitments in Central America, to stop arms shipments, and to work with the U.S.

to resolve regional issues, it is by no means assured that the Cubans will be.

Effects on Other Regions of Conflict?

Both superpowers have apparently decided that many of their Third World clients are too expensive, bring too few benefits, and represent an inordinate and no longer tolerable drain on resources. Especially when the clients themselves become involved in conflicts, they often cause enormous grief for their sponsors but very little gain. Both superpowers are tired of these struggles, drained by them, disillusioned with their incursions into Third World areas of marginal strategic value, and desirous of extracting themselves from the obligations that such involvements incur.

And yet, the United States and the Soviet Union are far from agreeing on a set of rules of the road for disentangling themselves from Third World conflicts. Both sides remain wary and distrustful of each other, often wanting to continue to try to secure advantage even while the process of extricating themselves is going on.[27] As the superpowers seek to establish greater cooperative relations at some levels, they also eye each other suspiciously, each is not sure if the other can be trusted, and they continue at other levels in many of these regional conflicts to keep a hand in. Soviet and American leaders have apparently now concluded that seeking resolution of various regional conflicts is important to their overall relations; but the U.S. and the USSR are a long way from reaching agreement, written or informal, on the operating codes that will govern in these circumstances or that would put their relations on a new basis.[28]

Although the two superpowers may be awkwardly stumbling toward such, there is as yet no generalizable model that can be applied to the resolution of Third World conflicts. Each conflict is different, with different actors, different problems, and different superpower interests. What worked in Afganistan is not really applicable to Angola, and what worked for a time in southern Africa may not have much relevance in Central America. There may be a mood and climate on the part of the superpowers to move toward resolution of some of these regional conflicts but there is as yet—and perhaps cannot be—a generalized formula for doing so. Not only is each regional issue sui generis but the stakes of the superpowers in each are different as well. At the same time, the resolution of a problem in one area creates a dynamic that may lead to resolution of problems in other regions.

Of the regional conflicts, and keeping in mind the ongoing nature of many of these conflicts, the Central American one proved to be the most protracted, the most difficult to resolve. Or else for a long time it was not in the interests of the superpowers to resolve the conflict. Or perhaps it was lower on their priorities. But in 1988 and 1989 there was considerable movement on the Nicaraguan issue, with both the U.S. and the USSR exerting pressure to help resolve some of the military and political aspects of the issue. But it was really the fortuitous outcome of the 1990 election, in which the opposition defeated the Sandinistas, that fundamentally changed the equation. Not only is the balance of power in the region now far more favorable to the U.S. than it was before that election, but the process itself has now generated a momentum that could conceivably lead to the resolution of other aspects of the Central American regional problem as well.

CONCLUSIONS AND IMPLICATIONS

The United States was lucky on Nicaragua. No one expected the Sandinistas to lose the February 1990 election. Everyone assumed that the machinery was in place and that the Sandinistas would win. The Sandinistas controlled the media, the electoral machinery, the bureaucracy, military and secret police, the youth and other groups, and vast patronage. They were the best organized. U.S. foreign policy was sufficiently certain that the Sandinistas would win that it had already begun talks with them concerning a settlement: the U.S. would allow the economic embargo to expire and would agree to discuss bilateral issues, while the Sandinistas would stop interfering in the internal affairs of their neighbors, stop arms shipments to El Salvador, and stop trying to destabilize neighboring governments. At the same time Soviet arms shipments to Nicaragua had been cut off and the U.S. and the USSR were discussing other steps to resolve the regional conflict, although these talks seemed for a long time to be going nowhere.[29] But the victory of Violeta Chamorro changed all the givens in the area and rendered moot most of the issues that before seemed so difficult. It is now, as they say, a "whole new ball game."[30]

The Nicaragua turnaround left many issues still unresolved (the Contra resettlement and reintegration, the future of the Sandinistas and their relations with the elected regime, the capabilities of the Chamorro government, the ultimate future of Nicaragua), but it also fundamentally changed the political equation in the region and introduced some new dynamics. The victory of Chamorro put increased pressure on the FMLN in El Salvador to reach an agreement with the government, and it also isolated and added to the pressure in Cuba. The Central American conflict was by no means solved but there is no doubt that several important steps were taken toward a resolution of the multifaceted problems there and that the momentum and processes put in march by the change in Nicaragua allowed for new hope of resolution of other regional problems.

We should bear in mind, however, that even with the increased U.S.-USSR cooperation over Nicaragua, the severe problems in the area will not be resolved and the conflicts there will not go away immediately. The superpower conflicts in and over Afghanistan, Cambodia, southern Africa, and the Middle East are by no means over despite some partial cooperation between the superpowers toward resolution of these other regional issues. The struggle over Afghanistan goes on; in southern Africa the conflict is not over; Cambodia and the Horn of Africa remain problematic to say the least; and there are few signs of imminent resolution of Middle East issues. We should not expect the complex issues of Central America to be neatly or easily resolved either. The guerrilla movements in El Salvador, Guatemala, and elsewhere, after so many years of fighting, will not just fade away quietly; and there is some doubt as to just how much the Soviets can control them. So despite the breakthrough in Nicaragua, conflict in the region will go on—although hopefully on a reduced scale and with some greater prospect of resolution.

A strange and troubling paradox now enters here: even if further superpower agreements can be reached on Central America, for example El Salvador, that will not solve the area's immense social and economic problems and it could well exacerbate them. The issues are not just East-West (the Cold War) but also North-South (poverty, underdevelopment, dependency). Under Secretary Baker, Central America had already been shifted from the front to the back burner, and additional settlements on the East-West agenda would take the region off the hot plate of attention altogether. Such agreements would enable the U.S. to extract itself even further from what has been a difficult and divisive policy area, but the result would likely be a new era of "benign neglect" and of very little attention to Latin America's manifold internal problems. We would of course continue sporadically to deal with the debt, drugs, and immigration issues but those do not generate the same heat or funds as a long-term, steady, anticommunist containment policy. Nor do they provide the basis for the sustained, positive, long-term, and mature policy that all experts on the region are agreed is necessary.[31] With the crisis in Central America constantly before us in the last decade the United States has been forced to pay the region attention and take it seriously, but with the strategic threat (Soviet expansionism in Central America) now reduced or removed the U.S. might well revert to its traditional policy of ignoring the area.[32]

Latin America is already low on the U.S.'s list of priorities; and while solving the divisive Nicaraguan and El Salvadoran imbroglios would surely bring foreign policy benefits, it would also remove virtually the last reasons for the U.S. to pay attention to the region. "Benign neglect" of course is not usually so benign: it results in allowing small problems to fester into larger ones, historically calling forth new rounds of hand-wringing and interventions on the U.S.'s part. If we could have confidence that we could put our relations with Latin America on the same normal, regular basis that we maintain with Western Europe and that we would have a sustained, multifaceted assistance program for the area, then there would not be cause for worry; but there are few indications that the U.S. is about to do that. Further agreements with the Soviets over Cuba and El Salvador might be beneficial from the superpowers' point of view; but if that means less aid and involvement, it could be disastrous for the rest of Latin America.[33]

Finally, therefore, we should be under no illusions that an agreement between the superpowers on some aspects of Central America will altogether end the Cold War in the hemisphere. The guerrilla struggles in several countries will doubtless go on, the Soviet Union will remain Argentina's largest commercial partner, the Soviets will likely continue with their involvement in Peru, and the machinations of Cuba and Castro will doubtless go on. There are no panaceas for peace anywhere in the area and an agreement between the superpowers will not solve Latin America's pressing and multiple domestic problems. Foreign policy specialists will know that, but it is important nonetheless that we not allow the possibilities for superpower agreement on *some,* perhaps quite limited, Central American issues to turn into wishful thinking that the area's problems have thereby been resolved and that we need not pay it attention anymore. Such a conclusion, which is easy for policymakers and the public to fall into since their attention span to any one issue is usually short, would not serve our interests or those of Latin America. And, since everything has a trade-off, we end on the paradox that while a superpower agreement on Nicaragua and possibly other countries would undoubtedly benefit the U.S. foreign policy position, it could well have a harmful effect on the U.S. attention and assistance prospects for the region.

Part III

THEORETICAL PERSPECTIVES

8

State-Society Relations in Latin America: Toward a Theory of the Contract State

STATE-SOCIETY RELATIONS: AN OLD AND A NEW FOCUS

From time immemorial political analysts have been concerned with the interrelations between the state and/or government *and* the component, constituent societal groups on which it is based and which it is presumed to reflect. Aristotle was the first to give systematic treatment both to changes in state-society relations and to the idea that the relations of the state to the society must be kept in harmony and equilibrium, that a state that ran too far ahead of, or fell too far behind, public sentiment as expressed through its major class and societal groups spelled trouble in terms of state-society relations. Both situations might produce disequilibrium, discontent, and revolution within the system as a whole. Hence Aristotle and a long line of political thinkers that followed argued for a just ordering of state-society relations to ensure that the state reflected, more or less, the sentiments of civil society and that public policy would continue to be in accord with the demands of the broader nation.

For a long time modern political analysts concentrated on the state part of this equilibrium, not the societal. That is, they studied the formal-legal structures of government—constitutions, laws, formal divisions of power—and left socioeconomic matters to other disciplines. That reflected the legal—even legalistic—background of most of the leading analysts, their training in the law and constitutionalism, and the prevailing emphasis on the formal rules and procedures of government.

Beginning around midcentury with the rising focus on interest groups and interest group theory, however, the pendulum began to swing back the other way. That is, the societal determinants of public policy (public opinion, political culture, interest groups) received heavy emphasis while state institutions were now generally relegated to the status of dependent variables. Government decisions on various public policy issues were presumed to reflect merely the balance of power of the societal and interest groups that had a hand in their formulation. This focus on the "input" functions was deemed particularly appropriate in studying the developing nations, at least according to the most influential book on the subject,[1] since they were in any case thought to have weak central state institutions but perhaps strong class, sectoral, and corporate associations.

In recent years, a new emphasis has been given to *state-society* relations. That is, a new stress has come to be placed on *both* the state *and* societal groups, as well as the interrelations between them.[2] Many scholars have come to see that while in some areas public policy reflects, or is even determined by, the interest group struggle, in other areas the state has a certain independence and even autonomy in shaping public policy. The state is not merely a neutral referee presiding over the conflict among rival interests, as in the liberal theory, nor is it merely a part of the "superstructure," determined by underlying class conflicts and domination, as in the classical Marxian formulation. Rather, the state has increasingly come to be seen as a crucial independent actor, reflective of the interest group or class context, but also to some degree itself shaping policy outcomes, in part conditioning and molding the structure of class and societal relations as well as itself being shaped by them. Certainly the dynamic *inter*relations between state and society have become a subject matter of renewed, stimulating, and controversial interest.

Latin America provides a particularly exciting laboratory to examine anew the whole theory and political arena of state-society relations. For Latin America has long had not only powerful corporate and interest groups—the Church, the army, the oligarchy, and the like—but it is also a culture area in which the role of the state has long been assumed, or in some cases wished, to be a powerful one. No Latin American would ever make the mistake, as did American interest group theory, of saying that the state and who controlled it were unimportant, that the state was merely a neutral referee in the interest group struggle. Rather, the idea of the state in Iberia and Latin America has always implied a strong directing state, tutelary and sometimes authoritarian, but seldom weak— at least in aspiration—and certainly not neutral. Who controls the central state apparatus, and the groups that have special access to it and its favors (patronage, jobs, spoils, power, contracts, status, prestige, money), is a central preoccupation throughout Latin America, perhaps *the* central preoccupation. That is why the competition for control of the state system and the use of violence and various forms of strong action to attain it and keep it is often so intense.[3]

But it is not just the Latin American state systems that are, or seek to be, strong; its major corporate and interest groups tend to be powerful as well. Such agencies as the Church, the army, and the economic elites, the trade unions, the university, and the bureaucracy, in fact, are throughout Latin America not mere "interest groups" in the North American sense but, more fundamentally, *corporate* agencies, parts of the backbone of Latin American "society," inseparable from it, and fundamental to its continued existence. Hence in Latin America we have a tradition of both strong states *and* strong corporate or societal interests—albeit a limited number of them. Indeed, it is one of the major tenets of this chapter that the arenas of conflict and interchange between the state and these component societal units constitute among the major arenas of Latin American political life, perhaps *the* major arenas, on whose successful management the possibilities of any government rests and by the mismanagement of which most governments fall. More specific hypotheses dealing with these themes are set forth below.

The issue of state-society relations, and frequently of competition between the state and societal groups, has a long history in Iberia and Latin America, going back to medieval times. In both Iberia and Latin America such strong societal or corporate agencies as the military orders, the Catholic Church, the towns, the landed elites have a history that often predates that of the state. Frequently these groups feel, therefore, that they have greater legitimacy than the state, that they stand prior to and above the state with inherent rights and a special place in society that no mere state or government should touch. But over time a centralizing state also emerged, competing with these societal groups, claiming sovereignty over them, and culminating in the sixteenth-century Hapsburgian model of a powerful, imperial state system strongly established in both Iberia and Latin America.

In Iberian and Latin American history, henceforth, sometimes the state would be dominant, sometimes the societal or corporate units. The competition was often fierce and bloody. It was frequently, in recent times, covered over with the language and rhetoric of democratic competition, or else democracy and the several state-society competitions coexisted side by side. In any case, I contend that these arenas of Iberian and Latin American state-society relations (state-military relations, state-Church relations, and the like) have been and remain among the most important, and yet least studied, of these nations' political processes and dynamics. The state-society arena has by now been modernized to include the realms of state-labor relations, state-peasant relations, etc., as well as the more traditional groups; but the arena of state-society relations (for example in the new "organic laws" of the armed forces or the efforts to renegotiate the *fuero militar*) is still present and crucial for understanding the political systems of Iberia and Latin America.

LIBERAL, MARXIAN, AND CORPORATIST CONCEPTIONS OF STATE-SOCIETY RELATIONS

There are two major paradigms in the social sciences for treating state-society relations: the liberal and the Marxian. Neither gives sufficient attention to the role of the state.

In the liberal paradigm the state is generally considered a mere filter of the interest group struggle. If, as Theodore Lowi tells us, the dominant ideology of the United States is interest group liberalism,[4] then the state's role is to sort out and balance these contending interests and to evolve policy from a reconciliation of, and compromise among, conflicting group interests. In David Easton's well-known formulation, which for a long time served—and may still—as the dominant one in political science, the political system consists of the "inputs" of the various interest groups, plus a kind of "black box" or policy-neutral state system into which these "inputs" are fed, and "outputs" or public policies that reflect the balance, or imbalance, of the input pressures being fed in.[5]

Of course interest group theorists recognize some role for the state in "the system." The state must sort and sift among the contending interests and may even regulate them to some degree—though in a laissez faire polity as in a laissez faire economy like the United States, such regulation is kept to a minimum. But the dominant metaphor is that the state serves as a kind of impartial umpire among the contending interests. The interplay of these interests and their influence in the Congress, bureaucracy, and other decision-making bodies is clearly where the action is according to this interpretation—not in the state itself. To use an economic image again, under liberalism the polity, as well as the economy, is based on the marketplace principle of virtually unlimited, open-ended, "free" interest group competition. Although the state may oversee and referee this interest group struggle, it has little independent strength of its own and practically no autonomy as a political actor. In interest group liberalism the state has been relegated to the role of a "dependent variable."

In the Marxian theoretical paradigm (though not in the actual practice of Marxist-Leninist regimes) the role of the state is remarkably, perhaps astoundingly, parallel. The state is considered a part of the "superstructure," reflective of and determined by underlying class and economic factors. In Marx's classic formulation in the *Communist Manifesto*, the state is portrayed as the "executive committee of the bourgeoisie." Just as in feudal society the state was a reflection of landed interests, so in capitalist society the state serves and reflects the interests of the new dominant class, the bourgeoisie. But note that in both feudal and capitalist society, the state is again a dependent variable, reflecting and determined by the interests of the prevailing class, while having little autonomy of its own.

It is not necessary to straw-man these theories, all the easier then to blow them away. Obviously most political analysts, even the strongest advocates of an interest group approach, recognize some degree of autonomy for the state—why else would our universities have separate courses on the courts, the Congress, or the presidency? Similarly with Marxian theory. In a quite lucid and undogmatic analysis of the Eighteenth Brumaire of Louis Bonaparte, Marx has a perceptive analysis of how the state, although still reflective of the overall class configuration, may achieve a degree of autonomy from all classes. And in the most recent effort to perform another of the periodic "salvage operations" on Marxian theory, a number of analysts have sought to reconcile the classic *theory* of Marxism, which presumes a state structure determined by class factors, and the *facts* of a state system in various parts of the world that seems to operate independent from them.[6]

The fact remains, however, that in both theoretical paradigms, the liberal and the Marxian, the state's role is relatively marginal. While both models concede the state some importance and even some, at times, autonomy, the real dynamics are located in the interest group struggle, for the liberal interpretation, and in the class struggle, for the Marxian. Both accord the state subsidiary importance; both, in social science terms, analyze it as a "dependent variable." In neither is there much attempt actually to analyze the autonomous powers of the state—its relative independence, in some circumstances, from either the interest group or the class struggle.

None of these comments are meant to deny the importance either of interest groups and their competition or of classes and class structure. Indeed, in this study the importance and relevance of these institutions and groups are taken for granted as givens. Nonetheless it is striking that in both the liberal and the Marxian interpretations the state plays such a minimalist role. For many countries, especially those in Latin America, such an interpretation is inadequate and inaccurate. Nor do the liberal or Marxian approaches, therefore, provide us with a sufficient or complete explanation for comprehending Latin American politics and society. Particularly in dealing with state-society relations in a part of the world,

Latin America, that has a history of both strong and, relatively, autonomous state authority, other explanations must be employed.

CORPORATISM AND THE CORPORATIST FRAMEWORK

This is where corporatism and what elsewhere I have called the "corporatist framework" and explanatory paradigm are particularly useful and pertinent.[7]

In these other writings I have analyzed at length the political theory and political sociology of corporatism and organic statism as they apply in Latin America; the political economy and political dynamics of such systems; the biases of such corporatist and organically structured systems as well as the possibilities for their transcendence; right, center, and left variants of corporatism and organic statism; as well as creeping corporatism in other nations. There is no need to repeat all those materials here. However, a number of the more salient points about corporatism, the state, and the corporate groups or units that make it up, particularly as the analysis pertains to Iberia and Latin America, ought usefully to be emphasized.

1. "Corporatism" as here used refers not just to the manifestly "corporatist" regimes of the interwar period (Salazar's Portugal, Franco's Spain, Vargas's Brazil), but to a longer history and tradition of organicist-corporatist theory and structure of sociopolitical organization, what Ronald Newton has referred to as "natural corporatism."[8] Corporatism in this sense means the tendency to view the political community as the sum total of the functional interests in the society (armed forces, Church, landowners, unionists, etc.), with each of these interests deemed to have a defined position and right to participate. In contrast with the individualism ("one-man-one-vote") of liberalism, under corporatism participation is in considerable measure determined by sector, societal group, or functional "corporation" (which thus includes entities like the university as well).
2. Because of its long tradition of organicist-corporatist thought, its Catholic-corporatist conceptions, its grounding on Roman law and organization, and the strength of such traditional corporate groups as the army, the Church, the bureaucracy, the guilds, the university, the parish, and the *municipio,* corporatism has long been particularly, but obviously not exclusively, strong in Iberia and Latin America. Corporatism is not exclusive to Latin America for other countries

have also experienced corporatism, but it is especially prevalent and long lasting there, and the particular forms that it has taken (Catholic, Thomistic, organic-statist with historic Christian overtones, as well as newer and more democratic variations) have been uniquely derived from Iberian and Latin American history. Thus seen, corporatism is not just a response to crisis,[9] nor to a particular class configuration,[10] but a recurring, permanent, almost "natural" feature of Latin American life.[11]

3. Corporatism can nonetheless take both a variety of forms (Catholic, secular, bureaucratic-authoritarian, liberal-pluralist, statist, societal, associational) *and* have a variety of causes. That means that corporatism can take democratic forms (as in Venezuela), distinct authoritarian forms (as in Mexico or in Pinochet's Chile), and various combinations of these (as in Argentina or Brazil under military rule). We concede of course that Latin America is structured along both class and corporate lines, but here we are concerned chiefly with the latter. Similarly, we concede that Latin American organic-corporatism can come not just from history and tradition but also from the demands and exigencies of modern-day state requirements, as well as the felt need by many Latin American regimes to get a surer, firmer handle on contemporary economic pressures.

4. Latin America has a history of not just strong corporate agencies but strong *state* organization as well. Indeed, the bureaucratic-authoritarian-paternalist, or "Hapsburgian," model that emerged in Iberia from the twelfth to the sixteenth centuries and was then carried over to the New World remains, even today, the model to which many Latin Americans aspire. It is no longer the only model but it certainly has continuing strong roots and support: witness the powerful strength of conservatism and the Right in such countries as El Salvador, Mexico, Colombia, Guatemala, Chile, Brazil, and Argentina.

5. Centralized statism is tempered, however, by the continued and recently renewed vitality of societal groups, of Latin America's "*fuerzas vivas,*" where popular sovereignty is ultimately presumed to reside. Much of Latin American history can be read as an effort to create such strong societal and associational organizations where none had existed before, to correct the historic "*falta de organización*" that almost all classic Latin American sociology sees as the bane of the area's history and the crucial factor in its underdevelopment.[12] State and society require continued balancing and the achievement of a just equilibrium. Corporatism may take Rousseauian/democratic as well as authoritarian forms.

6. The strong role of the state in Latin America implies not so much a system of more or less free associability and complete laissez faire for interest groups, as in the United States, but often of state licensing, regulating, policing, and chartering of the interest or corporate group life. This usually involves the setting of qualifications for these groups for recognition as legitimate political actors, the granting of "juridical personality" to those that have been duly recognized, and the giving of privileges or maybe even monopoly power to especially favored groups. The juridical definition of the rights and obligations, place and position, of both the state and the several major corporate groups is important both to our exercise here and to our understanding of Latin American politics, which is usually organized on a much more formal and legalistic basis than is the case of the United States. Under democracy, these relations are currently all being renegotiated.

7. Implied in the above, and as a corollary to it, is the fact that while there is a considerable pluralism of groups in Latin American society, that pluralism often represents a limited pluralism, rather than the virtually unlimited (some would now say "anarchic") pluralism of the United States. In Latin America, thus, not only are the rights of the various corporate groups considerably more restricted and legally confined than in the United States, but their numbers are much more limited as well. In contrast to the plethora of groups and the advantages of crosscutting (and hence limited and tempered) loyalties in the United States, in Latin America the number of such groups, often enjoying state-granted monopoly or quasimonopoly power to speak for an entire "class" or sector of the population, is quite limited.

8. Implied also in this discussion of "juridical personality," the legal status of the various corporate groups, limited pluralism, statism, and the like is a conception of a bureaucratic polity, an administrative state system rather than a liberal one. In such a bureaucratic or administrative state, the givens, the parameters, the expectations, the structures, *and* the behavior of groups and individuals tend to be different than in the liberal or laissez faire polity. The several groups do not always deal with each other directly but rather indirectly through the bureaucratic structure of the state system, again enhancing the power and authority of the state. Hence also the "bureaucratic phenomenon," the immense size of the bureaucracy and the notion that all problems should be dealt with administratively through the state rather than directly between groups and in the "marketplace," either economically or politically.[13] For example, labor-management relations in Latin America are seldom just that; instead they almost

always involve the state as well (or the labor ministry) as an "interested" and frequently decisive "third party." Hence labor protests are often directed primarily toward influencing the government rather than involving collective bargaining directly with employers.

9. Much of the politics of Latin America, historically as well as at present, may thus be seen in terms of the following major arenas:

a. The competition within and among the various Latin American corporate or interest groups to capture the state system for themselves or to secure special favors from it.

b. The efforts of virtually all states and regimes, often weak in legitimacy and effectiveness but nevertheless strong in their aspirations and in terms of the ideals of Iberian and Latin American political theory, to extend their sovereignty and authority over heretofore distant or heretofore neglected geographic areas and policy arenas—to say nothing of previously "undomesticated" or only minimally formed societal groups—and thus to fill the historic organizational void. That explains the organization and cooptation by the state historically of much of the Latin American business and middle classes—and the efforts by the state—not always successful—to coopt and control the labor and peasant sectors.

c. The parallel effort by these societal groups to preserve a degree of usually contractually defined independence and autonomy from the state, to preserve their "liberties." Later in this chapter, these relations of mutual interdependence between the state system and its component corporate groups are referred to in terms of a "contract state," and some preliminary comments are offered that are designed to set forth a theory of the Latin American contract state. Most often these state-society relations are defined constitutionally, in special charters, or through what are called "organic laws" that define the relations, let us say, of the army or the university to the state. Indeed, these relations are fundamental to understanding Latin American politics. Furthermore, although there are some parallels, the politics of these state-society relations are defined and take place in a context that is quite different from North American interest group liberalism. In the latter the struggle is chiefly *between rival interest groups;* in the case of Latin America the struggle may at times and does take place among rival interests, but it chiefly occurs as *between the state and the major corporate interests* (the Latin use of that term, we have seen, implying something far stronger than U.S.-style interest groups), or with the state serving as a mediator among rival interests. This distinction between the

U.S. and Latin American systems is critical for understanding the differing contexts and practices of much of U.S. and Latin American politics. Recently these relations have been rendered far more complex by the reemergence of the electoral arena alongside the more bureaucratic state-society ones.

PURPOSES, DEFINITIONS, AND HYPOTHESES

The purpose of this research note is to explore, in a preliminary and tentative way, the interrelationships between the Latin American state systems and their component corporative groups. It is my contention that these areas of state-society relations constitute among the principal arenas of Latin American politics, and that an understanding of them is critical to an understanding of politics, change, and breakdown in the area as a whole. It is recognized of course that there are other important arenas— the electoral one, the class one, the international one, for instance—but we view the arenas of Latin American state-society relations as both critical and almost entirely unstudied. It is our purpose to explore these arenas of state-society relations *systematically,* by fashioning indices for the more precise measurement of the relations of the state with any given corporative or societal group, and *comparatively,* employing data for all the twenty Latin American countries. The overall goal of the project is to facilitate and contribute to a better comprehension of Latin American state-society relations, and hence to contribute to our understanding of politics in the area and how this may change over time.

Several definitions set forth at the beginning will help facilitate the analysis:

Corporatism is defined here as the organization of society and polity in terms of their component vertical, sectoral, and/or professional units— the Church, the army, the university, and the like. In a modern corporatist system it is usually the state that licenses, structures, and controls interest representation through the organization of officially sanctioned, often noncompetitive groups and associations established mainly in terms of legally prescribed functional categories. But, except under the most extreme of dictatorships, these societal units also maintain some autonomy from the state, increasingly so under democracy.

The state is here defined as the authoritative decision-making public body within the polity. It is, following Weber,[14] the continuous, administrative, legal, bureaucratic, coercive agency of the polity, a mechanism for legitimated political domination and control. It is more than a referee among rival interest groups but usually less than a totalitarian system. Special emphasis should also be placed on the term "legitimated," implying that a state may by its actions lose as well as gain legitimacy. Implied also in this definition is that while the state may and usually does reflect civil society, it also has the authority to shape that society and the demands made by it on the state.

Society is here defined, in keeping with Latin America's own frequent use of the term, as the articulate, *organized*, recognized, hence legitimated and participatory element within the nation. Implied in the above, and in contrast to the North American conception, is that one does not necessarily become a member of political "society" in Latin America by the mere act of being born; rather, one becomes a member of "society"—and thereby acquires certain rights as a political participant to have one's voice heard and to bargain—through incorporation into one of the duly constituted groups or "power contenders" within the system.[15] This is also, as indicated, the Latin American definition of popular sovereignty: it is these groups that provide a regime with its right to rule, not always the popular will as expressed in regular elections. Hence when a Latin American speaks of "society" or "the nation," he or she means the general population only in the most restricted of senses; a more common interpretation in the literature of the area is that "society" and "nation" refer to the *involved, organized,* and duly *recognized* component units or sectors of the population: religious institutions, the military, municipalities—in short, the major societal and corporate groups. This conception of political society hints at why state-society relations in Latin America provide such a critical area for study, and why it is in such systems that the unorganized poor have so long been neglected.

In this projected study I shall be exploring the interrelations of state and society in Latin America. I shall seek to show the importance of examining these relations in terms of what has been called a "corporative" or "organicist," or "state-society" as distinct from or in conjunction with, a liberal framework. My research will focus chiefly on the political, legal, and juridical relations between state and society. This focus is not meant to deny the validity, albeit partial, of a liberal approach to understanding Latin America, for surely the democratic openings occurring there merit our applause and support. Nor is it meant to invalidate the validity of a class interpretation of Latin America state-society relations; indeed, I take it as a given, and so obvious as to require no further explanation, that classes and class structure are crucially important in

Latin America. However, since Latin America has historically been, and remains at present, structured along *both* class *and* corporative lines, emphasis on the one to the exclusion of the other provides only a partial explanation. Hence my focus on the important political, legal, and juridical and *corporative* parameters of Latin American state-society relations, not as an alternative to these other approaches but as a necessary complement to them.

These arenas of Latin American state-society relations, I hypothesize,—of state-Church relations, state-army relations, state-university relations, state-labor relations, and the like—constitute among the major arenas of Latin American politics, critical for an understanding of the area. This form of strong state politics and of complex interrelations between both a strong state and strong corporate units is largely unknown in the United States because our traditions are different, our state structure has historically been weak, and because we had, unlike Latin America, no feudal or quasifeudal past to help give rise to such structures. I hypothesize further that a focus on these arenas of state-society relations also sheds light on the contemporary change process throughout the area and, through the pressures and crises that system is currently undergoing, on the potential for democratic stability or, alternatively, for revolutionary upheaval. This model provides a sense of the ebb and flow of Latin American state power versus that of its component corporate groups, of the comings and goings of various groups seeking to capture or hang on to power, of changes in the relative power of the several groups over time, and of the all-important role of the state in all these machinations.

TOWARD A THEORY OF THE CONTRACT STATE

The above considerations represent a new way of thinking about and conceptualizing Latin American social and political life. They begin to get at how *Latin Americans* often view their political practices and institutions, as distinct from the institutional and ideological blinders through which most outsiders view the area.

The ideas presented here in preliminary form need to be fleshed out in more complete and concrete form. It is my hope and intention to undertake a more comprehensive study that details the structure, history, and dynamics of state-military relations, state-Church relations, state-labor relations, state-university relations, etc., in *all* the Latin American nations.

The project relates closely to work that I have been doing on mediating structures.[16] Thus far that research has been concentrated on mediating structures in the United States (churches, schools, unions, neighborhoods, families, communities), but I am now moving forward with a project giving it a comparative and foreign policy focus.

Finally, we hope to elaborate soon a full-fledged theory of the Latin American, or Iberic-Latin, "contract state." The "contract state" is based on the idea that so much of Latin American political life swirls about and is based upon those "contractual" arenas of state-society relations described preliminarily here. The "contract state" idea clearly has strong roots in Iberian and Latin American history, and it remains strong today in contemporary practice.[17]

The "contract state" idea not only serves as a useful shorthand, or heuristic device, for enabling us better to understand Latin America politics, but it also enables us better to distinguish that politics from other systems—for example, from American-style liberalism and constitutionalism or from European-style parliamentarism, from a system of laissez faire politics on the one hand and from complete statism on the other. Once again, Latin America seems to occupy an intermediary or "mixed" position on this spectrum (it has both liberal and corporative institutions); the "contract state" conception helps us get at precisely what those differences and similarities are. At the same time, the "contract state" idea enables us to avoid some of the problematic features of several of the alternative explanations discussed earlier.

I believe the "contract state" idea to be an especially useful approach for understanding and coming to grips with Iberia and Latin America. Some of the dimensions and reasons for suggesting the appropriateness and special relevance of that approach have been analyzed preliminarily here. A further elaboration and examination of the ideas suggested will be presented in a subsequent volume. I hope eventually to elaborate a full-blown theory or model of the "contract state" as it applies to both Iberia and Latin America.[18]

9

Rethinking Political Development: A Look Backward over Thirty Years, and a Look Ahead

Looking back over the last twenty or thirty years in comparative politics, one is struck by how closely the dominant concepts and models in the subfield are related to actual events and the broad currents sweeping the world of nations, to attitudinal and mood changes in the United States itself (where most, but by no means all, of the comparative politics literature is written), and to intellectual and methodological innovations within the larger field of political science. It is not that comparative politics exactly follows the headlines (although it may do that too), with their almost daily and often fickle flights from one dramatic crisis or area to the next; but it does tend to reflect the long-term trends in public and/or elite opinion that help determine which geographic or issue areas, or which intellectual approach, are to receive priority. Such fluctuations in our thinking, attention, and priorities have also affected the field of comparative politics and its changing emphases, research priorities, and conceptual perspectives over the last several decades.

The purpose of this article is to trace in broad, general terms these developments and interrelations over the last thirty years, to show how comparative politics developed from its earlier formal-legal approach to a more vigorous and genuinely *comparative* discipline, to trace the rise of the dominant political development school and its decline, to analyze the approaches that supplanted it as well as the fragmentation of the field, and to assess the current condition of the discipline—most particularly the question of why and how the political development approach may be staging a considerable comeback. In all of these trends we seek

Reprinted from Kenneth Paul Erickson and Dankwart Rustow (eds.), *Comparative Political Dynamics: Research Perspectives for the Turn of the Century* (New York: Harper and Row, 1990), under the title "Political Development Reconsidered—and Its Alternatives"; published also in *Studies in Comparative International Development* 24, no. 4 (Winter 1989–90): 65–82.

to show how the field interacts with and is part of a larger national, international, cultural, and political environment. For as American (and maybe global) politics and policy-making have become increasingly divided, fragmented, and in disarray in recent years, comparative politics has seemed also to follow these trends. Ultimately, we ask, is this new ferment, lack of coherence, and fragmentation a pathetic sign of the state of the field or is it an indication of intellectual health and vigor?[1]

TRADITIONAL COMPARATIVE POLITICS AND THE DOMINANCE OF THE POLITICAL DEVELOPMENT APPROACH

Traditional comparative politics is universally thought to have been dominated by a parochial, formal-legal, and institutional approach. That is the charge that Roy Macridis, in his tub-thumping, flag-waving, and very influential little book, raised against it in 1955.[2] Macridis, representing a new generation of comparativists who were more influenced by the recent approaches in political science than by the older approach that had been heavily dominated by lawyers and legalists, wanted a comparative politics that concentrated on informal and dynamic aspects: public opinion, interest groups, political parties, process variables, input functions, decision-making, and the processes of change.

That approach, which soon became the prevailing one in comparative politics, corresponded to others that we might call global. For our purposes, the most important of these were the emerging cold war in the 1940s and 1950s and the sudden emergence in the late 1950s and the early 1960s of a host of new nations onto the world scene.

The interrelations between these three events—a more dynamic comparative politics, the cold war, and the new or emerging nations—have yet to be analyzed adequately, in my view.[3] Some U.S. officials, and doubtless a few scholars as well, saw the fashioning of a body of literature dealing with the emerging nations purely as a means by which U.S. foreign policy could control and dominate these countries for cold war purposes. Other scholars saw the constructs of development theory as purely an intellectual approach, a way of understanding and probably of encouraging development, but not a means of manipulation. Still others—a majority I would guess—saw some (maybe varying degrees of) interrelations between U.S. cold war strategies and a theory to analyze and help shape the politics of the developing nations but generally saw no incompatibility between the two, perhaps thought of them as complementary, or thought both goals were worthy of pursuing at once.

By the 1960s the political development approach had emerged as the dominant one in comparative politics. Some scholars continued to labor in the vineyards of the more traditional institutional approaches and others continued to write first-rate books on Western Europe. But the developing nations were clearly where the action was, particularly so with the election of John F. Kennedy, the creation of the Peace Corps, whose mood was carried over into the effort to *bring* development to the emerging nations and not just to analyze it, the growth and new programs of the U.S. Agency for International Development, which sought to put development into concrete, realizable programs, and— among other events—the Cuban Revolution and then the Alliance for Progress, which focused enormous attention on Latin America and the Third World and reemphasized powerfully the cold war considerations that undergirded the U.S. government's development efforts.[4]

Considerable variation existed among the several leading writers and approaches to development—differences that have been blurred in our memories over the years or that have been purposely subordinated to the goal of lumping all "developmentalists" together for the sake of more easily critiquing or discrediting them. First, there are disciplinary differences: the more deterministic approaches of economists such as Rostow[5] or Heibroner,[6] for example; the more sociological—but in their own ways also deterministic—approaches of Deutsch,[7] Levy,[8] Lipset;[9] and to my mind the more sophisticated, subtle, and nuanced political science approaches of Pye,[10] Apter,[11] Weiner,[12] and others.

Among the political scientists, considerable and important differences also existed. Gabriel Almond, who employed the structural-functionalism and pattern variables of Talcott Parsons,[13] was by now the chairman of the Social Science Research Council Committee in Comparative Politics; his and James S. Coleman's 1960 book, *The Politics of the Developing Areas*,[14] was a pathbreaker in the field and perhaps the most influential of the genre. The SSRC/CCP was the dominant group in the comparative politics field,[15] producing during the 1960s a series of volumes through the Princeton University Press that charted new ground in such areas as political culture, political parties, and so on.[16]

But not all development-oriented political scientists shared Almond's views or his approach, and even within the SSRC/CCP not everyone was so enamored of structural-functionalism and Parsons' pattern variables. In addition, many area specialists believed at that early time that the use of a common set of categories for all nations was like comparing apples and oranges and that the effort to stuff all the world's culturally diverse political systems into one overarching scheme was artificial and false.

They also read the area-specific chapters, which followed Almond's long and theoretical introduction in *The Politics of the Developing Areas,* as an attempt to impose supposedly universal categories on areas where they didn't fit very well and did a disservice to a better understanding of these regions.

At the same time that there was a sniping from afar, in graduate seminars and other less public forums, other close-up members of the SSRC/CCP were pursuing their own research agendas in ways that did not seem to owe so much to the Parsonian-Almondian approach. Still others—and one thinks particularly of Guy Pauker in this regard—began the study of developing nations as a committed Parsonian but after actually spending time in Indonesia came back convinced that the pattern variables were not very useful. Some members of the actual SSRC/CCP have said that to their recollection Almond was the *only* one of their group who really accepted and was enthusiastic about the pattern variables. It may be that the reason Almond remained so committed to this intellectual scheme, as distinct from many of his colleagues, was his later admission that prior to his writing of *The Politics of the Developing Areas,* he had never visited any of the developing nations.[17]

Nor should one discount the possibilities for change, growth, modification, and amendment within the developmentalist approach. For example, the Cambridge scholars who were members of the Joint (Harvard-MIT) Seminar on Political Development (JOSPOD) continued to explore new development-related topics every year for over twenty-five years, and to grow intellectually and develop new concepts or refine old ones in the process.[18] Other members of the SSRC/CCP continued to expand their understanding of development as well.[19] In addition, a whole new generation of graduate students, fortified with the developmentalist ideas and conceptual armature, went out to the Third World in the early-to-mid-1960s and came back with dissertations that often obliged their mentors to modify their views. Finally, critics from within the establishment such as Samuel P. Huntington (though not a member of the SSRC/CCP) published a devastating critique of the earlier developmentalist approach, challenging the view that socioeconomic modernization and political development went hand in hand, were mutually supportive, and that the latter was somehow automatically produced by the former.[20]

What is required, first of all, therefore, is a considerable disaggregation of earlier development theory. There is a rich body of literature "out there" which deserves to be read and considered anew. It is not a monolithic "school" nor were its principal advocates all of one mind on these issues. Rather, right from the beginning there were nuances, diverse views and approaches, and a wealth of scholarship and ideas. Far too often the developmentalist approach has been dismissed with a blanket condemnation. Its principal figures have been all lumped together in one amorphous category. While certain of its intellectual thrusts seem in retrospect to have taken us in some wrong directions, this early focus on the developing areas yielded rich insights and a vast literature. It is a shame that this literature is not paid more attention than it is at present, because the wealth of information contained therein is still a marvelously fertile ground for the student of developing nations.

The second, related point to remember is that the criticisms of development theory (analyzed in the next section) were not necessarily applicable to the whole body of thought and research—although that has been the practical result—but only to some of its (I would say) most vulnerable published work. That is, the criticisms have been most strongly leveled against the writings of Almond, Lipset, and Rostow. These are taken as the paradigm writers in the developmentalist school. But it seems to me these are, in some of their particulars, the easiest works to strawman or to criticize; further, I am not sure that their writings are—or were—representative of the entire development approach. The field is far too rich, varied, nuanced, and diverse for us at this stage to dismiss (or smear) an entire body of work only because a few of its leading spokesmen went too far, said some things that can easily be criticized, or exaggerated the universality of their model.

CRITICISMS OF DEVELOPMENTALISM

During most of the 1960s the "developmentalist" approach was the dominant one in comparative politics. Although other comparative politics scholars continued to write in different genres and from other points of view, the political development paradigm became the prevailing one. That appeared at the time to be the most intellectually stimulating approach; that was where the money was, in the form of research grants and opportunities; that was where the most prestigious publication outlets (*World Politics,* the Princeton University Press) were; and, since political development had also been accepted as a major goal of U.S. foreign policy toward the Third World, that was the route through which the opportunity to influence policy lay.

But eventually the criticisms of developmentalism and the developmentalist approach began to build.[21] The criticisms came from diverse directions; eventually the cumulative impact was devastating—so much so that today's graduate students, while acquainted with the criticisms, hardly know the original literature at all, no longer read it, and tend to treat it (if at all) dismissively in their seminars in one brief session. A listing of some of the main criticisms follows.

First, the political development literature is criticized as biased and ethnocentric, derived from the Western experience of development and of doubtful utility in non-Western areas and only limited utility in the incompletely Western ones. For societies cast in traditions other than the Judeo-Christian, lacking the sociopolitical precepts of Greece, Rome, and the Bible, without the same experience of feudalism and capitalism, and not having experienced the cultural history of the West, the argument is, the Western developmental model is either irrelevant or of meager usefulness.[22]

Second, it has been argued that the timing, sequences, and stages of development in the West may not be replicable in today's developing nations. With regard to timing, it can be said that countries whose development is occurring in the late-twentieth century face different kinds of problems than those whose development began in the nineteenth century. In terms of sequences it appears, for example, that rapid urbanization may precede industrialization in the Third World whereas in the West just the reverse occurred; and when one speaks of stages, rather than capitalism following feudalism as in the West, in the Third World the two have most often been fused. The result is that virtually all our interpretations based on the Western developmental experience—ranging among the political behavior of the middle class, the presumed professionalization of the armed forces, the demographic transition, and other key indicators of modernity or the transition thereto—need to be rethought and reconceptualized when applied to the Third World.[23]

The international context of today's developing nations, third, is quite different from those of yesterday. That factor also was ignored in most of the development literature, which in the 1960s focused almost exclusively on domestic social and political change. Few countries have ever developed autonomously and in complete isolation; but it is plain that today's developing nations are caught up in a much more complex web of dependency and interdependency relations, cold war conflicts, alliances and blocs, transnational activities, and the "world culture" (Lucian Pye's term) of tastes, communications, and travel than was the case of the early modernizers. These international connections need to be factored into any theory of political development.[24]

Fourth, the critics argue, the political development literature often misrepresented the role of traditional institutions. In much of the literature traditional institutions were treated as anachronisms, fated either to fade away or be destroyed as modernization went forward. But in most modernizing nations, traditional institutions have proved durable, flexible, and long-lasting, adapting to change rather than being overwhelmed by it. They have served as filters of modernization and even themselves as agents of modernization. A much more complex understanding of the interrelations between tradition and modernity is required.[25]

In the developing nations, fifth, the sense is strong that the early political development literature raised false expectations and created unrealistic goals for these societies to achieve. Almond's original functional categories seemed reasonable and nonethnocentric enough; but in actual practice "rule adjudication" was taken to mean an independent judiciary, political parties and an independent legislature were required, and countries that lacked these institutions were too often labeled, "dysfunctional." Hence the development literature frequently skewed, biased, and distorted the political processes working in the developing nations, forced them to create Potemkin village-like institutions (such as political parties) that looked wonderful on paper but proved to be very ephemeral, or, alternatively, obliged them to destroy their own traditional institutions, which might have been viable within their own contexts.[26]

A sixth criticism is that political development was part of a larger cold war strategy fomented by the United States to keep the Third World depressed and "in chains." Two distinctions need to be pointed out here. The first is between those who did have such a blatantly cold war strategy in mind,[27] and those who more simply wanted to analyze development and, often in addition, wanted to help the emerging nations to achieve it. Frankly, most of the scholars who wrote on political development preferred both goals and saw no contradiction between them: that is, they favored development and thought that in the same process both United States and Third World aspirations and interests could be achieved.

And that leads us directly to the second distinction. Many of those who wrote the early development literature shared the general United States attitude of that time of the need to contain the Soviet Union and prevent the developing nations from going communist. But the way to do that, they all but universally agreed, was not to keep the Third World countries depressed and in chains; instead it was to help stimulate their development, to help make them viable, to promote economic growth and political institutionalization by which they could themselves be in a condition to resist communist appeals. So there was clearly a cold war motive behind much of the early development analysis, but it was emphatically not to keep these nations depressed but rather to build them up socially, economically, and politically.[28]

Seventh, the political development perspective has been criticized as wreaking downright harm on the developing nations. The focus on political development sometimes had the effect of helping to destroy or undermine indigenous institutions within the Third World that were often quite viable, provided some cultural or social "cement," and might have helped these nations bridge some transitions to modern forms. Instead, because many intellectuals as well as government leaders within the Third World accepted the developmental perspective and the seemingly inevitable progression from "traditional" to "modern," these traditional institutions (family or patronage networks, clan or tribal groups, etc.) had to be eliminated for development to occur. The result in many developing nations is the worst of all possible worlds: their traditional institutions have been largely destroyed, their modern ones remain inchoate and incompletely established, and they are hence left not with development but with a political and institutional vacuum.[29]

One final criticism of the political development approach needs to be made, and that is that its early leaders were themselves not always sufficiently adept politically. There were rivalries for leadership within the political development movement as well as resentments by members of the SSRC/CCP against the leadership; some of these rivalries and bitter feelings are still alive and strongly felt even thirty years later. More important from the point of view of the receptivity of the political development approach was that the SSRC/CCP, which dominated the field for at least a decade, failed sufficiently to broaden its base, bring in adequate numbers of new members, and incorporate the research findings and concepts of comparativists other than themselves. Year after year, as the SSRC/CCP volumes came out over the decade of the 1960s, they had the same editors and, for the most part, the same contributors. Very little fresh blood or fresh ideas were introduced, a fact that stimulated resentment among many other comparativists who also had important and worthwhile things to say. Later, quite a number of these persons would turn out to be among the foremost critics of the developmentalist approach.

These criticism of the literature of political development were powerful and quite devastating. Eventually, by the end of the 1960s, not only were these criticisms widespread but other factors were operating as well. So many case studies of developing nations had now been written in which the developmental approach itself was found wanting that eventually the assumptions of the approach itself were questioned, no longer so much the countries themselves and their "dysfunctionality" in terms of the developmental criteria. Samuel Huntington weighed in with his powerful critique, suggesting that socioeconomic modernization and political development, instead of going forward hand in hand, might well work at cross purposes. The Vietnam war provided another blow since in some quarters the war was presented as a disastrous consequence of a misplaced emphasis on political development by the United States. In addition, some of the early writers on development were viewed as supporters of the war or even its "architects."

A generational factor was also involved: the political development literature was largely fashioned by one generation of scholars and by the end of the 1960s that generation was beginning to pass in favor of a younger generation who were critical of their forebears or who simply had other ideas. And that gets us to the final reason for political development's demise: fad and fancy. Political development was in part a product of the early 1960s, of the enthusiasms of the Kennedy administration, of the Alliance for Progress, and of "the Peace Corps mood of the times" (Almond's phrase). But by the late–1960s both that era, that fad, and that body of literature had largely come and gone. By then other fads and fashions had come into existence: dependency theory, corporatism, political-economy, bureaucratic-authoritarianism, a revived Marxism, others. The analysis turns next to a treatment of these new approaches.

NEW AND ALTERNATIVE MODELS

The decline in the consensus undergirding the political development approach had brought a variety of other approaches to the fore. In part these changes were related to logical and/or methodological flaws in the developmentalist approach itself; in part they were due to broader changes within the larger society. One is tempted to draw parallels between the decline of the developmentalist approach in the 1960s and the decline of the American societal and foreign policy consensus, and to relate the rise of multiple approaches in comparative politics in the decade that followed to increasing divisions, even fragmentation, in American society as a whole. But it may be that such "cosmic" conclusions are larger than we are justified in reaching at the present time.

The decline of the older consensus in the field need not necessarily be lamented. As set forth in the previous section, there *are* major problems with the political development approach. And the new approaches have, for the most part, made a contribution to the discipline. The trouble is, as with development theory, that there are "vulgar" as well as more sophisticated versions of most of these newer approaches which need to be sorted out; and furthermore many of these newer approaches have now in the 1980s also, like political development, run their courses and begun to be supplanted. By what, we must ultimately ask, and what therefore is the future of the field?

Dependency Theory

Dependency theory grew directly out of dissatisfaction with the developmentalist approach and specifically out of the criticism that development theory ignored international or "dependency" variables, such as international market forces over which the Third World had little control, multinational corporations, and the machinations of U.S. embassies abroad.[30] Now of course there are dependency relations in the world as well as complex relations of interdependence, and I think we all recognize that U.S. embassies (as well as others) and various transnational actors such as the MNCs do sometimes muck around in the internal affairs of other nations. The trick in utilizing dependency theory, therefore, is to distinguish between those writers who use the theory pragmatically to shed light on the role of international actors operating within the borders of Third World nations, or otherwise controlling their destinies,[31] and those who would use the theory as an ideological weapon, usually from a Marxist or Marxist-Leninist perspective, to flagellate the United States.[32] A sophisticated dependency theory can be a useful tool of analysis, but the more vulgar ideological kind should be viewed as purely a political instrument.

Corporatism

The corporatist approach similarly arose out of discontent with development theory and was meant to shed light on political phenomena which both developmentalism and dependency theory only inadequately explained. Two schools of thought within corporatism emerged early on. One viewed corporatism as a general pattern of political cognition like liberalism and Marxism and, because of that area's particular history and traditions, seemed to have had an especially strong impact on the nations of the Iberic-Latin (including the Philippines) culture area.[33] A second view took corporatism as a general model of the political system, without particular regional or cultural affinities, implying a certain kind of relationship between societal structures and the state, and therefore present in a wide variety of regimes.[34] These views need not be seen as incompatible; indeed the two perspectives can be used fruitfully in conjunction with each other rather than as polarized approaches.[35]

Corporatism has now been found to be present, in different forms, in virtually all political regimes. Its very ubiquitousness, however, has diminished its utility as an explanatory device. The result is that the corporatist approach has suffered a different fate than dependency theory: corporatist features, it is now acknowledged, may be found in varying degrees almost universally; the utility of corporatism as an explanatory device is widely recognized among scholars; the corporatist approach has been accepted in the literature as a contributing but not a complete or sufficient explanation; and meanwhile the field has now gone on to other things. The corporatist approach has been superseded not out of controversy anymore (although some still goes on from time to time) but out of acceptance and, hence, a certain boredom.[36]

Political Economy

The early writings on political development largely ignored political-economy variables. In part that was because in the 1950s when the theory was first formulated, the barriers between the social science disciplines were sharper and interdisciplinary work was less appreciated than is the case today. In part also, it was because development studies had previously been dominated by economists and sociologists, and in the new development literature a conscious effort was made to emphasize the autonomy of the political variables. It further seems likely that, given the cold war origins of some of this literature (recall Rostow subtitling his classic 1960 book, "A Non-Communist Manifesto"), a conscious effort was made to stay away from political-economy explanations that could too easily be confused with Marxism.

And, like dependency theory, that is still the problem with the political economy approach. In subtle, sophisticated hands,[37] the political economy perspective can be a useful and insightful one. In less sophisticated hands, or among those who consciously wish to use it that way, the political economy approach has a tendency to tail off into a Marxian interpretation with, again, greatly varying levels of sophistication as opposed to vulgarity.

Bureaucratic Authoritarianism

Bureaucratic-authoritarianism (or B–A) arose out of the self-same disillusionment with the developmentalist approach as did a number of these other schools, and was particularly aimed at explaining the rash of military coups that occurred in Latin America in the 1960s and early 1970s. The term *bureaucratic*-authoritarianism was used to distinguish the newer more institutionalized military regimes in Argentina, Brazil, Chile, Peru, and Uruguay from the older, more personalistic or *caudillo*-dominated military regimes of the past.[38]

Bureaucratic-authoritarianism is a good term, for in fact the newer Latin American authoritarian regimes were more bureaucratic, more institutionalized, more "developed" than those in the past. The trouble was that this useful contribution was accompanied by an attempt to explain the B–A phenomenon through a convoluted argument that pointed to the crisis of Latin America's growth strategy of import substitution as *the* cause of bureaucratic-authoritarianism and thus shaded off into a kind of economic determinism which the evidence could not sustain.[39] Like so many of the approaches examined here, B–A marked a significant contribution if shorn of its ideological baggage and so long as a useful but still partial explanation was not elevated to the status of a single and all-encompassing one.

Marxism

I know of very few scholars who do not find the general Marxian paradigm of use in providing a map, a broad-gauged explanation, for the transition from feudalism to capitalism. That is what has made the Marxian explanation popular intellectually in the developing nations for that is precisely the transition through which they are presently going. The trouble with this approach comes when it is used to explain the transition from capitalism to the next stage, when it is applied to specific groups where it does not fit very well (the Church or the armed forces, for instance), and when it is used as a rigidly ideological formula rather than as a flexible tool of analysis.[40]

In addition, the socialist countries have found that Marxism is not a very useful guide in providing for an efficient and productive economy; their intellectuals have abandoned Marxism almost to a person, and many of the developing nations—once enamored of Marxism—are no longer so attracted to it. In the present era Marxism and especially Marxism-Leninism appears to be valued as a formula for gaining, consolidating, and hanging onto power, but as a way to achieve either political freedom or economic efficiency it is no longer valued.

Many of these newer explanations have provided useful contributions to comparative politics. Quite a number have by now been successfully integrated into, and are widely accepted in, the broader field. It should be remembered that they provide partial explanations, not complete ones; and that they too, like the political development approach, have gone through a virtual life cycle of birth, growth, flourishing, acceptability or cooptation, and then a gradual fading away.

In another work,[41] I have suggested that the disappearance of the consensus that used to exist about the political development approach and the rise of these other, competing new ones is not necessarily an unhealthy sign for the discipline. The existence of a variety of approaches has stimulated a healthy discussion and ferment in the comparative political discipline and reflects the methodological and political realities in which we and the field live. In that earlier work, therefore, I suggested three priorities of research: continued refining of these several separate approaches, efforts at building connecting bridges among these "islands of theory," and continued attempts to fashion larger syntheses incorporating elements from these several theories. To these three I would now add a fourth task: grappling with the revival of the political development approach and comprehending the newer political phenomena emerging around us which may also point back to a revival of developmentalism.

POLITICAL DEVELOPMENT REVISITED

In the early 1960s, when the last major experiment in democratic development in Latin America took place, great hope existed that democracy, development, peace, and security would be closely correlated. Intellectual justifications for such correlations were provided in the development literature of that period, and most particularly in the writings of W. W. Rostow, S.M. Lipset, Karl Deutsch, and others. Using his famous aeronautical metaphor, Rostow demonstrated—based on the European and U.S. experiences—that as countries developed economically, they also tended to become more middle class, more pluralistic, more democratic, more stable, more socially just, and more peaceful.[42] Lipset and Deutsch in path-breaking articles[43] at that time showed the close correlations between literacy, social mobilization, economic development, and democracy. An obvious foreign policy lesson also followed from this research: if we can help developing countries to be more literate and middle class, they will consequently become more democratic and more able to resist the appeals of communism.

But correlations do not imply causal relationships, and in Latin America as well as many other developing areas in the 1960s a wave of military coups swept the civilian democratic governments out of power. Greater literacy and social mobilization did not lead to democracy and stability but to upheaval and, ultimately, under military governments, to repression. The middle class proved to be not a bastion of stability and democracy but deeply divided and very conservative, often goading the military to seize power from the civilian democrats. By the late 1970s, none of the correlations were correlating very well: democracy had collapsed, seventeen of the twenty Latin American nations were under military authoritarian rule, the developmentalist literature was rejected and in shambles, and the new, postdevelopmentalist interpretations—dependency theory, corporatism, Marxist explanations, bureaucratic authoritarianism—were in their heyday.[44]

But since the late 1970s, nations as diverse as South Korea, the Philippines, and the Republic of China have embarked on some remarkable transitions to democracy. In Latin America the figures of a decade ago have been almost exactly reversed: eighteen of the twenty-one countries and over 90 percent of the population are either democracies or en route to democracy. This transition in so short a time has been nothing less than amazing. Not only has this given rise to a whole new approach and body of literature ("Transitions to Democracy")[45] in comparative politics, but it also forces us to reconsider and maybe resurrect the older, discredited developmentalist approach. At least six factors are at work here, demanding our attention.

What Works in Development

By this time we have some thirty years experience with development. Our discussions no longer need to be focused entirely at the conceptual and theoretical level, as they were to a large extent in the 1960s. With the proper qualifications, we now *know* what works in development. We have a three-decade-long track record, we have abundant case histories, and we have sophisticated comparative studies. We know what are unsuccessful development strategies and what are successful ones. Overwhelmingly, the evidence now points to the conclusion that what works in development is democracy, security, open markets, social modernization, stable institutions, and peaceful, moderate change[46]—all the elements that Lipset, Rostow, and the early development literature posited as necessary.

A World Political Culture in Favor of Democracy

The concept of a "world political culture," first articulated by Lucian Pye,[47] is and always will be imprecise and difficult of empirical verification. Nevertheless there can be no doubt that in the last decade a remarkable transformation that can be called global has occurred. No one wants corporatist, bureaucratic-authoritarian, organic-statist, or Marxist-Leninist regimes anymore. In Asia, the Soviet Union and Eastern Europe, and in Latin America the sentiment in favor of democracy is overwhelming. Public opinion surveys in Latin America indicate that over 90 percent of the population in virtually every country favors democracy. *Glasnost* and *Perestroika* may have ushered in one of the most fundamental transformations of the late-twentieth century: political opening and democracy within communist regimes. A host of authoritarian regimes in diverse parts of the world—"friendly tyrants," as one research report labels them[48]—have been swept from power. Though the measures are inexact, few of us can doubt that a revolution of very profound dimensions in favor of democracy has begun to sweep the world.

U.S. Foreign Policy

Most of the transitions to democracy that have occurred have been the products of indigenous forces and only secondarily of external ones. Nevertheless in some key countries at critical times, a U.S. policy in favor of democracy has also been crucial. A strong democracy/human rights agenda has been pursued by the United States both for strong ethical and moral reasons and because it is our history as a nation to pursue such crusades, and for strong practical reasons: it is in our interest to do so. The most recent campaign for democracy and human rights began under President Carter and it continued in somewhat altered form under President Reagan. Carter emphasized human rights and helped begin the process, while Reagan gave it a broader democracy focus and emphasized that human rights tend to flow from American strength, not American weakness. By this point human rights and democracy have acquired a consensus of bipartisan support and it is inconceivable that any future U.S. administration could have a successful foreign policy without these components.[49]

The Decline of the Other Models

By this time not only have the major explanatory models—corporatism, Marxism, bureaucratic authoritarianism—largely run their course and been accepted, at least in their fundamental contributions, into the discipline, but the regimes based upon these models have either been discredited and/or overthrown as well. Cuba, Nicaragua, and the Soviet Union are no longer viewed as viable models by very many people anymore, while the "Nasserist" (progressive, nationalistic) military of Peru, the generals in Brazil, and the corporatist regimes of Portugal and Spain were thoroughly discredited and are no longer with us. The demise or discrediting of the older "models" along with the resurgence of democracy have given rise to the sentiment that maybe the developmentalist paradigm had (and has) something to recommend it after all.[50]

Changed Political Attitudes in the United States

After Vietnam, Watergate, the relative economic decline of the United States in the 1970s, and Jimmy Carter's "malaise," the sense was strong in the United States that we had nothing to offer the world. Our self-confidence had been eroded by events both at home and abroad. But during the 1980s, as the economy recovered and then flourished, American self-confidence began to recover. Contrary to the earlier "ethnocentrism" literature, the sense grew that maybe the United States was not such a bad place after all—at least as compared with most others—that it still had a great deal to offer the rest of the world. There are many criticisms that can be raised against it but undoubtedly Allan Bloom's book[51] struck a responsive chord. That book emphasized the democratic and civilizing values in the Western cultural tradition; it pointedly suggested, in contrast to much of the prevailing cultural relativism, that some cultures (the Western one) are in fact more democratic, more humane, and more civilized than others (let us say, the Iranian one).

Development in the Short Run—and in the Long

The democratization, development, and modernization that have occurred in many Third World areas in the last decade force us to reassess the Lipsetonian and Rostowian theories. Lipset, Rostow, and the entire development approach and school were thoroughly discredited in the 1960s and 1970s—and often for good reasons, as outlined in the first part of this chapter. They and their followers, as well as many U.S. government officials, tended to portray the relationship between development and democracy in ways that proved far too simple, implying a causative relationship that did not exist, basing their theories of development too heavily on the Western and European experiences, and thus for a long time helping lead astray both development theory and the policies that flowed from it.

But we now need to face the fact that while Lipset and Rostow (and their schools) were wrong in the short run, they may still prove to have been correct in the long run. That is, while there is no necessary, automatic, or causative relationship between development and democracy—as some of the early developmentalists themselves pointed out—there are tendencies, correlations, and long-term relationships that cannot be denied. It is therefore necessary, I believe, to begin a serious reexamination of the earlier development literature to see what should be saved and what jettisoned. There may well be more worth saving than would have seemed likely ten years ago.[52]

For example, we learned in the 1960s that there was no necessary correlation between democracy and the size of the middle class; indeed in many countries it was the middle class that plotted to overthrow democracy. But now in the 1980s it is the middle class that has led the opposition to military authoritarianism and is convinced, having tried other models, that democracy is much to be preferred. Employing other indices yields further correlations: the armed forces are now both more professionalized and more in favor of democracy than they were twenty years ago. Literacy is now far greater and so is the spread of democracy. Economic development over three decades has gone forward and so has the desire for democracy increased. The relationships that did not correlate very well in the 1960s now seem to be correlating very well indeed.[53]

These strong correlations raise the distinct possibility that while Lipset, Rostow, et. al., were too optimistic and hence mistaken in the short run, in the longer term their correlations (and the predictions that went with them) may yet prove to be correct. One decade (the 1960s) was simply too short a period for the developmentalist propositions to be adequately tested. Moreover, the more sophisticated theories of development recognized that these were long-term processes, that the transitional period was almost by definition likely to be chaotic, and that there were bound to be many setbacks on the road to development. But over the course of the decades now, we have a longer time period to observe, we have a considerable experience with development, and the earlier correlations and assumptions of the development approach have begun to look better and better.

The fact is that the base for democracy in Latin America as well as in East Asia is bigger, more solid, and more promising now than it was in the 1960s. The middle class is larger, there is far greater affluence, bureaucracies are better trained and more experienced with development, the associational and institutional life has grown and become better consolidated, literacy is far higher, vast social changes have occurred leading to pluralism, the military is better educated and more professional, per capita income is higher, more persons are better educated, the private sectors are larger and more active, and so on.[54] These changes may well mean that the current openings to democracy in much of the developing world may prove more than just cyclical, popular now but subject to a new round of coups when the next crisis comes. When civil society was weak and development just beginning for many countries in the 1960s, an authoritarian regime might have seemed to some a possible alternative; but as development and pluralism have gone forward into the 1980s a new wave of military coups seems increasingly unlikely—at least in the better institutionalized and more viable countries. It may be that the developmental changes of the last quarter century and more have been sufficiently profound that not only can many countries look forward to a stabler future based on development and democracy, but also the processes involved force us to reconsider the main premises of the development approach in a newer and more positive light.

CONCLUSION AND IMPLICATIONS

The field of comparative politics has become increasingly fragmented since the 1960s. There is no one approach that dominates the field nor is there an approved body of theoretical knowledge on which all or even most scholars can agree. Since the decline, discrediting, and demise of the developmentalist approach, the field has lost its earlier unity. Perhaps this is a reflection of the increasing fragmentation within the discipline of political science more generally and in the United States itself. Whatever the ultimate answers to those questions, it is clear that what exists in comparative politics is separate subsections within the field, each with its own apostles, theory, and research work, and with usually limited efforts to connect one subsection of the field with another. To employ again the metaphor used earlier, we have "islands" of research work and theory, with often limited attempts to construct causeways and linkages among these diverse archipelagos, and almost no central, overarching structure or theory that would provide unity to the field as a whole.[55]

It seems unlikely any time in the near future that the unity that reigned in the 1960s in the comparative politics field as a whole will be restored. Nor am I at all certain that such unity is desirable. The unity that centered around political development in the 1960s, I believe, while contributing valuable new insights and approaches, also led us down some wrong trails and blinded us to phenomena and approaches that did not seem to fit comfortably in the developmentalist approach. My own view is that the field has been greatly enriched by the variety of approaches and perspectives that came to the fore in the 1970s.

But those approaches have also largely run their course and their useful contributions have been incorporated into the field. Now we are in a new era, no longer of corporatism, bureaucratic authoritarianism, and organic-statism, but an era of vast social and political changes and of quite remarkable transitions to democracy. These changes have made the once all but moribund developmentalist approach look better and better, and certainly deserving of a second consideration. The developmentalist approach looks far better in retrospect and from a long-term perspective than it looked in the late 1960s and 1970s. Shorn of its ethnocentrism, its biases, and its blindness—all critiqued earlier in this article—the developmentalist approach and paradigm contain a rich body of sophisticated literature and a large storehouse of theory and insight from which we can still—and again—profitably learn. The developmentalist approach will unlikely ever recapture the central place in the field that it enjoyed in the 1960s—too much has changed, and so have we and the field—but it certainly can retake its place as one of the major half dozen or so approaches here surveyed—another one of the "islands of theory" from which the painstaking task of constructing drawbridges to other islands and to the mainland can now take place.

10

Political Culture and National Development

Since the Enlightenment, what we now call the social sciences have come to eschew "culturalist explanations" of political, social, and economic behavior. Over the past two centuries, and particularly since Marx and Durkheim, we have tended to think that scientific and technical advances, economic interrelationships, and institutional arrangements determine the way people think and behave, and not culture. It is interesting and significant that both Marxian analysis and recent non-Marxian developmental analysis (as found in the writings of S. M. Lipset or W. W. Rostow,[1] for example) tend to downgrade or even manifestly reject the cultural variables that help shape development, in favor of "grand theory" in which presumably universal sociological and economic factors play the major role.

No one would deny, of course, that the great motor forces of scientific and technological advance, economic development, and institutional change are among the critical factors in stimulating modernization processes. At the same time, explanations from the point of view of political culture, in amateurish hands, run the risk of dangerous simplification, national stereotyping ("Englishmen do this," "Spaniards do that"), and the employment of unacceptable racial and ethnic biases.

THE POLITICAL-CULTURAL IMPERATIVE

Nevertheless, the importance of cultural variables cannot be ignored. Some scholars, among them Daniel Bell and Clifford Geertz, suggest that cultural factors are as important in shaping national development as the others previously listed, even arguing that it is often culture that conditions the form, pace, and style of economic development instead of the other way around.[2] In their view, what Marx called the "superstructure" (culture, ideas, belief systems, traditional ways of doing things) influences

Reprinted from *Fletcher Forum of World Affairs* 13 (Summer 1989).

the substructure (economic and class relations) as much as or more than the latter shapes the former—or at least interacts with it in far more complex ways than the apostles of grand, often unidimensional, systems theory have been willing to admit. At the same time, in the hands of sophisticated analysts such as Lucian Pye, Gabriel Almond, Samuel Huntington, and Sidney Verba, the comparative study of political culture has moved far beyond the old, unacceptable "national character" studies to become far more precise, empirical, and rigorous, and to provide a major tool for understanding the political differences between regions and countries.[3]

In both Marxian and non-Marxian development theory, traditional political culture was presumed to give way under the onslaught of modernization, either through revolution or by more gradual processes. But in research project after research project over the past three decades focused on the developing nations, traditional political culture and institutions have proved to be remarkably long-lived and persistent. Rather than being swept aside by the tides of history, or consigned to history's ash cans, these institutions—whether in Asia, the Middle East, Africa, or Latin America—have repeatedly shown themselves to be flexible and accommodative, most often bending to change rather than being overwhelmed by it. Many of these traditional institutions, such as India's caste associations or Latin America's extended patronage networks, rather than having been discarded as modernization proceeds, have themselves modernized. In the process, they have converted themselves into interest associations, and thus, have bridged the gap between traditional and modern. These institutions have provided for political-cultural continuity as well as change.

Religion was one of those "traditional" cultural forces that was supposed to disappear as modernization went forward. But who studying the Middle East, in the face of the revival of Islamic fundamentalism, can say with certainty that religion is a thing of the past? Nor can Latin America's historic Catholicism be simply waved aside as an artifact of the past; rather, the political struggle there involves different factions *within* the Catholic Church (and, increasingly, between the Church and the rising evangelical sects), not between religion and the supposedly inevitable forces of secularism. As Daniel Bell has remarked, "From Voltaire to Marx every Enlightenment thinker thought that religion would disappear in the twentieth century because religion was fetishism, animistic superstition. Well it's not true," Bell continued, "because religion is a response, and sometimes a very coherent response, to the existential predicaments faced by all men in all times. Empires have crumbled, political systems have crumbled, economic systems have crumbled. The great historical religions have survived."[4] The modernization-begets-secularization thesis has just not stood up.

Religion is, however, but one of the features of political culture on which our comparative studies of development ought to concentrate. Others include legal systems, traditional social organizations (such as the family or clan), patronage mechanisms, ideologies and belief systems, and historic forms of social and political institutions. All of these are part of a broad "political culture." Yet none of them can be accounted for entirely on the basis of scientific or technological change, or economic or class structure. In fact, much of what we find in the political culture persists independently of these other forces, often defying the best-laid schemes of the grand systems builders.

CULTURE, CORPORATISM, AND LATIN AMERICAN DEVELOPMENT

In my own earlier research on Latin America, I tended to emphasize those political-cultural features inherited from the feudal-medieval (and thus preEnlightenment) mother countries: Spain and Portugal.[5] These features included powerful strains of authoritarianism, elitism, hierarchy, patrimonialism, and corporatism. I saw corporatism, then as now, as the product of two main influences.

The first was Latin America's historical and cultural tradition, strongly influenced by Catholic precepts and the peculiarly Iberian history of the Reconquest, the achievement of national consolidation according to the Hapsburgian model (top-down, absolutist, and distinct from the Lockean liberalism model). This tradition was also affected by the particular (and continuing) organic relations to the state of such corporate agencies as the military orders, the Church, the town, and the universities. The political arena largely focused on the state's efforts to expand and consolidate its power over these groups, and on the corporate entities that make up society to maintain their autonomy from the state. In this sense, corporatism is a product of a particular world view derived from an Aristotelian-Thomist synthesis; it is a general pattern of political cognition comparable to liberalism or Marxism.[6]

The second influence leading to the persistence and even expansion of corporatism, a factor later emphasized by Philippe Schmitter and others, and elevated into a veritable cottage industry of new writings,[7] was not historical but contemporary: the modern state's need to control and harness the Latin American development process through the creation of state-sponsored and directed trade unions, peasant associations, and other corporate bodies. This second form of corporatism was, of course, not unique to Iberia or Latin America but existed in a variety of forms in different areas.

Several influences were at work in shaping the concept of political culture I used with regard to Latin America, and particularly the emphasis on corporatism as one essential ingredient in it. The first was dissatisfaction with the other paradigms then available—developmentalism and Marxism—neither of which, after a point, seemed to fit Latin America very well. Second, related, was the effort to develop a paradigm that *did* build upon Latin America's own history and dynamics, including its powerful, persistent traditions of organic-statism and corporatism. Third was research experience in Brazil, Mexico, Central America, the Dominican Republic, Venezuela, Argentina, Spain, and Portugal. All, in regimes of the Left and of the Right, in military contexts as well as democratic ones, seemed to have one or another form of persistent corporatist institutions.

The fourth influence was my earlier training as an historian, under Irving Leonard, Donald Worcester, Lyle McAlister, and Alva Curtis Wilgus. One cannot have studied Roman law, the writings of Thomas Aquinas, the *Siete Partidas,* the "organic laws" governing state-church or state-town relations, the "*fuero militar*," or Spanish colonial administration without coming away with a profound appreciation of the immense, and continuing, impact of these institutions and ideas on Latin American life. Indeed, I would argue, contrary to those social scientists who believe that Latin American "history" began only with the Cuban revolution, that one cannot understand Latin America at all unless one first come to grips with the heavy hand of the hemisphere's history, which includes powerful political-cultural influences.

Political-cultural approaches have not always been appreciated by some Latin American intellectuals or by some North American scholars. For what such explanations do is to place responsibility for Latin America's continuing underdevelopment directly on Latin America itself rather than allowing it to be ascribed (far preferable, from the Latin American viewpoint) to US machinations, as in dependency theory. Latin Americans also resent the paternalism involved, the notion that the United States must be the model for them to follow, and that they themselves have nothing to contribute. Ironically, when a theory did come along, such as corporatism, that *was* derived from Latin America's own history and traditions, the region decided it did not like that theory and rejected it.[8]

Some US scholars also had problems with the corporatism idea. The

Marxist Left, of course, had to reject it because the theory clashed with their faith that it was class structure that determined political culture and never the other way around. Now, however, some enlightened Marxists have rediscovered the independence of culture as a political variable. The noted *"dependencia"* writer Enzo Faletto has just published an article on political culture and democratization in which he concludes that "structural conditions are insufficient for democracy to arise and take effect."[9]

Non-Marxist scholars also had very mixed feelings. Although not rigid economic determinists, they nonetheless often tend to believe that socio-economic forces are the chief explanatory factor in development and that culture is important only because it seems to "get in the way." As liberals, they cannot abide the determinist elements present in some political culture writings which seem to suggest that, despite their diligent reform efforts, Latin America seems *always* fated to be authoritarian, elitist, and organic-corporatist. If that is so, then how can political-culturalists explain Latin America's inspiring, recent transition to democracy?

At this point, several of the more fevered criticisms of political culture research need to be addressed. Political culture is certainly not a "racist" explanation as some of the old national character studies might have been. Rather, it looks systematically and empirically, with the appropriate qualifications, at *patterns* of political beliefs and orientations; it tries to understand other societies on their own terms. If such examinations of cultural factors are "racist," then the entire field of cultural anthropology might as well pack up its tents.

Nor does emphasis on political culture imply a deterministic "culturalist" explanation. Rather, it simply says that political culture is one important variable among several (class, economic factors, political institutions) that shape political outcomes and, therefore, is deserving of serious attention. Just because a scholar *chooses* to write about political culture because that person finds it interesting does not mean he or she thinks other factors are unimportant. So far as I know, not a single serious scholar who writes about political culture has claimed that this factor is important to the exclusion of all others; nor has there been on the part of scholars of political culture an attempt to elevate political culture into a single-causal explanation.

Rather, political culture is generally viewed as an important factor which, under the impact of both Marxist and non-Marxist political economy or systems theory, has not received the attention it deserves. As a matter of fact, most serious scholars in this field see political culture, economic and class determinants, and political-institutional factors as interrelated in all kinds of complex and changing ways. They would prefer to remain open-minded concerning the question of whether it is the economy that determines the culture, for example, or the culture that helps shape the kind of economy and developmental patterns that emerge. It seems to most of us that these questions need to be kept open for discussion, investigation, and empirical testing, and should not become simply a matter of assertions that border on religious faith.

Nor are political-cultural explanations ruled out by the recent transitions to democracy in Latin America. First, the more careful analysts of political culture have always recognized that, at least since the nineteenth century, two traditions—an authoritarian-corporatist one and a liberal-democratic one—have uneasily coexisted in Latin America, often alternating in power. At present, the liberal-democratic one is (temporarily?) ascendant. Second, while at the formal-institutional level (and in some cases more deeply than that) democracy in contemporary Latin America has triumphed, below the surface many institutions—the Church, the Army, labor relations, lord-peasant relations, the state structure—often remained dominated by authoritarian-corporatist-patrimonialist features. Third, change has occurred, including in Latin America's political culture. The area is now more urban, affluent, literate, developed, and modern than it was thirty years ago, when the last great, but soon aborted, movement toward democratization began. Opinion surveys in country after country show that democracy has a firmer foundation now than it had during the heyday of the Alliance for Progress in the early 1960s. As socioeconomic development and modernization have gone forward, the political culture has also been transformed, albeit shakily in some countries, toward support of democracy. Again, the more sophisticated analysts of political culture have consistently recognized that political culture is not static and unchanging but always shows both continuous and changing features.

A RENAISSANCE OF POLITICAL CULTURE

Political culture is presently enjoying a renaissance. Samuel Huntington, Aaron Wildavsky, Harry Eckstein, and Lucian Pye—all among the leading figures in the profession—have recently published major books and articles using the political culture approach.[10] Westview Press, perhaps the leading publisher of Latin American and developing-areas books in the country, has recently begun a new political-culture series; Harvard University's Center for International Affairs also has initiated a faculty seminar on political culture. Three major articles dealing with political culture have been published in the *American Political Science Review* in the past two years; in the most recent of these, Professor Ronald Inglehart of the University of Michigan argues that "it is time to redress the balance in social analysis"—toward greater attention to political-culture variables. His empirically-based research indicates that political culture is a crucial link between economic development and democracy, that political culture is an important independent variable, and that the peoples of different countries and areas have reasonably durable cultural attributes that often have major economic and political consequences.[11]

In anthropology, Clifford Geertz's emphasis on "thick description"— essentially political culture—has been widely lauded.[12] In economics and sociology, Tony Barnett's recent book on development stresses that the development process cannot be understood in terms of technological advances alone but that economic, political, *and* cultural factors must also be taken into account.[13]

Even psychoanalysis, which has always assumed that its categories were universal, has now moved toward greater cultural relativism. "The prevailing psychological maps we assume in the West to be universal simply do not apply to people in much of the world," states New York psychoanalyst Alan Roland. "You just can't do psychotherapy with a person from Vietnam or El Salvador as you would with a Boston housewife," says Harvard Medical School psychiatrist Arthur Kleinman; "the ethnocentric arrogance of Western psychotherapy is being challenged head on by the growing recognition of the problems of treating non-Western immigrants." Kleinman concluded, "There are some psychiatric disorders, like depression and schizophrenia, that are universal; but even among them the power of culture to radically shape symptoms is profound."[14]

Meanwhile, even in Latin America where dependency theory ("blame it all on the United States; never look inward—at least not publicly!") holds sway, some grudging recognition of the political-cultural variable is beginning to surface. Chilean scholar Norbert Lechner has just published an influential book on political culture and democratization[15]; already noted is the fact that one of the leading advocates of the primary importance of economic factors in determining political outcomes, Enzo Faletto, is now arguing that the "structural factors" stressed by dependency theory are inadequate to explain democracy's rise and consolidation in the area. More traditional Latin American thinkers—Zea, Paz, Faoro—have long wrestled seriously and honestly with the weight of their own countries' political culture.

Even more important have been the effects of the recent East Asian economic miracles on Latin America. Latin America cannot and does not wish to emulate East Asia sociologically, but it does recognize it is losing out economically to the various Asian "tigers" and suffering by comparison with them. East Asia had all the features that Latin American dependency theory complains about—US multinationals, dependency on US markets, etc.—and yet Asia turned these features to developmental advantage while Latin America still insists on blaming them for its underdevelopment. But if East Asia and Latin America had these "structural features" in common, and one turned them to advantage while the other remained mired in underdevelopment, then it must be factors other than the structural ones that explain their differences. Among scholars as well as many Latin Americans, even though the latter cannot always bring themselves to say so publicly, the sense is growing that the missing explanatory variable may well be culture.

CONCLUSIONS

It seems obvious to me that political culture remains an important variable in explaining development, or the lack thereof. If the red herrings and straw men ("racism," "culturalism") can be stripped away, political culture in well-trained hands (devoid of national stereotyping or determinism) can be a powerful source of explanation and interpretation. Anyone who would study Latin America, for example, without paying serious attention to key political-cultural variables simply does not understand the area. Such variables must include religion and the Catholic Church, the code law legal system, the values and preferences that Latin Americans hold, the critical role of *"fueros"* and the corporate organization of society, and the role of history and tradition.

At the same time, political culture should not be thought of as *the* only explanatory variable, to the exclusion of class structure, political institutions, economic development, and doubtless other factors as well. A partial but still incomplete explanation derived from political culture should not be elevated into the status of a single or all-encompassing one. This is, it seems to me, where the interpretation offered in Lawrence E. Harrison's book, influential in some quarters, goes astray.[16] First, although Harrison says in his preface that he recognizes other forces besides culture are important in explaining Latin American underdevelopment, those factors never figure subsequently into his analysis; it is plain from his analysis that he believes culture is *the* most important factor. Second, Harrison pictures Latin American culture as static and unchanging when, in fact—as in the recent transitions to democracy—that culture is undergoing profound transformation.

Third, it is clear that Harrison is immensely hostile to Latin American culture, wants to abolish it entirely as if Latin America were some *tabula rasa* whose cultural slate could be wiped clean, and argues essentially that Latin America cannot develop until it takes on US-like virtues. Clearly, this will not do: Latin America cannot simply start anew as if there were no history, sociology, or culture there that is important or worth preserving. The issue is not whether to abolish Latin American culture and start anew (impossible, of course) but to adjust to and work within Latin America's existing institutions and culture, while trying to nudge the region toward greater efficiency. Surely, this is a more interesting and complex view of political culture than the rigid and unidimensional picture presented in the Harrison book, and represents a more realistic approach to Latin American development. It may surprise some analysts to read this author's criticism of a culturalist explanation, especially given the fact that he and I are sometimes lumped together in the same footnotes. In fact, Harrison's book goes so far beyond my own sense of the usefulness of political culture as *part* of a broader, more complex, and multifaceted explanation that I wish here to disassociate myself from his position.[17]

On the Latin American side, there are also problems. Not only are "dependency" (dependency, of course, exists in Latin America; *dependency* is an ideological construct) and structuralist interpretations still prevalent, but Latin America has yet to come to grips with its own political culture. Corporatism was one of the characteristics of historic Latin American political culture, but in the Latin American mind corporatism has been associated with authoritarianism and militarism. So as Latin America has repudiated its authoritarian regimes in the past decade, it has also felt obliged to repudiate corporatism.

In their rush to embrace the new "transitions to democracy" literature, however, Latin American scholars and public officials have not faced squarely the fact that they have essentially moved from an older authoritarian (or state) form of corporatism to a newer form (neo-corporatism) that is more societal and pluralist in character. But it is still *corporatist*, in the realms of labor relations, interest group relations, state-society relations, and many areas of public policy, which means there are still cultural and institutional continuities as well as changes in the recent processes of openings to democracy. Unless and until Latin America recognizes this reality of cultural continuity, not only will Latin Americans continue to misinterpret their own societies and politics, but, in failing adequately and realistically to acknowledge the continuing critical role of such important *corporate* institutions as the armed forces, countries such as Argentina also run the risk of seeing the very transitions to democracy that have been so heartening in this past decade destroyed in the process.[18]

Part IV

COUNTRY AND REGIONAL STUDIES

11

Turnaround in Nicaragua: The Larger Implications

INTRODUCTION

While there have been many heartening openings toward democracy and freedom in Marxist-Leninist regimes recently, surely one of the most stunning occurred in Nicaraguan on February 25, 1990. On that day Nicaraguan voters went to the polls in massive, unprecedented numbers, repudiated and ousted Daniel Ortega and the Sandinista government, and elected opposition leader Violeta de Chamorro as president of the country. Although other women have served briefly in the presidency in Latin America, Doña Violeta is the first woman ever *elected* to the presidency—and by a decisive, near-landslide margin at that.

The opposition's election came as a surprise to nearly everyone. All the preelection polls showed that Ortega and the Sandinistas would win. The Sandinistas controlled the jobs, the patronage, the television, the economy, as well as immense coercive power. Between the Sandinista party, the military and the militias, the public bureaucracy, and the Sandinista-controlled popular associations (for women, students, peasants, nearly everyone), the regime already commanded at least one-third of the voters. In addition, any government in Latin America that cannot manage to control its own elections is usually thought of as incompetent. So how could the Sandinistas lose?

No one thought the Sandinistas would blatantly rig the election or the ballot counting. Too many international observers would be on hand for that. Instead, the assumption was that the "fix" (jobs, promises to the faithful, intimidation where necessary) would be on long before the observers got on the scene.[1] Nor did the Sandinistas ever conceive that their own people would repudiate them. The Sandinistas did not hold this election in order to lose. But lose they did, on a massive scale, in one of the most amazing victories for democracy that we have seen in a period filled with numerous democratic triumphs.

Reprinted from *The World and I* 5 (April 1990), under the title "Nueva Nicaragua."

THE SANDINISTA REGIME

Under Sandinista rule, the Nicaraguan economy went into a tailspin. Per capita income dropped steadily during the 1980s until Nicaragua achieved the dubious distinction of nearly matching Haiti as the poorest, most miserable country in the western hemisphere. As the economy ran downhill, the regime's vaunted social programs in health, education, and agrarian reform areas also had to be curtailed. Misery spread—and so did disenchantment with the Sandinistas.

The causes for the regime's economic shortcomings have been variously described, depending on one's political point of view. The Sandinistas and their foreign supporters blame all the problems on the United States, of course, on the economic sanctions imposed and on the U.S.-funded Contra war. The regime's foes blame it all on Sandinista incompetence and mismanagement. Actually, both sets of factors were critical. There is no doubt the sanctions and the Contra war hurt, and hurt badly. But incompetence on the part of the Sandinista leaders who had never before run an office let alone a government was also critical. The global depression of the early 1980s also hurt, as did continuing low world market prices for Nicaragua's export products.

What of the nature of the Sandinista regime? At the top (the nine-man Sandinista directorate) the regime was clearly not just Marxist but Marxist-Leninist. This element provided both the leadership and the direction to the regime. There were sometimes personal or program differences among these leaders, but even the regime's staunchest supporters conceded the leadership to be Marxist-Leninist.[2]

At lower and often less articulate levels, the regime was Marxist, often vaguely so, but not necessarily Leninist. In virtually every government office the mix would be slightly different. Hence the confusion oftentimes over whether the regime was monolithically Marxist-Leninist or only Marxist.

At still lower levels, there was greater diversity: Marxist, Marxist-Leninists, reform Catholics, social democrats, and humble, often minimally educated persons who wanted change. At this level too, a good share of the economy (maybe 50 percent) remained in private hands. These facts help explain the widely divergent views in the United States about Nicaragua, and why the policy debate has so often been polarized. At the top we saw only the Marxist-Leninist element in command, a particularly *feo* (ugly) group committed to imposing a Marxist-Leninist dictatorship—in aspiration if not quite yet in actual implementation.

But at lower levels all those thousands of Americans who traveled to

Nicaragua, churchpersons and other generally well-meaning types ("political pilgrims," in Paul Hollander's apt phrase), found considerable diversity as well as sweetness and light. The partial pluralism that continued to exist at lower levels was purposely used by the Sandinista regime to gain favorable publicity and support for its cause, and also to disguise the leadership's true intentions. But between these diametrically opposed views of the revolution, there could be no meeting of the minds. And the policy debate hence waxed vigorously—and often viciously—at the same time.

THE U.S. POLICY RESPONSE

The United States was never so strongly supportive of the old Somoza regime as the Sandinistas and their supporters have often claimed.[3] Nor was the United States initially hostile to the Sandinista revolution. In fact, it was precisely while the U.S. was still aiding Nicaragua that the regime became sharply more Marxist-Leninist and less pluralistic, abandoned democracy as its announced goal, and allied itself with Cuba and the Soviet Union. Because the belief among too many persons is exactly opposite of the facts, it needs emphatically to be stated that the United States was not the cause of Nicaraguan revolution nor was it U.S. policy that caused it to veer off in a Marxist-Leninist direction.

The debate over U.S. policy in Nicaragua was the most polarized of all our foreign policy debates in the 1980s. In the Congress the debate was often bitter, with strong posturing on both sides—in part because few Nicaraguans vote in the United States, the electoral stakes are small, and hence congressmen can say and do stupid things on Central America that they would never be able to do on other areas.

Even in the celebrations of the restoration of democracy in Nicaragua, one cannot escape the partisan recriminations. Was it the Reagan policy of isolating Nicaragua, slapping on the embargo, and funding the Contras that ultimately *forced* the Sandinistas to hold the 1990 election? Or was it the Democrats' support of Oscar Arias and the Central American "peace plan" that led to a democratic opening? Republicans and Democrats have been reliving once again the 1980s debate.

Actually, both sets of factors were important. There can be no doubt that without the U.S. pressure there would have been no elections in Nicaragua and that political pluralism, already precarious, would have dwindled to the vanishing point. But it is also the case that (former) Congressman Jim Wright's peace plan, which President Reagan eventually signed off on, was instrumental in beginning a process—largely carried out by the Central Americans themselves—of negotiations, of quid pro quos, and of mutually applied pressures that obliged both El Salvador and Nicaragua to begin dealing with their oppositions, to open up political space, and to bring their moderate as well as most radical oppositions into the political process.

The U.S. government, like the rest of us, was so convinced of a likely Sandinista victory in February that it had begun secret negotiations with the Nicaraguan regime even before the election. The polls as well as CIA soundings had indicated a Sandinista victory. The U.S.-funded National Endowment for Democracy had been only partially successful in getting money to the opposition and was itself sure the Sandinistas would win.[4] So the U.S. had begun negotiations to reach a settlement of the differences between the two countries. However, the victory of Chamorro solved those problems—and led to some new ones.

Now the questions will center on how much we can do for Nicaragua, and when. With Panama, the Soviet Union, and Eastern Europe already lined up for aid, to say nothing of our own domestic budget shortfalls, this is a difficult time for Nicaragua to be competing for U.S. largesse. On the other hand, it is in our interests to help Nicaragua not only democratize but also recover economically—and it is probably our obligation as well.

The tasks will be enormous. Nicaragua is broke, deeply in debt, its economy devastated. The transition from a form of statism that benefited chiefly Somoza to state socialism under the Sandinistas was a difficult one, and so will be the transition back to a more open market system. Waste and inefficiency are rampant. Thousands of jobs, patronage positions, and sinecures will be on the line; there will be great debates over how much of the economic patrimony inherited from the Somozas or nationalized by the Sandinistas should be returned to private hands or kept in the public domain.

The debate in the United States will also be sharp. It is a measure of how deep the political divisions are over this issue that even in the midst of celebrating a democratic victory in Nicaragua we continue to argue for partisan advantage. The Democrats suggested we get the funds for Nicaragua by scrapping the Strategic Defense Initiative and the B-1 bomber; the Bush administration resisted those pressures. Some wanted to lift the sanctions immediately as a reward to Nicaragua, but cooler heads expressed the advantages of keeping at least some sanctions in place until Chamorro is inaugurated and the Sandinistas have surrendered their control. The debate was similarly renewed over cutting off all aid to the Contras or providing some further assistance to facilitate their resettlement.

LARGER RAMIFICATIONS

While the democratic victory in Nicaragua was heartening, there are implications of these dramatic events that go beyond that country. Hopefully, once the dust settles, Nicaragua will no longer be such a divisive issue in the U.S. domestic politics, polarizing the debate, poisoning the climate, and on a smaller scale producing nasty confrontations reminiscent of the debate over Vietnam.

The democratic victory removes another satellite from the Soviet orbit, and obviously also renders moot the difficult issue of Soviet arms shipments to Nicaragua. It also removes a pillar of support from under the Marxist-Leninist FMLN in El Salvador, since Nicaragua will no longer serve as a refuge, training ground, inspiration, political mentor, and arms shipper to the guerrillas. The reestablishment of democracy in Nicaragua may well make the peaceful settlement of El Salvador's bloody, long-time insurrection more possible.

Chamorro's election and the ousting of the Sandinistas isolate Fidel Castro even more. Already out of step with the political openings elsewhere in the communist world, and now with no other supportive Marxist-Leninist regimes in the western hemisphere, Cuba is increasingly alone. Plus, Castro is facing internal divisions and rumblings of discontent unprecedented in the previous thirty-one years of his revolution. It is no longer merely wishful thinking to ask, is Castro next?

FUTURE PROBLEMS

In addition to the economy, Nicaragua faces many future problems. The Sandinista leadership has been particularly adept in the past at manipulating and maneuvering in power, and we should not expect that to end just because they lost the election. The victory for Chamorro and her coalition was a democratic opening and carries considerable legitimacy, but in Central America elections have traditionally been only one route to power among several and they do not always convey definitive legitimacy throughout a fixed term of office.

The Sandinista leadership *loves* being wined and dined in Moscow and in the socialist and social-democratic salons of Europe; it loves being the center of global attention and controversy; and it will be very hard for them to go back to the obscurity of being out of the limelight in a small, everyday country again. For Nicaraguan young people, the revolution was a profoundly liberating experience (in a cultural and social as well as a political sense), and it will be hard—maybe impossible—for them to go back to chaperoned dates and greater parental control. Among the mass population, the mobilization has been intense and expectations have been raised very high, and these hopes will also have to be reined in somehow.

The Sandinista army, the militia, the secret police, and the mass associations have all been thoroughly indoctrinated politically under Sandinista regime control; whether and how their loyalty can be transferred to a new elected government are very difficult matters to assess. The huge public bureaucracy loyal to the Sandinistas will similarly have to be reduced in size, made more efficient, and depoliticized; but in what manner and if this can be done at all will be divisive and potentially explosive matters.

Nor is the new governing coalition without its problems. Chamorro woefully lacks administrative experience, is not well informed on economics, and needs to be well advised on virtually all policy matters. Her coalition, the United Nationalist Opposition (UNO), consists of fourteen fractious parties from the far Left to the far Right that is certain to start fragmenting now that its common goal, defeating the Sandinistas, has been realized.

But a focus on the splintered parties is only the surface aspect of a deeper problem: Nicaraguan politics is basically a can of worms consisting of long-time family rivalries, personalistic ambitions, backstabbing, clan and almost "tribal" feuds, clean versus dirty business and political dealings that often go back for generations, and a nasty, vindictive style of politics that reflects the personal, family, and clan feuding. Some of us, to no avail, had warned Elliot Abrams and other policymakers about this feature way back when the U.S. first got deeply involved in Nicaragua. This is the part of Nicaraguan politics that is the most difficult for outsiders to penetrate and fathom, and the most frustrating. Yet such divisions and the inability to coalesce and to work together politically is a critical facet that has been the bane of U.S. policy toward Nicaragua at least going back to the Carter administration; it may well serve to undermine a concerted U.S. policy once again.

CONCLUSION

The Nicaraguan election provided a political opening and opportunity that should cheer democrats everywhere. After ten years of fumbling and disaster under the Sandinistas (as compared with forty years in Eastern Europe), Nicaragua has a chance again to make a correction and go in a democratic direction. Hope is high but the obstacles are many.

Whether through luck or skill or both, the Nicaraguan election represented a significant triumph for the Bush administration. Not only do the Nicaraguan events satisfy Secretary of State James Baker's domestic criteria of removing these nasty Central American issues from the front burner, getting them out of the headlines, cementing a working relationship with the Congress, and enabling President Bush to ride a crest of popularity right through the 1992 election; but they may also be looked upon as a genuine foreign policy triumph. Reaganites can claim vindication of their Contra policy, Democrats can say their peace process worked, and meanwhile a Marxist-Leninist regime has been removed from power in Nicaragua and democracy restored. The motives may not always be the purest but the outcome is certainly favorable and, all in all, it is not a bad tradeoff.

We need to assist massively this democratic experiment in Nicaragua while also keeping a wary eye on the Sandinistas. At the same time we need to watch, hope, and press forward on the even larger but closely related agendas of El Salvador, Cuba, and the Soviet Union.

12

Mexico: The Unraveling of a Corporatist Regime?

with the assistance of Carlos Guajardo

INTRODUCTION: THE UNIQUE CASE OF MEXICO

Mexico is unique among the authoritarian regimes friendly to the United States. Not only does it share a porous, 2000-mile border with the United States, but it is probably more interdependent with the United States on a host of issues—water resources, pollution, energy supplies, tourism, investment, trade, finances, migrant labor, debt, drugs, agriculture, to say nothing of politics and diplomacy—than any other country in the world. What happens in Mexico has profound implications for the United States and *vice versa*.

Mexico is a developing Third World country bordering an industrialized First World country, with all the attendant tensions to which this gives rise. Moreover, for a time in the 1980s there was a risk that Mexico might have gotten sucked into the maelstrom of the Central American conflict. Hence Mexico is one of those critical locales, rather like the Caribbean Basin, the Middle East, and southern Africa, where the North-South vortex of conflict and the East-West one intersect. Given its location, importance, and complex interdependence with the United States, Mexico may be second only to the Soviet Union in terms of its significance for US foreign policy.

Mexico is also distinctive in terms of the nature of its "tyranny." It does not have a single tyrant as did Chile (Pinochet) or Pakistan (Zia), nor is it a full-fledged dictatorship. Rather, Mexico has a corporatist-bureaucratic-authoritarian regime which has functioned for 60 years and may well survive long into the future—notwithstanding Zbigniew Brzezinski's comment that Mexico would become the "next Iran." If it is a

Reprinted from *Journal of Interamerican Studies and World Affairs* 30 (Winter 1988–89); also published in Adam Garfinkle and Daniel Pipes (eds), *Friendly Tyrants* (New York: St. Martins, 1991).

tyranny at all (the Mexican system allows for a considerable degree of openness and freedom), Mexico is an institutionalized tyranny or, better, a system of institutionalized authoritarianism. Mexico is more akin to Jordan under the Hashemites, South Africa under the apartheid regime, or Taiwan under the KMT (Kuomintang)—all institutionalized regimes— than it is to the more personalistic dictatorships of Suharto, Stroessner, or Mobutu. It often is difficult for personalized dictatorships to survive the decline or demise of their single leader, but authoritarianism of the more institutionalized sort may go on for a considerable period.

THE MEXICAN BACKGROUND

Mexican Authoritarianism

Mexico is a corporatist-bureaucratic-authoritarian regime, one that emerged out of the chaos and bloodshed of the Mexican Revolution.[1] The regime was put together on a largely *ad hoc* basis and designed for less than glorious purposes: to preserve the *de facto* power ambitions of President Plutarco Calles (since he was constitutionally forbidden from perpetuating himself in office), and to control the disintegrative forces emerging out of the Revolution. The system helped provide an answer to the continuing disorder that followed the Revolution in the 1920s, but was not the product of any great ideological breakthrough or some early romance with a single-party regime. Rather it was a pragmatic response to a crisis situation, a response that has been perpetuated and now has become institutionalized.

The system is *authoritarian* in the sense that one party, the *Partido Revolucionario Institucional* (PRI), has monopolized the national political life for six decades.[2] It is *bureaucratic* in that it is a *machine* and a *system* that governs Mexico, not any single individual. It is *corporatist* in that the PRI incorporates within its ranks the major corporate or functional groups in Mexican society: workers, peasants, and the so-called "popular" sector which is supposed to include all others. The corporatist system is not only monopolistic, in the sense of organizing Mexican political society into a number of officially-sanctioned, non-competitive units—thus excluding large segments of the population who are not so organized—but it also is badly outdated.[3]

Corporatist-authoritarian regimes like Mexico's typically seek to incorporate, under state direction, the newer social and political forces arising from modernization while excluding, and sometimes suppressing, non-cooperative groups. The system is based on assimilation and coöptation. It also requires a constantly expanding economic pie so that new "pieces" can be handed out to the rising groups without the old ones being deprived. However, when the economy turns stagnant and even contracts—as it has in Mexico during the 1980s—there are no new pieces to hand out, and the accommodationist political game quickly turns sour. Tension and violence usually increase and the political system begins to come unglued.[4] That has been Mexico's situation recently.

Such corporatist-bureaucratic-authoritarian regimes like that of Mexico typically do not collapse in chaos in the same way that the regime of a Marcos, a Batista, a Trujillo, a Somozo, or the Shah has done. It is precisely the fact that they are *bureaucratic* and institutionalized that makes regimes like Mexico's longer-lived and less prone to complete, sudden breakdown than the personalized tyrannies. Instead, in countries like Mexico, the process is often long-term, involving a gradual unraveling rather than a precipitous overthrow. The final *putsch* to oust such a regime may be administered by a revolutionary cabal (military or civilian), but usually the process of decline is gradual and plainly visible to all long before it happens. The decline and eventual collapse of the Portuguese and Spanish corporative-authoritarian regimes—one of which was finally toppled by revolution, the other by a very fast evolution—seem to offer the most likely possible scenarios for Mexico.

In all these cases, the corporatist-bureaucratic-authoritarian regime had some basis of popular support when it began, but over the ensuing decades became more closed, ossified, "dinosauric," and unable to respond either to new realities or to new demands being placed upon it.[5] That is precisely the question for Mexico at present: whether the system has enough flexibility and resiliency to respond to the new circumstances brought on by modernizing changes and pressures or whether it will become steadily more discredited, inefficient and, finally, prone to collapse or even overthrow. Such an eventuality would have incalculable implications for US foreign policy and, given that long, weakly-policed border with Mexico, for US domestic politics as well.

The Mexican regime is not a blatantly repressive or dictatorial one. It is authoritarian rather than totalitarian. It is not terroristic: it does not employ techniques of wholesale torture; it does permit a considerable amount of individual and group freedom. It allows pluralism, albeit mainly of a limited and officially-sanctioned sort. It uses patronage and corruption to cement support and to keep its followers in line. It also employs limited repression, and it seeks to balance control with openness. Mexico is a one-party state (although opposition groups are allowed) whose party machinery, organized by the PRI, has monopolized political life for over half a century. It is an executive-centered system as well, in which the president is the repository of such vast powers as to rival the ancient Aztec emperors and the Spanish viceroys. In addition to the PRI and the presidency, power is lodged in a "revolutionary family" (heirs to the revolution of 1910), which includes high bureaucrats, military officials, former presidents, cabinet and autonomous agency officials, and other governmental officials and political influentials.[6]

Although the PRI, in the past, has proven capable of solving many kinds of problems pragmatically and of surmounting crises, it now faces a situation in which an accumulation of problems threatens to destroy its absolute power. Heretofore the PRI usually handled opposition to its power through coöptation, fraudulent elections, limited repression, or a combination of these. At present, however, the PRI and the entire Mexican system face a situation of not one, but several, delicate problems.

Mexico is suffering from its worst economic crisis in this century, one which seems unlikely to end anytime soon. Unemployment and underemployment combined are estimated to be above 50%. One million persons will enter the labor force every year for the next 15 years. This means that the Mexican economy must grow at a rate of at least 5% annually to provide jobs just for new entrants alone, regardless of those presently unemployed. With oil prices expected to remain low for the foreseeable future, and no apparent immediate solution to Mexico's immense foreign debt ($105 billion), a 5% annual growth rate is highly improbable. On the other hand, the "lucky" Mexicans who do have a job have suffered a 40% decrease in their real wages over the past 5 years. At the same time, businessmen do not seem willing to return the capital they have deposited in foreign banks (estimated at $70 billion) until they perceive a stable economy. With the economy in such dire straits, social problems also are mounting.[7]

Politically, the worsening economic crisis and the widespread corruption have led many Mexicans to demand change, reform, and democracy. Mexico's problems are increasingly being viewed as political as well as economic. The corporatist PRI, organized for a rural, uneducated Mexico, may no longer be functional in the urban, educated, interdependent Mexico of today. The unemployed include not only the Indians migrating to the cities but also educated persons with high expectations. It is no longer certain that Mexico's leaders can deal with the growing discontent directed at the PRI and the system as a whole. The system may have lost its legitimacy.[8]

The PRI won the 1988 presidential election, but the victory did not heal the deep divisions within the Party and may have exacerbated them.

Never since the PRI was formed had a candidate of the official party faced so much opposition, both within and without the dominant party. Fidel Velásquez, leader of the Confederation of Mexican Workers (*Confederación de Trabajadores de México* or CTM)—one of 3 main corporate pillars of the system—opposed the official party candidate, Carlos Salinas de Gortari, because of the austere economic policies he had advocated while serving as cabinet minister. Leaders of the oil workers' union, probably the most powerful union in Mexico, stated publicly that they were not satisfied with the Salinas nomination and might instruct their members to vote against the PRI if Salinas did not repudiate the austerity measures then in effect. PRI "kingmaker" Carlos Hank González also hinted that the Party was "teetering" in power. Although all these pronouncements must be taken with a grain of salt as representing efforts to acquire greater influence in the government for the group or individual speaking, they indicate the depth and breadth of discontent within the dominant party machine. The PRI was shocked by its poor electoral showing in 1988 and the strength of the opposition.

Opposition Forces

Although the PRI has never lost a presidential election in the 60 years of its existence, it has allowed opposition parties to function so long as they are "loyal" (i.e., non-revolutionary) and have no possibility of taking power. The PRI has even "structured" past elections to give the opposition minority representation in the Congress, and to demonstrate how "democratic" Mexico really is but, again, only so long as that opposition stays loyal. By now there are opposition elements in the country which are not only "disloyal," but which also have the potential to destabilize, or conceivably even to take over, the system.

The heretofore strongest party in the opposition, the PAN *(Partido Acción Nacíonal),)* has been unable to acquire a strong national following and gain support among the lower classes, due both to an image as a party of the rich and to its pro-US posture. By the same token, neither have the forces of the Left been able to muster large and consistent support due, primarily, to fragmentation and lack of organization. Nevertheless, the opposition has begun to build up strongholds in certain parts of the country. Most supporters of the Left are found in slums of the major cities and in the southern rural ("Indian") states. The PAN is strongest in urban areas (especially among the middle-class) and throughout the north (especially in those states which border on the United States).[9]

Rising disenchantment with the PRI has led many Mexicans to support the PAN. However, this support is thin and arises more from discontent with the PRI than from the attraction of the PAN platform. In addition, a lack of capable, dedicated leaders has led many Mexicans to despair that the PAN could ever offer a viable alternative to the PRI. Fernando Canales Clariond, the PAN candidate defeated for the governorship of the state of Nuevo León in 1985 in a rigged election, abandoned his followers, refused to head up the demonstrations organized to protest the fraud, and declined to run for the mayorship of Monterrey, the "capital" of the northern industrial heartland of Mexico and a PAN stronghold, where he had a good chance of winning. Similarly, another PAN gubernatorial candidate and two of his allies began a hunger strike to protest PRI manipulation of the vote in his state, only to abandon the protest later and leave his supporters holding the bag. In Mexico, these half-hearted protesters were known derisively as "Gandhi wanna-bes."

In 1988, the PAN presidential candidate was Manuel Clouthier, a wealthy landowner, who ran an appealing populist campaign. He was so effective on television that the two state-owned channels prohibited his appearance. While campaigning in León at the same time as Salinas, he drew twice the crowds as the PRI candidate (who also was roundly booed). When Clouthier challenged Salinas to a debate, Salinas refused under pressure from PRI leaders who did not want to give the PAN candidate any more publicity. Despite his good showing, Clouthier lost the presidential race—that is the Mexican system; nevertheless, he may have triggered a new dynamism within the opposition. Clouthier and the PAN got 17% of the vote in the 1988 election, but later he was killed in an automobile accident.

On the Left, Cuauhtemoc Cárdenas, son of Mexico's famed populist/socialist president of the 1930s, in 1985 began what he called the *Corriente Democrática* (Democratic Current). Now organized as a party, Cárdenas teamed up with Porfirio Muñoz Ledo, former president of the PRI and leader of its reform wing. They drew their support from Mexico's traditional Leftist groups and parties, which are strong among intellectuals and which have some (usually limited) resonance among the lower classes. The new movement was greeted skeptically at first: how could former PRI officials (both Cárdenas and Muñoz Ledo) campaign in the name of democracy? Nevertheless, using his father's name as his strongest weapon—as well as widespread disenchantment with the ruling party—Cárdenas also ate into the previously solid public support for the PRI. With Clothier garnering followers from the PRI's Right, and Cárdenas

(31%) from the Left, the 1988 election was one of the most interesting—perhaps the most competitive—in Mexico's history. It may serve as a prelude to a more open political system in the future.

As yet, however, such a more genuinely pluralist system seems quite far off, if it develops at all. Because of the economic-*cum*-political crisis, there is a foul public mood in Mexico. This malaise has been expressed in simmering public discontent which translated, in the 1988 election, into large-scale defections from the PRI to the opposition parties. However, the PRI controls far too much spoils, patronage, opportunities, contracts, jobs, graft, favors, and even coercive power for a complete breakdown and loss of power to happen quickly. Nor is it the case that there have been many protest movements, let alone any inkling of social revolution, in Mexico despite its manifold problems. Some anomic movements have been organized, an occasional individual will chain himself to the gates of the cathedral in Mexico City, and there are small-scale protests by the opposition. The usual indicators of trouble in Mexico are all on the rise: alcoholism, drug abuse, domestic violence, and church attendance, but no sign of large-scale social or political protests. So there may be more resilience, more elasticity, a greater capacity to cope in the Mexican system than some observers think. It is yet to be seen if the discontent revealed by the 1988 election will change all this.

US Views about Mexico

Most people in the United States do not spend a lot of time or energy worrying about very many foreign countries, certainly not in Latin America; Mexico is one of the few exceptions. That is because so many have gone to Mexico as tourists or have (or have had) established connections with it in any of the myriad ways characteristic of neighboring countries with a long common border. This attention displays a further sectional, or regional, breakdown: seen from the perspective of New York or Washington, the chief issues in US-Mexican relations are the debt, conflicting views of foreign policy, and the future political stability of Mexico. Viewed from the US Southwest, however, the chief issues are (1) illegal, inadequately-controlled Mexican migration into the United States and (2) the resultant problems of schooling, housing, water, social services, and crime to which this continuous flow gives rise.

Virtually everyone in the United States wants to have good relations with this southern neighbor. The list includes US growers who depend on cheap Mexican labor, politicians in the Southwest who want to head off the influx of even greater numbers of illegal immigrants, the large number of US citizens who either live in Mexico or visit there as tourists, businesses who see Mexico (particularly the strip just across the US border) as one of the few places in the Third World in which they are still willing to invest, and the US State and Defense Departments, who (a) recognize US dependency on Mexican petroleum resources, (b) understand the disastrous foreign, as well as domestic, policy consequences that would follow if Mexico were to become destabilized, and (c) would much prefer not to have to lead a "Black Jack" Pershing-like invasion or occupation of a collapsing—or Cuba-leaning—Mexico. Such a destabilization not only would send millions of Mexicans (as distinct from the current hundreds of thousands) fleeing north across the US border—thus compounding the problems already mentioned—but also would have disastrous consequences for US foreign policy in many ways. If, in recent years, El Salvador and Nicaragua have posed divisive, wrenching foreign policy problems for the United States, a destabilized, Left-leaning Mexico would make those problems pale by comparison.

Persons opposed to good relations with Mexico have tended to be few in number because Mexico has never presented a tyranny as oppressive as, for example, Haiti or Chile, and because the media have never paid it that much attention. Therefore, those who raise the "Mexico issue" have usually been scholars, those with a special interest, ideologues, reformers, and/or political missionaries of various sorts, although attention to Mexico's problems has recently become more prevalent. For the most part, the "missionaries" have wanted to bring US-style elections, US-style democracy, US-style human rights, and US-style economic and bureaucratic principles and organization to Mexico—none of which would likely work very well in that context.

The distinction that should be made is between those who would pursue a reform agenda despite this inappropriate context, and the pragmatists who push for change on the one hand, but recognize the realities of Mexico and US-Mexican relations on the other. For example, former US Congressman Jack Kemp has been an advocate of privatization in Latin America as a way to increase efficiency and productivity; still, he recognizes that too vigorous a pursuit of this agenda in Mexico might destabilize the whole Mexican system. Given the importance of Mexico and the length of the US/Mexican border, Mexico is the last nation whose socio-political institutions the United States would want to undermine in the name of reform. Congressman Kemp recognized this fact, although other ideological "true believers" in a US mission there do not.

More recently, Mexico has gained damaging notoriety due to alleged unwillingness to clamp down harder on drug traffickers, corruption, hoodlums who may prey on US tourists, and tardiness in prosecuting those responsible (apparently including some Mexican military officials) for the deaths of two officials of the DEA (US Drug Enforcement Administration). Publicity over these issues has stimulated a great deal of "Mexico-bashing" in the United States, including a US Senate resolution which criticized Mexico severely. Of course, Latin America has long been an area which the United States could pick on in various ways without having to worry about retribution either in a foreign policy sense (because Latin America is weak and "unimportant") or from domestic constituencies. The United States had finally begun to put its relationship with Latin America on a more even keel,[10] until the drug traffic and the bad publicity regarding Mexico threatened to undo all the gains made, to poison US public opinion toward Mexico, to revive anti-Latinism, and, once again, to make Mexico in particular—and Latin America in general—a scapegoat for US frustration. If this new development continues, not only will it sour US-Latin American relations, but it will be disastrous for US foreign policy as well.

It may well be, however, that this debate between defenders and opponents of close relations with Mexico is not the best way to treat the issue. It is more important to recognize the complex interdependence which now exists between two close—but very different—neighbors, and all the problems to which this gives rise: culture conflict, tourists who are (or feel) victimized while traveling in Mexico, immigration, the drug traffic, debt and investment issues, the "bureaucratic politics" of US foreign policy, in which different US government agencies send confusing, if not contradictory, signals to Mexico, and the various sensitivities, or lack of same, which are amplified by proximity. We are neighbors of Mexico but, as in the title of Alan Riding's book, "distant neighbors" indeed.[11]

Viewed in this light, Mexican problems have a way of becoming US problems. That is the real US foreign policy concern. It is not so much a question of praise for, or criticism of, Mexico; rather, it is the United States' fear that Mexico's problems—drugs, corruption, economic mismanagement, lack of democracy—will not only undermine and destabilize the Mexican system, but also produce disastrous consequences for the United States. Mexico's problems become magnified and more visible by proximity and by the constant flow of people across the border. As a result, the US debate over policy is chiefly between those who want to push Mexico hard toward reform before disaster strikes, and those who believe that Mexico still has the ability to work out its own solutions—thereby solving US problems with Mexico at the same time.

Relations with the United States

US relations with Mexico are among the most complex in the world. *First* of all, Mexico is very important for US foreign policy. To appreciate how important, all one need do is conceive of a Cuba-, Nicaragua-, or Iran-like revolution taking place in next-door Mexico and the vast range of dilemmas to which this would give rise, not to mention, *second,* the problems and mismatches generated by the close proximity of a developed and an underdeveloped country sharing a long, porous border. *Third* is the "bureaucratic politics" problem: the fact that US policies (diplomatic, drug, energy, and strategic) often work at cross-purposes, are contradictory, or operate in a context where one agency of the US government plunges ahead without coordinating its actions with—or even informing—other agencies with responsibility in other areas.

A *fourth* factor consists of the ups-and-downs of US-Mexican relations, historical as well as current: a history of intervention, insult, mutual recrimination, and slights (both real and imaginary). *Fifth* is the fact that US-Mexican relations take place on many levels and with significant overlaps. Relations at the official level are only one, and probably a quite small, part of the picture. These must be considered in the context of literally millions of other exchanges: with tourists, business transactions, flow of workers and commerce across the border in both directions, and so forth. There are direct relations between US and Mexican cities, states, interest groups, and individual citizens—e.g., "local" foreign policies as it were, few of which are ever coordinated.[12]

Consequently US-Mexican relations are characterized by seemingly endless layers of complexity. For example, when President Reagan, early in his term, proposed the idea of a North American accord to integrate the economies of Canada, the United States, and Mexico in a common market arrangement, the idea was rejected by high Mexican government officials on nationalist, protectionist grounds. Meanwhile, such a North American common market has come into existence *de facto* and in part, in the form of a multitude of informal arrangements. At lower bureaucratic levels, Mexican officials candidly admit that such a common market is not only inevitable but already in process, even though their leaders cannot say so publicly.

Mexico has enormous importance for the United States not only on economic issues, but also on strategic ones. Given US proximity to Mexico, any turmoil in the latter would redound on the United States. Undoubtedly, any social unrest would send hundreds of thousands, if not millions, of Mexicans fleeing north across the border. If guerrilla activity were to begin in Mexico, the United States might be forced to militarize its border or, perhaps, even to intervene militarily. Should crisis erupt in the Middle East and oil supplies from the Persian Gulf be cut off, the United States might want to occupy southern Mexico in order to ensure a safe supply of oil. However, Mexico, with 80-million people and a vast territory, is not Grenada; the implications of such a military action would be grave, difficult for the Department of Defense even to contemplate, let alone carry out, and immensely costly both in terms of US-Mexican relations as well as public opinion in the US. So far, by-and-large, the United States has focused on other, smaller issues instead of the larger ones that might cause political and social unrest in Mexico.

The drug traffic is now a major concern. However, the United States has not always dealt with this issue diplomatically. It continues to blame Mexico for supplying, or trans-shipping, most of the drugs consumed in the United States, whereas it may be that the root of the problem lies within the United States. For Mexico, as for the rest of Latin America, producing drugs for the US market carries powerful incentives: (a) it is enormously profitable; (b) it is rational economically; (c) it adds to the GNP; (d) it earns foreign exchange; (e) it is labor- (rather than capital-) intensive; (f) it is produced with low-level technology that is next-to-impossible to eradicate; and (g) it involves high-level political and military officials who cannot, realistically, be touched. Instead of its current (futile) concentration on cutting the supply, the United States should devote more effort to cutting domestic demand. However, such a shift in emphasis is not only more difficult but entails the raising of thorny domestic issues, such as those involving civil liberties and US domestic politics. The Mexican position is that the United States focuses on control of the supply side of this traffic because it is unable (or unwilling) to attack the demand side; as a result, Mexico has become the scapegoat for what is essentially a US domestic problem. The drug traffic carries the potential for becoming a disaster for US-Mexican relations and may, inadvertently, give rise to an outcome which the US most wants to avoid: the destabilization of Mexico.[13]

Immigration is also a major US concern. Nevertheless, it is beyond the power of the Mexican government to control it effectively. Although the United States has a legitimate right to protect its borders, laws like the Simpson-Rodino immigration bill, if strictly enforced, could hasten the possibility of upheaval in Mexico by closing an important escape valve for unemployed Mexicans, and thus the very explosion inside Mexico that the United States hopes to avoid.

From the US viewpoint, there were also problems with Mexico's foreign policy toward Central America and the Caribbean. Mexico sees itself as a Latin American country which, *ipso facto,* has a better understanding of the region than does the United States. Mexico prides itself on a revolutionary tradition which may serve as an example to other Latin American countries, and which it uses not only to justify its role as "honest broker," but also to tweak the nose of the United States, to pacify Mexico's domestic Left, and as a rationale for demonstrating independence on foreign policy issues. It is not surprising that the United States and Mexico have found it difficult to have a meeting of the minds on hardly any aspect of their respective positions toward Central America, although Mexico has moderated its position in recent years and begun to tone down anti-US rhetoric. While the United States obviously prefers the quieter position, it should not forget that such rhetoric serves a useful purpose in pacifying more radical elements on the domestic Mexican political scene, thereby also contributing to the US interest in preserving Mexican political stability.[14]

Overall, the most important issues in US-Mexican relations are economic. Trade is of mutual concern and has recently taken a turn for the better. In the past, the United States has imposed high tariffs on many imports from Mexico, whereupon the latter has reciprocated by raising its own protectionist barriers against US goods. One recent positive step was to allow US companies to own 100% of their investments inside Mexico. Equally beneficial to both sides are the foreign-owned factories along the Mexican side of the joint border *(maquiladoras),* which are able to import their raw materials duty-free, take advantage of cheaper Mexican labor, and provide jobs for many Mexicans at the same time. However, even here, there are some thorns among the roses: 80% of the *maquiladora* employees are women, mostly new entrants into the labor force, which means that little dent is made in existing Mexican unemployment figures. In addition, location of the *maquiladoras* along the border naturally attracts families to the area and makes it possible for the husband to cross over to the US side to work, thus exacerbating the immigration problem.

For Mexico, its biggest problem is its enormous debt and the limits this imposes on economic growth. Just paying the interest alone is a tremendous drain on the economy. Neither reschedulings nor bail-outs have resolved the debt issue. Although the austerity measures imposed by the IMF (International Monetary Fund) have probably strengthened their economy in the long run, these are politically and socially costly in the short run. It is not at all certain that Mexico is any better off now (1989) than it was in 1982 when the debt crisis began. No satisfactory resolution is yet in sight. Only a form of debt relief or forgiveness will really do it for Mexico but that, of course, means that someone else—probably the US taxpayer—must bear the cost.[15]

Even with all these problems operating, the United States has recently begun to put its relations with Mexico on a more mature basis which, with the appointment of a skillful, tactful ambassador, will undoubtedly facilitate improvement in US-Mexican relations.

CRISIS OR POTENTIAL CRISIS

Precipitating Events

Despite the fact that Mexico has often, even consistently, opposed the United States in international fora, it is highly unlikely that it would go so far as to provoke a crisis. Not only is the United States the source of most of Mexico's imports, but it is also the consumer of 60% of Mexico's exports. Any confrontation with the United States would immediately cut Mexico off from its most important market. As a newly industrialized country (NIC) with an annual per capita income of about $2,500, Mexico is unlikely to jeopardize economic well-being in favor of ideology.

Still, some issues remain to threaten US-Mexican relations. There is the issue of Central America: Mexico viewed the Sandinista government in Nicaragua as representing the forces of revolutionary nationalism whereas the United States viewed it as a communist puppet regime. In the past, Mexico worked to undermine the US policy of opposing the Sandinistas but did not have the economic, or other, leverage necessary for continued opposition. Indeed, Mexico appeared to have moderated its policy on Central America in exchange for US economic help. Former President Miguel de la Madrid halted oil sales to the Sandinistas and even refused Fidel Castro's invitation to visit Cuba.

Even the debt problem appears to be amenable to negotiation. Under a recent agreement which did not quite find the number of bidders expected, Mexico sold a part of its public debt at less than face value in return for assurances from the US Treasury that it would guarantee the paper. The agreement leaves the US banks with less paper value but with a virtual immunity against any type of default on that share of Mexico's debts. Although such small steps do not, in and of themselves, solve the debt problem, they do make it less severe and less likely to provoke disaster—which may be about all that can be expected. It is now quite widely recognized in Mexico that any attempt to take strong action, either alone or with other debtors, would only exacerbate the situation.

At the same time, the United States seems willing to accept a greater share of the costs of solving the problem.

Barring some unforeseen event, relations between the two neighbors seem to be getting better as we head into the 1990s.

US Opinion Trends

Not too long ago, the US perception of Mexico was that of a democratic, pluralist country (or at least moving in that direction). However, during the 1980s that perception reversed itself to depict the Mexican government as corrupt, inefficient, undemocratic, and drifting (if not already locked) into authoritarianism. Both members of the US media, as well as some officials of the US government, have drawn attention to evidence of corruption within the PRI and its unfortunate tendency to "steal" elections when it was deemed necessary. There is also evidence that the US government may have fostered this vilification campaign against Mexico for reasons of its own—drugs, Central America and, perhaps, other issues—even to the extent of providing some of the evidence. Unfortunately, this campaign backfired by provoking Mexico into a defensive, nationalistic, and anti-US posture, rather than by encouraging the Mexican government to rid itself of those corrupt members who do, unfortunately, exist within its ranks—which was the probable motive behind the US campaign.

Some US citizens have admittedly been victims of crime while in Mexico, although the media may well have given such incidents undue attention; it is certainly safer to visit Mexico than almost *any* US city. Nevertheless, Mexico often appears on US television screens as the scene of many disasters, not only of earthquakes and debt problems, but also as a place where tourists are preyed upon, where drug traffickers are protected by corrupt officials, and DEA officials are murdered with impunity. The fact that Mexico has paid a high price in number of its police killed in the course of combating the drug traffic is seldom mentioned, nor the fact that the office of the Mexican Attorney-General spends up to *half* its budget on the drug eradication program. Neither is much coverage given to the way in which US border patrol officials treat illegal Mexican immigrants.

Mexico's image in the United States had undergone considerable deterioration over the last ten years, a development which could make Zbigniew Brzezinski's characterization of Mexico as the "next Iran" almost a self-fulfilling prophecy. However, under President Salinas Mexico's prospects and its reputation have both been rising.

Predictions

Contrary to many "scare" predictions, the destabilization of Mexico or a severe crisis in US-Mexican relations is extremely unlikely. The Mexican system has resources, vast amounts of patronage, resilience, and extensive accommodative capacity—to say nothing of vast coercive power which it has not yet even begun to use. If the Mexican economic crisis should continue indefinitely, however, and the system begin to exhaust its supply of patronage and spoils, then trouble could well loom ahead, although such a scenario is not yet in sight.

While highly unlikely at the moment, scenarios which could cause problems in the future might include:

1. The spread of the Central American crisis into Mexico—e.g., the appearance of a Castro-like guerrilla movement in Mexico's southern states.
2. The accession to power of a "Nasserist" (Left-wing, anti-US) military.
3. Election of a Left-wing nationalist, Yankee-baiting populist to the presidency.
4. Mexican declaration of a complete, unilateral default on its foreign debt.
5. A Mexican deal with Fidel Castro by which Mexico permits establishment of a Soviet/Cuban base on its territory in return for a pledge not to instigate a Leftist *foco* in Mexico (the deal becoming public knowledge).
6. Accession to power of a Right-wing military regime violently repressive of human rights, i.e., the Pinochet option.

At the moment, none of these worst-case scenarios are on the horizon. More likely is the spread of disarray, making Mexico much more difficult to govern. For example, persistence of the recent economic crisis could easily lead to political crisis and massive increases in migration to the United States. It is typical of bureaucratic-corporatist-authoritarian regimes that they are unable to adjust or accommodate to new realities, which usually leads to a process of unraveling.[16] In the early stages, such a process of pulling apart is gradual, "quiet" rather than dramatic. If the unraveling process goes on long enough, such as a decade or two, the *coup de grace* to the system may be administered violently. As Merle Kling has cogently argued,[17] in a culture and context of accustomed and accepted political violence, the range of possible political outcomes is far broader and more open-ended than in a democratic context.

The United States would not tolerate a regime hostile to itself in Mexico. Almost certainly it would take action either to undermine such a regime or, even, to intervene. At this stage, it is premature to anticipate that a Leftist, anti-US regime might assume power in Mexico. Mexican political thinking covers a broad spectrum (as in the United States) ranging from anti-US nationalism to those with mixed feelings toward their northern neighbor, from pragmatists who "go along to get along" to those who truly love and admire the United States. In this context of love-hate, as well as ambivalent, attitudes, it is unlikely that US/Mexico relations would suffer any major breach.

Could an anti-US regime arise out of Mexico's present socio-political problems—a Cárdenas government, for example? This seems unlikely, given the current strength of the PRI and its devotion to the national self-interest. Could a repressive military government come to power in response to national crisis, breakdown, or attempt at Leftist revolution? Certainly in the event of either scenario one predictable consequence would be an increase in refugees streaming toward the US border. Certainly the United States would seek to negotiate with such a regime to help restore order and provide for a democratic restoration, but US action in this situation would be limited unless the regime posed a threat to US security.

POLICY ASSESSMENT

Ramifications of US Policy Decisions

Mexico is big, important, complex, populous and, as such, cannot be treated as a banana republic. Furthermore, it is characterized by a form of *institutionalized* authoritarianism which is deeply-embedded and far-reaching, so that for the US to apply pressure to alter the system in any fundamental way (as with Duvalier or Marcos) would take decades at best or, at worst, be counterproductive. In addition, since Mexico is located next door to the United States, any possible benefit which might accure from applying pressure would always have to be weighed against the potential for harm which might result from inadvertent destabilization.

Thus far, US policy is cognizant of these possibilities and has opted for restraint. This is not to say that there is not a school of thought among US policymakers which would prefer to adopt a more direct approach to remake Mexico in the US image. There still is little coordination of policies regarding Mexico among US agencies and private groups involved in commerce—broadly defined—with Mexico, a situation which sometimes produces serious gaffes. However, overall, the United States has not sought to destabilize Mexico because of policy differences between the two countries, recognizing that change cannot be imposed from without, no matter how good the intention, but that efforts at reform must be nourished slowly, not transplanted instantly.[18] Even the most ideologically committed members of the US Congress recognize that Mexico requires special treatment and that an aggressive policy toward Mexico is almost certain to be self-defeating.

These considerations mean that the usual swords and stilettos that we use to get rid of other tyrants must be sheathed in the Mexican case. We cannot bribe an entire corporate regime into retirement, we cannot provide for its safe haven, and we cannot—in the last resort—assassinate it.[19] For all the reasons already discussed—size, complexity, neighborliness, an institutionalized regime—none of these techniques will work in the Mexican case. We can provide some nudges and pushes, if applied sensitively, to help Mexico to reform itself; but much more than that we cannot and should not do. And we would not be successful if we tried. In the situation of multiply-layered complex interdependence which characterizes our relations with Mexico, a more aggressive policy is almost certain to be self-defeating.

Prescriptions

The essential dilemma with which the United States must wrestle in terms of US-Mexico policy, of course, is how hard the United States can press Mexico without running the unacceptable risk of destabilizing the Mexican system. Even the most aggressive reformers have acknowledged that if the United States pushes too hard on Mexico, the whole house of cards that is the Mexican system will likely come tumbling down. Avoiding such an eventuality in Mexico ought to be right up there with (or near) avoiding nuclear war in the US list of foreign policy priorities. As a result, US policies, in general, have been sensible and appropriately restrained.

Most are agreed that Mexico as well as the United States would be better off in Mexico were more democratic, had a more open social and political system, and a freer, less statist economy. Part of the problem of US relations with Mexico and of US efforts, generally well-meaning, to bring such changes to Mexico, is that the Mexicans themselves are not at all certain what democracy would mean or look like in their context and whether it is desirable or not. Is Mexico amenable to a policy of democratic reformism? Does Mexico really want democracy? In what form? Will democracy and a less inclusive statism actually be functional, effective, and viable in Mexico? The United States tends to assume that the answers to these questions are all affirmative, but Mexicans are not so sure. Of course, US assessment of what an appropriate US policy toward Mexico is should be based on how the United States answers these critical questions.

The problem for policy is that in Mexico there are complex answers to these questions, which alone should give the United States pause before rushing in too quickly with its own preferred solutions and running the risk of destabilizing the system. In surveys, Mexicans tend to prefer democracy but also want democracy in the form of a strong, statist, nationalist, and integralist form that is not altogether different from the system Mexico has now. A small percentage (15–20%) would prefer, within this organicist integralist context, to go in a Left-wing direction á la Allende or perhaps the Nicaraguan regime. Roughly the same percentage (and thus a small minority) want to go in the direction of Anglo-American style (Lockean) democracy.[20]

The real division in Mexico, therefore, is between those who have a large stake in the present system (and they are many in number) and wish to continue it—a system based on patronage, favoritism, and the near-monopoly of the PRI—and those who would reform it sufficiently to head off a crisis. The former element, which is powerful within the Party and state apparatus, favors the maintenance of a strong, controlled, disciplined, monolithic, authoritative (if not authoritarian) political system—with just enough safety valves to allow pent-up pressures to escape but not so many as to allow real pluralism, competition, and the potential for a loss of power to develop. The second group recognizes that Mexico must go toward democracy and must reform itself, but wants this to proceed ever so slowly, by evolutionary means, without provoking instability. The type of democracy that this element has in mind, however, is still a Rousseauian form (organic, integral, top-down, presumably where the elites will still interpret and give meaning to the "general will") and not the genuinely competitive, hurly-burly, chaotic form of US-style democracy.[21]

The debate in Mexico, therefore, is not about whether to restructure itself in the US mold—and that fact should hopefully give pause to those US groups who would vigorously seek to do so. That position is a distinctly minority position in Mexico and will remain so. The only real question is whether Mexico will try to maintain its present system unaltered—and there are powerful elements there who wish to do so—or whether those who want to open up the system a little bit to some limited democratic reformism will have a chance. It must be understood that even the reformers want only a little more democracy—a little more open, a little less ossified, a bit more dynamic—and not genuine equality and pluralism.

Now if that fact can be accepted—that Mexico does not necessarily want US-style democracy and that it may be not only imprudent but downright destabilizing for the United States to insist otherwise—then it may be possible to devise a sensible and rational policy toward Mexico. Such a policy would involve some nudges, pushes, and urgings in a reformist direction but no heavy-handed campaigns. The United States surely can suggest and even urge certain (probably limited and small-scale) reforms on Mexico, but it cannot—nor do the Mexicans want the United States to—remodel their whole system. This may be called a "prudence model" of Mexican democracy and of an appropriate US policy response—one that recognizes limits on what the United States or Mexico can do, that focuses on the possible and the realizable rather than the romantic and the wishful, and whose possibilities for success outweigh the possibilities for disaster. Such a prudential policy would serve the United States' best interests as well as those of Mexico, and would be based on recognition of where Mexico is *now* in terms of its possibilities for change and reforms rather than envisioning some far-off ideal that is not only unattainable in the present circumstances but may well be destructive both of current Mexican institutions and the cement that holds that system together, *and* of the possibilities for decent, stable, US-Mexican relations.

Future Anticipations

To a large extent, the future stability of Mexico depends upon the ability of the United States to remain far-sighted in its decision-making. Mexico needs the cooperation of the United States in order to emerge from its present economic crisis. The US position on such matters as trade and debt strongly affects Mexico's ability to deal with these problems. Such considerations surely will gather strength in the years ahead and may already surpass politico/diplomatic considerations in order of priority.

Consequently, as economic issues become paramount, the best way for the United States to influence Mexico's domestic and foreign policies is through the carrot of increased trade, investment, and enlightened border policies. So long as such trade-offs can be kept from offending Mexican nationalist sensitivities, economic help of this sort can be offered in exchange for acceptable policy reforms. For example, negotiations over debt relief—however disguised for US domestic political purposes—

can be (and have been) linked to Mexico's increased neutrality toward Central America.

Since Mexico's democratization and government efficiency are important to the United States, the latter must take care to pursue this goal tactfully. Mexico is protective of its sovereignty (as are most countries) and will resist blatant attempts by the United States to infringe on this prerogative. Hence, a *quid pro quo* approach might be effective. For example, in return for the United States agreeing (as it has under the amnesty provisions of the Immigration Reform and Control Act of 1986) to allow a larger number of immigrants to stay in the United States, the PRI might be persuaded to recognize some opposition victories in Mexican mayoral or gubernatorial elections.

Increasing both public and private, formal and informal contacts between the two countries can be equally effective, and acceptable, stimuli for positive change. On the public level, encouragement can be given to more cultural exchanges, more "partner" relationships, and those smaller-scale efforts best carried out by agencies like the Inter-American Foundation and the National Endowment for Democracy.[22] Informal contacts at lower levels—as in the informal movement toward a North American common market—can accomplish a great deal. Hopefully, change in Mexico will evolve along with an increase in private, informal contacts with the United States at multiple levels, accelerated by the revolution in communications and commerce which draws the two nations together, changing cultural (including political-cultural) models toward democratization through interdependence with the United States. Undoubtedly, informal contacts will democratize Mexico more than anything on an official level.

Easing the debt burden is in the interests of both countries, since it would allow the economy to grow, which, in turn, will foster a reduction in political tension. The United States should accept the fact (as it currently is doing) that the debtor countries cannot pay back the enormous sums that are owed and that a situation of impasse benefits no one. Instead of simply lending money just to pay the interest, as an earlier version of the Baker Plan suggested, the United States should absorb some of the costs and urge countries like Germany and Japan to do the same. Although that is currently the situation *de facto,* a formula still must be found to create an intermediary institution—partly funded by the US—that would enable debt relief to be provided in a disguised, or more palatable, form. Mexico had some good years in 1986 and 1987 in terms of its trade surplus, but most of the money earned went for interest payments and not into investment and growth. If the United

States really wants political stability in Mexico, easing the debt burden should carry a high priority on its agenda.

On the other hand, this may pose yet another quandary: the possibility that economic recovery may only postpone, not solve, Mexico's many political problems. If oil prices doubled tomorrow, Mexico would be in great shape economically, but incentive to political reform might go down the drain. Such an economic windfall might well revive the boom-and-bust mentality of the 1970s and 1980s during which corruption flourished. Yet corruption can undermine the benefits of a stable, growing economy as well as prospects for democracy. It may be that Mexico needs to go through an economic wringer in order to force the people and the government to instigate real reform.[23] If any of these processes proceed too fast or too abruptly, however, the result is less apt to lead less to democracy than to a new, worse form of authoritarianism (Left or Right) or, even, a return to the kind of chaos Mexico has experienced in the past (1910–1930).

The discussion points to a dilemma, maybe a series of them. On the one hand, Mexico needs to expand its economy to head off fragmentation and social unrest; yet, on the other, only severe economic hardship would appear to provide the incentive for reform needed for longer-term development. Policy appropriate for the short run—moderation, restraint—may not be appropriate for the long run. This is the tightrope which the United States must walk in its dealings with Mexico. If the United States pushes too hard, its efforts will be self-defeating. If it exercises benign neglect, Mexico (in the familiar pattern of earlier corporatist-authoritarian regimes) likely will continue to unravel until a point is reached where the regime—like Portugal in the early 1970s[24]—disintegrates or is overthrown. Not only does this require a delicate balance by the one on the high wire, but an equally delicate balance by those who control the financial (and a number of political) strings as well. Mexico may develop as Spain did—toward a more liberal and democratic, but still partially corporatist, regime—but the possibility of corporatist breakdown à la Portugal is a contingency which must also be borne in mind.

EPILOGUE

In a 1973 article which received considerable attention and often provoked controversy, the author set forth a model which he called the "corporatist framework," for the study of socio-political change in Iberia and Latin America.[25] Mexico was one of the main examples cited of such a corporately-organized society and polity, but, in the discussion of the corporatist model itself, in the last part of the article, where the author talked about the decay, fragmentation, unraveling, and potential for disintegration within corporatist regimes, little attention was given to Mexico. Now Mexico may begin to serve as an illustration of the latter process as well.

In Portugal in the early 1970s, Marcello Caetano tried to modernize, update, and revitalize his country's moribund corporatist institutions, as the Mexicans are now doing. He attempted to usher in limited change while continuing to operate within the older corporatist-authoritarian framework. In so doing, he discovered that, in the altered circumstances of the 1970s, he could neither go back and resurrect the older system of corporatist-authoritarian controls, nor fast-forward enough toward a genuine liberal democracy without infuriating the old guard and precipitating his own overthrow. The result was a disastrous temporizing on the part of government, a spiraling crisis and, ultimately, revolution. It may yet be possible for Mexico to avoid such a breakdown; but the fact must be faced that this has been the fate of many corporatist-authoritarian regimes which went on too long and modernized insufficiently. Certainly, many of the same ingredients are present in the Mexican case.

13

The Dominican Republic: Mirror Legacies of Democracy and Authoritarianism

Among Latin American nations, the Dominican Republic has been one of the most unfortunate and least successful in its efforts to develop a system of stable democratic rule.[1] In its 150 years of independence, the authoritarian tradition and legacy have been powerful, and the democratic weak. In all that time, the Dominican Republic has enjoyed only twenty-five years, or one-sixth of its history, under what can loosely be called "democratic government," and one-third of those years have come within the last ten. Democracy in the Dominican Republic, when it has existed at all, has been weak, tenuous, unstable, and uncertain—and that remains the case under the present democratic regime.

A democratic breakthrough has occurred, nevertheless, and one would be wrong either to overestimate its importance or to underestimate it. Dominicans still sometimes exhibit rather ambivalent feelings about democracy, but there can be no doubt that there has been a significant shift toward democratic rule. This change is related to other, broader transformations in Dominican society: greater affluence; a larger middle class; economic development; changing political culture; and changes in the international environment. The shift is therefore not limited to a change in political institutions at the top but is based on profounder and deeper alterations in that often unfortunate nation. For this reason it would be very difficult for the country at this stage to revert to its more authoritarian and repressive traditions. That could now be accomplished only with such bloody repression, á la Pinochet in Chile, that it would be very difficult to bring off, but not impossible. That is why, while democracy is established and now even more institutionalized than ever before in Dominican history, its future is not entirely certain, cannot be taken for granted, and bears close scrutiny.

Reprinted from Larry Diamond, Juan Linz, and Seymour Martin Lipset (eds.), *Democracy in Developing Countries: Latin America* (Boulder, CO: Lynne Rienner Publishers, 1989).

Few North Americans would disagree with the definition of democracy employed in this study, encompassing regular elections, civil liberties, and separation of powers, which after all derives from and is close to the Lockean, Madisonian, Anglo-American understanding and tradition.[2] In Latin America, however, where historic political roots lie in a Thomistic-Suárezian and, later, Rousseauan tradition, a somewhat more ample and broader definition must be used.[3] In Latin America, the pluralism that exists is usually more controlled and limited than is the unbridled and virtually anarchic competition of U.S. interest-group pluralism.[4] "Participation" is also understood somewhat differently, often in organic, corporate, and group terms as much as through the individualistic form of participation—"one-man-one-vote"—of the United States.[5] Similarly, civil and political liberties are often defined differently from the U.S. understandings, or with distinctive nuances, or with a different sense of priorities than is true in the Anglo-American tradition.[6]

These differences of meaning are crucial because they lie at the heart of the Dominican Republic's efforts to achieve democratic rule. Historically, Dominicans have imported forms of democracy derived from the Anglo-American tradition, including constitutions that were simply translations into Spanish of the U.S. Constitution, which have not always worked very well in the Dominican context. When democracy failed to work or produced anarchy and breakdown, Dominicans reverted to their other, authoritarian, historic tradition. *Never* in history have the Dominicans been able to find a formula that blends these two traditions, or one that takes into account their own, somewhat distinctive meanings of democracy. Today, the quest for such a formula goes on, which is why we must remain both hopeful and at the same time somewhat skeptical about the permanence of the present democratic system in that country.

HISTORICAL OVERVIEW

The Dominican Republic is a nation of nearly 6 million people on 19,386 square miles (48,464 square kilometers) of territory.[7] It occupies the eastern two-thirds of the island of Hispaniola, the second largest (next to Cuba) of the string of islands rimming the Caribbean Sea. The Dominican Republic, Catholic, Spanish-speaking, and Hispanic, shares Hispaniola with French-speaking Haiti, which the Dominicans are wont to portray as black and "African."

The Dominican Republic has a per-capita annual income of about

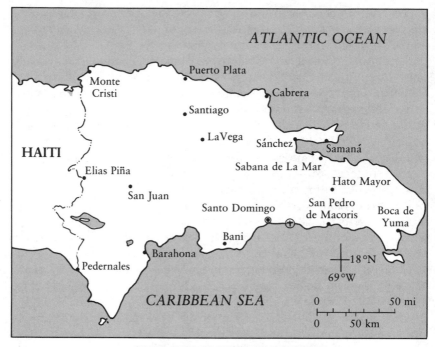

THE DOMINICAN REPUBLIC

$1,200. The country has experienced impressive economic growth in the last twenty years and is no longer among the poorest of the Latin American countries. It is now about 55 percent urban, reflecting the recent growth of the manufacturing, commercial, and service sectors. Literacy has climbed to about 70 percent. The changes in the last three decades in terms of the modernization of virtually all areas of life have been nothing short of remarkable.[8] These changes have laid the basis for the emergence of a more democratic system.

It has not always been this way. Indeed, the Dominican Republic has one of the most chaotic and disruptive histories in all of Latin America. This history has strongly shaped not only the nation's development, or, properly put, the absence sometimes thereof, but also its attitudes toward democracy.

The Colonial Past

At the time of Columbus's landing on the island in 1492, Hispaniola ("little Spain," the name the Spaniards gave to it) was peopled by the

Taino and Arawak Indians. Neither had very large or complex societies, compared to the vast Aztec, Mayan, and Inca civilizations that the Spaniards would later find on the mainland.[9]

The Spaniards established the first permanent European settlement in the New World on Hispaniola, calling it Santo Domingo. Here the first university, the first cathedral, and the first monastery in the Americas were founded. It was on Hispaniola that the first Spanish social experiments in colonial rule were carried out.[10]

Before its arrival in America, Spain had had considerable experience with conquest and colonization. The reconquest of the Iberian Peninsula from the Moors had just been completed the same year that Columbus discovered America, and the Spanish conquest of America may be looked on as almost a continuation of that reconquest. Indeed, quite a number of the hierarchical and authoritarian practices and institutions that Spain carried to America were reflections of the same institutions recently established in Iberia.[11] The "democracy" of Spain's middle ages—the system of representation by estates, the autonomy of cities, the rule of law— had been eliminated by the sixteenth century in favor of absolutism and authoritarianism; and it was this later, or "Hapsburgian," model that was carried over to the New World.[12]

On Hispaniola, the Spaniards established the practices and institutions of imperial rule that would later be extended to the rest of the Americas. The Spaniards conquered and subjugated the native Indians. They milked the colony of its gold and silver. They forced the Indians to work in the mines under inhuman conditions that resulted in rapid decimation of the native population. More or less simultaneously, a *hacienda* or slave-plantation system was established in which the Indians were obliged to perform exhausting manual labor.[13]

The Spanish colonial system represented a whole way of life—political, social, military, religious, legal, and intellectual, as well as economic. This system was imposed on Hispaniola during the sixteenth century, and it remained the dominant pattern for centuries thereafter. It remains strongly present today, representing an alternative to the current and emerging liberal-democratic system. It therefore behooves us to know more about that system and why it has been so long-lasting.

The Hapsburgian system, in all its manifestations, was a rigid, top-down, hierarchical, and authoritarian system that still has powerful echoes in the Dominican Republic.[14] Politically, it was a system of absolutist authority proceding from all-powerful king to captain-general to local military conqueror *cum* oligarch. Each unit in the hierarchy exercised absolute authority, allowing for no challenge or questioning from below. There were no hints of democracy or grassroots participation.

Socially, the system was similarly rigid and hierarchical. The Spanish conquerors occupied the highest place in the hierarchy. There was a very small "traditional middle class," often mestizo or mulatto, of soldiers, artisans, and craftsmen. At the lowest levels, as serfs or virtual slaves, was the native Indian population. As the Indians began to die out, the Spaniards began to import African slaves to do manual labor. Importing African slaves did not change the social structure of the colony, however; it only meant substituting one lower class for another. The basic two-class system was thus established and remained intact. It was reinforced by racial criteria, so that the class barriers to social advancement became virtually impossible to overcome.

The economy was similarly exploitive, mercantilist, and feudal. A small elite milked the colony dry for its own benefit and that of the Spanish Crown. Almost nothing was reinvested in the colony for internal development; that would not have been in accord with the mercantilist philosophy then prevailing. The religious, legal, and educational systems established under the Spanish colonial system were similarly hierarchical and authoritarian. There was no preparation in self-rule, let alone democratic self-government.[15]

Since that was the prevailing mode, it should not be surprising that the Spanish colonial structure was established in this fashion in the early sixteenth century. What is surprising is that it lasted so long: through three centuries of Spanish colonial rule, on into the independence period of the nineteenth century, and even to the present. For even now, the sixteenth-century Spanish model of a bureaucratic-authoritarian state serves as an alternative to the liberal one, a top-down system that has by no means disappeared from the Dominican consciousness.

The first half-century, 1492–1550, was the "glorious" period of Spanish colonial rule on Hispaniola. After that, the colony was ignored and abandoned and became bedraggled. The population declined, the more enterprising Spaniards went off to the richer colonies of Cuba and the mainland, and Hispaniola went into a centuries-long depression from which it is still recovering. It became a run-down and backward way station in the vast Spanish empire. Important for our purposes is the fact that its main institutions also declined: the church; the university; the *hacienda*.[16] From this point on, Hispaniola would face the problem not just of overcoming its authoritarian Spanish past but also of creating institutions—any institution—to fill the void. The colony of Hispaniola was characterized chiefly by disorganization, by what Dominicans would later refer to as a *falta de civilización* ("lack of civilization"). Not only did the island lack any liberalizing and democratizing institutions; it lacked any institutions at all on which a viable postindependence political order could be based.

The second problem is the island's strategic location, commanding two key passageways into the Caribbean: that between North and South America; and that between the Isthmus of Panama and Mexico *and* Western Europe or North America. This important strategic location means that Hispaniola has been frequently shelled, occupied, and pressured by the larger powers. In the colonial period, the Dutch, British, and French all sought to wrest control of the island from Spain. The French eventually succeeded, in the eighteenth century, in taking the western third of the island from Spain and converting it into a valuable sugar colony based on slave labor, from which the later independent nation of Haiti sprang. In the independence period, Spain and France again, then Britain, Germany, the United States, and the Soviet Union all sought to conquer the island, secure bases there, or use the island as a pawn in larger global power struggles. Never would the Dominican Republic be able to develop autonomously. Rather, it was always caught up in, and always a pawn of, these larger international struggles, which served further to retard its possibilities for democratic progress.[17]

The Independence Period

At the end of the eighteenth century Spanish Hispaniola was a bedraggled backward colony, with nowhere near the wealth, the importance to Spain, nor the institutional base of a Mexico, a Peru, or an Argentina, for example. It had neither the strong church, strong oligarchy, nor strong *hacienda* system of a more traditional or conservative society nor the nascent liberal or liberalizing institutions of a more democratic and modernizing one. Indeed it is the absence of any institutions of any sort that would now plague its life as an independent nation.

Dominican independence was set in motion by events occurring outside its borders. In 1795, as a result of the wars in Europe precipitated by the French Revolution, Spanish Hispaniola was ceded to France. Soon, the first of a series of slave revolts broke out in Hayti (as Haiti was spelled before its independence) aimed at overthrowing white, French colonial oppression. The rebellion and upheaval soon spread to the Spanish end of the island. French Hayti achieved its independence, but in 1809 Spanish-speaking Hispaniola was reunited with Spain.[18]

In 1821, the Dominican Republic declared its independence, but before independence could be consolidated, Haitian columns again overran the entire island. Haitian rule, 1822–1844, was cruel and barbarous, and it left an indelible mark on the Dominican Republic. The Haitians freed the slaves but also burned the plantations, slaughtered the cattle, drove out the Hispanic elements, and provoked social and political chaos. Hispaniola had always lacked, since 1550, an organizational infrastructure; now, whatever institutions it did have were largely wiped out. The once-proud colony reverted to a more primitive form of existence.[19]

The twenty-two years of Haitian occupation, and continued Haitian raids and incursions after that, gave rise to a further development important to the main theme of this chapter: a widespread desire for strong authoritative (if not authoritarian) rule as a way—as Dominicans viewed it, the only way—of keeping out the Haitians. Haiti's rule had not only been destructive, but it was also by a black nation that the Dominicans viewed as "African," "uncivilized," and "barbaric." Henceforth, they would make strenuous efforts to expand their military and secure strong, authoritarian rule. Dominicans might admire democracy and representative government in the abstract, but in their own country they felt authoritative rule was necessary to preserve an entire white, Western, Hispanic way of life. In the mid-nineteenth century, when racial theories were still in vogue and long before the Civil War settled the issue in the United States, these were powerful and compelling arguments in Dominican eyes.[20]

As Haitian rule proved increasingly corrupt and inefficient in the early 1840s, sentiment among the Dominicans for independence increased. A group of secret societies was organized that led the independence fight. These societies were infused with the ideals of republicanism and of the French Revolution. Led by the charismatic Juan Pablo Duarte, the Dominicans not only threw off Haitian rule in 1844 but also adopted a liberal and democratic constitution patterned after that of the United States. It provided for separation of powers, civilian control over the military, an independent legislature and court system, regular elections, and a long list of civil and political rights.[21]

From this point on, there would be two political and constitutional traditions in Dominican history. The first, the authoritarian, was older and well-established. It went back to the island's "golden era" in the sixteenth century. It would continue to dominate for at least a century and a quarter of Dominican independent life, strengthened by fears of Haiti and the absence of strong institutions. It was powerful in the army, the church, the rural areas, the traditional landed class, and the rising business and commercial elites. But alongside this tradition, competing with it and even occasionally coming to power for short-lived stretches, was a liberal and democratic tradition. It remained for a long time a minority strain in the Dominican Republic but gradually gained strength, especially in the urban areas, among intellectuals and a part of the middle class, and eventually among students, workers, some businessmen, and some peasants. From then on, Dominican politics would have to be viewed not as a single hierarchical, "Hapsburgian" pyramid, but as two competing paradigms and ways of life, existing side by side, seldom overlapping or intermingling, touching sometimes but usually locked in mortal combat, rivals to control the pinnacles of power and the state system from which money, influence, patronage, public policies, and spoils all flowed.[22]

The first problem with liberal democracy in the Dominican Republic, when independence was achieved in 1844, was that it bore absolutely no relation to underlying Dominican social or political realities. To this point, Dominicans had had no experience whatsoever in democratic self-government. None of the measures contained in the Constitution had any grounding in Dominican experience or realities. The realities that did exist—the church, the landholding system, the class structure—were hardly supportive of democratic governance. On the contrary, a liberal constitutional framework had been superimposed on a social structure that was still cast in authoritarian molds. It could not possibly last or work.[23]

The second problem is that Dominicans did not all or necessarily want democracy, or want it all that much. They admired liberal representative government (what they knew of it) in the abstract and as it worked in the United States. But they were not fully convinced of its efficacy in the Dominican Republic. The Dominican Republic was too unorganized, too chaotic, too "uncivilized" for democracy to work; it had no existing democratic institutions. On top of that, Haiti's assaults continued intermittently all through the later 1840s, 1850s, and 1860s. Only a strong government and a strong military, Dominicans reasoned, could repel the more populous Haitians and provide a degree of domestic order.[24]

The third problem was underdeveloped socioeconomic conditions. In 1844, the Dominican Republic was about 98 percent illiterate and 90 percent rural. There was practically no middle class. The economy was run down and had been devastated further by the Haitian occupation. The social and economic base, to say nothing of the political traditions, on which a viable democracy could be based were simply not present.

Hence a recurring pattern developed in Dominican history. A new liberal-democratic element would rise up every generation (1840s, 1870s, 1900s, 1920s, 1960s, 1980s). With high expectations and with great flurry and romance, they would launch a new democratic opening that ordinarily lasted from a few weeks to a few years. The democratic elements would prove inept or unable to solve the country's immense, underdevelopment-related problems and, hence, in the absence of a strong institutional structure, would quickly be replaced by authoritarian men-on-horseback. The authoritarians would stay in power for extended periods of twenty to thirty years, until the next generation of liberal democrats rose up. The question we face today in the Dominican Republic is whether this cycle has finally been broken, or whether it will repeat itself.

Within months of taking office, Duarte and his fellow democrats were replaced by military authoritarians. Duarte himself was weak and incompetent, he lacked any administrative experience, and the only semi-strong institution in the country was the independence army. For the first thirty years of the Dominican Republic's independent life, in fact, two rival men-on-horseback, Buenaventura Báez and Pedro Santana, alternated in the presidency. Báez served five times as president, and Santana four. Both men were preoccupied with holding the infant and underinstitutionalized country together—as well as with reaping profits out of the public treasury for themselves. Both strove to ward off Haiti's assaults, which meant developing a larger army and searching for an outside "protector." Spain, France, and the United States were all approached with protectorate plans, and from 1861–1865, Spain reoccupied the country. But Spain was also driven out, and the country reverted to its familiar chaos alternating with strong-arm rule. The Haitians were in fact kept at bay during these thirty years, but that success came at some sacrifice of national sovereignty and with the further cost of continuing complete lack of institutionalization of democratic government.[25]

In the 1870s, there was a second brief interregnum of democratic rule under Ulises Espaillat. Espaillat promised to administer the nation's finances honestly and to govern constitutionally. Espaillat was in the tradition of Duarte, long on ideals but weak on practical realities. He proved unable to manage the contentious forces in the nation, especially the regional *caudillos* and their private ragtag armies, and soon fell from power. He was succeeded by another dictator, Ulises Heureaux.

Heureaux governed for seventeen years, from 1882 to 1899. He was a corrupt and brutal tyrant, but he was able to govern. As had the Báez and Santana regimes, his strong-arm rule did manage to keep the Haitians out. But Heureaux was not just a bloody dictator. He was a new breed of authoritarian who provided both stability and development. In this, he was very much like Porfirio Díaz in Mexico and was part of the same Latin American preoccupation, so widespread at that time, with a positivist philosophy of order and progress.[26]

Under Heureaux, the Dominican Republic took off economically for the first time. The developmentalist accomplishments of Heureaux and, later, Trujillo were due as much to international business cycles as to the policies of these authoritarian rulers; but they did provide a climate of stability in which investment increased and the economy could flourish, and they made sure they received the credit for the accomplishments. In the 1880s and 1890s, new roads were built, telephones introduced, dock facilities built. The population increased, foreign capital began to pour in, lands under cultivation increased, the first manufacturing was introduced, exports increased. The tempo of economic life quickened and a new business and middle class began to grow. Prosperity expanded; some real national infrastructural development went forward. But note: All these accomplishments came about under authoritarian auspices, not democratic. Another plus was thus added to the arguments for Dominican authoritarianism: Not only did authoritarianism help preserve peace and keep Haiti away, but it also seemed to be responsible for progress and prosperity.[27] Meanwhile, Heureaux had piled up an immense foreign debt.

Following Heureaux's assassination in 1899, disorder and instability again set in. In 1905, Ramón Cáceres came to power, ushering in another of those brief interregnums of well-meaning democratic rule. The economy was in ruins, and democracy again fell victim to *caudillismo* and the feuds among the rival elites. Cáceres was also assassinated, and the country again fell back into chaos.

Meanwhile, the U.S. presence in the Dominican Republic had been growing incrementally. European creditors had been threatening to use gunboats to collect unpaid debts; hence in 1905, under the Roosevelt corollary to the Monroe Doctrine, U.S. tax officials had been sent in to administer the country's customs receipts and to help pay off its large foreign debts. In 1907, U.S. Marines were sent in to protect the customs agents. In 1909 and again in 1912, the Marine contingent was increased. In 1916, faced with continued instability and also the outbreak of World War I, President Woodrow Wilson authorized the Marines already on the island to assume control. The full-scale occupation lasted from 1916 to 1924.

Although this interpretation will doubtless be controversial, the U.S. Marines' occupation may be looked at in terms comparable to the rule of the "order-and-progress" dictators that came before and would come after. Albeit at first, the occupation forces tried to work through the local political institutions, eventually they tired of the effort, suspended the Constitution, and ruled by decree—as a long line of Dominican dictators had done. The Marines disarmed the population, stripped the regional *caudillos* of both their irregular private armies and their source of funds (the local customs house), and created a centralized constabulary to maintain order. Moreover, the progress brought by the Marines was considerable. Not only did they introduce baseball and chewing gum; they also built highways, water systems, docks, telephone lines, sewerage systems, bridges, and other infrastructural projects. In all these ways, the Marines' rule was remarkably similar to that of Heureaux. It could be added that neither Heureaux nor the Marines were hesitant to use force and repression against those who opposed them.[28]

Following the Marines' withdrawal the pendulum again swung briefly to the democratic side. A new constitution was drawn up, largely drafted in the U.S. Embassy and following closely the U.S. model. In the elections of 1924, supervised by the Marines, Horacio Vásquez was elected president.[29] Vásquez presided over another of those brief democratic interruptions in what otherwise has been a long authoritarian tradition. But Vásquez, in 1928, illegally extended his term of office, thereby undermining his government's legitimacy, which, since it had been established by the U.S. occupation forces, was shaky to begin with. Vásquez became sick, further weakening his hold. He neglected to create a political party, and the nation's institutional infrastructure, after the Marine occupation, was almost nonexistent. In 1929, the world market crash occurred, and in 1930, the bottom dropped out of the Dominican economy. Plotting by the elites and *caudillos* was renewed. That same year, General Rafael Trujillo, head of the Marine-created National Guard, seized power; he would rule for the next thirty-one years and add some further ingredients to the long tradition of Dominican authoritarianism.

The Trujillo Era

The dictatorship of Generalissimo Rafael Trujillo, 1930–1961, was a far more complete or "total" dictatorship than anything the Dominican Republic had seen up to this point. Trujillo began his rule as a rather typical man-on-horseback, but, using modern organizational, technological, and informational techniques, his dictatorship eventually came to resemble the totalitarian regimes of Europe in its repressiveness and extent of centralized control.[30]

Trujillo dominated all areas of Dominican national life. He controlled the armed forces and turned them into an instrument of internal occupation and repression. He created a single party to serve as the political machinery of his dictatorship. He dominated and controlled, privately or through the state, about 50 percent of GNP. He stamped strict controls on all group and associational life: trade unions, businessmen, professional associations, etc. He created a vast national spy network and introduced, after World War II, technologically proficient terror, torture, and surveillance techniques. He controlled education and the media. With those forces he could not absolutely control, such as the church or the U.S. Embassy, he worked out mutually supporting arrangements. No group or institution could remain independent of Trujillo's control.[31]

Several aspects of Trujillo's dictatorship merit particular attention in this context: First, he absolutely eliminated whatever early stirrings of democratic rule—nascent political parties, interest groups, and the like— had begun to emerge in the early part of the century and in the 1920s. By the end of the long Trujillo era, there was no foundation—no leaders, no institutions—on which a new democratic order could be based.

Second, Trujillo was, like Heureaux, an order-and-progress dictator. He presided over a period of unprecedented economic growth. Although enriching himself in the process, he built roads, bridges, public buildings, curbs, docks, highways, and more. He greatly expanded agricultural production and exports. Manufacturing, commerce, and industry also expanded several times over. Percapita income more than doubled, though it remained terribly unevenly distributed. The stability and discipline of his regime attracted foreign investment. Trujillo did not stay in power for thirty-one years by blood and terror alone; rather, there were real economic accomplishments of the regime, and not all the profits ended up in the dictator's foreign bank accounts.[32]

Third, the development and modernization that occurred were closely related to the kind of regime Trujillo's was. Beginning in the 1930s in the underdeveloped society of that time, the Trujillo dictatorship was also rather primitive, limited largely to political and military controls. But in the more developed nation of the 1950s, Trujillo's controls could also become more complete and pervasive in dominating civil society. As the regime took on more and more "totalitarian" characteristics (thought control, mass indoctrination, technologically efficient terror), it also became more and more problematic that democracy could be built in its aftermath.

Fourth (and related), the regime became more explicitly corporatist and bureaucratic-authoritarian. Trujillo was a man of action and certainly not an intellectual or institutional innovator; but his advisers were caught up in the wave of corporatist sentiment that swept Europe in the interwar period, and they gradually introduced more and more modern corporatist features into the regime. These included organic-integralist ideas and the sectoral organization of society and representation. Similarly, by the 1950s, the regime was no longer just a personalist dictatorship but had become more and more bureaucratic-authoritarian. In this regard (though not in others), the Trujillo regime was like the regime of Generalissimo Francisco Franco in Spain. That is, it always remained a personal dictatorship, and no one ever had any doubt where ultimate decisionmaking authority resided. But under the impact of societal and economic modernization, both these regimes also became more complex and sophisticated over the years, necessitating modern bureaucratic structures to go along with the personalist dictatorship. A bureaucratic-authoritarian model thus grew up alongside of but did not supplant the older system of one-man rule.[33]

Finally, because Trujillo's rule was so total, its collapse provoked a near-total vacuum. In terms of democratic institutions, the Dominican Republic was only slightly more advanced in 1961, when Trujillo was assassinated, than it was in 1844, when independent life began. It had developed some institutions in the interim, but very few were democratic. There were no democratic political parties operating in the country (though there were numerous exile groups), no autonomous associations or economic interest groups, no independent press or judiciary, no experienced democratic leaders, no practice in democratic ways. After 127 years of independence, the authoritarian tradition remained dominant, and the democratic one was pitifully weak. That would change dramatically, however, in the period after 1961.

Democratizing the System

Following Trujillo's assassination, the Dominican Republic went through another of those brief democratic interims that has traditionally followed the collapse of dictatorship. But conditions had changed: The country was more affluent, more socially differentiated; the United States (fearing another Cuba) poured in economic aid. Democratic forces were far stronger than ever before, in part because the blood and excesses of the

Trujillo regime had thoroughly discredited the historic authoritarian model. Had Trujillo ruled more moderately and not been so greedy or cruel, the historic authoritarian model, tempered by paternalism, might have been able to hang on. Instead, Trujillo had ruled as a tyrant, had overstepped the bounds of permissible behavior that a long tradition of Iberian and Latin American political theory had established for "just princes," and therefore by his own doing had helped justify his people's "right to rebellion."[34]

The rebellion that came, however, was not limited to a circle of elites at the top. The original assassination plot was limited to elite elements, but almost immediately it spilled over into popular demonstrations.[35] This change was related to other, vaster changes that had occurred in Dominican society during the long Trujillo era. A sizable middle class (perhaps 20 percent of the population) had emerged, there was a large working class in the capital city, students and others had been mobilized, and rapid urbanization had resulted in a large unemployed *lumpenproletariat* in the capital's downtown streets, who could be recruited for political demonstrations. In the years 1961–1965, a veritable "explosion" of political participation occurred, which meant in long-range terms that the country could never go back to its earlier, "sleepier," semifeudal past.[36]

Initially, Trujillo's son and heir, Rafael, Jr., or "Ramfis," tried to continue his father's regime. But societal pressures built up, and in November 1961, he resigned the military position he had held and fled the country—along with virtually the entire Trujillo family. For the next two months, a former Trujillo puppet, Joaquín Balaguer, tried to preserve continuity by agreeing to share power with a Council of State, but in January 1962, he too was forced into exile. The Council of State, without Balaguer, continued in power.[37]

In the meantime, the United States had become heavily involved in internal Dominican affairs. The United States was interested in a democratic outcome in the Dominican Republic, but its main concern, in the immediate aftermath of the Cuban Revolution, was to prevent a "second Cuba" in the Caribbean. To this end, the United States had pressed the Trujillos to liberalize and even attempted to push them out of power, but not precipitously or in a way that would upset stability or lead to a Castroite takeover. Strenuous efforts were made to control the post-Trujillo transition, in contrast to the post-Batista transition, which the United States had not controlled. The dilemma for U.S. policy was captured by President John F. Kennedy: "There are three possibilities in descending order of precedence: a decent democratic regime, a continuation of the Trujillo regime, or a Castro regime. We ought to aim at the first, but we really cannot renounce the second until we are sure that we can avoid the third."[38]

The Council of State ruled during 1962. It carried out some modest reforms and prepared the way for elections in December. The elections were won by a two-to-one margin by Juan Bosch and his populist Dominican Revolutionary Party (PRD). Bosch was a socialist, a democratic, and a charismatic but mercurial leader who had lived in exile for over twenty years. His base of support was workers, peasants, and young people. He sought to bring a democratic revolution to the Dominican Republic and to carry through much-needed social reforms. But Bosch ran into the implacable hostility of the Dominican military, the church, and the economic elites. The country became polarized. The U.S. Embassy also became suspicious of his socialist orientation. Bosch's personal idiosyncrasies and his and his party's inexperience of governing also weakened his position. After only seven months in office, Bosch's government was overthrown by a military coup.[39]

Power then returned to the conservative elite and upper-middle-class elements who had governed under the Council of State. But the new regime proved to be corrupt, inefficient, and repressive. It could no longer, after the explosion of participation of the previous two years, return to the more traditional and "sleepier" politics of the past. Resentments began to build up among the trade unions, the middle class, and intellectuals. Even the business community became disillusioned with the existing government. Meanwhile, the PRD plotted to stage a constitutionalist and democratic comeback.[40]

The explosion came in April 1965. A PRD–led popular and middle-class–based revolution succeeded in toppling the government. It was on the verge of defeating also the regular armed forces. At that moment, fearing the revolution would be taken over by Castro-Communists, the United States intervened. In the next few weeks, the United States sent in 22,000 troops, occupied the country, quashed the revolution, and installed an interim government. The democratic revolution in the Dominican Republic, which had as its goal the restoration of Bosch to the presidency and the government that had been ousted in 1963, was thus snuffed out by the greatest democracy on earth. The irony was not lost on the embittered Dominican people; anti-Americanism increased.[41]

By 1966, the contending forces in the Dominican civil war had been pacified, new elections were scheduled, and the bulk of the U.S. forces had been withdrawn. The winner of the 1966 presidential election was Joaquín Balaguer, the shrewd political leader who had once been a puppet president under Trujillo. He presented himself as an efficient administrator (in contrast to Bosch), as a populist, and as a peacemaker to a population now fed up with upheaval. Balaguer ruled for the next twelve years. Although it may be characterized as semidemocratic or pseudo-democratic, his regime was in the tradition of Santana, Báez, Heureaux, and Trujillo; it merits close scrutiny.[42]

Balaguer was, to begin, a deft politician. He cleverly played off contending political and military forces, meanwhile enhancing his own power. This was no mean feat in the more complex and pluralistic society that the Dominican Republic had become.[43]

Second, he presided over a period of unprecedented economic growth. Largely fueled initially by money from the United States, the Dominican economy achieved such increases as to be dubbed the "Dominican miracle." The economic and social development of the Balaguer era gave rise to a general economic quickening that affected all areas of the national life, and it helped swell further the size of the middle class.

Third, Balaguer used repression, albeit selectively. His was not a bloody regime as Trujillo's had been. Rather, he was careful to stay within constitutional bounds. He was not averse to having the police and armed forces use repressive tactics, including "disappearances," especially against PRD labor leaders and political organizers; but he managed to avoid the violence being associated with him personally. Instead, Balaguer quietly went about depoliticizing the population, lowering the decibel rate, avoiding confrontations, and calming down the country from the frenetic politics of the early 1960s.[44]

Fourth, Balaguer's regime was, therefore, more in the long traditions of Dominican *dictablandas* (soft dictatorships) as opposed to *dictaduras* (hard dictatorships). His was a regime that blended constitutional precepts and considerable freedom with tempered authoritarianism, as contrasted with Trujillo's bloody excesses. Balaguer provided order, stability, and discipline but without going beyond the generally acceptable standards of Dominican society. He was also a builder and developer of his nation. For these reasons, his regime remained popular; Balaguer still has widespread popularity today, as witness his return to power in 1986, after an 8-year absence, in a genuinely fair and competitive election, and his reelection in 1990. He represented one of the two main streams in the Dominican political tradition—the authoritarian one, now blended with various democratic overlays—and was careful not to overstep the boundaries of permissible behavior. He did not become a tyrant; he was not discredited as a leader. A Balaguer or Balaguer-like option, therefore, was a possibility for the Dominican Republic, however undemocratic or pseudodemocratic it might be. That occurred in 1986, and, given the country's opposing democratic and authoritarian traditions (which Balaguer deftly and sometimes incongruously reconciles), it could well be a possibility for the future.

Nonetheless, by 1978 Balaguer's earlier regime had run its course. Balaguer himself was older and feebler. He had a less-firm control on the levers of power. The bloom was off the economic "miracle." Democratic pressures were again rising, as they have periodically in Dominican history, but this time they were stronger and were coming at shorter intervals.

In the 1978 election, Balaguer faced a formidable foe in the person of Antonio Guzmán of the PRD. The PRD was both populist and the best-organized political party in the country. Guzmán was clearly ahead in the balloting when the armed forces, still fearful of Bosch's party from past experiences, stepped in to try to secure a Balaguer victory. This time, the United States intervened on the part of the democratic forces, putting immense pressure on the regime and threatening to cut off all aid. The ballot count resumed, and Guzmán and the PRD emerged victorious. Since 1978, the Dominican Republic has been governed democratically, including the most recent Balaguer administration.[45]

Guzmán represented the right wing of the PRD, and he served until 1982. Even with Guzmán's suicide (widely attributed to the uncovering of corruption in the regime and perhaps even in his family) in the closing weeks of his administration, constitutional procedures were followed. His successor, Salvador Jorge Blanco, also of the PRD, was elected in 1982. Both Guzmán and Jorge carried out significant social reforms, though within a context of increased economic difficulties and austerity. Both respected freedom and civil liberties, both ruled democratically. This was, in short, a reassertion, once more, of the country's alternative and democratic tradition, long submerged or popping out only temporarily, but now in full blossom.[46]

Guzmán and Jorge provided eight years of uninterrupted, PRD–led, democratic rule. It was the longest continuous period of democracy in Dominican history. Both presidents took steps to curb the military, to respect human rights, to rule constitutionally, and to provide for social and economic reform. Democracy appeared more strongly consolidated than ever before. But both these presidents were hamstrung by deteriorating economic conditions in the late 1970s and early 1980s that forced unpopular austerity measures, by rising corruption within the large state bureaucracy, and by patronage demands pushed by the PRD's own stalwarts.

In 1986, the PRD put up an unpopular candidate, Jacobo Majluta, who was tainted with the earlier corruption, while an opposition coalition nominated the venerable Balaguer. Balaguer was legally blind and quite infirm, but again his appeal—based on populism, efficiency, prosperity, and a blending of the traditions of democratic and strong rule—proved attractive. Juan Bosch was also a candidate and, though finishing a distant third, drew votes from the PRD. Balaguer won the election by a narrow margin; indeed, the margin was so narrow and sufficiently questionable that the vote count was temporarily halted, and the military threatened to annul the results. Eventually, after considerable machinations involving the armed forces, the U.S. Embassy, and the outgoing PRD government, Balaguer was declared the victor. In 1990, in another contested election, Balaguer again beat out Bosch.

Currently, the Dominican Republic has a democratic system that could be called "emergent" and only partially stable. But it also shows tendencies toward being only semidemocratic and perhaps even, depending on the definitions and criteria used, partially authoritarian.

Hence, the questions we must ask ourselves are whether the present democratic system will be permanent, or if it too will prove but temporary. Has authoritarianism been eliminated or superseded; has democracy now finally achieved majoritarian support; or will we continue to see an alternation between the two? Alternatively, have the Dominicans now achieved, in the system of Balaguer, something of a fusion between the two, a formula for blending and reconciling these two powerful, alternative forces in their long political history? If so, they will have hit on a formula that the country has long sought, and which other Latin American countries have also long tried to achieve. Should that formula work, the Dominicans will have developed a genuinely indigenous, developmentalist framework—an achievement whose significance would reach far beyond the small island of Hispaniola and that would be of interest to many other Latin American and Third World nations.[47] Unfortunately, because of Balaguer's infirmity and the country's continued severe economic problems, it seems unlikely that in the Dominican Republic this formula will achieve any greater success than have others in the past.

THEORETICAL ANALYSIS OF THE HISTORICAL PATTERN

Having traced the historical evolution of the Dominican polity, we now turn to a dissection of it. That is: What are the major social, economic, cultural, historical, political, and external factors that account for the major historical developments reviewed above? Our purpose is to explain the transitions to and from democratic rule, to and from authoritarian regimes, as well as the periods of persistence of democratic and/or authoritarian rule. So as to facilitate comparative analysis as well as to determine which of the general theoretical variables concerning democratic development are especially salient, we focus here on the following nine variables: political culture; historical evolution; class structure; ethnic and religious cleavages; state structure and strength; political institutions; political leadership; development performance; and international factors.

Political Culture

Most Dominicans believe in democracy—at least in the abstract. That is, they are supportive of representative government, constitutionalism, regular elections, and basic human and civil rights. Moreover, such democratic sentiment has been growing in the Dominican Republic and, by this time, may even represent majoritarian opinion. The problem is not that Dominicans are natural "Fascists" or that they love authoritarianism. The problem is simply that they are not convinced, given their chaotic history and absence of institutions, that democracy works well or as intended in the Dominican context.[48]

The Dominicans have had considerable experience with democracy, and most of it has not been good. Duarte was a romantic idealist who was quickly overthrown; the same is true of Espaillat in the 1870s. Cáceres was a good president, but under his rule U.S. customs agents and Marines came in, and the Dominicans lost their sovereignty. Vásquez ruled ineffectively in the 1920s and paved the way for Trujillo. Bosch was similarly ineffective as a political leader and later launched a revolution that produced chaos, bloodshed, and U.S. intervention. Guzmán killed himself, and Jorge's regime was plagued by corruption and economic contraction. Democracy does not, in the Dominican Republic, have a great and glorious history.

The Dominicans are suspicious of democracy for some other, quite sound reasons. The history of repeated Haitian invasions in the nineteenth century, and the continuing fear of Haitianization of Dominican culture and society even today, has led them to think that only strong, authoritarian regimes can withstand Haitian pressures. Second, the Dominicans know their own sad history well, especially the historic absence of institutions, the chaos, the disorder. From their point of view, only a strong government can keep this underinstitutionalized country from fragmenting and falling apart. Third, Dominicans look at the success stories in their history and ask who provided the most progress, the most development. The answer is, again, not the democrats but authoritarian or authoritarian/paternalist rulers like Heureaux, Trujillo, and Balaguer. These men all were, quite literally, builders of their country. In Dominican eyes, it is not the democratic but the authoritarian regimes that are associated with success. Democratic legitimacy has been difficult to build and sustain because the performance of the democratic governments has been weak, while that of the authoritarians has been strong, and also because of the lingering suspicions of the inadequacies of democratic rule.

These sentiments have been present even more broadly within the political elite, historically, than among the mass of the population.[49] It is the elites that most fear Haitianization—by which they no longer mean invasion from Haiti but rather the rising up of their own lower (and darker) classes. It is the elite that requires order, stability, and discipline for its economic profit-making. And it is the elite, especially its *nouveaux riches* elements, who have been most strongly supportive of Trujillo and Balaguer. In this sense, support for authoritarianism has a class base—though it should also be emphasized that *all* within the elite, those on the Left as well as on the Right, tend to prefer top-down rule. The question we must wrestle with now is whether in the present circumstances elite interest in order and stability is best served by supporting authoritarianism or democracy. Increasingly—and it is a very significant departure—elite sentiment has swung around to support moderate democratic regimes.[50]

The other complicating factor is the politicization of social and economic life. In the Dominican Republic, this has not reached an acute stage as yet, but it is increasing. Under the impact of the "revolution of rising expectations," social and economic relationships are increasingly being related to political issues and posed in political terms. Questions of employer-employee relations, state-owned enterprises, class relations, etc., are being increasingly politicized. To the degree this trend is emerging, it does not augur well for stable, moderate democracy.

A more democratic political culture has thus emerged in recent years in the Dominican Republic, but it is still tenuous. Democratic beliefs and values—in particular the legitimacy of democratic institutions and practices—are stronger than before, but they are still unevenly held and not held all that strongly even by those who profess them. In past times of crisis, Dominicans have abandoned democracy and opted for an authoritarian solution, or for some blend of strong central control coupled with considerable individual freedom. This is particularly true among the political elites, whose commitment to democracy may be quite fickle. Nor is it clear at this stage how strongly Dominican social institutions— the church, the armed forces, religion, family, clan, community, work life—are conducive to or supportive of democratic values. The alternative authoritarian tradition is still strong, and it could at some point make a comeback.

Historical Evolution

The Dominican Republic felt the full force of Spanish colonial administration, strongly authoritarian in all its aspects, during its first fifty years (1492–1550); but after that the colony was largely ignored by Spain. Colonial neglect did not assist the Dominican Republic to develop nascent democratic institutions, however; instead, it resulted in the absence of institutions of any sort. Hence, at the time of independence, the Dominican Republic had neither the liberal institutions of a democratic polity nor strong traditional institutions derived from the colonial era, which might have provided stability during the transition to independent nationhood. This institutional vacuum accounts in large measure for the country's alternation after independence between chaos and authoritarianism.

Although independence from Spain came relatively peacefully, the subsequent 22-year Haitian occupation was not only oppressive but also destructive of those few institutions the country had left: the church; the *hacienda;* the landed oligarchy; the university. The conditions under which the Dominican Republic ultimately achieved independence were bloody and destructive, not peaceful and gradual. Moreover, the country had had no opportunity or training in democratic self-government, and there had been no opportunity for a system of more competitive politics to develop prior to independence.

Furthermore, when independence finally was achieved, the Dominicans adopted an inappropriate constitutional framework. In essence, they took the U.S. Constitution, translated it into Spanish, tacked on the French Bill of Rights, and made no effort to develop a constitution reflective of indigenous traditions. Shortly thereafter, when democratic government was overthrown, a constitution was adopted that provided a more authoritarian form: powerful executive; weak Congress and courts; special position for the armed forces, and so on. Although the Dominican Republic has had by this time nearly thirty constitutions in its life as an independent nation, in fact there has been an alternation between two main forms: one liberal and democratic; and the other Caesarist or Bonapartist. Never has the country developed a constitution that reflected an indigenous design or tradition, and never has it fashioned a stable and lasting formula for governance that effectively reconciles its democratic and its authoritarian currents.[51]

In sum, the nation never had the opportunity to acquire experience with democratic institutions prior to independence. Political competition began before there were any well-grounded institutions to handle such competition. Nor were democratic institutions adapted to the country's unique conditions, built upon, or integrated with its cultural and historical traditions.

Class Structure

The Dominican Republic has a rigid class structure, reinforced by racial criteria. Racially, the country is about 5 percent white, about 60 percent mulatto, and about 35 percent black. Those at the top of the pyramid are both wealthy and white, or light mulatto. The middle class is chiefly mulatto. The lower classes tend to be black and darker mulatto. Race and class are thus closely intertwined. The divisions between the classes are both clear and deep; in addition, Dominicans are very conscious of racial background and class background and positions.[52]

Historically, the white ruling class has dominated the presidency, the cabinet, and the highest positions of governmental authority. Land, commerce, industry, banking, and the learned professions have similarly been dominated by this same element.

In the last fifty years, the mulatto middle class has emerged as a major and new force. The middle class now numbers about 20 to 30 percent of the population. Its avenues of social mobility have included the armed forces, the university, smaller-scale business, and the bureaucracy. Trujillo emerged out of this mulatto middle class and brought along with him into power fellow mulatto middle-class officers, as well as civilian sycophants. Because of this, some authors see the long Trujillo era (1930–1961) as effecting a class and racial change in the Dominican power structure: from white elitist rule to increasingly mulatto middle-class rule.[53]

The middle class has emerged as a dominant force in Dominican national affairs—some would say *the* dominant force. The middle class is now preeminent in many of the country's leading institutions: the bureaucracy; the church; the university; the military officer corps; political-party executive committees; the trade-union leadership. While this class has become numerically far larger and influential in all these institutions, it also remains deeply divided on social and political issues. It is dependent on the state for jobs, favors, and contracts; it is also dependent on foreign capital and therefore cannot be considered a strong, autonomous, or indigenous bourgeoisie. It is likely that this element will emerge (and perhaps it already has) as a force for moderation and stability, but so far there are few signs of a happy, liberal, stable, middle-class society emerging in the Dominican Republic.[54]

The working class has similarly grown in size in the last half-century, but it is weakly organized and dependent on the state. Only about 8 to 9 percent of Dominican workers are unionized, and there is an immense pool of unemployed laborers, whom employers can hire if workers become too demanding. Moreover, the unions are deeply divided between Communist, Socialist, Christian-Democratic, and U.S. Embassy-sponsored movements. Organized labor is by now a force to be reckoned with in Dominican society, but by itself it cannot—unlike some other groups—determine political outcomes.[55]

The peasant element is numerically the largest but politically the weakest of all Dominican groups. There are now peasant cooperatives and peasant political organizations, but these tend to be small and not very effective as interest groups. Neither they nor the trade unions are entirely free to organize independently of the state or employers. The distribution of land is very unequal, with most of it concentrated in the hands of civilian or military elites, but there is a large class of peasant smallholders and subsistence farmers. The Dominican countryside thus remains backward and semifeudal, dominated by patron-client relationships, though it is also increasingly socially differentiated.

On balance, the social and class structure of the Dominican Republic does not augur well for democracy. However, the growth and affluence of the middle class—and therefore the possibilities for stable democracy—are far greater now than they were a generation ago.

Ethnic and Religious Cleavages

For the Dominican Republic, ethnic and religious cleavages are not a major problem. In fact, in these areas the country is quite homogeneous. Catholicism is the religion of over 90 percent of Dominicans. While many do not actively practice their religion, and while Protestant sects have grown significantly in recent years, religion has not been a major source of societal cleavage. Indeed, one can say, given the divisiveness of Dominican history and its class structure, that religion and a Catholic political culture help provide the cement that holds the country together and gives it national identity.[56]

Nor is ethnicity a major divisive issue. Although the Dominican Republic has a social system in which race and class are mutually reinforcing, the country has remained remarkably free of racial hatred or racially inspired violence. Prejudice does exist with regard to darker-skinned persons, and Dominicans are very conscious of racial backgrounds and features. But there has never been a race war nor is there intense racial bitterness. There are no black-power movements in the Dominican Republic, nor anything resembling apartheid or "Jim Crow" laws. Rather, the Dominican system has been one of gradual assimilation: of blacks into the mulatto category and of mulattos into the "white" or upper classes. In this sense, prejudice is as much cultural as racial, and therefore it is possible to move up in the social-racial scale. Money, education, clothes, and position are all "whiteners" in the Dominican Republic.

The country's other ethnic groups are small and numerically insignificant. There are small communities of Chinese, Lebanese, Japanese, North Americans, Jews, and Western Europeans. To varying degrees, these elements have been integrated into Dominican society and into the political class. Most of the foreign communities, however, maintain a considerable degree of separate existence. They are not generally bothered by the Dominicans (though there have been instances of occasional friction), and they themselves have not pushed for separate power. The numbers involved in these foreign communities are simply insufficient for serious ethnic cleavage or conflict to develop.

The Dominican Republic is, therefore, more or less homogeneous religiously, culturally, and ethnically. Whatever subcultural cleavage exists is not centralized around two or three but dispersed among numerous small groups. Nor has subcultural cleavage resulted in separatist terrorism or civil strife.

State Structure and Strength

The Dominican state system has historically been weak. It performed few functions; it was not always able to preserve stability or maintain public order. The biggest change came with the Trujillo era. Trujillo built up enormously both his own power and that of the central state. He divested the country's regions of their residual power; he built immense new ministries that reached into more and more areas of national life. He greatly increased the size and strength of the armed forces, using them as an instrument of his dictatorship. The economic-control mechanisms of the central state were also greatly strengthened during the Trujillo era, both to increase the power of the dictatorship and to enrich the ruling family. By the end of the Trujillo era, the Dominican Republic was a far more centralized system—militarily, politically, and economically—than it had been before.[57]

The extensive role of the state in the economy, and of state ownership, has roots in and derives from the Trujillo era. Not only did Trujillo centralize economic decision making; he also used his dictatorial control to amass immense personal wealth. When he was killed, the vast Trujillo holdings were taken over by the government. These included factories, airlines, steamship companies, sugar mills, and land holdings—the total amounting to about 50 percent of Dominican GNP. At the time (1961), the Dominican Republic had the second-largest state sector in all of Latin America, behind only Marxist-Leninist Cuba. This was achieved through inheritance, not expropriation.[58]

The large Dominican state sector has major social and political consequences. The state corporations have become, over the last quarter-century, gigantic patronage and employment agencies: corrupt, bloated, and inefficient. Another consequence is that the private accumulation of wealth has come to depend in large part on having a position in or access to the state. The immense size of the state sector has also meant it is virtually impossible for private entrepreneurs to compete in the same economic areas. Finally, because of the sheer size and numbers of persons employed by the state, social and cultural groups and voluntary associations have little check on state power, nor can they retain much of an autonomous existence. The sinecures, jobs, and opportunities for enrichment through the state sector help explain why the electoral and, sometimes, extra-electoral struggle to control it has been often heavily suffused with violence and fraud.

Turning from the state's economic functions to its more manifestly political ones, we find a mixed record in maintaining public order. The Dominican state has not only been authoritarian historically, but it has also—particularly its military and security forces—often been arbitrary. Opposition politicians and groups have frequently been intimidated, beaten, repressed, and even killed. At times, the security forces have operated outside governmental control, engaging in terrorist activities and settling political and other scores with or without the supervision or even knowledge of the political authorities. In most circumstances, the state has been able to control protest movements and riots, often using violent methods to do so, but there is that unforgotten instance in the

1965 revolution, when a ragtag people's army defeated the regular military apparatus and caused its disintegration. Overall, the assessment is that military repression has frequently had a negative effect on democratic institutions; further, that it has sometimes tipped the balance between civil and military authority away from the former.

The armed forces as an institution deserve special mention in this context.[59] The military has long been extremely suspicious of democratic movements and of civilian control. Civilian "meddling" in the affairs of the armed forces has often been answered by military involvement in politics. The military tends to think of itself as a special institution with special obligations, above the Constitution. It is also a major avenue of social mobility for ambitious middle class mestizo youths, and it is frequently a means to achieve wealth and power, often illegally, on a grand scale. The armed forces therefore occupy a special place: They think of themselves as a proud and professional institution, but their performance has often left a great deal to be desired, and they are often resented and hated by the civilian population. Hence, the potential for conflict between military and civilian authorities or amongst rival factions within the military remains great. The efforts of recent civilian democratic governments to change these corrupt and repressive practices remain of uncertain effect.

Summing up, we can say that the authority of the national state has been effectively established in the Dominican Republic. Indeed, the power of the state has gone beyond an effective minimum: State power is heavily concentrated and centralized; the state has immense power over the economy; and the state is not always effectively limited by autonomous intermediate groups. Nor has the state always been able to maintain order and national security by democratic means. The armed forces frequently operate above "mere" civilian control and are not fully committed to democratic principles.

Political Institutions

Despite the large number of constitutions promulgated in Dominican history, in fact the constitutional tradition has been quite continuous. The large number of constitutions relates to the Dominican practice of promulgating a new basic law every time there is an amendment or even a modest change in constitutional wording or procedures. But actually, all the constitutions have duly provided for separation of powers, a presidential system, basic human rights, and so on. The difference has been in the different emphases given these provisions. Recall that the

Dominican Republic has two major political and constitutional traditions: one more authoritarian and the other more democratic. But the differences even between these two traditions have not been all that great. The more authoritarian constitutional tradition provides for a stronger executive, a significant role for the armed forces, wide emergency powers, and, at least historically, a special position for the Catholic church. But even in the Dominican Republic's authoritarian tradition, provision is made for a congress and a judiciary, though not usually on a coequal and independent basis. The country's democratic constitutional tradition, by contrast, provides for a somewhat weaker executive, a stronger congress and court system, subordination of the armed forces to civilian control, separation of church and state, fewer emergency powers, and a more extended list of human, political, social, and economic rights.

The problem in Dominican constitutional history, as we have seen, has been to reconcile these conflicting traditions, both of which have considerable resonance in Dominican national history. And it is interesting that, in their provisions for a strong executive, for example, these two traditions are not all that far apart. Both the supporters of the one point of view and the supporters of the other have come to recognize a certain validity in the other group's position. It is therefore especially significant that in the most recent Dominican constitution, that of 1966, a major effort was undertaken to blend the authoritarian and the liberal traditions. The executive remains powerful, but Congress and the judiciary are elevated in importance and have achieved some greater degree of independence. Human rights are emphasized, but there is also provision for the exercise of broad emergency powers. The position of the armed forces remains ambiguous. Importantly, both the authoritarian government of Balaguer, which promulgated this constitution, and the democratic regimes that succeeded him after 1978 have been able to live with and function within—not always happily or comfortably but so far without repudiating the basic law—this constitutional framework.[60]

The Dominican political-party system has historically served to perpetuate and reinforce the country's deep divisions. The parties in the past tended to be the personal followings and/or machines of one or another family, clique, and clan. To an extent, many of them have these same characteristics today. But since the Trujillo period, more broad-based and ideological movements have emerged, and there is some evidence now of greater continuity and permanence to the parties. The Center-Left is dominated by the PRD, the country's best-organized political party. There is a small Communist Party and several other small groups on the far Left.[61] Bosch's Party of National Liberation (PLN) has been gaining in strength.

The Center-Right was long dominated by the Reformist Party, the personal machine of President Balaguer. It was caudillistic, devoid of ideology, and poorly organized. The weakness of the party system on the Center-Right is due in large part to the fact that this social element, led by wealthier and middle-class Dominicans, has historically had other routes to power open to it besides popular appeals and elections: family and interpersonal connections or even a military coup, for example. The Christian Democratic Party had also long tried to lay claim to the center of the political spectrum. In addition, there are a number of farther-Right and other personalistic parties, who may present candidates from time to time. For the 1986 election Balaguer managed a merger of the Reformist and Christian Democratic parties into the Partido Reformista Social Cristiano (PRSC), which represented a wedding of his machine with the ideology and organization of the Christian Democrats. Hence overall, the trend has been away from temporary and personalistic factions and toward a more broad-based and lasting party system centered around two relatively moderate parties: the PRD, somewhat to the left of Center, and PRSC, to the right of Center.

Since Trujillo's demise in 1961, the Dominican press has been remarkably free. It consists of four vigorous dailies in the capital city, over 100 radio stations (a large number for a country so small), and seven commercial television stations. Freedom of the press has been generally respected; the press has taken on an active political role in presenting alternative viewpoints and, overall, has been one of the great bulwarks of Dominican democracy in recent years.[62]

Political Leadership

At the end of the Trujillo era, the Dominican Republic faced an almost complete vacuum of political leadership. Trujillo had concentrated all power in his own hands and had taken pains to ensure that other leaders would not come to power. Many potential leaders were killed or jailed; others were forced into exile where they lost contact with the realities of their own country. By the end of Trujillo's 31-year rule, the Dominican Republic had practically no leaders with domestic political experience, and none with experience, so important in the modern world, in international agencies, banks, and lending institutions. This lack of leadership showed up immediately in a succession of short-lived post-Trujillo governments.[63] To a considerable extent, the Dominican Republic's repeated failures of democracy may be attributed to the lack of vision, ingenuity, and political skills on the part of its democratic leaders.

It takes a long time to build up cadres of political leaders, and in the last twenty-five years the Dominican Republic has come a long way. Within the parties, the private sector, the state-owned enterprises, and the professions there is now a corps of trained and experienced leaders who can run the government. That marks a major change from the Dominican Republic's earlier experiment with democratic government in 1963, when Juan Bosch could not find enough trained persons to man the cabinet, let alone all the other agencies that needed to be staffed.[64]

The general assessment is that the quality, skill, effectiveness, and innovativeness of leadership, and of democratic leaders in particular, has improved greatly in the last quarter-century. More and more, leaders have become committed to democratic processes, not always or necessarily because they are committed to democracy *per se,* but because they see now democracy as providing coherence, order, stability, and continuity to the polity. However, since the Dominican Republic's political system is based strongly on patronage and has a patronage-intensive style of politics, U.S. standards of honesty and probity in managing public accounts cannot always be taken for granted.

Development Performance

Unfortunately for the proponents of Dominican democracy, it has been the country's authoritarian leaders who have been the most successful in providing for national economic growth. Heureaux, Trujillo, and Balaguer: these are the presidents credited with being the Dominican Republic's great developers. It is they who built the roads and highways, the port facilities, the transportation systems, the curbs and sewerage systems, the bridges and public buildings, the water supplies and electrical grids. It is these authoritarian presidents who are given credit for the great spurts of national economic growth. Under Balaguer, in the 1960s and 1970s, for example, the Dominican Republic's growth rates averaged 6 to 7 percent per year and in some years were in double digits—right up there with the miraculous growth rates of Japan, West Germany, and Brazil. Many Dominicans still consider the Balaguer regime as the best government they ever had. (This is less true for Trujillo; his regime is now too far back for most Dominicans to remember, and he was too brutal). These accomplishments help explain Balaguer's continuing popularity today.

By contrast, the country's democratic leaders have not been very successful developers. Juan Bosch's regime, in 1963, was so chaotic and disruptive that little in the way of economic development could or did take place. Guzmán was inaugurated in 1978, when the Balaguer "miracle" was already in decline, and when the second oil shock (1979) devastated the Dominican economy. Jorge Blanco was forced to preside over such a severe austerity program that it cost the PRD significant political support and undermined the possibilities for social reform. Jorge Blanco had campaigned on the promise that he would bring economic as well as political democracy to the Dominican Republic, but the world economic downturn, which began in 1979 and continued—and worsened—thereafter, prevented him from carrying out these ambitious goals. It is not possible to say, therefore, that Dominican economic growth under democratic rule has been sustained and reasonably well distributed. The rapid growth has come under authoritarian governments; development under democratic regimes has been inconsistent and uneven.

On the other hand, the socioeconomic changes since the early 1960s (the end of the Trujillo era) have been impressive and indicate how much broader and more propitious the socioeconomic base for democracy is now as compared with earlier. Literacy has increased from 50 to 70 percent. Per-capita income is triple what it was in 1960. The country is 70-percent urban and 30-percent rural, just the reverse of what it was thirty years ago. What might be termed the "participatory population" (those involved in the money economy, who are informed, who vote, etc.) is also far higher. The manufacturing and industrial sectors are far larger, and, as indicated, there is more wealth and a larger middle class. Because of these changed socioeconomic conditions, the Dominican Republic is becoming a country where a more open and democratic system may become the rule rather than just an occasional interlude.

International Factors

Historically, it has been the next-door Haitian threat that has led Dominicans to prefer strong and authoritarian governments as the only way to preserve their independence as a nation. By now, the Dominican Republic has achieved military parity and even superiority vis-à-vis Haiti, and the populations of the two countries are now also about equal, between 5 and 6 million in each. Currently, the Dominican "great fear" is of Haitianization internally; that is, a rising-up of their own lower classes, who tend to be darker. In modern times, this has served as a main rationalization for authoritarian rule.

The Dominican Republic remains highly dependent internationally.[65] It is dependent economically on the prices, or quotas, that the large importers—mainly the United States—will pay for its exports, chiefly sugar. Since world sugar prices are so low (about 8 cents per pound, way below production costs), the state of the Dominican economy is especially perilous. It is vulnerable to changing world-market prices, to changing consumer habits (the preference for artificial sweeteners), and to the quotas set by the major importers. The country is also heavily dependent on the United States for capital, foreign aid, investment, technology, and other markets.

The Dominican Republic lies within what the United States considers its sphere of influence. It is close to Cuba and Puerto Rico and commands the key passageways into the Caribbean, to the Panama Canal, and to the entire isthmus of Central America. Because of its key strategic location, the Dominican Republic has long been buffeted about in international crosswinds, as a pawn of the major powers of which the United States is only the most recent.[66]

The United States' interests in the Dominican Republic are primarily strategic, which means its attitudes toward Dominican democracy have often been ambivalent. The United States long supported the Trujillo dictatorship, since it assumed that Trujillo would best support its interests in the area. When Castro came to power in neighboring Cuba, the United States reasoned that right-wing dictators like Batista or Trujillo, rather than preserving stability, might instead provide the conditions under which communism would flourish. Hence, the United States moved to depose Trujillo and install a moderately conservative regime, which would enable the United States to control the Dominican transition in a way that it had not controlled the Cuban.

The United States supported Bosch (but only half-heartedly), and there is some evidence of U.S. involvement in his ouster. In 1965, the United States intervened militarily to put down the PRD-led democratic revolution. The United States subsequently supported Balaguer with mammoth amounts of economic assistance in the late 1960s; but then turned around and supported his opponent in the 1978 elections. Since 1978, the United States has been supporting the existing democratic governments, because they are perceived as best preserving stability and U.S. security interests in the country. It is, so far as the support of democracy is concerned, a spotty record. The United States' main interests are strategic, and it is not always the case that democracy was viewed as best securing that priority.

Summing Up

The Dominican Republic has not had a long, consistent, or particularly happy experience with democratic government. There is now a clear pattern of evolution toward democratic rule; but the historical experience has not been particularly auspicious. In this section, we try to explain and summarize the country's overall degree of success (or lack thereof) with democratic government, cutting across the preceding analysis of discrete developments and abstracting from them the most important explanatory factors. We try to offer some summary judgments of the general historical, cultural, social, economic, and political factors that have been most important in determining the country's overall degree of success or failure with democratic government.

Dominican political culture historically has not been conducive to democratic rule. We consider this a very important explanatory factor. Dominican political culture, inherited from Spain, has been absolutist, elitist, hierarchical, corporatist, and authoritarian. Democracy has been a more recent addition to the Dominican tradition and, up until recently, was neither very popular nor deep-rooted. In many areas and institutions of Dominican national life, the authoritarian tradition and practices persist.

Spanish colonial rule left the Dominican Republic with no experience in democratic rule. Equally damaging to the Dominican democratic possibilities were Haiti's continuous assaults and occupations, after independence had initially been achieved. That left the Dominicans not only without democratic experience but downright fearful that weak institutions, which they equated with democracy, would lead to complete destruction of the nation.

Dominican class structure, reinforced by racial criteria, has been rigid and immutable. There is a certain fluidity in Dominican society because of its mixed racial character, and because prejudice is more cultural than racial. Nevertheless, class and race have served as virtually insurmountable obstacles to egalitarianism and greater democracy.

Ethnic and religious cleavages have not been particularly important in hindering democracy. The Dominican Republic is rather homogeneous on both these scores. We would not, in the Dominican case, judge this to be an important factor in explaining democracy or its absence.

The Dominican state structure has historically been weak, so weak that it actually retarded the possibilities for democratic growth. More recently, the state structure has become larger and stronger but not so much so as to have a major damaging effect on democracy. We judge the Dominican state system to be relatively neutral so far as its impact on democracy is concerned.

Two political traditions, authoritarian and democratic, coexist in the Dominican Republic, and these are reflected in the country's political structures and two main constitutional traditions. Now an effort is being made to combine and reconcile these two conflicting traditions. An emerging political-party system in which the two main parties are close to the middle of the political spectrum, coupled with a free and vigorous press, have added further to democracy's possibilities.

The country's political leadership has been thin—and kept purposely so by its authoritarian leaders. The democratic leadership has not been experienced or skillful. Now that is changing, as a corps of able and experienced leaders has emerged—a development that augurs well for future democratic development.

The Dominican Republic has generally been more successful in achieving economic development under authoritarian regimes than it has under democratic ones. Many Dominicans therefore associate progress with authoritarian rule. By the same token, they tend to associate incompetence, inefficiency, lack of progress, and now even austerity with democracy. Over the long run, these associations will probably change, but they remain a difficult factor for the country to overcome.

The Dominican Republic is both a dependent nation economically, and one that lies within the U.S. sphere of influence. It is unlikely the country can quickly break out of its dependency relations, though it has by now considerably diversified its economic base and trade relations. Nor is it certain the country would be better off that way. Existing within the U.S. orbit strategically has produced mixed results for Dominican democracy, though in the present circumstances it appears that U.S. strategic interests and those of Dominican democracy may be meshing.

The most important factors overall in explaining Dominican democracy or its absence would thus seem to be political culture, decolonization (by which we mean the Haitian experience), class structure, political structure, and international (dependency) factors. Important—but less significant than these others as explanatory variables—would seem to be political leadership and development performance. Of less importance or even irrelevance in the Dominican case would seem to be ethnic and religious cleavages and state structure and strength. These last factors either are not salient to the Dominican case, or else their effects were the reverse of what the general theoretical model for all developing nations hypothesized.

These same factors, in more or less the same order of importance, have influenced the present, more optimistic prognosis for democracy in the Dominican Republic.

1. Dominican political culture is now far more supportive of democratic rule. Admiration for authoritarianism and authoritarian solutions diminished significantly because of the repression of the Trujillo experience; and support for representative, democratic government has increased significantly. In addition, the international political culture, with its enthusiasm for democracy and human rights, is now more supportive of Dominican democracy.[67]

2. The possibilities for Haiti's continued assaults have now been minimized, as the Dominican Republic has achieved military and population parity with Haiti. Indeed, one could say this factor has all but been eliminated as a contributory cause of the retardation of democracy in the Dominican Republic.

3. Class structure remains crucially important but there are now ameliorating effects. There is more general affluence, and the standard of living has increased appreciably in the last two decades. The now sizable middle class, while not the rock of stability and democracy that some writers predicted,[68] has emerged as a balancing force in the political arena, oriented toward preserving stability and a moderate, middle-of-the-road government.

4. The political structure also shows some hopeful signs. Especially encouraging are the present Constitution (which achieves a working balance between the nation's more democratic and its more authoritarian aspects); the political-party system's evolution toward the moderate middle; the growing strength and autonomy of associational life; and the sheer persistence of and practice under existing democratic institutions.

5. The international environment has also become more promising. The Dominican Republic has managed to renegotiate some of its ties of dependence, particularly its relations with the United States. In addition, the United States has come to see that its strategic interests can best be served by supporting and identifying with moderate democratic governments. In addition, on a global level, democracy is the goal toward which almost all nations and peoples now aspire.

In addition to these major factors, it can also be said that Dominican leadership is now better and broader than it was, and that the developmental performance and overall achievements of the two most recent democratic governments are viewed—relatively speaking—more favorably than before.

All these factors add up to a considerably altered set of conditions now, as compared with the past, that point toward a more favorable situation for democracy in the Dominican Republic today than at any time in history. The societal base, the cultural environment, the political structure, and the international setting all provide a foundation on which democracy may be enabled to both thrive and endure.

FUTURE PROSPECTS AND POLICY IMPLICATIONS

The preceding discussion seems to indicate a more optimistic conclusion regarding the future prospects for democracy in the Dominican Republic. To a point, such a conclusion can be justified. But democracy still hangs by some terribly weak threads in the Dominican Republic. Dominican democracy remains subject to buffeting by a variety of crosscurrents; threads could snap and break at just about any time. Democracy is firmer than before, and the overall societal conditions more supportive of it, but that by no means rules out the possibility for extrademocratic elements staging a takeover.

Three themes command our special attention in this final section. The first is the impact of the world economy on the prospects for Dominican democracy. The world economic recession that began in 1979 and deepened thereafter has had a devastating effect on the Dominican economy. The Dominican Republic is going through the worst economic slump since the Great Depression of the 1930s. Unemployment is up, social problems are mounting, per-capita income is declining, and there are fewer and fewer pieces of the economic pie to hand out to more and more clamoring groups. The country has been forced to carry out a severe austerity program that, in 1983, produced large-scale food riots, which were met by police repression. The country's economic problems are undermining the viability of its recently established and still-fragile democratic institutions.[69]

It has been the case historically that when the bottom drops out of the Dominican economy, the bottom has usually dropped out from under the political system as well. It should be understood that we are talking here of the possibilities for undermining not just the government of the moment but an entire system of more-or-less moderate, more-or-less democratic, more-or-less prudent and centrist politics built up with so much difficulty over the past thirty years. That is what makes the present economic crisis so serious: It has the potential to subvert and destroy an entire set of democratic political institutions that, with much nurturing, have grown, developed, and become better-institutionalized in the three decades since Trujillo.

A second major theme requiring analysis is the ongoing Dominican search for an appropriate developmental formula. Earlier, when Dominican authoritarianism was still both in bloom and in power, I suggested that such a formula would likely mean joining the country's corporatist-authoritarian and democratic traditions.[70] Subsequently, I have suggested that few Latin American nations would likely make it to being full-fledged democratic systems, but that the best we could probably hope for was a transition from a "closed" (authoritarian, top-down, nonparticipatory) to an "open" (more pluralist, freer, more competitive, quasi-democratic) corporatist regime.[71] Understandable at the time it was written, when Latin America corporatism and bureaucratic-authoritarianism were still in full flower and power, the prognosis may have been unduly pessimistic.

It is still my view that countries such as the Dominican Republic need to find a formula to blend and somehow reconcile their authoritarian and democratic traditions. They need to devise a framework in which their organic, integralist, and corporatist forms can be joined with their liberal and democratic preference. They need, in short, to be able to blend their Thomistic-Suárezian-Rousseauan traditions with the Lockean-Jeffersonian one.[72] But given the recent transitions to democracy in so many Latin American countries and the obvious strength of democratic sentiment, in the Dominican Republic as elsewhere in Latin America, one can now be more optimistic about the prospects for a more firmly based and solidly institutionalized system of democracy there. Our expectations can now be enhanced to encompass not just a more open corporatist system, but a full-fledged democracy. Dominican democracy must still reach its accommodation with and adjust to the currents of organicism, corporatism, and Bonapartism still strongly present in Latin America—that is, it must be indigenous and genuinely Latin American and not just imported—but we can now be more optimistic that it will be real democracy nonetheless.

The third and last concluding theme concerns whether the Dominican Republic is, in the present circumstances, reverting to its earlier authoritarian, quasi-democratic, and paternalistic basis. Recent criticisms of the existing Dominican government have suggested precisely that point. These criticisms suggest that in the use of authoritarian methods against rioters in the spring of 1983, in the use of patronage by the government to secure its hold on power, and in the use of strong executive power, the Dominican Republic was returning to its historic authoritarian and *caudillo* forms.[73] The 1986 reelection of Balaguer gives rise to the same disturbing thought.

Some of these trends toward tightened controls are in fact under way, but another interpretation may be given to them besides the one given by critics. One may concede that the government's tactics in some of these instances have been questionable (and we do not have the space to discuss these here in detail), but without drawing the same inference as do the government's foes. For one may also see these steps as an attempt by a democratic Dominican government to adjust realistically to that other, more historic, organic-corporatist-authoritarian Dominican tradition. In the use of patronage, in the employment of executive power, and in government assistance to trade-union, peasant, and professional associations, we see attempts by a manifestly democratic regime to accommodate and reconcile itself to that other tradition. One cannot govern democratically in the Dominican Republic without such accommodation. Historically, when the one Dominican Republic that is liberal and democratic has tried to govern entirely without the other Dominican Republic that is not, that has been a formula for instability and anarchy. One can remain a democrat while also recognizing realistically that to prevent national breakdown and the historic pattern of alternation between democratic and authoritarian rule, compromise and reconciliation between these "two families" of beliefs and sociologies is absolutely necessary. That is also what the reelection of Balaguer seems to indicate.

Hence, in the long run, it is the great independence hero Bolívar, not Saint Thomas and Suárez on the one hand nor Locke on the other, who provides the model for Latin American, including Dominican, democracy.[74] Bolívar recognized Latin America's profound democratic aspirations, yet he also recognized realistically the powerful centrifugal forces tearing the continent apart and forcing it to opt for authoritarianism. Hence, he fashioned a formula that combined democratic rule with strong leadership, that incorporated certain Rousseauan and organic forms into a liberal-constitutional arrangement. It is a formula still valid today, one from which both the Latin American nations undertaking a democratic transition and those on the outside who are encouraging them in that direction can profitably learn.

Among policy recommendations directed toward the industrialized countries (especially the United States) that emerge from this study, therefore, the following would seem to be of particular, overall importance:

1. Provide economic relief (aid but especially trade) so that the current economic crisis not only does not undermine the economy but is prevented from tearing down democratic political institutions.
2. Provide assistance to democratic political groups in ways that relate to Dominican needs and aspirations and are not based on ethnocentric notions.
3. Exercise patience and understanding, so that Dominican efforts to find a developmental formula uniquely their own, which combines and seeks to reconcile their conflicting traditions, which responds to and builds upon their own historical experience rather than that of others, are not met with knee-jerk rejection and hostility.
4. Reorient U.S. strategic interests in ways that support moderate democratic regimes rather than disrupt them.[75]

14

Is Cuba Next? Crises of the Castro Regime

Everywhere one looks, communist regimes are in deep trouble. Whether one is talking about the Soviet Union, Eastern Europe, the People's Republic of China, Afghanistan, Ethiopia, Angola, Mozambique, or other Third World Marxist-Leninist regimes, profound transformations—and considerable economic, social, and political unraveling—are taking place. In Nicaragua and Eastern Europe, a number of communist governments have been swept from power; others are wobbly and may be on their last legs. Although the dimensions and specifics have varied from country to country—and though the nature of the crisis is different in well-institutionalized countries like the Soviet Union and only weakly established ones like Ethiopia—there are general patterns to be observed as well. These transformations are shaking the remaining communist states to their very foundations. The challenges are so deep and widespread in fact that they add up to a *profound and systemic* crisis of communist regimes, not just a temporary crisis of the moment.[1]

Cuba has appeared to be the one exception in this picture. Cuba has emphatically rejected Soviet-inspired *glasnost* and *perestroika*. Seemingly alone among communist regimes (even North Korea has opened a dialogue with the South), Cuba has refused to change in any fundamentals from within or to acknowledge the new international realities and to adjust its policies accordingly. Cuba has made no bows whatsoever toward the newer currents of openness, democracy, change, freedom, and pluralism now sweeping the world; its foreign policy remains similarly dominated by "old thinking" rather than anything new. Fidel Castro still dominates the Revolution in a one-man and highly personalistic fashion, and the entire apparatus of the totalitarian state—single-party regime, secret police, thought control, cult of the leader, absence of human rights, absence of choice, monopolistic state-controlled interest associations—remains locked in place. While the rest of the world is changing, Cuba

Reprinted from *Problems of Communism* 40 (January–April 1991).

appears not only to be rigid and unchanging but even to have tightened the screws of totalitarian controls.

The image we have of Cuba as rigid and uncompromising, as rejecting the kinds of democratizing currents that have occurred in the Soviet Union and Eastern Europe, is essentially correct. And yet this image serves to disguise the severe tensions existing in Cuba as well. Below the surface Cuba is not the severe, blustery regime that its public stances and the demeanor of its "maximum leader" would lead us to believe. Rather, Cuba and its Revolution are in deep trouble, signs of discontent are everywhere, and the basic tenets of the Revolution—the shift from capitalism to socialism and the shift away from the U.S. and into the Soviet camp—are being questioned as never before. The uncompromising bluster of the regime is a sign of weakness, not of strength; the hardening of totalitarian controls means not that the Revolution is strong but that it is in deep trouble.[2]

CUBA: THE CRISIS OF A COMMUNIST REGIME

All the world's communist regimes have recently faced, or are currently facing, crises of unprecedented dimensions.[3] These crises have been so severe in many cases that they have led to the unraveling, fragmentation, and institutional decay if not destruction of what the literature had led us to believe were strong, monolithic Marxist-Leninist regimes. The several crises facing the communist states are interrelated; cumulatively, they imply a crisis of *systems* and not just of particular governments. I propose to discuss these crises in terms of seven factors: the crisis of ideology, the crisis of institutions, the crisis of society, the crisis of leadership, the crisis of economy, the crisis of morale, and the crisis of external relations. When considered cumulatively, these seven areas of crises add up to a profound challenge to the existing Cuban regime.

The Crisis of Ideology

Now thirty-two years old, Cuba's is still a relatively young revolution. Over the years the regime has taken great pains to emphasize its ideological purity and its moorings in Marxism-Leninism. One might expect, therefore, that ideology would be stronger in Cuba than in some other communist regimes.

But in fact that does not appear to be the case. Cuba is intensely nationalistic and its Marxism-Leninism is strongly infused with nationalistic sentiment. Its nationalism is considerably stronger than its

Marxism-Leninism, however, leaving the regime without a solid ideological base. "Socialism" has become a slogan, but among most Cubans adherence to it is neither strong nor deep. In the absence of very much else (poor economic performance, mounting crises), nationalism only goes so far in holding the regime together and giving it purpose. The problem has several dimensions.

The first problem is Fidel Castro. Castro was never much of an ideologue. A nationalist, yes, a skilled political operator, a charismatic figure, a man of immense ambition and self-importance; but a Marxist-Leninist of only doubtful credentials. In the best analysis ever done of the question, a study by the Department of the State at the behest of an apprehensive Eisenhower administration in the last months of the dying Batista regime concluded that there was "no evidence" that Castro was a communist.[4] Therefore Castro's 1961 declaration that he was a Marxist-Leninist, had always been a Marxist-Leninist, and would always be a Marxist-Leninist came as a considerable surprise to objective observers, to Castro's closest aides, and probably to Castro himself. The declaration of Marxism-Leninism was purely pragmatic and calculating: a means to tweak the United States and to secure assistance from the Soviet Union. In fact, now as then, Castro remains impatient with ideology, seems not to have seriously read Marx or Lenin, is still more a nationalist than an ideologue, and makes the appropriate rhetorical bows to Marxism-Leninism but has not yet internalized it fully. Castro is a Marxist-Leninist of necessity, not of conviction.

At lower levels, the levels of the regime's apparatchik, the regime is even less Marxist-Leninist. As in all communist states once the first generation of revolutionaries begins to pass from the scene, a new generation takes over that hardly remembers the heroism of the early revolutionary struggles and is less ideological. These "new men" (few women have made it to the level of the Communist Party Executive Committee in Cuba) are pragmatists and bureaucrats, often impatient with the ideology and wanting mainly for themselves and their country to move ahead. These Cuban officials at middle ranks know how to mouth the Marxist-Leninist slogans but they seldom let ideology get in the way of ambition or practical action. The Marxist-Leninist ideology is in any case sufficiently vague that almost any activity can be rationalized under its rubric. Hence public discussion in Cuba is laden with ideological posturings but private conversations with middle-to-upper ranking officials can and do take place on a purely pragmatic plane.[5]

At the mass level, Marxist-Leninist ideology carries almost no resonance at all. This is still the situation after strenuous efforts over thirty-two years to infuse ideology and political content into the educational system, the mass media, and all areas of national life. The Cuban people have just not bought the message. Many are still attracted to "socialism" as an ideal, but just as many blame socialism for their present problems. The slogans remain omnipresent on walls and billboards and the Cuban people are nationalistic; but infused with Marxism-Leninism, no. The ideology is not relevant to most Cubans' lives, it is too abstract and "foreign," and the Cubans have more important concerns (food, housing, depressed living standards) on their minds than ideology. In public Castro has pushed the ideology, emphasized "moral incentives" over material ones (an admonition that after thirty-two years of hardship has worn very thin), and sought to create a "new Cuban man." But so far there are few signs that the ideology has deeply infused Cuba or that it has been internalized by very many.

Meanwhile, Castro's appeal among the Latin American Left has declined precipitously. As Latin America during the 1980s moved back toward democracy, and as the obvious failures of Cuba and other socialist regimes became manifestly apparent, the attractiveness of Marxism-Leninism and of the Cuban Revolution as a model for other countries to emulate lost their appeal. In country after country, throughout the hemisphere, USIA surveys reveal, the population prefers not Marxism-Leninism (or authoritarianism either) but representative, democratic government.[6] Many on the Latin Left have abandoned guerrilla campaigns in favor of electoral politics. The steam has gone out of the hemispheric revolutionary ethos.

Perhaps the most telling current sign of ideological weakness in Cuba is that the regime has lost its direction, its sense of purpose, its vision. In years past the Cuban leadership consoled itself even among all the hardships by saying that it represented the wave of the future. But almost no one believes that anymore, either in Cuba or elsewhere in what remains of the socialist world. Few Cubans at middle-to-upper levels are convinced that they are still in the vanguard of history. This shift in how its own leaders think has done much to sap energy from the Revolution. The Revolution has lost its self-image.[7] In the process its self-justifications ("sacrifice now for a better future") have been undermined and so has a great deal of the legitimacy of the regime. There is presently lots of paralysis in Cuba and no one is sure of where the country is going. The global crisis of Marxist-Leninist ideology has not only drained enthusiasm from the regime but has also undermined its very purpose and reason for being. Cuba has seen the future—and it has proved to be a shambles.

Hence with neither Fidel Castro, the apparatchiks, nor the general public believing strongly in Marxism-Leninism, and with the fundamental legitimacy of the Revolution being questioned for the first time, the regime has a severe ideological crisis on its hands. The moral foundations of the Revolution are being eroded, nationalism in the absence of much economic growth has proved an insufficient and rather tired basis, and very few people really believe the ideology anymore—if they ever did. What has taken its place? Nothing so far—except that as in all communist regimes we have now witnessed the rise of a new generation that is neither very ideological nor dedicated to sacrifice, the rising influence on that generation of the wish for material goods, and an increasing desire for the basic bedrocks of Western civilization: not just rock music, Coke, and jeans but also freedom, democracy, and human rights. These "countercultural" trends now rising in Cuba, in ways parallel to their earlier development in Eastern Europe and the Soviet Union, may augur as much trouble for the regime in the future as does the decline in attractiveness of the regime's Marxist-Leninist ideology.

The Crisis of Institutions

The Cuban Revolution has never been strongly institutionalized. The Cuban tradition historically has been one of personalism in politics, not bureaucratic organization. During the late 1950s Fidel Castro came to personify the Revolution and during the 1960s he was its one-man decision maker. He was universally referred to by his first name, a sign of both affection and personalization. Castro's style was to ride around the island in his jeep, soaking in the plaudits while also making ad hoc, spur-of-the-moment decisions about agrarian reform, industrialization, and other matters that he knew little about. Castro's personal style was highly publicized at the time and to some it seemed romantic and endearing. But it helped ruin the effort at agricultural diversification in Cuba, produced a series of wrong decisions about industrialization, and helped precipitate the downward turn of the Cuban economy. Cuba has still not recovered from these early mistakes. But through it all Castro remained the great *caudillo* (man-on-horseback; nowadays, jeepback) of the Revolution, a heroic and romantic picture to be sure but one that proved ruinous economically for Cuba.[8]

During the 1970s, with Cuba now absolutely dependent on the Soviet Union for its livelihood, the Soviets insisted on greater regularity, normalcy, and rationality in decision making. The Soviet system is rationalistic and bureaucratic, and the Soviets neither understood nor appreciated the flamboyant, populist, and charismatic style of Fidel Castro.

They insisted that the Revolution settle down and become more routinized. Hence an elaborate bureaucratic structure was put in place, modeled on that of the Soviet Union, that presumably would rationalize Cuban decision making.

But after two decades of "bureaucratization," Fidel Castro still makes all the important decisions in Cuba. Small, routine matters can now be handled in the bureaucracy but on the large issues Castro remains the key person. Without his approval, almost nothing gets done. Castro must still be consulted on virtually everything—including often the small issues supposed to be handled bureaucratically. Hence despite the growth of a "bureaucratic model" of decision making, the personalistic or charismatic one continues to coexist alongside of it, often completely overshadowing the more routinized one.[9]

Cuba thus has the worst of all possible worlds. On the one hand it has Fidel Castro, a clever man but one whose megalomania, resentments concerning the United States, incredible ego, poor decisions, and fantastic sense of self-importance (the world is his stage, not just Cuba) have been both the cement and the undoing of the Revolution. But now Castro is aging and fading (more on this below), a man whose bluster and sheer presence are no longer sufficient to keep the Revolution on track. Castro still has considerable moral authority as the *líder máximo* of the Revolution, but increasingly he is being ignored or bypassed by the rising younger generation. The unraveling that will almost certainly follow Castro's demise is the fate to which all regimes so heavily based on one-man charismatic rule ultimately are doomed.

At the same time the bureaucratic institutions created a few short years ago to please the Soviets remain tenuous. It is the familiar Latin American pattern of creating perfect institutional structures on paper for the outside world to see and admire, meanwhile operating by means of other structures. At the most basic, grass-roots level the Committees for the Defense of the Revolution (CDRs), neighborhood and block associations that chiefly performed vigilante functions, have not been well received by most Cubans and have begun to fade into obscurity. They are seldom utilized anymore and for fewer purposes; certainly the CDRs that regularly spy on and report any deviance among neighbors could not serve as a future base for representative and democratic government.

The several mass organizations for youth, women, etc., whose creation in the 1960s was greeted warmly by supporters of the Revolution, are now viewed as simply organs of the state, subordinate to state authority, and official mouthpieces of the regime. Their memberships are declining as more and more Cubans—like their Eastern European and Soviet counterparts before them—have come to value genuinely pluralist and independent associations.

The bureaucratic structure patterned after the older Soviet model has become just as venal and unproductive as its parent. It is riddled with graft, sinecures, special favoritism (increasingly so), shortages, and inefficiencies. Plus it has little actual decision-making authority. Cuba seems unhappily to have combined the worst features of Soviet and Latin American bureaucracy. Hence in the current crisis where Cubans are waiting once again for directions from Castro as to the future course of the Revolution, so far they have not received many answers; worse, it is no longer clear that Castro can still take Cuba in directions it may not want to go.

The Communist party has become like the parties in other communist regimes, an elite organization whose members are dedicated mainly to hanging onto power and preserving their own "percs" and privileges. At Cuba's lovely Verdedero Beach, an entire, separate peninsula has been reserved for the grandiose mansions of high Party officials, access to which is prohibited by metal gates and armed guards. Party members monopolize all positions of influence in the regime, and the Party itself has come to serve as an avenue of upward mobility for able, talented Cubans seeking to rise to the top of the pyramid. But these are all self-serving functions; many observers are not convinced that the Party has the cadres and trained leaders to govern Cuba after Castro eventually departs from the scene.

That leaves the army, headed by Fidel's little brother Raúl. Raúl is the heir-apparent, the Soviets' favorite because his orthodoxy is unquestioned; but Raúl has several chips on his shoulder, is not well liked by the Cuban people, and lacks Fidel's presence and charisma. The Cuban armed forces are the largest, best-trained, best-equipped, and by far the most experienced military in Latin America—perhaps in the world, given their involvement in so many armed conflicts in recent years, ranging from Central America to southern Africa to Ethiopia to South Yemen to Cambodia.

But the armed forces have not been immune from the growing divisions and even dissension in Cuban society more generally. Many Cuban families lost sons in Angola; several thousand troops also returned from the African campaigns with AIDS. The trial and then execution of General Arnaldo Ochoa and several of his aides on drug-running charges also revealed fissures within the armed forces. The earlier prediction was that once Castro goes, and given the debilities of the bureaucracy and the Communist party, if there were any sign of the regime coming unraveled, the army might well take over. That could still occur—or the army could serve as the power behind the throne propping up a Party dictatorship. But now in the wake of the Ochoa trial a new complication has arisen: the possibility of the army also fragmenting, with various civilian factions aligned with different military factions and all of them competing for power. In any of these cases, with the army in power, so close to the surface of power as to make the familiar civil-military distinction all but meaningless, or with military factions overlapping with civilian factions and competing for power, one wonders how much has really changed from the praetorian politics of prerevolutionary Cuba.

Crisis of Society

Cuba does not have any serious ethnic or regional-separatist movement with which to contend, as do the Soviet Union and some Eastern European states. But it does have a number of other social cleavages with which it must deal and that have the potential to change Cuban society fundamentally or to tear it apart.

To begin, there are sharp generational differences.[10] Castro himself is now in his sixties, paunchy, graying, and balding; most of the old guard of the Communist party are in their seventies. The old guard monopolizes most of the important positions in the regime, meanwhile separating itself more and more from the daily life of the Revolution and ruling in an increasingly imperious manner. The next generation, consisting of many very talented Cubans, persons in their forties who may only dimly remember the Revolution of the late 1950s and who are the Cuban version of the Soviet gray flannel suit types—not ideologues but bureaucrats and technicians—is not only impatient with the inefficiencies of the old leadership but also wants to take over their percs and positions—the sooner the better. In interviews, many of these younger-generation officials were remarkably candid in saying that they thought the Revolution took some wrong turns in the early 1960s and in criticizing the senior leadership, even Castro.

By now, however, there is also a third revolutionary generation of young people in their early twenties and teens. Cuba, like other Third World countries, has a very young population with over a majority under twenty-five years old. Despite all the educational thought control, the propaganda of the government over thirty years, and the concerted effort to create the "new Cuban man" (socialist, loyal to the Revolution, not self-serving) by concentrating on the youth, the regime seems to have lost the battle. It may have been more successful in the countryside (although in this century the countryside has never ruled Cuba), but among youths in Havana little evidence exists that the new man or woman has emerged. Cuban young people have also been strongly affected by what Lucian Pye once called the "world culture"[11] of rock music (including now its protest lyrics), dress, and behavior emanating from the West. They want more freedom, they would like to be able to travel, and they wonder why they must continue to sacrifice for a regime that does not seem to be going anywhere. These young people are patriotic and nationalistic, and doubtless many of them would be willing to defend and maybe even die for the Revolution; but discontent is simmering among the youth, as among the general population, and in the present difficult circumstances of Cuba it will not do anything but get worse.

Cuban young people interviewed by the author found the regime boring and out of date. Unless one is a part of the university-educated elite and a member of the Party, there is not much to do or look forward to. A person cannot travel, move, change jobs, or do much of anything without the regime's permission. Few incentives exist beyond the "moral" ones, and after three decades these admonitions to work and sacrifice more are wearing thin. Cuban young people have no money to spend and nothing to spend it on even if they had some. During the week there is nothing to do in once-lively Havana, and on weekends the big thing to do is to walk (no one has cars) to the waterfront area for an ice cream cone. That is the extent of social life because restaurants and clubs like the Tropicana (whose show is a relic of the Batista era, designed for tourists, with the showgirls wearing bananas and coconuts on their heads à la some old Carmen Miranda movie) are too expensive, Cubans may be refused entry, and they are there mainly to earn foreign exchange from the few visitors in Cuba. A later, more risqué show at the Tropicana is reserved for high Cuban officials; once again, common people are excluded.

Nor have the regime's vaunted social programs worked as well as claimed. The Cuban economy has been in difficult straits from the beginning (discussed below), but for a long time the regime and its sympathizers abroad consoled themselves by pointing to its successes in social programs: housing, health care, and education. The housing program, by Castro's own admission, has been the least successful: the housing situation in Havana is terrible and rapidly getting worse as old homes deteriorate and few new houses are built to replace them, while the apartment houses built by the state in the suburbs and interior towns are shoddy and never enough to keep up with demand.

Cuba earlier made major studies in medicine, but now it is facing renewed shortages of medical personnel and facilities; and indications are that malnutrition and malnutrition-related diseases are again on the rise and that life expectancy is going down. Similarly with education: in the early 1960s Cuba concentrated heavily on education and significantly reduced illiteracy (which even before the Revolution was very low—25 percent—by Latin American standards). But since that early spurt, the educational efforts have flagged and functional illiteracy is again rising. The economy simply has not generated the resources to maintain the educational or other social programs at adequate levels. In addition, there is some, although still inconclusive, evidence that the earlier figures may have been "cooked"—that is, exaggerated to show the regime in a better light than it deserved.[12]

Meanwhile, because of the unfulfilled promises, discontent with the Revolution has been rising. The regime is increasingly isolated, Cubans are becoming more cynical, they are tired of waiting for promised "better times," tired of the endless sacrifices for what looks like a gloomy future. The Cubans complain mightily that they never have enough money, that there is nothing to buy in the shops, that their currency is worthless. Like the Russians and Poles, they are increasingly impatient with the rationing and the long lines, with the shoddy goods they finally receive at the front of those lines, and with the special stores and privileges enjoyed by the Party and regime elite. Cuban society is not only fraying at the edges; it is beginning to unravel.

Crisis of Leadership

Fidel Castro has passed his sixtieth birthday and is visibly aging. His famous beard is now gray and scraggly, he is no longer the young, dashing, dynamic leader of yesterday, and up close he looks old and pasty. There are reports that he has lung cancer. To put it crudely, it now looks like although the CIA's exploding cigars failed to get him, the real things may have.

Crude jokes circulate in Havana about the longevity of Castro's rule, which is now thirty-two years. Some Cuban cynics mutter that Castro wishes to surpass the record of Paraguay's Alfredo Stroessner (thirty-five years) as the longest-lived dictator in all of Latin America in the twentieth century. There was a wild celebration in Asunción when Stroessner surpassed the previous thirty-one–year record of the Dominican Republic's bloody tyrant Rafael Trujillo, and now Fidel has surpassed Trujillo as well. A certain perverse pride exists among dictators in these matters.

Cubans are also beginning to question and make jokes about Castro's *machismo.* In Latin American society, when a regime's masculinity is questioned and joked about, that is usually a sure sign that a long-lived dictator is in trouble, that he will soon face serious challenges. It is the metaphor of the bullfight: the bulls *know* when the bullfighter is scared, past his prime, and vulnerable. New challenges to the *lider's* position begin to be contemplated. It is that time in Havana, a time of thinking about and making incipient challenges to Castro's long rule. When the leader's own people start making crude jokes about the leader's immortality or even virility, it is time for him to start thinking about stepping down—or to turn up the terror, which also in due course usually produces the regime's demise.[13] Fidel Castro appears more and more like one of those aging, rotting tyrants out of the fictional bestseller *One Hundred Years of Solitude*—ironic since the author, Gabriel García Márquez, has long been a Castro admirer.

Castro is seen even by his own subordinates as increasingly out of touch. He is still honored and deferred to by subordinates as the great hero of the Revolution; Castro still has considerable moral authority. But while honoring him in the breach, they also increasingly ignore his advice. At a press conference in Havana held for some visiting Latin American journalists, for example, the visitors laughed at Castro's jokes and were properly deferential, but it was plain they did not take him overly seriously either. They said "Yes, Fidel" and "You're right, Fidel" but without either enthusiasm or conviction. While Castro remains the great spokesman and *caudillo* of the Revolution, he is also seen as anachronistic and is less and less listened to. As in Spain in the early 1970s with Franco, the post-dictatorial transition has begun in Cuba even while the dictator is still in power.[14]

What will happen once Castro goes is very uncertain and—with the malaise of so many Marxist-Leninist regimes—increasingly more so. Cuba has a large number of bright, able, skilled, middle-level persons in the Party and in the regime, but none of them has the charisma or the stature to fill Castro's shoes. And with the bureaucracy so inefficient, it is doubtful that Cuban communism could survive without major alterations unless there is a single charismatic person to hold it together. But Castro, fearing potential challengers to his absolute authority, has never allowed anyone else to build up a personal base or to have responsibilities that might have provided training for the succession. Those who have developed such ambitions, such as General Ochoa, have usually been quickly disposed of. The Soviets have also been worrying about the problem of the succession, and their solution has been to try to strengthen the Party and improve the bureaucracy. But these steps may not be enough to hold Cuba together in the post-Castro era.

Raúl Castro, the armed forces head, may already have been designated to succeed his brother Fidel. Raúl is said to be a more orthodox communist than Fidel and to be more acceptable to the Soviets. But he is said to have been involved in some shady dealings, is thought of as petty, and lacks his older brother's sense of the historic. Raúl may lack Fidel's charisma but with the Russians' support and as head of the armed forces he has some obvious advantages.

It seems highly unlikely that when Castro leaves the scene, the Cuban regime will disintegrate. It seems far more likely that a combination of Raúl, the army, and the Party will provide continuity. Nevertheless, one should not discount the tensions and pressures, both internally and stemming from the external environment. Fidel's are *very* big shoes to fill; the regime faces numerous internal tensions; and pressures from the outside (Moscow, Washington, and Miami) are intensifying. Once the great *líder* of the Revolution departs, it would not be surprising to see some of the threads that hold the regime together begin to fray, come apart, maybe even unravel over the long term. If these developments were to be accompanied by widespread expressions of discontent in Havana, an uprising in one of Cuba's provinces, or an exile invasion, the regime could very quickly have a severe crisis on its hands.

The Crisis of the Economy

The Cuban economy has long been a troublesome issue for the regime.[15] Now the economy promises to become an even worse disaster, undermining further the regime's claims to accomplishments in the social area, destroying morale and hope, and ultimately threatening Cuba's communist stability.

Some perspective is necessary. Before the Revolution Cuba was one of the highest (third in manufacturing, first in transportation, fifth in per capita income) ranking nations in Latin America on various indices of economic development. Cuba was not at all, as the regime's propaganda and its foreign apologists tried to portray it, a backward, poverty-ridden country.

During the first decade of the Revolution, 1959–69, the Cuban economy was ruinously managed. Ché Guevara, one of the heroes of the Revolution, was put in charge. Guevara may have been a heroic guerrilla fighter but he knew nothing about economics and was a terrible administrator. First Cuba tried heavy industrialization but after building expensive factories it found that it could import the products cheaper than it could produce them domestically. The still-empty factories (white elephants) that dot the Cuban countryside are illustrations of the classic mistakes of an incompetently run, centrally planned economy. Meanwhile, Cuba neglected agriculture, which was soon in ruins. Then in the late 1960s Cuba went back to "king sugar" on a massive scale; industrialization was abandoned.

Today Cuba is far more dependent on its historic single crop, sugar, than it was before the Revolution. Sugar accounts for approximately 90 percent of Cuba's export earnings, as compared with only 75 percent thirty-five years ago. The shift back to sugar has come at a time of disastrously low prices for sugar internationally and when everyone knows that sugar has no future in world markets. At about eight cents per pound, the world market price for sugar is about half of Cuba's production costs. But in recent years most countries, including the United States, Western Europe, and the Soviet Union, have become largely self-sufficient in sugar, thanks to increased sugar-beet production. Many grocery stores give away five-pound bags of sugar free as a promotion, always a sign of low world market prices. In addition, consumer preferences are changing: we now drink light beer instead of sugared beer, diet colas instead of the real thing, and saccharine in our coffee. Finally, technology has overtaken the Cubans: sweeteners can now be produced in laboratories (what are called "left-handed sugar molecules") in ways that yield real sugar but without the calories. When this product comes on the market in a few years, it will devastate the few remaining economies still heavily dependent on sugar. Recognizing these dismal trends, other historic sugar producers like the Philippines and the Dominican Republic have been diversifying out of sugar. But not Cuba, which has become more rather than less dependent on sugar.

Cuba's efforts to diversify its economy have meanwhile foundered. Industry is practically nonexistent, there is no business or commerce to speak of, diversification in other crops has not worked out chiefly because Cuba's "natural" market, the United States, is closed to it, and tourism—though now being encouraged again—is still in its primitive stages. The hotels are old and dingy (though some new ones are being built), service (which to the socialist Cubans smacks of subservience) is practically nonexistent, the soap doesn't produce lather, and the toilet paper is more like sandpaper—familiar problems in socialist tourism. Our group, which stayed in the Havana Libre (the Havana Hilton in earlier times), was forewarned that the rooms would all be bugged, but of course the Cubans also managed to blame that on the preceding Batista regime—as though the technology had not been upgraded in the last thirty years. Recently a deal was worked out between Cuba and a Spanish consortium to build new hotels, upgrade the service, and hire and fire whom the Spanish choose; but Cuba's relations with Spain are now at a very low point, and it will take years and maybe decades before Cuba is ready for large-scale tourism again. Plus such tourism, by bringing in foreign ideas, tastes, and lifestyles, has the capacity to further undermine the regime, as it did Franco's a quarter of a century ago.

Cuba's economy is in such deep trouble that both its economists and its people despair. Earlier the hope had always been held out by the regime that sacrifices now would result in improvements later on. But almost no Cubans maintain that hope anymore. Sacrifices have just led to more sacrifices, never to improvements. The prospects for the Cuban economy are dismal. Cuba is trying to become more self-sufficient but meanwhile the standard of living is actually declining. The regime has put the country on a "war" footing, with greater rationing of scarce goods, reductions in food allotments, bread rationing, and calls for still more sacrifices. The Cuban people do not *look* healthy: it is said that the only fat things in Havana are the cigars, and even those have suffered a decline in quality. The possibilities are growing—and most Cubans recognize this—that the economy may *never* recover. But if the economy fails to deliver, the social programs that are the regime's chief claim to accomplishment will continue to run down. The regime cannot in this day and age continue to exist on the basis of "moral incentives" alone; eventually it must start to deliver real goods and services—or else!

Cuba's economic performance has been dismal in comparison not just with neighboring capitalist countries but also with socialist ones. Previously, poorer countries like the Dominican Republic, which historically has always lagged behind the more richly endowed Cuba on various indices of economic development, has by now passed Cuba in terms of per capita income. The larger countries of South America and Mexico have all, economically speaking, left Cuba in the dust. The English-speaking islands of the Caribbean have similarly prospered while Cuba has floundered. Even in Central America, beset by immense social and political problems in part caused by Cuba's meddling and sponsorship of guerrilla activities, economic performance has been better than Cuba's.

The most interesting comparisons are with other socialist or formerly socialist nations. In that comparison Cuba also comes out badly. Even with their upheavals and economic inefficiencies of recent years, for example, Eastern Europe, China, the Soviet Union, and North Korea have all done better than Cuba. Cuba is in fact the only one of the socialist countries, to say nothing of the capitalist ones, that has shown almost no growth at all in the last thirty years. In some key sectors Cuba is still trying to catch up to the production levels of the 1950s.

Into this economic breach caused by bad planning and disastrous economic management came the Soviet Union. Soviet subsidies became the major factor in the Cuban economy, helping to keep afloat this island economy that would otherwise sink beneath the Caribbean. The Soviet subsidy, chiefly in the form of paying inflated prices for Cuban sugar that the Soviets do not need and providing Cuba with cheap petroleum, was in the range of $5 billion per year, or $14 million per day. This subsidy is more than the United States provides to any country in the world. Since Castro's purse strings are in Moscow, it is clear that the Soviet Union is often able to dictate Cuban policy, both domestic and foreign. As Robert Packenham's careful analysis has shown, what the Cuban Revolution has done over thirty years is both to devastate the economy and to substitute one form of dependency (on the United States) by an even worse kind (the Soviets).[16]

But that was all before the economic and political disintegration of the Soviet Union. In a time of economic hardships at home, the Soviets are not eager to take on more Third World basket cases and they have become increasingly impatient with the Cuban one. Soviet and Eastern European officials in Havana are unanimous in their derogatory comments about the Cuban "management style" and especially about Fidel Castro—comments often laced with cultural and racial prejudice. Cuba is probably still too valuable a proxy in the Third World and too much a thorn in the side of the United States for the Soviets simply to give up on it. However, the Soviets are now decreasing their trade with and aid to Cuba and telling the Cubans they will have to find new markets and be more on their own.[17] The declining economic support from the Soviets explains Castro's testiness toward them in recent speeches, his willingness to open Cuba to greater tourism, and his desire to gain access to U.S. markets. Meanwhile, the directives have gone out to the Cuban people: still more sacrifices, greater self-sufficiency, more rationing, and the economy placed on a "war" footing.

Crisis of Morale

After thirty-two years of revolutionary upheaval, of fiery speeches but limited real accomplishments to show for all the sacrifices, Cuba is facing a crisis. In addition to all the concrete manifestations of Cuba's troubles discussed earlier, a good deal of the spirit has gone out of the Cuban Revolution. The people on the street are grumbling, no one enthusiastically supports the Revolution, the image of the regime's invincibility is fast fading. The élan is dying, among both Cubans and Cuba's earlier supporters abroad. Cuba is like Poland in the 1970s, with vast discontents, widespread cynicism and murmuring of complaints, and the portents of greater upheavals to come.

Cuba no longer represents the wave of the future, only a dismal past. Some Cubans still go through the motions of waxing enthusiastic for the Revolution (that is expected and even required of them) but genuine emotion is lacking. What was earlier felt as an intoxicating explosion and surge of liberation and heady optimism in the first years of the Revolution is no longer there. It has become a dull, mostly boring routine. By the same token the liberating appeal that the Revolution had for the rest of Latin America in the early 1960s has now gone—except in very limited intellectual circles and among persons who have not seen Cuba firsthand.

Cuba is not a very happy country. There is little spontaneity, enthusiasm, or joie de vivre. The vitality and restless energy for which Cuba was famous have been sapped. The endless lines, shortages, and rationing have taken an enormous toll. Little money is available to spend and, in any case, the shops—except the special stores reserved for the elite—are empty of goods to buy. Once dynamic and bustling Havana has become a dull, gray, crumbling city. The *system* has grown to be a burden that Cubans bear but no longer have enthusiasm for.

Many Cubans recognize, further, that democracy and human rights are the future of Latin America, not Marxism-Leninism. Cuba has made some half-hearted efforts to align itself with these trends but since it has no democracy and its human rights record is abysmal, these steps are seen as hollow and hypocritical. Cuba has repeatedly arrested those who dare to speak out in favor of human rights; its record on human rights is so bad that it has by now prompted United Nations investigations. Some members of the regime recognize that Cuba is out of step with the times and the democratizing currents in Latin America. They even express their disappointments to visitors while also recognizing that they cannot do much to change the system—at least until Castro is gone. They also understand that for a Marxist-Leninist regime, especially, to be so out of step with *history* is very dangerous for its future.

Cuba is sullen and its people often bitter. They don't like but cannot change the system, so they have resigned themselves to it. There is widespread complaining, which the regime often tolerates as a safety valve to let off steam, but no real organized opposition. The Committees in Defense of the Revolution and the totalitarian controls take care of that. In my long walking tours around Havana in neighborhoods off the main streets, countless people would sidle up and pop the question, "How can I get to Miami?" For Cuba is an island fortress and it is not easy to get in or out. One cannot, as in Central America, pay a few gratuities to get across the borders and into the land of milk and honey, the United States. One senses in Cuba what one also felt in Eastern Europe before the recent revolutionary openings: widespread discontent but, because there is little one can do about it, also bitterness, resentment, and fear. Cubans are suffocating, sense their isolation, and know the bell is tolling for the regime; yet they are also demoralized, sullen, repressed, and understand that public expressions of discontent would bring them only trouble. Defections, however, are on the rise; and my estimate is that, if the boats were made available à la Mariel and they were free to go, fully a third to a half of the Cubans would leave.

Even among high-ranking Communist party, foreign ministry, and government officials with whom I met—privately and in places where the conversations could not be overheard—the sense is strong that the Revolution has failed and requires new direction. There is now widespread questioning of Castro's leadership and thinly veiled criticism of the system. Even more surprising, since it came from senior officials, was the idea that Cuba had taken some wrong steps, made some wrong decisions in the early 1960s, and now wishes it could take them back. The two most important mistakes indicated by these officials were (1) the decision to transform Cuba into a wholly socialist economy rather than a more mixed kind; and (2) the decision to cut Cuba off entirely from the United States (its main, closest, and best market and still—not the Soviet Union—the chief magnet and focus of attention for most Cubans) and to realign itself entirely within the Soviet orbit.

But these are the two main initiatives that define the nature of the Cuban Revolution. Take them away and there is no more reason for the Revolution. So when such comments come from high government officials, it means that they are questioning the very bedrocks of the Revolution. But these are also realistic persons: they know that there is no turning back the clock and that they are stuck with the system they have. That is probably what makes Cuba now such a sad and melancholy country: the widespread sense of terrible mistakes made but an equally strong sense that it is now too late to do anything about them, that Fidel and the leadership could *never* admit that they had made mistakes even if privately everyone acknowledges that, and therefore that they are condemned to live with the system they have, however woeful it may be.

Cuba's Isolation Internationally

Cuba and its Revolution have become increasingly isolated internationally. The heady days of Cuba's leadership in the nonaligned movement and as an inspiration to revolutionaries everywhere are over. On all fronts the regime seems to be out of step with its own area and with the world.[18] Given Cuba's other debilities, one cannot be sure how long the Revolution can stand up under all the pressures.

To begin, Cuba has lost almost all its allies and supporters within the Caribbean/Central American region. The Grenadan revolutionary regime has been ousted, Nicaragua's Sandinistas have been repudiated by that country's electorate, and Castro's latter-day buddy, Manuel Noriega, lies rotting in a U.S. jail. In addition, and with Soviet pressure, the Faribundo Martí National Liberation Front (FMLN) guerrillas have been weakened and have hence entered into negotiations for peace with the government in El Salvador. Even Mexico, which had long befriended the Cuban Revolution and used that policy to tweak the United States, is now putting distance between itself and Cuba. All these changes have left Cuba without significant allies and supporters anywhere in Latin America.

During the 1980s Cuba succeeded in reestablishing normal state-to-state relations, broken since the early 1960s, with a number of Latin American countries, and has heralded that as a triumph for the Revolution and a defeat for the U.S. policy of isolating Cuba. But there is another and far more persuasive explanation. For the fact is that Cuba is now dealing from a position of relative weakness and the states with which it reopened relations, from relative strength. Unlike in the 1960s, very few of the Latin American nations feel threatened by Cuba any longer, by the example of its revolution or by its sponsorship of guerrilla movements within their borders. The Cuban Revolution is no longer attractive to these other countries' populations nor do they feel intimidated any longer—except perhaps El Salvador and one or two other of the small and weakly institutionalized countries—by Cuba's capacity to stimulate violent threats to their stability. Rather than a sign of Cuba's success, therefore, the new diplomatic relations with other Latin American countries is a sign of their success, their greater confidence and institutionalization, and of Cuba's debilities. Reestablishing relations with Cuba may carry some trade advantages for the other Latin American countries, enables them to satisfy their own domestic lefts, and is a sign of their maturity and self-confidence. They are emphatically *not* a measure of Cuba's revolutionary successes; in fact, just the opposite is the case.

Meanwhile, Cuba has lost further ground diplomatically and politically elsewhere in the world. When a large number of Cubans seeking political asylum took refuge in the Spanish Embassy in Havana, Cuba invaded the embassy, treated Spain and its diplomats shabbily, and thus squandered all the goodwill that it had tried to develop with Felipe González's socialist government. Cuba's relations with other West European socialist parties and governments, and with the Socialist Internationale, has also been eroding. Cuba's many human rights abuses, its economic failures and mismanagement, and its rejection of any Soviet-style *glasnot* and *perestroika* have further harmed the regime's reputation in Western Europe. Meanwhile, as the regimes in Eastern Europe have democratized and undergone transformation, they are also reassessing their older close relations with Cuba and finding the regime less than satisfactory. Vaclav Havel has been particularly pointed in urging Cuba to try a whiff of freedom.

The problem for Cuba is that it is simply out of touch and out of step with global trends. The winds in the world are blowing toward greater freedom, democracy, and human rights, not less as in Cuba. All over, people want the freedom to travel, to speak as they please, to behave as they please, to dress as they please, to listen to rock music as they please—not dull conformity as in Cuba. What we might call the "global culture" (freedom, human rights, consumerism) is having its impact worldwide—but not in Cuba. Cuba is one of those unfortunate countries, along with Albania, North Korea, and Vietnam that not only remains locked into an essentially Stalinist political structure but also refuses to change. However, even in these latter Stalinist holdouts, at least some modest change is now under way; Cuba, in contrast, has refused to bend at all and seems intent on strengthening its repressive armature rather than opening the country up.

All these and other trends have increasingly estranged Cuba from its longtime friend and sponsor, the Soviet Union. The Soviets have long despaired of Castro and Cuban decision making and have tried to introduce greater rationality. They have also long subsidized the Cuban Revolution because Cuba was a useful ally and proxy, capable of wreaking vast destabilization on Latin America and driving the United States to do some irrational things. But now the Soviets can no longer afford this enormous drain on their economy, Latin America is not viewed as an important place for their diplomacy, and their relations with the U.S. are clearly far more important to the Soviets than their relations with Cuba.[19]

Cuba has explicit rejected Mikhail Gorbachev's calls for *glasnost* and *perestroika* in favor of a call for "rectification."[20] Rectification means essentially a return to moral incentives, ideological purity, central planning, and one-man rule—all the elements of the 1960s that got Cuba in so many difficulties in the first place. Rectification has been portrayed in the press as Castro's answer to Gorbachev's challenges, an alternative to the Soviet and East European reforms. It is probably that—and also considerably less. For *glasnost* and *perestroika* in Cuba, if ever tried, have the potential to be profoundly destabilizing. Only a secure and well-institutionalized country could manage such transformation successfully. Cuba emphatically is not well institutionalized. The real reason for Castro's rejection of the Gorbachev formula, hence, is fear that his own power would thereby be eroded and his revolutionary regime possibly destroyed. Castro himself recognizes the weakness and discontent in his regime and has concluded that he and the Revolution cannot take such chances. While Castro is still in power, there will be little *glasnost* and *perestroika*.

Cuba lies so close to the regime's "enemy," the United States, is so far from the Soviet Union, is so isolated internationally, and has such internal weaknesses that it feels it cannot take a chance on such a thoroughgoing reform. But Castro has to respond in some way to the changes occurring in the Eastern Bloc and to maintain a rationale for his own actions, and so he has decided on rectification as the slogan. But rectification is a dead end, a throwback to the past, a reversion to all the past policies that had so damaged the Revolution. Seen from inside Cuba, rectification is not a progressive step but a reactionary one. It symbolizes not strength but fear of change. Like Cuba's foreign policy "accomplishments" in recent years, rectification is a sign of weakness, not of success.

At the same time the Soviets keep putting the pressure on. They have been meeting with the Cuban business community in Miami to talk trade and commerce.[21] They are talking of using Miami instead of Havana as a hub for the Soviet airline Aeroflot. Their aid and subsidies to Castro are all declining. All these steps have added to the isolation of Cuba—and to its paranoia.

CONCLUSION

After thirty-two years one would expect the Cuban Revolution to have consolidated itself, to have become institutionalized, and to have cemented its base, to be secure and self-confident. But in fact what one finds in Cuba is terrible insecurity, often weak institutions, a lack of self-confidence, severe uncertainty about the future, a nonconsolidated regime. Cuba faces all the general crises faced recently by other communist regimes—a crisis of ideology, a crisis of institutions, a crisis of society, a crisis of leadership, a crisis of the economy, and a crisis of morale—and it faces additional crises that these other states do not, stemming from its international isolation and its preoccupation with and proximity to the United States. Rather than constituting a strong and well-entrenched regime, Cuba seems very precarious and vulnerable indeed. Cuba is, to be sure, a totalitarian state with all the mechanisms of control characteristic of such regimes, but upon close examination it is apparent that the strings that hold the whole system together are quite thin and weak. In these facts we also have reasons both for Cuba's frenzied diplomatic activity in recent years and for its strong rejection of Gorbachev-like reforms of *glasnost* and *perestroika*.

Cuba has all the problems faced by Eastern Europe and the Soviet Union in the 1980s—and more besides. We now realize just how fragile, despite their totalitarianism, these states were, so the news of Cuba's vulnerabilities should not come as a great surprise. Still, after more than three decades in power, one expects to find a strong, monolithic regime; instead one sees a weak, debilitated state, seething with tensions and uncertainties, fragile and not at all confident about the future. The Cuban economy is (there are no other words for it) a disaster area, the regime is only incompletely institutionalized, and societal tensions are rising. Castro's leadership is being increasingly questioned, the morale of the Revolution is very low, and the regime seems to have lost its ideological and programmatic direction. The Cubans do not like their Soviet and East European "allies" (who live in unfriendly compounds with high walls and make racial and cultural jokes about them), and now at the official level relations have soured as well. Thirty-two years after the Revolution it is still the United States—and its culture as well as policy—that remains the chief preoccupation in Cuba, not the Soviet Union.

It is from these weaknesses, tensions, and discontents that one also explains Cuba's recent policy initiatives. Cuba's reaching out to various Latin American countries and their reciprocity stems from Cuba's weaknesses and these other countries' strengths, not the other way around. It also stems from Cuba's profound unhappiness with the Soviet Union and the feeling that the Soviets have abandoned both socialism and Cuba. Cuba realizes that the Soviet Union cannot continue propping up its economy so massively as in the past and therefore it needs to expand its trade and diplomatic contracts with other nations. Similarly with rectification: this new strategy of going back to strict ideology and central control is not something Cuba follows out of choice but because it recognizes its weaknesses, the simmering discontents, and fears that if it follows a Soviet or East European policy of openness and pluralism, the entire edifice of Castro's rule may tumble down. The new Cuban foreign policy and rectification reflect Cuba's weaknesses, not strength.

Cuba is not about to collapse tomorrow. It still has considerable strengths and reserves, including a massive coercive apparatus. Castro's personality and moral legitimacy, despite all the fissures and explosive pressures, will probably hold the Revolution together at least for a time. Meanwhile, the gradual unraveling of the Cuban social, economic, and political fabric will continue. Once Castro leaves the scene it may be that Raúl, the army, and the Party will be able to hold the regime together in altered form. But my strong impression after two visits to Cuba and numerous interviews with high officials is that Cuba is a veritable boiling cauldron of tensions and simmering discontents. Hence to the many Cubans in Miami whose bumper stickers proclaim "Next Year in Havana," the advice would be, don't pack your bags yet. On the other hand it might not be a bad idea to at least get them out of the closet.

15

South American Domestic Politics and Foreign Policy

This chapter explores the domestic bases for foreign policy changes in South America and their implications for U.S. policy. It focuses on the following areas: the transitions to democracy in the region, rising nationalism, strengthened political and economic institutions, European influences, the debt crisis, the drug issue, public opinion, and the search for new social and political models. In all of these areas, South American and U.S. priorities and agendas are becoming increasingly far apart. Clearly the changes that have been occurring in South America call for a major rethinking and reassessment of U.S. strategies in the area. Given the sclerotic U.S. political condition and quasi-paralyzed foreign policy, however, its will and capacity to make these adjustments remains very much open to question.

South American countries have changed enormously in the last twenty-five years. They are no longer weak, underdeveloped countries certain to follow the U.S. lead on most issues. Rather, in the last quarter century, much of South America has emerged from underdevelopment to occupy positions as middle-range powers and Newly Industrialized Countries (NICs). The economies of Argentina and Brazil are major forces to reckon with in the world arena. Moreover, these and other South American countries have become far more modernized and institutionalized in both a political and an economic sense.[1] Greater affluence and development have been accompanied by stronger nationalism and more assertiveness in international affairs. While Argentina, Brazil, Chile, Venezuela, and Peru, and even Bolivia, Ecuador, Paraguay, and Uruguay, are still dependent on the United States in some ways, they have become increasingly independent in others. Independence has been indicated by reestablishing relations with Cuba, staking out increasingly nonaligned positions, and

Reprinted from G. Pope Atkins (ed.), *South America into the 1990s: Evolving International Relationships in a New Era* (Boulder, CO: Westview, 1990).

generally becoming more and more inclined to "go it alone" in international affairs. These more independent positions are widely accepted and applauded by South American populations. The U.S. presence and position have undergone slippage, and a certain estrangement has set in with a growing separation and distancing from the United States.[2] Especially given their new-found economic power and the role of a number of the South American states as middle-level actors on the world's stage, these changes carry immense implications for U.S. foreign policy.

U.S. policy in Latin America has always been crisis-oriented. Rather than paying serious and sustained attention to the area and thus anticipating new developments with a coherent, informed, rational, and long-term policy, the United States instead has reacted to crises only after they occur and in an ad hoc, often ill-informed, and usually fickle way. Once the crisis-of-the-moment passes, the United States again tends to ignore the area, turn to issues and areas it presumes to be more important, and resurrect the older policy (or non-policy) of benign neglect—until some new crisis again forces its way onto the front pages. These attitudes and reactive strategies also help explain the neglect, indifference, and inattention to the critical changes that have been occurring on the South American continent, changes that will also, inevitably, carry major implications for U.S. foreign policy.[3]

DEMOCRATIZATION

The general trend toward democracy in Latin America in recent years has been heartening.[4] The corporatist and bureaucratic-authoritarian regimes that prevailed in the 1970s have now, for the most part, been replaced. Whereas a decade ago, two-thirds of the Latin American countries were under one or another form of military and authoritarian control, that proportion has now been reversed: over two-thirds of the countries (if one includes Mexico) representing more than 90 percent of the Latin American population are now governed democratically. In the South American continent, Argentina, Bolivia, Brazil, Chile, Ecuador, Peru, and Uruguay have all made dramatic returns to democratic rule. Bolivia, Ecuador, Paraguay, and Peru are perhaps shaky democracies, but democracies nonetheless.[5]

The United States has been strongly supportive of these democratic transitions, bolstering democracy at the rhetorical level, assisting it to flower, and even putting pressures on nondemocratic regimes to move toward democracy. It is true that most of the impetus to democracy in South America in recent years has come from South Americans themselves and not directly from the United States; but the United States has been a vocal and active supporter of democracy in the region and has tried to assist in the consolidation of democratic regimes once they are in place.[6]

U.S. motives in supporting these thrusts have been both ethical and strategic. As a democracy itself with a certain missionary tradition of trying to bring the benefits of democracy to other countries, the United States is naturally pleased that Latin America is now also, finally, achieving democracy. The strategic reasons are at least as important. Democratic regimes, the United States has found, tend to be less bellicose, less involved in their neighbors' internal affairs, less inclined to conflict, and in general cause fewer problems for the United States than other kinds of regimes. Strong democracies are the best guards against communism and Marxism-Leninism on the one hand and repressive authoritarians on the other—both of which cause the United States no end of trouble. In addition, although it took the Reagan administration some time to learn these lessons, standing for democracy is the best and surest way to get the Congress, the bureaucracy, the media, church and human rights groups, and public opinion—to say nothing of U.S. allies—to support the goals of U.S. policy. For the United States, then, a properly-conceived democratic posture is not just the moral and right thing to proclaim; it also serves important strategic interests.[7]

It should not be thought, however, that having a larger number of democracies in South America represents a cure-all for U.S. foreign policy problems there. Unfortunately that is the conclusion that too many analysts, inside and outside the government, have reached: that once Latin America achieves democracy, then all the issues that separate them will also be resolved. It is true that recent Presidents Alfonsín (Argentina), Febres (Ecuador), García (Peru), Paz (Bolivia), Sanguinetti (Uruguay), and Sarney (Brazil) were probably the most moderate and most democratic collection of leaders we are likely to see for a long time. That is by no means to say, however, that differences have been ameliorated. Furthermore, there seems to be no serious and coordinated effort within the U.S. government to deal with the continuing disagreements between the United States and these governments or their successors—however democratic they may be or, in one or two cases, precisely because they are democratic. At least six major areas of concern command our attention.

First, important countries like Argentina and Brazil have some fundamental disagreements with the United States over basic national interests. These differences will not be ameliorated by any change of regimes in Buenos Aires or Brasilia.[8]

Second, the very process of democratization has opened up new vistas, new promises, and also new fads to the South Americans. By no means should it be assumed that all of these new perspectives will be favorable to U.S. interests; indeed quite the contrary is likely to result—in the form perhaps of greater sentiment for nonalignment, stronger anti-Americanism, and more articulate, widespread, and more publicly-expressed opposition to specific U.S. policies.

Third, the form that Latin American democracy has taken (in Argentina, for example) is far closer to European-style democracy (as in France, Spain, or Italy) than it is to the U.S. system. That is not necessarily a barrier to good relations, but it does complicate the issue (and the lives of many U.S. administrators abroad and their programs) and it does not provide the common political-cultural basis of agreement that the United States enjoys with some other countries.

Fourth, Latin American democracy may be inclined to take some radical directions. Among South American intellectuals and church people particularly, the insistence is often strong that the transition to democracy in their countries has so far been only partial and incomplete. They will concede that "some" progress has been made, but only "bourgeois democracy" has been achieved. Now, they believe, it is necessary to take an additional step, which in the Marxian lexicon they use is inevitable, toward a more "advanced" and "progressive" form. They wish to be on the "cutting edge" of a new kind of democracy. By this they often mean socialism, "economic democracy," and perhaps even Marxism, but of an "independent" sort. None of these postures would seemingly bode well for U.S. policy.[9]

Fifth, the democratic regimes that have come to power in South America have not at all been in agreement with U.S. policies on a host of issues: trade, debt, Central America, strategic policy, the Falklands/Malvinas controversy (in the Argentine case), nuclear weapons, and so on. Argentine President Alfonsín, for example, emphasized that while his country was Western in geographic location, culture, and political institutions, it would be even-handed, almost neutralist and nonaligned, in its foreign policy. He was prepared to admit no legitimate strategic interests to the United States in all of Latin America.[10] Clearly this will not do from a U.S. perspective, because the United States does perceive legitimate strategic interests even in the Southern Cone. Alfonsín was not alone in these sentiments, however; the foreign ministries of Brazil, Peru, and Uruguay have pushed in many of the same directions.

Sixth, U.S. contingency planning has made no provision for dealing with a reversal of the current democratic trends. The United States may have allowed its hopes and wishes for the area to get ahead of serious analysis. Some academic literature tends to see democracy as the inevitable end product of an historical evolution that, once achieved, is unlikely (except by a full-scale fascist regime) to be reversed.[11] Democracy in Bolivia, Ecuador, Paraguay, and Peru is very fragile, however, and could be overthrown at any time; and in Argentina, Brazil, Chile, Uruguay, and Venezuela democracy is not as well consolidated, let alone institutionalized, as North Americans would like to think. The United States needs to be prepared in a policy sense if democracy were to be overthrown—especially, as has usually been the case in the past, if several overthrows occur at about the same time.

This is not to say that the United States should not warmly applaud and support the several transitions to democracy in South America. It should and does. But the United States also needs to recognize that not all the outcomes of those transitions will be benevolent toward the United States. Furthermore, the United States needs to develop contingency planning should the democratic trends be reversed.[12]

NATIONALISM

The new democracy in South America has helped unleash new forms of nationalism as potent political forces. Nationalism existed under the previous military regimes in their national security state forms.[13] The new nationalism, however, is more widespread and reaches to the popular level, and, consequently, is more explosive.

The rising new nationalism in South America takes several different forms. One is a new sense of pride in things Latin American and a corresponding insistence on doing things in a Latin American way. This includes pride in the new political institutions and a desire to develop indigenous democratic institutions and models. We may yet see significant experimentation with new institutions in South America, with indigenous and particularly Latin American ways of doing things (although there may be violent disagreements over what precisely that implies), or with particular and (it will be argued) uniquely Latin American combinations of Western and indigenous models.[14] In particular, with the near-simultaneous transition to democracy in Spain and Portugal and in South America, we are likely to see a new sense of pride in Iberian-Latin institutions and an effort to set them in marked contrast to Anglo-Saxon ones.

A second manifestation of the new nationalism is a growing resentment of U.S. officials operating in the South American countries and increased difficulties on their part in working with their South American counter-parts. Unlike the early 1960s, when U.S. personnel, know-how, and the Alliance for Progress money that went with them were, for the most part, warmly welcomed, the jobs performed by U.S. agencies are now much more difficult. Relations are seldom easy and often strained.

Polls and survey data are quite mixed in their conclusions about South American public opinion. Many South Americans still admire the United States and its accomplishments, affluence, and technology. The degree of admiration for U.S. political institutions, however, has declined. Most South Americans prefer their own cultural and social institutions: the family, strong interpersonal relations, and informal and relaxed lifestyles. They do not view U.S. cities, crime and violence, government and its leadership, or military institutions as something to aspire to or imitate. Admiration for U.S. institutions is much stronger among the older and fading generation than it is among the younger and rising generations.[15]

A third aspect of nationalism is generational in a broader sense than indicated above. The older generation of South American democratic leaders—including the likes of Eduardo Frei, Rómulo Betancourt, Galo Plaza, Fernando Belaúnde Terry, and Felipe Herrera—understood and admired the United States or knew how to function as if they did. In contrast, the newer generation now coming to power as agency heads, as cabinet officers, and even as presidents, grew up intellectually in the 1970s with Marxism and dependency theory, with the U.S. efforts directed against Salvador Allende in Chile, with U.S. aid to and close relations with the military-authoritarians of that era, with a United States that had ended the Alliance for Progress and viewed Latin America through the prism of "benign neglect," and with the twin U.S. traumas of Vietnam and Watergate. For this generation the United States is no longer the model to emulate, and an underlying hostility lurks beneath the surface.

A combination of nationalist resentments have come together over the debt issue. While most South American governments have acted respon-sibly on the matter of debt, their people are becoming increasingly im-patient. They blame the foreign commercial banks, the International Monetary Fund (IMF), and most of all the U.S. government for their economic woes. Moreover, even in educated circles the assumption is strong that the IMF, the commercial banks, and other international lend-ers operate at the behest of the U.S. government. The stagnation, high unemployment, poverty, underdevelopment, and inability to accommo-date the massive debt are blamed on the United States, not on their own corrupt or inefficient governments. Waiting in the wings to take political advantage of these bitter sentiments are populist and demagogic politicians, such as Luiz "Lula" da Silva in Brazil. Unlike the present leadership, these demagogues would repudiate the debt entirely and garner immense political backing in the process—regardless of the dire consequences for their nations' economies.[16]

International bankers and U.S. government officials find it difficult to understand the emotional depth of these nationalist sentiments. They cannot comprehend how some South American leaders might sacrifice their nations' future credit worthiness, realizing that assets would surely be seized and all foreign credits would immediately be canceled if such an "emotional" step as repudiation of debts were taken. These analysts, however (as I have written elsewhere),[17] underestimate the strength of Latin American sentiment on this issue. This is not to predict that all of South America is about to repudiate its debts tomorrow. It is to say, however, that one should not miscalculate the Latin American willingness to suffer heroic sacrifice for some glorious (however futile) cause. Those who are inclined toward such underestimation should read again the Ernest Hemingway novels about Spain—or perhaps García Marquez![18]

It should also be said that right-wing Latin American nationalism and anti-Americanism are as prevalent as the left-wing varieties. Moreover, it is difficult to detect when some fine lines have been passed. In Peru, for example, a logical policy for the United States might have been to extend economic aid despite President García's anti-American rhetoric and wait for his term to end. But García had already crossed the line that separates rhetorical anti-Americanism for domestic political purposes from the real thing. He was anti-American in private as well as in public; he needlessly (and perhaps foolishly) antagonized Secretary of State George Shultz and thereby hurt Peru's interests. In Chile, it is the right-wing anti-Americanism that is virulent, particularly as a result of U.S. pressures on strongman Augusto Pinochet. The Southern Cone has a long history of right-wing anti-Americanism and one should not underestimate its xenophobic manifestations.[19]

INSTITUTIONALIZATION

It is probably fair to say that South American institutions now are stronger than they were the last time democracy prevailed in the region in the early 1960s. The point has general theoretical interest as well as relevance to the analysis of foreign policy. Most students of Third World development, especially those of Latin America, have been highly critical of the influential writings of W. W. Rostow and their incorporation into

U.S. foreign assistance programs (Rostow was influential as head of policy planning at the State Department). Rostow, and numerous other early scholars of development, seemed to argue that development followed an inevitable, automatic, and universal path that led to a socially just, pluralist, affluent, democratic, moderate, and middle-class society that looked like an idealized version of the United States itself. The Latin American experience in the late 1960s and early 1970s, however, seemed to invalidate the Rostow formulations; a wave of military coups occurred, democracy was halted, the middle class often proved to be reactionary rather than progressive, and pluralism and social justice were attacked. All of Rostow's assumptions seemed wrong.[20]

The return to democracy in South American countries may force us to reassess Rostow's formulations. There is more affluence in South America now than in 1960 when Rostow wrote, the middle class is considerably larger and more secure, the lower classes are often better off, there is a stronger sense of social justice, literacy is more widespread, pluralism is better established, the associational life (business groups, labor unions, political parties, civic associations of all sorts) is far stronger, and there has been a gradual evolution toward democratic rule. In short, the social base is now far stronger and more solidly supportive of democracy than it was thirty years ago when the Alliance for Progress, in consonance with Rostow's ideas, was launched.[21] It may be, therefore, that the era of dictatorship and bureaucratic-authoritarianism of the 1960s and 1970s was only an aberration or temporary interruption, and that the "inevitable" and "universal" effects of modernization have in fact worked their inexorable effects toward moderate, middle-of-the-road democracy. That Rostow may be correct in the long run (though wrong in the short) is something that most scholars of development are not ready to admit, but we should be prepared to acknowledge that he may have been prescient.

All this implies that democracy in South America has a considerably stronger base than previously, that South America's historic associational and institutional vacuum has begun to be filled, and that the chances of consolidating and sustaining democracy are now better. One should not overstate this point, however; it remains necessary to make some sharp distinctions about the type and degree of institutionalization with regard to the individual countries of the region.

It is useful to distinguish first between social, economic, and political institutionalization. In South America, it seems clear that in the last twenty-five years considerably more social and economic growth has occurred than political development. Urbanization, social change, rising literacy, economic modernization, and rising living standards have all gone forward at rapid rates; but political development—democratization, institutionalization, associational life—while improving, has lagged behind. We now know that social change, economic growth, and political development are not automatically correlated; indeed, socioeconomic change may even undermine and disrupt political development.[22]

Second, we must distinguish between democratic and authoritarian institutionalization. While attention has generally been focused on the transitions to democracy in many countries, in Chile and Paraguay institutionalized authoritarianism proved for a long time very difficult to overcome. Furthermore, one should not forget the strong authoritarian tendencies still present in the countries that have made the transition to democracy, which could reassert themselves under certain conditions.

The distinction between countries needs also to be made. The situation and conditions in each country are different; no single transcendental process is at work in South America. Argentina under President Alfonsín was more democratic than at any time in the last sixty years; but there were also signs of the old fragmentation, and the strength of the non-democratic and antidemocratic forces should not be underestimated. Brazil's President Sarney consolidated his position, but he was still looked upon by all sides as a weakly legitimated and transitional president. (The question is, "transitional" to what?) Bolivia is economically bankrupt and politically chaotic; it is a miracle that Bolivian democracy has lasted as long as it has. Ecuador has a "tempered democracy": An elected government, but one where the familiar disintegrative processes continue—*pronunciamentos* by military leaders, a congress in the hands of the opposition, efforts to impeach the president, threats by the army to dissolve the Congress, and other rumblings from the barracks.[23] Uruguay has not solved its pressing economic problems and, like Argentina, the polity remains fragmented. In Chile and Paraguay democracy is still very new.

Hence, while it is probably accurate to argue that the developmental theories of Rostow and others deserve a close reexamination based on the longer-range trends in Latin America toward democratization, in the short term it is clear there is nothing automatic, universal, or inevitable about the process.

NEW MODELS

All of the older models of development in Latin America are dead. None of them have worked as anticipated. The dysfunctionality of the development models ranges across the political spectrum from left to right.

The general discrediting (for different reasons) includes Cuba under Fidel Castro as well as Chile under Pinochet, the Nicaraguan Revolution as well as the earlier revolution of the Brazilian generals. In between stand a variety of other "models" that also have not operated very well: the "Nasserism" of the Peruvian military from 1968–75, the "socialism" of Michael Manley in Jamaica, the "corporatism" and bureaucratic-authoritarianism of a number of military regimes in the 1960s and 1970s, and "populism" and the various other "isms" tried earlier.[24]

Nor is the United States regarded any longer as the premier political and economic model to emulate. This stands in marked contrast to the situation 140 years ago when, as the report of a commission to rewrite the Argentine constitution put it, "the democratic government of the United States represents the last word of human logic"; and again, "the committee has been guided . . . by the provisions of a similar constitution recognized as the most perfect, viz., that of the United States."[25] One cannot conceive of a South American politician saying anything similar today.

The current situation also stands in sharp contrast to that of thirty years ago when the United States stood as the political, economic, and moral exemplar. Then came the assassination of John F. Kennedy, racial conflict, Vietnam, student protests, urban violence, Watergate, Jimmy Carter's national "malaise," economic downturn, Ronald Reagan's conservative free-market ideology, the decline of American competitiveness, and so on. None of these events, persons, or processes enhanced U.S. prestige in South America. In fact, over the past quarter century, the elements in American society that Latin Americans most admired have steadily eroded. The size and strength of the U.S. economy and its technology evoke a grudging and perhaps jealous admiration, but this is based on pragmatic needs rather than any emotionally positive response. In this and other ways, U.S. relations with South America have become more a marriage of convenience than anything resembling a love match. South America knows that it needs U.S. capital, investment, technology, and access to markets, but little sentiment exists to be like the United States in very many particulars.[26]

Curiously, while the United States has declined as a model, South American efforts to fashion indigenous models have not worked out very well either.[27] In the 1960s and 1970s, there was a considerable fascination in various countries with fashioning an indigenous model of development, or one that combined local features with the best of imported institutions. The features that would have to be accommodated in such a model, however, included corporatism, organic-statism, patrimonialism, and authoritarianism.[28] For some countries, it also implied bringing the Indian civilizations into the political process as full participants, and erecting a social, cultural, and political system based on significant Indian input. While many intellectuals were sympathetic to the idea of a genuinely Latin American model of development, they were divided over the specific ingredients that would be included. They much preferred, it turned out, a model—dependency theory—that blamed the continent's problems on outside (especially U.S.) influence, and the move to fashion a Latin American model of development declined.

Little remains with regard to agreement on an appropriate and desirable developmental model. The older Latin American designs are dead, the newer ones are moribund, and the U.S. is of diminished attractiveness. Consequently, many South Americans have tended to look toward Europe and to find certain "advanced" or "progressive" manifestations to be admired. It is not Margaret Thatcher's United Kingdom or Helmut Kohl's Federal Republic of Germany toward which South Americans most look. They are more attracted to Mitterrand's vision of a socialist France (while Jacques Lang and Régis Debray were seen as defining the regime, before Mitterrand began following a more conservative course) or to the Spanish socialism of Felipe González (while he, too, was taking an anti-American and pro-Nicaraguan stance and before reality set in there as well). In these ways South Americans are searching for a model that is not only an alternative to the U.S. example, but that stands as critical of it.

Other South Americans are not any more sure that "progressive" Europe (West or East) is any more an appropriate model for them than is the United States. They argue that neither the United States nor Europe provide models for South America.[29] More and more South Americans are concluding that only a pragmatic, eclectic, pluralist, and reasonable regime that is neither too far to the right nor too far to the left will serve them well. This helps account for the current presence in South America of more centrist, moderate, middle-of-the-road governments than ever before in hemispheric history.

THE DEBT CRISIS

Latin America, as we saw in chapter 6, has been going through the worst economic crisis since the 1930s. In country after country, the economy has turned stagnant or shrunk, living standards have fallen, and the gross national product has been set back to 1960s levels.[30] The burden of the decline has fallen heaviest on the shoulders of the poor.

The causes of the recent downturn are several. They include quadrupling oil prices during the 1970s, declining global markets for Latin America's primary exports, diminished U.S. aid during the 1970s era of "benign neglect," and extravagant and often wasteful spending by Latin America governments and state agencies. To help maintain existing economic levels in the face of these long-term downward trends, the Latin American governments and public sector enterprises borrowed heavily at high interest rates from commercial banks that were flush with petrodollars, with the encouragement of the U.S. government seeking to substitute private loans for public foreign aid. As long as the world economy was expanding, the loans did not appear to be onerous; once the global recession hit in 1979–80, however, it became impossible for the debtor countries to meet their obligations. Interest payments continue to be paid to the banks but virtually no principal. Meanwhile, the total debt for the continent soared to over $400 billion—enough to threaten not only the Latin American economies but the commercial banks and perhaps the international financial system as well.

Although the U.S. government has proved willing to step in during genuine emergencies, such as in the Mexican bankruptcy of 1982 and with the Baker and Brady plans to stimulate U.S. investment in Latin America and replenish the international lending banks, it generally prefers to let the parties to the problem—the commercial banks and the Latin American governments—work out solutions by themselves. The U.S. position is that these are regular commercial debts and the Latin American countries must honor their obligations. In practice, this has meant that the IMF imposes conditions on the Latin American countries, pronouncing them "credit worthy" and therefore eligible for more loans provided they put their internal economic houses in order. The conditions have generally included cutbacks in public services, reduced subsidies of such items as food and oil products, diminished social programs for the poor, decreased imports, wage freezes for or firings of employees in the public services, general belt-tightening, and increases in exports which are usually achieved at the cost of domestic consumption. None of these programs help increase the popularity of the government that carries them out; austerity has in fact proved to be unpopular at a time of rising expectations and more combustible nationalism throughout the hemisphere. Those most often blamed are the local governments, the banks, the IMF, and, especially, the United States. "Outside forces" are viewed as most responsible and as collectively serving as the handmaiden of U.S. interests.[31]

South Americans tend to see these loans as part of the northern nations' obligations to the southern ones. The massive transfer of wealth from the United States to South America that has occurred as a result of the unpaid debt is the main agenda item of the North-South "negotiations." Besides, some South Americans reason, this is money owed them for past decades or centuries of exploitation of their resources. The U.S. banks were in it for their own profit, the argument goes, and therefore the risks involved are the banks' responsibility. In any case, it is now the obligation of the banks and the U.S. government to help debtors out of the crisis. Rather than seeing unemployment and hunger spread and living standards decline, the United States and its banks (one and the same, in this way of thinking) have an obligation to come to their rescue and forgive the debt.

South American governments have so far rejected this popular notion concerning the debt. In the new climate of democracy and the necessity of government to respond to popular demands, however, this cannot last forever. Most governments of the area continue to pay lip service to their obligations to repay their debts. Everyone knows that they cannot pay in full but that the fiction must be maintained. By making some attempts at repayment, they can continue to qualify for more loans and avoid the ostracism and severe financial costs that an outright repudiation would bring. But demagogic politicians are waiting for the next round of elections; for nationalist reasons and to garner popular acclaim they would be willing to remove the oppressive debt in one fell swoop. They reason—perhaps accurately—that even if they repudiate their debts, the United States would eventually bail them out in order to serve the strategic interests at stake.

Distinctions must again be made among individual countries. Bolivia is in de facto default on the debt, although creditors do not publicly acknowledge the fact out of fear of spreading the possibility of repudiation to the larger debtors. Peru is, like Bolivia, nearly broke, so that former President Alan García's gratuitous statement that Peru would pay 10 percent of its earnings to service the debt was actually that much more than Peru had been paying. Chile's economy has gone through boom-and-bust cycles and in the 1990s experienced a boom of indeterminable length, which also had the effect of temporarily propping up the regime of Augusto Pinochet. Paraguay, a traditional economy now embarking on rapid growth, followed a conservative fiscal policy and did not borrow so heavily abroad. Argentina and Brazil are the key countries: they both have massive debt and have so far followed "responsible" policies of paying lip service to their obligation and obeying IMF conditions of imposing austerity in return for a continuing flow of new loans.

But in both countries there are powerful opposition movements that may come to power who are calling for outright repudiation and an end to the debt burden.

The debt issue is complicated because it is not just a financial one (the obligation to pay back the loans), but involves political, nationalist, and strategic issues of major importance as well. So far, the debt problem has been managed relatively successfully, but the possibilities of the strategy coming unglued also exist.

THE DRUG ISSUE

U.S. attitudes and policy toward drugs have gone through various permutations in recent years. First came a limited and lackadaisical effort to discourage drug use directed at the audience of U.S. consumers. That attempt failed in part because drug use was at that time widely thought to be a "lifestyle" issue on which persons could exercise "choices," and in part because the warnings coming from the Reagan administration fell on deaf ears. When it proved impossible to change American consumer habits, the focus shifted to the source of the drugs. Numerous efforts failed to persuade, cajole, or pressure South American (and other) governments into cutting off production. Since it most directly affected U.S.-Latin American relations, it is this second strategy that is the focus of the following remarks. The failure of this second strategy led to a third strategy, a much more multifaceted and sophisticated effort aimed at the U.S. public via television and other media, featuring prominent athletes and other opinion leaders. It was much more successful, partly because by then the medical evidence of the permanent damage done by drugs to the mind and body was overwhelming.

But let us return to the second stage of the anti-drug campaign, which most affected U.S.-South American relations. We concentrate here on the international dimensions of the problem and its potential to wreak havoc on U.S.-Latin American ties, leaving aside for now any moral considerations. We present a listing of why the issue is so complex and difficult and why the potential for severe damage to U.S.-South American relations arising out of it is so alarming.[32]

1. Drug use in a mild form is habitual and traditional among many Latin American indigenous elements, who chew coca leaves as a means of warding off hunger and pain. Unlike the United States, there is in Latin America no Calvinistic sense of sin or moral outrage at such widespread popular use of the drug.

2. Drugs (marijuana, poppies, coca) are a profitable cash crop for many Latin American farmers. They do not use the products themselves, there is no moral stigma attached to growing them, and their incomes are augmented four or five times as compared with growing more traditional crops. It is unreasonable to suggest that poor farmers give up this new income for the sake of a U.S. anti-drug campaign.

3. Most Latin Americans of the upper and middle classes do not use drugs, nor do their children. They therefore do not see the drug problem with the same urgency as do persons, especially parents, in the United States. Nor is the limited drug use in Latin America related to a rising incidence of crime and violence as it is in the United States. Drugs are not a major police problem for most South American countries. Until this changes—and there are signs that drug use by Latin American teens and others is spreading and thereby becoming a moral and a police problem—North Americans cannot expect Latin Americans to view the drug issue in the same scary way that they do.

4. Efforts to eradicate drug production do not cause the producers to disappear. Instead, they simply move on to another country. For example, Colombia's turn to drug production as a major export crop (now surpassing coffee!) developed only after the eradication campaign in Mexico forced the producers to move to another country.

5. Drug production by now is so widespread that it cannot be eradicated. Many areas of South America are seas of drug plants, rather like wheat in the American midwest. It is inconceivable that all this production can be eliminated.

6. The highly publicized campaigns to wipe out the production have not been effective. Production is carried out not in factories that are visible to helicopters and patrolling police, but in small, isolated, pots-and-pans processes located in dense jungles. No sooner is one of these primitive "factories" found and destroyed than more spring up in the same locale. The problem is so immense as to be unsolvable.

7. Large government operations, like the U.S.-run Operation Blast Furnace in Bolivia designed to drive the price of drugs down by eliminating markets and production, do not work very effectively. The Bolivian operation was very costly and cannot be often repeated; it was only a small drop in a very large bucket, and in the long run had almost no effect on prices or production. Nor does spraying of the drug crops work. It contaminates the environment, ruins nearby non-drug crops, and causes long-term disease and cancer in the population; hence, democratically-elected governments cannot permit it.

8. Many Latin American governments are not opposed to drug production as long as the producers do not threaten the government itself. It adds immensely to the GNP, keeps farmers happy, and enables the government to get away with fewer subsidies for its people and lower salaries to public employees.

9. The last point is an especially sticky one. The fact is that many local and even national officials in Latin America, as well as military and police officials, are in the pay of the narcotics traffickers. Neither the national governments nor these officials are prepared to cooperate with a drug eradication program that cuts into their own incomes.

10. The U.S. Drug Enforcement Agency (DEA) officials whom the United States sends to Latin America, unlike their State Department counterparts, often do not have strong backgrounds in the culture, languages, politics, or sociology of the area. They tend sometimes to ride roughshod over Latin American sensitivities and to ignore the conditions that make the issue so complex and difficult. Nor do the DEA officials always endear themselves to the State Department itself or to U.S. embassies abroad. Not only are there bureaucratic rivalries, administrative overlaps, and personal animosities involved, but their functions are entirely at odds. The job of the U.S. embassy mission is, by and large, to get along with, accommodate, and maintain good relations with the host government; that of the DEA in the same country is to provoke change and sometimes confrontation. The actions of DEA officials in South America in carrying out their mission has not always been welcomed by the rest of the embassy team.

It is unlikely, therefore, that the solution to the U.S. drug problem will come from Latin America. Realistically, it can only come from the United States itself through interdiction (which raises another set of problems), education, and ultimately changed mores and consumer habits. Efforts to solve a U.S. problem by putting pressure on or intervening in Latin American internal affairs will produce backlashes, generate ill will, and prove counterproductive. If the markets can be made to dry up on the U.S. side, which will certainly be a long-term process, then production will surely dry up on the South American side. The reverse is not true, however, because the unlikely reduction of Latin America production would only move it to Asia, the Middle East, or Africa. In the meantime, an insensitive and heavy-handed U.S. approach has the potential to wreak enormous damage upon our relations with South America.

PUBLIC OPINION

United States foreign policy in South America, and in Latin America in general, has had as one of its basic aims the promotion of democracy. Democracy as a goal of foreign policy has been pursued for both ethical and strategic purposes. The question remains, however, of whether Latin America wants democracy, or wants it all that much, or wants it in the same form that U.S. citizens envision, and whether—in the last analysis— the pursuit of democracy is a valid basis for foreign policy.[33]

The answer as to whether Latin America wants democracy is a resounding yes—but with important qualifications. In poll after poll in country after country, South Americans favor democracy and representative government. The surveys that exist indicate that when given their choice of alternative political systems, 80, 85, or 90 percent (depending on time and place) prefer representative rule.[34]

These same surveys also indicate that this is an abstract choice of preferences conceived in a vacuum. Although overwhelming majorities of South Americans prefer representative government, they are not certain that U.S.-style representative government will work in their countries. Democracy is good in the abstract, but their own countries, they sometimes believe, are too fragmented, too uninstitutionalized, or even too "uncivilized" for democracy to work. Based on their own national histories, they believe democracy leads to chaos, libertinage, and national breakdowns. Democracy is good and workable in the "Anglo-Saxon countries," but South Americans remain skeptical as to whether it works for them. Hence, if one asks South Americans the question that USIA pollsters seldom do—what they mean by democracy—the answer is almost always "strong" or "firm" government. About the same percentage that prefer representative government also favor strong government. This represents the two options that have always been open to South America: representative government versus strong or authoritarian government, democracy versus Caesarism. The surveys thus indicate that while representative government is the South Americans' first choice, if it does not work they may easily opt for the substitute of strong government.[35] This also means that the U.S. strategy of putting so many of its eggs in the one democracy basket may be an imprudent one.

Moreover, these same surveys show very little support for what we think of as democracy's supporting institutions. While 85 percent and more of South Americans prefer representative government, only about 30 percent favor political parties of any kind. They view political parties like George Washington viewed "factions," as divisive agencies detracting from the national purpose. An even lower percentage of South Americans—about 27 percent—view trade unions in a favorable light.[36] If the elementary civics and political science textbooks are correct that political parties and trade unions are essential to democracy and necessary for the pluralism that undergirds democratic life, then it is clear that South American democracy has a very weak institutional base. It may be that South Americans believe they can have democracy without a strong institutional life—perhaps not an invalid assumption if the model of democracy for South America is the direct democracy of Rousseau and the notion of an intuitively known "general will," and not that of Locke or Madison.[37] The third explanation arising from this data is that South Americans, when one probes beneath the surface, are actually not much in favor of democracy at all. Whatever alternative explanation is chosen, democracy—and with it U.S. foreign policy—seems shakier in South America than we may have thought.

This conclusion regarding the tenuousness of democracy in South America is reinforced by survey data on political attitudes among the lower classes. Representative democracy as the United States knows it is often supported by the South American upper and middle classes—but not necessarily the lower classes. These classes, like others in their societies, often support "democracy" in the abstract; but in practice they generally prefer a strong, nationalistic, paternalistic, populist, authoritative (if not downright authoritarian) regime, rather like Perón in Argentina. Between 40 and 60 percent of the population may support a Peronist-like system of statist nationalism that may verge on populist socialism. Once again, the portents for democracy and for U.S. foreign policy are not propitious if such attitudes prevail.[38]

South American attitudes toward the United States are similarly divided. On the one hand, a large majority of South Americans consider the United States to be a friend and admire its economy, technology, and national wealth. They tend to be envious of the strong democracy and representative government found in the United States and they admire the free speech, system of justice, and relative lack of corruption in American life. About half of the South Americans surveyed have a generally favorable impression of the United States while only about a quarter have an unfavorable impression. At the same time, South Americans make it clear that they are appalled by certain features (or what they perceive as features) of American life—the drug use, impersonality, lack of strong moral and religious values, erosion of the family structure—and believe their own moral and cultural values to be superior. Similarly, while most South Americans admire and respect the United States, they are strongly opposed to some aspects that have particular relevance for foreign policy. They are opposed to what is seen as U.S. militarism, interventionism (in Central America and the Caribbean), and heavy-handedness. Many South Americans were particularly opposed to the government of Ronald Reagan, which they saw as confirming all their worst prejudices about the United States as an uncivilized, gunslinging, lawless, dangerous, wild west country that shoots first and asks questions later.[39] (This attitude is largely based on movies rather than first-hand experience of the United States, and is often fomented and augmented by inaccurate or unrepresentative media coverage or by intellectuals with a political interest in presenting a distorted view.)

Complicating these relations is the fact that some South Americans are intensely jealous and envious of the United States. The hate stems not so much from what the United States does—its occasional gaffes and mistakes—but from what it is and stands for: success and modernity compared to South American failure and backwardness. To the extent this attitude is widespread, as it is in Argentina, the United States is certain to be envied and disliked regardless of what it says or does. There is certain to be a high degree of anti-Americanism, given these attitudes, no matter who is in power in Washington or in Buenos Aires. In that sense, U.S. relations with some of the South American countries may range from correct to frosty, but they are never likely to be "good."[40]

Overall, South American public opinion is probably more independent, less favorable disposed toward the United States, even more manifestly anti-American than it was thirty years ago. Then the U.S. image was overwhelmingly favorable in South America; but now the region is both more nationalistic and less pro-American. One suspects that this change has more to do with South America's greater development, independence, and assertiveness, combined with a perceived U.S. decline, than it does with any specific U.S. action or even set of actions over this period.

THE AGENDA OF ISSUES

Not only are the United States and South America diverging on the range of issues discussed above, but increasingly even the respective agendas of issues no longer contain the same items.

What are the basic or bedrock U.S. interests in South America? Essentially they may be summarized in a series of items.[41]

1. Security interests: Preventing "more Cubas," protecting the "southern flank," helping protect U.S. interests in the South Atlantic and the

South Pacific, guaranteeing the sea lanes, maintaining bases or listening posts, preventing "foreign powers" (viz., the Soviet Union) from securing a foothold or establishing bases, securing the borders, containing communism, assuring that in the event of a general conflict U.S. forces are not held up by having to deal with some local Soviet satellite in South America (the "economy of force" doctrine).

2. Economic interests: Maintaining access to the markets, raw materials, and labor supplies of the area; being able to invest and remit profits; opening up South American markets to U.S. products.
3. Political interests: Maintaining stability in ways that protect interests #1 and #2, allowing for change that is not radical.
4. Economic development and social progress: Assisting modernization that leads to these ends, both as a good in itself and because it contributes to interests #1, #2, and #3.
5. Democracy and human rights: Emphasizing these goals again both as ends in themselves (thus satisfying U.S. requirements for an ethical foreign policy) and because they also contribute to #1, #2, and #3.

What are the priorities of the South American countries? Not only are their priorities different from those of the United States, but the two lists converge hardly at all.

1. Regime survivability: This is the highest priority of any South American government. In a context of weak legitimacy and an uncertain tenure in office, where stability cannot be taken for granted, a regime must protect its own interests first and by almost any means. North Americans, who take stability for granted, seldom understand this need or the policies to which it often leads.
2. Sovereignty and territorial integrity: These doctrines are alive and well in South America where *realpolitik,* border issues, and irredentism are prevalent. Argentina's claims to the Falklands/Malvinas Islands are just the tip of the iceberg of the potential for inter-state conflict in South America.[42]
3. Economic development and social progress: This is a very high-order priority in South America, far higher than the U.S. preoccupation that is almost exclusively strategic.
4. Trade, commerce, investments, and markets: While the U.S. preoccupation is strategic, the South American one could be summed up in three words: trade, trade, trade. South America particularly wishes continued free access to U.S. markets, including especially capital markets, and is very much concerned with the protectionist thrust in

the United States Congress that would limit the entry of Latin American products.

5. Democracy and human rights (in their more advanced forms): Unless there is evidence to the contrary, it may be surmised that South America strongly favors democracy and human rights only partially for their own sake but in large part to qualify for U.S. and international aid and so they can show the world that they are as "civilized" as anyone else. These may not be noble or elevated reasons for favoring democracy, but perhaps such cynicism is warranted given South America's previous track record of loyalty to democratic precepts.

6. Security, stability, and order: These are concerns for internal order, what Jeane Kirkpatrick once called the "Hobbes problem" in Latin America,[43] not concerns for Cuban or Soviet-inspired insurrection— which is the U.S. preoccupation. In fact, with the exception of the *Sendero Luminoso* movement in Peru and a potential security problem in Colombia, the South American subsystem is currently freer of leftist insurrectionary threats than at any time since the 1950s. The very absence of such threats enables South America to flaunt the United States in ways it would not have done before and to stake out more independent foreign policy positions.

7. A place in the sun: South America wishes, perhaps even above the other priorities listed, to be afforded a sense of dignity, worth, and respect, and to be included among the "civilized" nations. They do not wish to be treated as "banana republics" or to be of interest only to U.S. vice presidents who must attend funerals there.

8. Independence: Most South American countries recognize their continuing dependence on the United States for economic, trade, and security reasons. But they also wish to diversify that dependence, to become more independent, and to open up relations with a broader spectrum of nations. The United States will have to adjust, probably painfully, to some of these transformations.

9. Alternative routes to development: While a major U.S. preoccupation in South America is regime stability, many South Americans are still casting about for an appropriate and innovative development formula. Such experimentation on their part is likely to produce ruptures of instability; many South Americans are willing to run that risk for the sake of achieving an authentic and genuinely indigenous model of development—which they have never really had in their 160-year history as independent nations—and probably to the considerable chagrin of U.S. strategic planners.

One is struck in reviewing these lists how far removed the U.S. priorities are from the South American ones. It is not just that the individual items are sometimes different, but that the entire agendas show very little convergence or complementarity. Moreover, even when there are items present on both lists—such as democracy, for example—it is plain that the parties often mean something quite different by that item or that their reasons for supporting it are quite different. The issue may not be subject to precise empirical verification, but one wonders if ever before have the two main parts of the Americas been so far apart.

CONCLUSIONS

Considerable signs of maturity are evident in U.S.-South American relations.[44] With most of the countries of the region, the United States has begun to put its relations on the same normal and regular footing that is the basis of its relations with much of Western Europe. This is not to say that there are no serious issues in U.S.-South American relations— there are, in fact, many of them—but it is to say that policy toward South America has become more routinized and no longer carried out on a crisis basis as was so often the case in the past. The causes of this new maturity in U.S.-South American relations are many, but undoubtedly important among them is the fact that the U.S. preoccupation with Central America has led to indifference and neglect toward South America. Such neglect is rightfully lamented by many scholars,[45] but among the unintended consequences has been a certain maturing of U.S. relations with quite a number of the countries of the area. There are many areas of bilateral and multilateral differences, but for the most part these are dealt with in the normal channels of negotiations and diplomacy rather than through some crash program for the region that is here today and gone tomorrow, or some CIA intervention. Given the previous U.S. track record in the region, I count such boring and even humdrum relations as steps in the right direction.

On the other hand, the range of issues that divide the United States from South America is large and growing larger. The community of interests that the United States and South America commonly shared historically as part of a New World order is dangerously thin. The "Western Hemisphere Idea"[46] of a commonality of experiences, histories, and aspirations shared by all of the Americas as distinct from their Old World forebears, may now finally be laid to rest. On virtually every issue and subject here discussed—democracy, nationalism, institutionalization, models of development, debt, drugs, public opinion, and the agendas of priorities—there are large differences that will not soon or easily be resolved. Not only are the policy and issue differences strong and increasing, there is as well increasingly little shared basis of understanding and mutuality of interests on which a firmer partnership and better relations can be forged.

It would require a major effort on the part of the United States and South America to begin working on these issues in a serious way, to manage ("resolve" would be too strong a word) them in an efficient, mutually satisfactory, and amicable manner, and to lay the basis for better future relations. Unfortunately, little of that is likely to happen, for U.S. foreign policy has been increasingly politicized on all sides and the entire American foreign policy system is increasingly immobilized and fragmented. Hence, we can expect little in the way of positive, concerted, and long-term policy at the highest levels of the United States government. Whatever new policy initiatives we see, therefore, are likely to come not from the top but from lower levels of the U.S. government. Moreover, such initiatives and solutions as are presented at these levels are likely to be partial, tentative, and incremental, as distinct from holistic and grandiose. Given past U.S. experience in the South American region, that may not be an altogether bad or inappropriate basis for U.S. foreign policy.

The winding down of the Cold War may lead at some levels to better U.S.-South American relations. The transformations in Eastern Europe and the economic troubles and political unraveling of the Soviet Union mean that the South Americans can no longer play the Third World "game" of balancing off the superpowers and gaining assistance from the U.S. in order to keep the communist wolf away. But with the Soviets no longer interested and unable to afford a global foreign policy, South America has been thrown back into the arms of the United States whether it wants to be or not. Prudent politicians in South America recognized and understood that fact and are already adjusting to take advantage of it. Such a marriage of convenience may lead to better U.S.-Latin American relations at a superficial level, and the newer emphasis on democracy and more open markets provides a basis for cooperation; but the recent international changes should not lead us to ignore the long-term trends toward estrangement.

Part V

TOWARD THE FUTURE

16

Saving Latin America from the "Black Hole"

Latin America is in very deep trouble. And when Latin America is in deep trouble it means that U.S. policy there will soon be in very deep trouble as well. It will not do for the United States to try to ignore the region or its problems as if they did not exist; our recent historical experiences with the area should have taught us the peril of failing to pay it sufficient attention. "Benign neglect" is no longer adequate as a basis for policy; as in Cuba in the 1950s and Central America in the 1970s, benign neglect allows small problems to grow into larger ones and produces disasters for U.S. foreign policy.

Latin America's current problems are profound, deep-rooted, and structural; they will not be easily resolved, and certainly not by a single presidential message or some new sleight of hand between Congress and the Department of State. Rather, they require deep thought, a multifaceted strategy, and a long-term, sustained commitment by the United States to the area.

The crisis in Latin America is economic, social, and political. Economically, the region has experienced no, little, or retrogressive growth during the entire decade of the 1980s; and the situation is not getting much better. There is very little capital going into the area from any source; and the little capital that is there, both foreign and domestic, is fleeing. Without capital, of course, there can be no development, and politics will soon turn into a zero-sum or a negative-sum game—that is, for every winner there will have to be a loser, or else everyone will turn out to be a loser.

Socially, the conditions in the region are getting worse. Hunger, disease, frustration, and hopelessness are all spreading. Social gaps are widening, inflation and austerity measures are devastating the middle and lower classes, and living standards are falling. The depressed and depressing conditions have come at precisely the time when modern communications

Reprinted from *The World & I* 4 (August 1989).

and the openings to democracy that have been so heartening in the area in the last decade have significantly raised popular expectations. Those are precisely the conditions—raised expectations at a time of declining living standards—that Crane Brinton and a host of experts have emphasized as *the* cause of revolutionary upheaval. Recent riots in the Dominican Republic, Brazil, Venezuela, and now Argentina have provided us with a foretaste of what is to come.

Politically, Latin America is again fragmenting and polarizing. The euphoria for democracy has passed. The prudent and pragmatic presidents (for the most part) who were in power in the 1980s may yield power to a new wave of populists and even demagogues. They will undoubtedly mismanage their economies as they have often done in the past, provoking further political unraveling. That will likely lead to new guerrilla challenges and again put immense popular pressures on the Latin American militaries to "save" the country. Such rumblings and polarization will cause major problems for U.S. foreign policy.

The question is not so much the terrible conditions in Latin America—on that we can agree. The real issue is what we should do about them.

ECONOMICS

The 1980s are looked on in Latin America as the "lost" or "negative" decade. Latin America has not yet recovered from the depression that began in 1982. In some countries per capita income has slipped back to 1960s levels, and Latin America's immense (approaching $500 billion) international debt has added enormously to the burden.

Some form of debt relief is undoubtedly necessary, as in the Brady corollary of the Baker Plan. But this is still a very delicate juggling act. Debt relief cannot be used (as it already is being used in some Latin American countries) as a convenient excuse to halt the reform of the region's often-corrupt, bloated, and inefficient institutions; nor can the private commercial banks be expected to absorb a full 50 percent cut in debt payments; nor, after the savings and loan bailout, can the American taxpayers again be asked to come to the rescue of the debtors, the creditors, and the international financial system.

It still remains the case that the only long-term solution is for Latin America to *grow* out of its present economic doldrums. But Latin American growth is not encouraged by slapping sanctions on Brazil, the region's leading success story, and by throwing up additional protectionist barriers that not only hurt Latin America's exports but also cause higher prices in the United States.

We need to help wean Latin America away from its historic mercantilist practices, but we must recognize that the required changes are not self-evident in Latin America nor will they come overnight. Too many political and patronage considerations are involved for that to happen quickly. By rushing too rapidly to spread free-market economies in the area we could easily destabilize the very countries we are seeking to assist.

Latin America has an uncanny capacity to absorb outside ideas; recently, it began to absorb the lessons of the East Asian success stories. Latin America knows it is suffering by comparison with the Asian "tigers," and while Latin America does not wish to imitate the hyper-organization of, say, Japan, it does recognize the need for greater rationality and organization of the national economic life and the need to become more efficient and competitive globally. Given the limits of the U.S. ability to help Latin America economically, this "learning from Asia" thrust may be the most heartening development in a long time.[1]

DEMOCRACY

The transitions to democracy that so many Latin American countries have experienced in the past ten years are deeply heartening and are among the greatest epochal changes of the late twentieth century.

But merely assisting the transitions to democracy in Latin America is not enough. Now democracy must be consolidated, and it must deliver. Otherwise, it will be known, as it already is known in Brazil, as "*democracia boba*"—"foolish democracy."

The stakes are tremendously high. For not only is it morally correct for the United States to stand strongly for democracy and human rights, but democracy also serves our national interests: Democracies don't try to destabilize their neighbors; they don't support guerrilla movements in the neighboring countries; they don't get in stupid wars (Argentina in 1982); they don't interfere in their neighbors' internal affairs; they are more stable than dictatorships; and they make it far easier domestically for the United States to defend its policies.[2]

The National Endowment for Democracy (NED), the semi-private agency created by Congress in 1983 to help foster democracy, has by now largely won its battles with its numerous early critics. And NED's activities have been generally prudent and wise.

Now is the time to increase NED's budget and expand its activities. It needs to move into the far more difficult area of helping to consolidate democracy through the building of democratic institutions rather than just assisting the transitions to democracy. And, both NED and the U.S. government need to help the still fledgling Latin American democracies *deliver* in the way of real goods and services, so as to prevent the polarizations and the dangers of military coups that now loom on the horizon.

MILITARY-STRATEGIC

U.S. defense strategy badly requires updating. Until very recently our focus has been preparation for a limited nuclear conflict (even though that is probably the *least likely* kind of conflict in which we might be engaged) or a largely conventional attack across the plains of central Europe. In this planning, Latin America is largely ignored, or it is dealt with through the doctrine of "economy of force."

While a war in central Europe seems highly improbable, far more likely are the kind of murky, politico-psychological guerrilla struggles that we saw in Southeast Asia and have recently witnessed in southern Africa and Central and South America. Paradoxically, even though these are the most likely types of conflict in which we will be engaged, they are the ones for which we remain woefully ill-prepared.

The Cold War is not yet over in Latin America. A recent study of U.S.-Soviet superpower relations and of various regions of conflict concluded that Latin America was the area where we could expect the *least* superpower cooperation.[3] In that region the Soviet Union gets enormous foreign policy mileage for very little cost, the local guerrilla movements have indigenous roots and can cause enormous havoc even without Soviet assistance, and Cuba remains committed to the fomenting of revolution even if the Soviet Union is not. Watching the upheaval in China and the spreading chaos in the Soviet Union, Castro is currently chortling with glee, for the recent events in the communist world have strengthened his position that economic reform and *glasnost* and *perestroika* do not work and lead only to problems.

So the United States needs to modernize its strategic planning, to keep its guard up, to recognize that Latin America is the center and not the periphery, to devise wise and politically informed strategies for dealing with the guerrilla forces, to continue its cooperative programs (in the Inter-American Defense University and elsewhere) with the Latin American militaries, and to continue advocating—despite the setbacks—the plans for regional defense forces.

DRUGS

The problems on the drug front are many. Essentially, because of infringements on civil liberties and other problems, drug enforcement personnel in the United States largely abandoned the effort to combat drugs on the domestic or consumption side and turned instead to the international side. But those involved were often woefully naive about international affairs and about Latin America in particular, and failed to comprehend why it could be quite rational economically for Latin American farmers and their governments to produce and export drugs.

The result has been an unending series of gaffes, mistakes, bureaucratic conflicts (between the State Department and the Drug Enforcement Agency, for example), and misunderstandings that not only failed to reduce the flow of drugs into the United States but also poisoned our relations with many Latin American countries.

There is no clear and easy solution to the drug problem. However, we are beginning to see that a successful strategy has to be pursued simultaneously on both the consumption and the production sides. On the production side, our interests are unlikely to be advanced by a purely law enforcement approach (putting everyone in jail who is involved in the drug trafficking, even if that includes armed forces heads, cabinet members, or the president himself). Rather, a successful antidrug campaign will work only as the Latin Americans and their leaders are convinced that drugs are also corrupting and ruining *their* societies as well as ours. Our goal must be to work with such leaders rather than against them. And in such countries as Bolivia, Colombia, and Peru, there are signs that such cooperative efforts are beginning to pay off.

CENTRAL AMERICA

Over the past 10 years, there is no doubt that U.S. policy has focused on several of the small countries of Central America, often to the neglect of the rest of the hemisphere. We need to move to correct that inbalance, even while recognizing we do have ongoing problems in Central America that must still command our attention.

In El Salvador, the conservative ARENA party has been elected to power. And it seems plain that we cannot abandon a democratically elected government in El Salvador just because we don't like the outcome that democracy may produce, though a handful of congressmen and some special interest lobbies would like to do so. Nor, because our interests are also vitally affected, can we abandon the Salvadorans in their struggle against the guerrillas. But we do need to keep up the pressure on the new Salvadoran regime to maintain centrist policies and not allow the hard Right to take over the party or the government. As seems almost always to be the case in El Salvador, our strategies need to be directed at least as much at the U.S. *domestic* political audience and debate as at that poor and traumatized country.

OVERALL

What is sorely needed is a sustained and multifaceted program for Latin America. Such a balanced and comprehensive view was set forth in the Kissinger Commission Report of 1984, but it was never adequately funded by Congress nor sufficiently pushed by the White House. Nevertheless, the ingredients for a constructive and positive policy for the area are all there.

Such a program would combine a strong democracy and human rights agenda with an updated strategic component, and would emphasize that an enlightened strategic policy could not be successful without a simultaneous commitment to democracy and human rights. The program would combine social and economic assistance with some necessary military assistance. It would emphasize working toward a resolution of the debt crisis but without absolving Latin America of the need for internal reform or passing the costs on to long-suffering U.S. taxpayers. The program would be as much directed toward building and consolidating democratic institutions as toward waging a vigorous antiguerrilla campaign and would again recognize the intimate relationship between the two. It would work to solve the drug problem, not by running roughshod over Latin American institutions but by trying to work cooperatively with them toward shared goals.

I would personally like to see U.S. assistance programs reoriented toward local, effective, small-scale, grass-roots organizations and activities rather than grandiose projects; but I have just about given up on the hope that USAID or the World Bank or the Inter-American Development Bank will ever see things that way. The Inter-American Foundation should consistently support good and worthwhile projects rather than at times giving funds to groups who hate the United States and are bent on our destruction. The United States could also do more in the way of basic health care, as the med-vac teams did in Honduras, because often simple inoculations can do more to help people and at the same time project a more favorable image of the United States than other government policies.

To be successful, such policies as recommended here must be supported and sustained from one administration to the next. They must be funded consistently by Congress in the face of other demands on scarce resources. And they must be bolstered by a diplomacy and a political commitment that helps put our relations with Latin America on the same mature basis that we have long maintained with Western Europe. Only by such a comprehensive and consistent program can we save Latin America from the "black hole" into which it is in danger of falling—and serve our own national interests at the same time.

17

The Democratic Breakthrough in Latin America: Challenges, Prospects, and U.S. Policy

THE DEMOCRATIC BREAKTHROUGH

In the past decade a remarkable breakthrough to democracy has occurred in Latin America. The changes in the region may, in long-range terms, be as significant as the parallel changes occurring in Southern Europe (Greece, Portugal, Spain), Eastern Europe, East Asia, and the Soviet Union. These turnabouts toward democracy in so many areas of the world must surely be ranked as among the most significant global transformations of the late twentieth century.

It was not very long ago that democracy in Latin America appeared to have very little future at all. In a survey that the author conducted in 1978,[1] twelve of the twenty Latin American countries (and the vast majority of the Latin American population) were governed under military-authoritarian regimes. In five of the other countries the armed forces were so close to the surface of power, or to acting as the real influence behind the civilian facade, as to render meaningless the distinction between civilian and military governments. That means that seventeen of the twenty countries were governed under one or another form of authoritarianism. The situation of human rights in the region was universally recognized as disastrous; repression and brutality were increasing. Among the twenty countries only Costa Rica, Colombia, and Venezuela continued to be governed democratically; and even about these there were many questions as to their stability and genuine commitment to democracy.

It was not just that democracy in Latin America appeared to be on the ropes but also, within academia and from a number of perspectives, a vast body of literature had pronounced it dead, dying, inappropriate, or irrelevant. This was, among academic scholars of Latin America, the heyday of corporatist, dependency, and bureaucratic-authoritarian inter-

Reprinted from *SAIS Review* 11 (Summer–Fall, 1991).

pretations of Latin America.[2] Both the corporatist and bureaucratic-authoritarian (BA, as it was called) interpretations carried the implicit assumption that discipline, authoritarianism, hierarchy, and strong central government were inherent, even "natural," or the result of inevitable cultural and socioeconomic forces in Latin America, while democracy was viewed as artificial, extraneous, almost "unnatural." The dependency interpretation suggested that democracy was largely irrelevant, that the real issue was international capitalism and its hegemony over local markets. All three of these perspectives, which achieved dominance in the 1970s, tended to shove democracy aside as an important consideration, to render it as a secondary variable.

But since the late 1970s, the situation has been reversed. Beginning with Ecuador and the Dominican Republic in 1978, then encompassing the important countries of Argentina, Bolivia, Brazil, Uruguay, and Peru, including the Central American countries, eventually Paraguay and Chile, and Mexico's reform program, even Nicaragua, a democratic wave has swept over the area. Even Haiti appears to have a chance of emerging in the democratic column.

It can now be said that nineteen of the twenty countries, and over 95 percent of the Latin American populations, live under democracy or under regimes aspiring or in transition to democracy. This includes various "halfway houses" (El Salvador, Guatemala)—more on this below—where the civilian, elected regimes and the military-authoritarian power structure continue to exist side by side; but no one doubts that such a "mixed" structure, imperfect though it is, is far preferable to the brutal, repressive, fully dictatorial regimes that existed in these countries in the mid to late 1970s. That leaves only Cuba as fully outside the democratic camp, and even in Cuba the winds of change may be in the air. Meanwhile, academic interpretations have turned away from the earlier focus on corporatism, bureaucratic authoritarianism, and dependency toward an emphasis on "transitions to democracy."[3]

CONSOLIDATED DEMOCRACY—OR MERELY CYCLICAL?

While the transitions to democracy in so many Latin American countries are surely heartening, the question remains as to how fundamental and lasting these changes are. Is Latin American democracy now consolidated, well institutionalized, and therefore permanent? Or is it merely cyclical, another one of those democratic waves that hits the area from time to time and then recedes? For the history has been that while many Latin

Americans desire democracy, democracy in the region has not heretofore proved very lasting, it has seldom delivered on its promises or worked very well, and it has often given rise to mismanagement and disorder. Over time the population then becomes disillusioned with its democracy, begins to demand order and stability, and seeks to have the army restore that stability. The cycle of democracy leading to military authoritarianism thus begins anew.

There is something to be said for the cyclical theory, for in fact that has in considerable measure been the history of Latin America. Immediately after independence in the 1820s the liberals were briefly in power, followed by authoritarian regimes (Rosas in Argentina, Santa Anna in Mexico) for the next twenty years. In the 1850s (obviously varying from country to country), the 1870s, and the 1890s other usually brief liberal breakthroughs occurred that were most often followed by a long authoritarian period. In the years of the worldwide depression of the early 1930s, no less than fourteen of the Latin American countries experienced military-authoritarian takeovers.

The next democratic wave came in the 1950s/early 1960s. A number of dictatorial and/or military regimes (Bolivia, Argentina, Cuba, the Dominican Republic, Venezuela, Brazil, Honduras) were overthrown. One journalist even wrote a book about this period, optimistically entitled "The Twilight of the Tyrants."[4] The changes toward democracy at this time corresponded with a shift in U.S. policy away from support of authoritarianism and toward the support of democratic development through the Alliance for Progress. But this brief democratic window was also quickly slammed shut. Beginning with Argentina in 1962, Brazil, the Dominican Republic, Peru, Honduras, and culminating in Chile and Uruguay, a new wave of military coups took place in the 1960s and early 1970s, bringing to power some of the worst human rights–abusing regimes ever in the history of Latin America. This wave of authoritarianism was the most recent one preceding the contemporary swing back to democracy.

The pattern of cyclical shifts from democracy to authoritarianism and back again has been regular and recurrent. It is so regular as almost to correspond, in a perverted sort of way, to Jefferson's famous call for a revolution at generational intervals. But if this cyclical pattern holds, we should expect that sometime in the next few years the pendulum will again swing back the other way. Latin America will become disillusioned with democracy (already occurring), democracy will be unable to deliver on its promises, disorder and societal decomposition will eventually result, and the familiar call will go out for the military to save the country from democracy's chaos. But eventually there will probably be a renewed impatience with authoritarianism and, once again, calls for democracy. That is how the cyclical theory works.

We all understand that there are many problems in Latin America that continue to make democracy precarious and a return to authoritarianism not entirely unexpected. These include vast socioeconomic problems, enormous class differences, weak political institutions, a political culture not always supportive of democracy, powerful drug lords, a powerful military apparatus, a weak underlying network of grass-roots civic associations, complex international pressures, and various extremisms of both left and right. Any one of these factors, and particularly a combination of them, could easily propel Latin America back toward authoritarianism.

The immense changes in the region in the last thirty years also need to be borne in mind, however. Let us use 1960 as our benchmark, both because we have good statistics dating from that period and because that was the time of the last great wave of democratization in Latin America. Today, Latin America is 70 percent urban and 30 percent rural, as compared with figures that were just the exact reverse of that in 1960. Today Latin America is 70 percent literate as compared with only 30 percent in 1960. Almost every country in Latin America has doubled its per capita income since 1960, and some have doubled it twice in that period. Even with the debt problem and the economic downturn in many countries of the early 1980s, most Latin America countries are far more developed and industrialized now than they were then. Their middle classes are larger and broader, the Latin American militaries have become better educated and more professionalized, a great deal of national infrastructure (roads, highways, airports, factories, port facilities, etc.) has been built in the interim, national communications grids now knit these countries together in ways that were not in place thirty years ago, political awareness and sophistication have increased, and in many countries a solid base for economic takeoff and development has been laid.

In the 1960s a vast body of what was called the "development literature" posited a close correlation between economic development and democracy. In the writings of S. M. Lipset, W. W. Rostow, Gabriel A. Almond, C. E. Black, Robert Heilbroner, and others,[5] the proposition was advanced that socioeconomic development would give rise to political development or democratization and further that such correlations were universal and well-nigh inevitable. U.S. aid policy under the Alliance for Progress was also based heavily on these assumptions, positing that if we poured in sufficient economic and social assistance, the countries of Latin America would become stable, democratic, peaceful, socially just, and anticommunist—just as we in the United States are.

These predictions proved to be woefully misconceived, at least in the short run, leading to a discrediting not only of the development literature but also of U.S. policy. With the wave of coups d'etat sweeping Latin America in the 1960s and with military-authoritarian regimes continuing to dominate during most of the 1970s, it was difficult to make the case that socioeconomic development and democracy were closely correlated. In fact, just the opposite argument was advanced by Samuel P. Huntington:[6] that rather than contributing to democracy, socioeconomic development may so raise expectations as to increase instability and undermine democracy, leading to military takeovers. That appears to be what happened to Latin America in the 1960s.

From the vantage point of the 1990s, however, the development literature looks far better than it looked ten or fifteen years ago. It may be that while the development school was wrong in the short run, it may yet prove to be correct in the long run. For we now find in present-day Latin America that increased literacy correlates well with democracy, urbanization correlates with democracy, economic development and the growth of a middle class correspond with democracy, and so on. All the correlates that did not correlate very well in the late 1960s and 1970s are now correlating very well indeed. One decade, the 1960s, was simply too short a time to measure the complex relations between development and democracy. These relations are surely not one to one; on the other hand, it would be equally incorrect to argue that there are no correlations at all. At a minimum, the development literature that posited a close relation between socioeconomic change and democracy merits a second look. For surely the relationship looks better now than it used to; it may also tell us a great deal about Latin America's future democratic prospects.

Let us make some distinctions. Democracy is probably quite firmly established in most of the more developed and well institutionalized of the Latin American countries: Argentina, Chile, Colombia, Costa Rica, Uruguay, Venezuela. Democracy is less well consolidated in the poorer and less institutionalized of the countries: Bolivia, Ecuador, El Salvador, Guatemala, Haiti, Honduras, Nicaragua, Paraguay, Peru. In these countries, or at least some of them, one would not be entirely surprised if the cyclical pattern were repeated, if military authoritarianism came back into power. There is a third group of what we will call "mixed" countries—Brazil, the Dominican Republic, Panama—where the levels of socioeconomic development are fairly high and democracy has been established, but where democratic institutions enjoy only weak legitimacy and could still be upset.[7]

The above comments mean that in assessing democracy's future in Latin America it makes little sense to talk about the continent as a whole. Rather, we must disaggregate and make distinctions among the countries. Democracy is likely to last in the most developed and institutionalized countries and it remains precarious in the less developed and institutionalized countries. Seen in this light, it seems likely that we may see an isolated instance of one or even several countries reverting to military-authoritarian rule. But these same data show why we should now be surprised if a whole *wave* of reversions to dictatorship were to occur. That possibility, given all the development in Latin America since the 1960s, seems highly unlikely. For even within the framework of cyclical patterns prevailing from the past, change has also occurred that makes the earlier experience unrepeatable in the present context.

THE POVERTY OF OUR NOMENCLATURE

One of the problems with analyzing the transitions from dictatorship to democracy in Latin America is the inadequacy of the terms used to conceptualize the process. Our thinking has been dichotomous: either dictatorship or democracy. But by forcing this either-or choice on Latin America, we have done the area and ourselves a disservice. Not only are these two terms alone inadequate to describe the complexity and diversity of the area but they also force upon us too narrow, too confined a range of choices.

First, the line between dictatorship and democracy ought to be seen as a continuous spectrum with many gradations, not as an either-or choice. Second, we need a nomenclature to describe the various points or "half-" or "part-way" houses on that spectrum. Not only will that reflect more accurately the realities of Latin America but it will also enable us to see more clearly the transitional processes involved. Third, employing a more complex terminology and set of categories will help us understand what is in fact part of the genius of Latin American politics and its politicians, by showing us how various "crazy-quilt," mixed forms and combinations may be constructed. It will be useful to know how one can perhaps move subtly from one category to a more democratic level without this necessitating full-scale social revolution or a reversion to military authoritarianism, which neither the United States nor most Latin Americans desire.

We propose here a seven-part classification (recalling that this is a continuum, so that various mixed forms are possible), rather than the two-part, dictatorship-versus-democracy dichotomy, which proceeds from most dictatorial (category 1) to most democratic (category 7):

1. Totalitarian,
2. Closed authoritarian-corporate,
3. Open authoritarian-corporate,
4. Elected government but military still powerful; a dual power structure,
5. Evolving toward full democracy,
6. Full (political) democracy,
7. Social or economic democracy.

Totalitarianism (category 1) is used here to summarize a syndrome of traits; it is employed in a technical, political science sense and not just as a term of opprobrium.[8] The traits defining totalitarianism are single-party state, cult of the leader, official ideology and indoctrination, absence of plural groups, state monopoly of the economy, technologically proficient terror and police control, and monopoly of control (in the same hands) of all means of armed combat. In Latin America only Cuba qualifies as a fully totalitarian regime, although Pinochet's Chile came close to qualifying in terms of most of the traits listed. Short of revolution or military defeat, it is extremely difficult—although perhaps not impossible—for a totalitarian regime to evolve toward a more democratic kind.

The second category, closed authoritarian-corporate, describes quite a number of recent dictatorial regimes in Latin America: Brazil, 1964–85; Paraguay under Stroessner, 1953–89; Argentina, 1976–83; Uruguay, 1973–85; the Dominican Republic under Trujillo, 1930–61; Cuba under Batista, 1952–58; Guatemala and El Salvador under military rule, 1972–79. These are full-fledged dictatorships with strict state control over many sectors of the population, but they are more authoritarian than totalitarian.[9] That is, they do not have a full-fledged ideology; they do not employ thought control; they may allow some, limited pluralism; etc. Nor is a closed authoritarian-corporate regime quite so difficult to nudge toward change as is a totalitarian one; the countries listed above serve as examples.

Closed authoritarian-corporate regimes may evolve into or gravitate toward more open, somewhat freer, authoritarian-corporate regimes. Such was plainly the case after Stroessner was replaced by General Andrés Rodríguez in Paraguay and in the last years of the Brazilian and Uruguayan dictatorships. These remained authoritarian regimes and were by no means democracies, but they allowed greater freedom for interest group activities and even opposition political parties. They may permit civil society, or parts of it, to be resurrected. Instead of the official, monopolistic labor unions, business groups, and other corporate interests of the closed authoritarian-corporate regimes, the open authoritarian-corporate regimes may permit a greater pluralism of interests and viewpoints. The transition from a closed to an open authoritarian-corporate regime is a major step in the transition to democracy: on the one hand the effort may fail and the regime may revert to a more closed or dictatorial form; but if it succeeds this may be just the opening that will enable democratic groups to surface, push farther, maybe even succeed.

Category 4 is where many of our "halfway houses" may be found. That is, a military regime may have agreed to hold elections, may have (as in Chile) already held elections in which its candidates lost; and now the difficult transition to democracy must be negotiated. The democratic opposition or a newly elected democratic regime does not wish the military to cancel the elections or restore the dictatorship, so it must enter into negotiations with the outgoing military regime. Compromises must be reached, usually involving amnesty for the military, recognition of the military's special place in society, or a dual power structure. The latter means that while the civilian government rules and has jurisdiction in some areas, the military continues to exist alongside it as a parallel and sometimes competing power structure. El Salvador and Guatemala are good examples. Purists of course will say these are not full democracies, which they are not; but the dual structure is still better than the purely dictatorial one, and a partial democracy is better than none at all. With careful coaxing and negotiations, furthermore, the scope of the civilian government may be expanded and that of the military gradually reduced.

Category 5, toward full democracy, overlaps with the preceding category and particularly with the last comments offered. Once elections have been held, then some of the most difficult steps often still lie ahead. This involves an ongoing political and negotiating process that does not end with the holding of elections. Is the military to be completely subordinated to civilian authority or will it still have a special political role and what, precisely, will that be? Can freedom be extended to all groups, including subversive ones, or must it still be restricted in some ways? Will officials of the old regime be punished for their participation in it or its atrocities, or will they enjoy full political rights? How will power be passed to a succeeding regime, and how many successive competitive elections are necessary before a regime is considered fully democratic? These are some of the most difficult issues that an emerging democracy must face; yet we have almost no literature devoted to it. We have abundant storehouses of useful knowledge on how to hold elections but very little on how to manage the at least equally difficult postelection issues. It is precisely in this phase where quite a number of Latin American regimes now find themselves.

Category 6 is full political democracy. Costa Rica and Venezuela surely qualify in this category; Colombia probably would as well if it did not have such severe problems of violence and narcoterrorism. Although they have only recently restored democracy, Chile and Uruguay—because of their strong civilian institutions and long prior histories under democracy—may rapidly approach this category as well. Other countries are similarly becoming more strongly democratized. At this stage there are still many problems and choices that these countries face. But the choices are democratic choices, often within the electoral arena, to be decided at the ballot box more than in the tense political arenas with few established rules where most of the issues discussed in previous categories must be decided.

We have listed social or economic democracy as the seventh category. Among some scholars as well as politicians, this is a logical, necessary, even (according to some) inevitable progression from the previous category of political democracy. But others argue forcefully that there is nothing necessary, let alone inevitable, about such a step; rather, like other essentially political questions, it should be decided in the electoral arena, by ballot box. If a country, having achieved full political democracy, wishes to take this step, that is up to the voters of that country. If they wish social and economic democracy, that is up to them; if not, that is their decision also. These are political choices that a mature democracy makes; the desirability of such changes is open to political debate within the country making the choice.

This seven-part classification offers numerous advantages over a simple dictatorship-or-democracy choice. First, it enables us to see the transition to democracy as a continuum with numerous stages along the way, rather than just as a dichotomous either-or matter. Second, it fits the often ambiguous, mixed, overlapping realities of Latin America better than does the two-part, dictatorship-or-democracy categorization. Third, it enables us to clarify the discrete issues and choices that a country faces at each stage of the transition. Fourth, it reemphasizes the point that the holding of elections is not enough; while elections are a major accomplishment en route to democracy, other equally difficult issues must still be faced for full democracy to be achieved. For in Latin America elections convey partial, not full, legitimacy; political jockeying and negotiations over power positions are thus a continuous process.

U.S. POLICY

It took some time for the United States to recognize and understand the advantages of a foreign policy based on the support of democracy. The issue has a long history in American foreign policy, relating to the old debate between "realists" and "idealists." Realists believed that the United States should be concerned above all else with defending its national self-interests regardless of whom that resulted in our being allied with; idealists, in contrast, wanted a foreign policy imbued with morality and ethical purpose, wanted the United States to be a "beacon on a hill" standing for democracy, human rights, and social justice, regardless of whom that resulted in our insulting. The realist school was summed up, briefly if crudely, in the words of John Foster Dulles, who once proclaimed that in the world, "we have no friends, only interests"; the idealist school was to be found in Woodrow Wilson's vow to "make the world safe for democracy" or Jimmy Carter's call at Notre Dame University to have human rights serve as *the* basis for U.S. foreign policy.

President Reagan was closer to the realist school, and as a result the U.S. came late to the process of assisting and supporting democratization in Latin America. Particularly in the larger, better-institutionalized South American countries, the main forces pushing democratization were indigenous. President Carter's human rights campaign, while not very effective in terms of concrete accomplishments while he was in office, undoubtedly had an effect in accelerating the loss of legitimacy of Latin America's military regimes; but the United States was not during the early 1980s actively and directly involved in trying to engineer democracy. It was the Argentines, the Brazilians, the Uruguayans, the Peruvians who ushered in democracy in their own countries, not the United States.

El Salvador provided the learning experience for the United States with democratization and with the numerous advantages of working with democratic governments. In that strife-torn country in the early 1980s the U.S. faced two alternatives, neither of which was attractive. It could allow the Marxist-Leninist guerrillas to achieve power and thus have to deal with all the negative consequences of having "another Cuba" in the western hemisphere; or it could back a brutal and rapacious military regime and thus have to face the continuous criticism of the Congress, religious groups, and other vocal lobbies concerning human rights violations. To extricate itself from this unhappy choice, the U.S. began pushing for a democratic opening that would provide a third and more attractive alternative. The U.S. urged, cajoled, lobbied, applied pressure, and poured in lots of money; it is a long and involved story whose details need not be repeated here. A series of elections were held that eventually elevated José Napoleon Duarte to the presidency. The U.S. now had a democratic government that it could support instead of having to choose between the unattractive alternatives of a guerrilla victory or a murderous military.

In the course of managing this process the Reagan administration learned some valuable lessons. In El Salvador it quickly realized that a democratic government was far easier to work with than any other type. A democratic government did not commit official murder, did not engage in stupid military campaigns, did not interfere in its neighbors' internal affairs, and was far easier for the U.S. Embassy to deal with. At least equally important in Washington, the administration learned that having a democratic government office in El Salvador defused congressional criticism, quieted the religious and human rights lobbies, enabled our allies to be sympathetic, got the public to support the policy, and in general caused far fewer headaches for U.S. policy. These domestic political considerations were certainly as important as anything happening "on the ground" in El Salvador.

The lessons learned in El Salvador in assisting a country toward democracy and propping it up if necessary later on were soon applied in Honduras, Guatemala, Paraguay, eventually Chile and Nicaragua. In Panama military intervention was used to get General Manuel Noriega out of power and a civilian, elected government installed. Meanwhile an intellectual and institutional infrastructure had been created to further the cause of promoting democracy abroad: President Reagan's 1982 speech to the British Parliament, two White House Conferences on Elections and Democracy Abroad, background work in some of the major think tanks, the Democracy Agenda, the National Endowment for Democracy, a State Department office on elections, agencies to provide election observers, etc. Democracy came to be at the core of U.S. foreign policy, and a cottage industry of agencies sprang up to promote it.

The motivations for this shift in policy, which surprised many observers due to the Reagan administration's earlier hostility to Carter's human rights policy,[10] were as much pragmatic and political as they were moral and idealistic. At the moral level, one can make the case that a foreign policy based on the promotion of democracy reflects American historic ideals and idealism, gives our foreign policy ethical purpose, and provides a set of principles that leaders as well as the public can believe in and support. At a more mundane level, the democracy focus helps give unity to the foreign policy agencies and provides the bureaucracy with something to believe in. We have also learned that democracies do not start wars (Argentina in the Falklands), do not try to subvert or destabilize their neighbors, do not aid guerrilla groups in neighboring countries, and do not muck around in their neighbors' affairs. Democracies make it easier for U.S. business and other groups to operate abroad and for the United States to carry on normal diplomatic relations.

Most important, democracies make it easier on an administration in Washington. Having democracies as our allies enables an administration to have good relations with the Congress instead of poisonous ones, to give it political space to carry out other important policies, to have good rapport with the media and less for them to wax indignant about, to have good relations with our allies instead of these being clouded by peripheral (e.g., Nicaragua) issues, to keep the religious and human rights lobbies off the administration's back, to reduce the nastiness and divisiveness of the domestic debate in favor of a more consensual and supportable policy. All these latter reasons for supporting democracy, which are especially powerful in Washington, can be summed up in one word: grief. Having an active and vigorous pro-democracy/pro–human rights policy—quite apart from any moral or ethical considerations—enables an administration to avoid great doses of grief and to carry out its policies in a more or less calm and reasoned fashion.

Academics and others will continue to debate whether the United States should so actively be seeking to "export" democracy,[11] but among politicians and foreign affairs officials the attractiveness of doing so, for the reasons listed above, is so powerful as to be irresistable. By this time there is widespread consensus, in both the Reagan and Bush wings of the Republican party, among virtually all politicians on the Democratic side of the aisle, and within all the foreign policy agencies, on the democracy agenda. Even "realists" like Henry Kissinger have now come to accept that for the United States to carry out a successful foreign policy requires a strong human rights component. This consensus is so strong that one cannot conceive how *any* future American administration of either political party could not have democracy and human rights at the heart of its foreign policy. The shift in this direction has been dramatic over the last decade and is probably not yet fully understood by the public or some university-based academics.

TOWARD THE FUTURE

The democracy agenda may offer the last great hope for U.S.-Latin American relations. Not only does the democracy focus enable the U.S. to put the turbulent house of its own domestic foreign policy-making in some order, but it may also provide greater cement and unity to U.S.-Latin American relations. For a long time the U.S. and Latin America have been drifting apart in terms of their interests and agendas; the democracy program may help correct or reverse that process. For the democracy agenda provides a means by which both U.S. security interests and Latin American interests in development can go forward at the same time. Rather than growing farther apart, the U.S. and Latin America may both be able to move forward amicably and compatibly on the basis of their shared interest in democracy.

It would be nice if we could end on this happy and optimistic note. But there is a complication: the end of the Cold War. Most of us probably welcome the winding down of the Cold War, and in some respects (the likely petering out of most Marxist-Leninist guerrilla movements, the decline of Cuba's troublemaking potential, resolution of some of the major conflicts in Central America) this development will be good for Latin America. However, we must also recognize that, for good or ill, and stripping all the rhetoric aside, the main and virtually only reason the United States has been interested in Latin America over the last forty years is because of the Cold War. As the Cold War winds down, therefore, U.S. interest and attention will likely decrease as well. Of course we will continue to have on-and-off-again interest in such issues as the debt, immigration, drugs, the environment, human rights, and others. But it is doubtful if these "new agenda" items will elicit the same sustained interest from the U.S. or the commitment of funds from the Congress that the Cold War did over nearly half a century. Already most Latin American governments are operating on the assumption that there will be less U.S. largesse for them in the years ahead.

The result is likely to be a new era of "benign neglect." As in other, past eras of benign neglect, there will be rhetorical flourishes about the importance of Latin America and U.S. interests there (the "New Partnership" of Nixon, perhaps President Bush's "Enterprise for the Americas" initiative), but little substance is put on these bones. Benign neglect, of course, is seldom very benign; and as in the 1950s and then again in the 1970s, it allows small problems to fester into larger ones. One hopes that this doesn't happen and perhaps with the end of the Cold War it won't. Nevertheless, the paradoxical note on which we end is that at precisely the time, through the democracy agenda, that the U.S. has a chance finally and at long last to put its relations with Latin America on a mature and mutually supportive basis grounded on a common interest in democracy, the winding down of the Cold War may well produce—

has apparently already produced—a renewed era of benign neglect that will undermine the vast potential that exists for forging better relations.

The present picture is thus a cloudy one. President Bush's initiatives in pushing the Central American conflicts toward resolution, the Brady Plan to relieve Latin America's onerous debt, the Enterprise for the Americas Initiative, and the North American free trade plan all deserve commendation. They provide a solid basis for a better policy. But Congress needs to put some financial flesh on the bones of these programs and to continue a sustained program of assisting Latin America's own efforts at political (democracy), economic (open markets), and bureaucratic (streamlining) reforms. Other areas, however, (Eastern Europe, the Middle East), also command our attention, and Congress faces strong demands from its constituencies that underfunded domestic programs receive greater budgetary support. Hence Latin America and a successful Latin America policy face an uphill fight, but then that is hardly new in the history of U.S. foreign policy. The newly democratic Latin American governments have many things going for them, but they and the region's friends in the United States will have to continue a program of advocacy if in the present circumstances Latin America is to get the attention and support it requires and if the administration's useful but sporadic initiatives are to be sustained as a mature policy.

Notes

Introduction

1. *Foreign Policy without Illusion: How Foreign Policy Works and Fails to Work in the United States* (Chicago and New York: Scott Foresman/Harper Collins, 1990).
2. The books and edited volumes included *Human Rights and U.S. Human Rights Policy* (Washington, DC: AEI, 1982); *Changing Dynamics of the Brazilian Economy* (Washington, DC: AEI, 1982); *Trade, Aid, and U.S. Economic Policy in Latin America* (Washington, DC: AEI, 1983); *Rift and Revolution: The Central American Imbroglio* (Washington, DC: AEI, 1984); *The Communist Challenge in the Caribbean and Central America* (Washington, DC: AEI and University Press of America, 1987); *The Iberian-Latin American Connection* (Washington, DC: AEI and Westview Press, 1986). Some of my more important essays, articles, and book chapters during this period were collected in *In Search of Policy: The United States and Latin America* (Washington, DC: AEI, 1984); and *Finding Our Way? Toward Maturity in U.S.-Latin American Relations* (Washington, DC: AEI and University Press of America, 1987). Also worth consulting during this period were the special issues of the AEI *Foreign Policy and Defense Review* we put out on Southern Europe, Central America, the Kissinger Commission, Panama, Puerto Rico, and U.S. strategic policy.
3. James L. Sundquist, "Research Brokerage: The Weak Link," in Laurence E. Lynn, Jr. (ed.), *Knowledge and Policy: The Uncertain Connection* (Washington, DC: National Academy of Sciences, 1978), 126–44; James A. Smith, *The Idea Brokers: Think Tanks and the Rise of the New Policy Elite* (New York: Free Press, 1991).
4. For a more complete discussion see Howard J. Wiarda, *The Democratic Revolution in Latin America: History, Politics, and U.S. Policy* (New York: Holmes and Meier, A Twentieth-Century Fund Book, 1990).

1. United States Policy toward Central America

1. For a full discussion see the chapter "The New Powerhouses: Think Tanks and Foreign Policy" in the author's *Foreign Policy Without Illusion: How*

Foreign Policy Works and Fails to Work in the United States (New York: Scott Foresman/Harper Collins, 1990).

2. The classic statement is Graham Allison, *Essence of Decision* (Boston: Little Brown, 1971).

3. See, among others, *Dictatorship, Development, and Disintegration: Politics and Social Change in the Dominican Republic* (Ann Arbor: Xerox University Microfilms Monograph Series, for the University of Massachusetts Program in Latin American Studies, 3 vols., 1975); *Latin American Politics and Development* (Boulder: Westview Press, 1989) with Harvey F. Kline; *The Distinct Tradition: Politics and Social Change in Latin America* (Amherst: University of Massachusetts Press, 1982); and *Corporatism and National Development in Latin America* (Boulder: Westview, 1981).

4. In the eyes of some, "understanding" means justification, rationalization, and sympathy. That means that the author, as some critics have put it, must be labeled a "fascist" for his efforts to try to enlighten and improve Reagan administration policy; while his sometimes colleague Abraham Lowenthal is similarly called a "crypto-fascist" for his writings that have likewise sought to understand the policy. The charges are of course ludicrous and, frankly, the author continues to prefer understanding to the lack thereof. For the debate see the thoroughly wrong diatribe by Keith Haynes, "Authoritarianism, Democracy and Development: The Corporative Theory of Howard J. Wiarda," *Latin American Perspectives* 15 (Summer 1988), pp. 131–50; as well as the author's response in the same journal, 16 (1989).

5. The information in this and the following paragraphs is derived impressionistically from interviewing leaders of both political parties, as well as participant observation in many of the organizations and processes cited.

6. Shirley Christian, *Nicaragua: Revolution in the Family* (New York: Vintage, 1986); Robert Pastor, *Condemned to Repetition: The United States and Nicaragua* (Princeton, N.J.: Princeton University Press, 1987).

7. John A. Reilly (ed.), *American Public Opinion and Foreign Policy* (Chicago: Chicago Council on Foreign Relations, 1980).

8. AEI was one of the key centers in which the planning and preparation for the transition was carried out.

9. Richard Nixon, *The Real War* (New York: Warner Books, 1980); *Mandate for Leadership* (Washington, D.C.: The Heritage Foundation, 1980); The Committee of Santa Fe, *A New Inter-American Policy for the Eighties* (Washington, D.C.: Council for Inter-American Security, 1980); Jeane Kirkpatrick, "Dictatorship and Double Standards," *Commentary* 70 (November 1979), pp. 34–45.

10. See the various "insider" books, by David Stockman, *The Triumph of Politics: Why the Reagan Revolution Failed* (New York: Harper and Row, 1986); Michael K. Deaver and Mickey Herskowitz, *Behind the Scenes* (New York: Morrow, 1988); Donald Regan, *For the Record: From Wall Street to*

Washington (New York: Harcourt, Brace, Jovanovich, 1988); and Alexander M. Haig, Jr., *Caveat* (New York: Macmillan, 1984).

11. Based on interviews with participants on both sides of the process.
12. On this process see the chapter entitled "The Washington Social Circuit" in *Foreign Policy Without Illusion.*
13. Hedrick Smith, *The Power Game: How Washington Works* (New York: Random, 1988).
14. A good, balanced account is Lou Cannon, *Reagan* (New York: G. P. Putnam's Sons, 1982).
15. Howard J. Wiarda, "The United States and Latin America: Change and Continuity," in Alan Adelman and Reid Reading (eds.), *Confrontation in the Caribbean Basin* (Pittsburgh: Center for Latin American Studies, University of Pittsburgh, 1984) 211–26.
16. For AEI see, among others, the various issues of the *Foreign Policy and Defense Review;* the Occasional Papers series of the Center for Hemispheric Studies; Mark Falcoff, *Small Countries, Big Issues* (Washington, D.C.: AEI, 1984); and, by the author, *In Search of Policy* (Washington, D.C.: AEI, 1984), and *Finding Our Way?* (Washington, D.C.: University Press of America, 1987).
17. See Wiarda (ed.), *Rift and Revolution: The Central American Imbroglio* (Washington, D.C.: AEI, 1984).
18. On the reasons why university academics have such a small foreign policy influence see the chapter on "Think Tanks and Foreign Policy" in *Foreign Policy Without Illusion.*
19. *Report of the National Bipartisan Commission on Central America* (Washington: Government Printing Office, 1984; New York: Macmillan, 1984). See also the *Appendix to the Report of the National Bipartisan Commission on Central America* (Washington: GPO, 1984); and the special issue of the *Foreign Policy and Defense Review,* Vol. V, No. 1 (1984) containing the Lead Consultant papers prepared for the Commission.
20. For a detailed, first-hand account see Constantine Menges, *Inside the National Security Council: The True Story of the Making and Unmaking of Reagan's Foreign Policy* (New York: Simon and Schuster, 1988).
21. This theme is more broadly discussed in "The Paralysis of Policy: Current Dilemmas of U.S. Policy-Making," *World Affairs* 149 (Summer, 1986), pp. 15–21.
22. See Barry Rubin, *Secrets of State: The State Department and the Struggle for U.S. Foreign Policy* (New York: Oxford University Press, 1987).
23. This is the major theme of *Foreign Policy Without Illusion.*

2. United States Policy in Latin America

1. For amplification see Howard J. Wiarda, *Finding Our Way: Toward Maturity in U.S.-Latin American Relations* (Washington, DC: AEI and University Press of America, 1987).

2. The "book" here referred to has now become the subject of serious scholarly work: Adam Garfinkle and Daniel Pipes (eds.), *Friendly Tyrants* (New York: St. Martin's Press, 1991).
3. For a fuller analysis see Howard J. Wiarda, *Latin America at the Crossroads: Debt, Development, and the Future* (Boulder, CO: Westview Press, 1987); also, chapter 6.
4. *The Times of the Americas* (May 31, 1989), 10.

3. "Friendly Tyrants"

1. Hans Binnendijk (ed.), *Authoritarian Regimes in Transition* (Washington, DC: Department of State, 1987); Guillermo O'Donnell, et al. (eds.), *Transitions from Authoritarian Rule* (Baltimore: John Hopkins University Press, 1987).
2. The ideas in this introductory section were given preliminary expression in Howard J. Wiarda, "Introduction: Dealing with Dictators in Decline," presentation made at the Public Policy Week forum of the American Enterprise Institute, Washington, DC, December 1985; and published in the special of the journal *World Affairs* devoted to this issue, 149 (Spring 1987).
3. See A. M. Rosenthal, *New York Times Magazine*.
4. See the discussion in Barry Rubin, *Modern Dictators* (New York: McGraw-Hill, 1987).
5. The debate between these position is especially well formulated in Garfinkle and Pipes (eds.), Introduction to *Friendly Tyrants* (New York: St Martin's Press, 1991).
6. Carl J. Friedrich and Zbigniew Brzezinski, *Totalitarian Dictatorship and Autocracy* (New York: Praeger, 1962).
7. Jeane J. Kirkpatrick, "Dictatorships and Double Standards," *Commentary* 70 (November 1979).
8. Howard J. Wiarda, *Dictatorship and Development* (Gainesville: University of Florida Press, 1968).
9. Hugh Thomas, "Cuba: The United States and Batista, 1952–58," *World Affairs* 149 (Spring 1987): 169–77.
10. Robert D. Crassweller, *Trujillo* (New York: Macmillan, 1966).
11. Richard Millett, *Guardians of the Dynasty* (New York: Maryknoll, 1977).
12. Gary Sick, *All Fall Down: America's Tragic Encounter with Iran* (New York: Random House, 1985).
13. An earlier version of this scale was presented in Howard J. Wiarda (ed.), Conclusion to *The Continuing Struggle for Democracy in Latin America* (Boulder, CO: Westview Press, 1980).
14. See Roy C. Macridis, *Modern Political Regimes* (Boston: Little, Brown, 1986).
15. On the concept of limited pluralism in authoritarian regimes see Juan Linz,

"An Authoritarian Regime: Spain," in E. Allardt and S. Rokkan (eds.), *Mass Politics* (New York: Free Press, 1970).

16. While such an approach is not strictly empirical, neither is it merely impressionistic. The Delphi method, as it is known, is somewhat more sophisticated than that.

17. On these distinct models of foreign policy-making see Graham Allison, *Essence of Decision: Explaining the Cuban Missile Crisis* (Boston: Little, Brown, 1971).

18. Roger Hilsman, *The Politics of Policy Making in Defence and Foreign Affairs: Conceptual Models and Bureaucratic Politics* (Englewood Cliffs, NJ: Prentice Hall, 1987); also Howard J. Wiarda, *Foreign Policy without Illusion* (Glenview, IL: Little Brown/Scott Foresman, 1990).

19. Don C. Piper and Ronald J. Terchek (eds.), *Interaction: Foreign Policy and Public Policy* (Washington, DC: American Enterprise Institute for Public Policy Research, 1983).

20. Howard J. Wiarda, "The Paralysis of Policy: Current Dilemmas of U.S. Foreign Policy-Making," *World Affairs* 149 (Summer 1986): 15–21.

21. I. M. Destler, Leslie H. Gelb, and Anthony Lake, *Our Own Worst Enemy: The Unmaking of American Foreign Policy* (New York: Simon and Schuster, 1984), esp. chapter 3, "Congress and the Press: The New Irresponsibility."

22. S. Robert Lichter, Stanley Rothman, and Linda S. Lichter, *The Media Elite: America's New Powerbrokers* (Bethesda, MD: Adler and Adler, 1986).

23. For a conceptual overview see Merle Kling, "Violence and Politics in Latin America," *Sociological Review* 2 (1967): 119–32.

24. An exception is Adam Garfinkle, *The Politics of the Nuclear Freeze* (Philadelphia: Foreign Policy Research Institute, 1984).

25. Joshua Muravchik, *The Uncertain Crusade: Jimmy Carter and the Dilemmas of Human Rights Policy* (Lanham, MD: Hamilton Press, 1986).

26. A. James Gregor, "The Continuing Crisis in the Philippines and U.S. Policy Options," *World Affairs* 149 (Spring 1987): 195–209.

27. The analysis here is indebted to the oral commentary presented by Richard Haass at the FPRI May–June 1987 conference on "Friendly Tyrants."

28. See, for example, John B. Martin, *Overtaken by Events: The Dominican Crisis—from the Fall of Trujillo to the Civil War* (Garden City, NY: Doubleday, 1966); but see also Howard J. Wiarda, *Dictatorship, Development, and Disintegration: Politics and Social Change in the Dominican Republic* (Ann Arbor, MI: Monograph Series of Xerox University Microfilms, 1975).

4. The Military and Democracy

1. Edwin Lieuwen, *Arms and Politics in Latin America* (New York: Praeger, 1960).

2. Howard J. Wiarda, *Critical Elections and Critical Coups: State, Society and*

the Military in the Processes of Latin American Development (Athens, OH: Ohio University Center for International Studies, 1979).

3. Tad Szulc, *The Twilight of the Tyrants* (New York: Holt, 1957).
4. See Howard J. Wiarda, *Dictatorship, Development, and Disintegration: Politics and Social Change in the Dominican Republic* (Ann Arbor: Xerox University Microfilms Monograph Series, 1975) Chapter IV.
5. José Nun, "The Middle Class Military Coup," in Claudio Veliz (ed.), *The Politics of Conformity in Latin America* (London: Oxford University Press, 1967) 66–118.
6. Alfred Stepan, *The Military in Politics: Changing Patterns in Brazil* (Princeton, NJ: Princeton University Press, 1971).
7. Guillermo O'Donnell, *Modernization and Bureaucratic-Authoritarianism* (Berkeley, CA: Institute of International Studies, University of California, 1973).
8. Lieuwen, *Arms and Politics.*
9. John J. Johnson, *The Military and Society in Latin America* (Stanford, CA: Stanford University Press, 1964).
10. L. N. McAlister, "Civil-Military Relations in Latin America," *Journal of Inter-American Studies,* 3 (July, 1961).
11. Elizabeth Hyman, "Soldiers in Politics: New Insights on Latin American Armed Forces," *Political Science Quarterly,* 37 (September, 1972) 401–18.
12. Robert Potash, *The Army and Politics in Argentina, 1928–1945* (Stanford, CA: Stanford University Press, 1969).
13. John Samuel Fitch, *The Military Coup d'Etat as a Political Process: Ecuador, 1948–1966* (Baltimore: Johns Hopkins University Press, 1977).
14. Luigi Einaudi and Alfred Stepan, *Latin American Institutional Development: Changing Military Perspectives in Peru and Brazil* (Santa Monica, CA: The RAND Corporation, 1971).
15. Frederick Nunn, *The Military in Chilean Politics: Essays on Civil-Military Relations, 1810–1973* (Albuquerque, NM: University of New Mexico Press, 1976).
16. Stepan, *Military in Politics.*
17. Ronald McDonald, "Civil-Military Relations in Central America: The Dilemmas of Political Institutionalization," in Howard J. Wiarda (ed.), *Rift and Revolution: The Central American Imbroglio* (Washington, DC: The American Enterprise Institute for Public Policy Research, 1984), 129–66.
18. Charles Corbett, "Politics and Professionalism: The South American Military," *Orbis,* 16 (Winter, 1973) 927–51.
19. Jack Child, *Geopolitics and Conflict in South America* (New York: Praeger, 1985).
20. Howard J. Wiarda, "The Latin American Development Process and the New Developmental Alternatives: Military 'Nasserism' and 'Dictatorship with Popular Support'," *Western Political Quarterly,* 25 (September, 1972) 646–90.

21. Abraham F. Lowenthal (ed.), *Armies and Politics in Latin America* (New York: Holmes and Meier, 1976).
22. Mark Falcoff, "Arms and Politics Revisited: Latin America as a Military and Strategic Theater," in Howard J. Wiarda (ed.), *The Crisis in Latin America: Strategic, Economic, and Political Dimensions* (Washington, DC: American Enterprise Institute for Public Policy Research, 1984) 1–9.

5. Europe's Ambiguous Relations with Latin America

1. Wolf Grabendorff and Riordan Roett, eds., *Latin America, Western Europe, and the U.S.: Reevaluating the Atlantic Triangle* (New York: Praeger/Hoover, 1985).
2. One of the better expressions is Fernando Henrique Cardozo and Enzo Faletto, *Dependency and Development in Latin America* (Berkeley: University of California Press, 1978).
3. Esperanza Duran, *European Interests in Latin America* (London: Routledge and Kegan Paul/Royal Institute of International Affairs, Chatham House, 1985).
4. Howard J. Wiarda, "The United States and Latin America: Toward the 1990s," *The Five College International Forum*, I (Fall 1988), pp. 24–31.
5. Richard Graham, *Britain and the Onset of Modernization in Brazil, 1850– 1914* (Cambridge: Cambridge University Press, 1972).
6. Dana Munro, *Intervention and Dollar Diplomacy in the Caribbean* (Princeton: Princeton University Press, 1964).
7. Michael Grow, *The Good Neighbor Policy and Authoritarianism in Paraguay: United States Economic Expansion and Great Power Rivalry in Latin America during World War II* (Lawrence, Kans.: University of Kansas Press, 1981).
8. Howard J. Wiarda, *The Iberian-Latin American Connection: Implications for U.S. Policy* (Boulder, Colo.: Westview Press/American Enterprise Institute for Public Policy Research, 1986).
9. Carmelo Mesa Lago, *Latin American Studies in Europe* (Pittsburgh: Center for Latin American Studies, University of Pittsburgh, 1979).
10. W. W. Rostow, *The Stages of Economic Growth* (Cambridge: Cambridge University Press, 1960).
11. *Finding Our Way? Toward Maturity in U.S.-Latin American Relations* (Washington, D.C.: University Press of America/American Enterprise Institute for Public Policy Research, 1987); and "United States Policy Toward Central America: A Retrospective of the Reagan Years," *Latin America and the Caribbean Contemporary Record*, James Malloy and Eduardo Camarra, eds. (New York: Holmes and Meier, 1990).
12. *Revolution in the Revolution: Armed Struggle and Political Struggle in Latin America* (New York: Grove Press, 1967).
13. The analysis in this section derives from Duran, *European Interests*.

14. Fernando Morán, "Europe's Role in Central America: A Spanish Socialist View," *Third World Instability: Central America as a European—American Issue*, Andrew J. Pierre, ed. (New York: Council on Foreign Relations, 1986), pp. 6–44.
15. See the Annual Reports of IRELA.
16. See Howard J. Wiarda, "Sixteen Reasons to be Pessimistic," *The Times of the Americas*, May 31, 1989, p. 10.
17. For elaboration on the future of the region see Howard J. Wiarda, "United States Policy Toward Latin America in the Bush Administration: Change, Continuity, and New Challenges," *Current History* (January 1990).

6. The Politics of Latin American Debt

1. Among the better books are William R. Cline, *International Debt* (Washington, DC, and Cambridge, MA: MIT Press for the Institute for International Economics, 1984); Richard E. Feinberg and Ricardo French-Davis (eds.), *Development and External Debt in Latin America* (Notre Dame, IN: University of Notre Dame Press, 1988); Pedro-Pablo Kuczynski, *Latin American Debt* (Baltimore, MD: Johns Hopkins University Press, A Twentieth Century Fund Book, 1988); John H. Makin, *The Global Debt Crisis* (New York: Basic Books, 1984); Barbara Stallings and Robert Kaufman (eds.), *Debt and Democracy in Latin America* (Boulder, CO: Westview Press, 1989); and Albert J. Watkins, *Till Debt Do Us Part* (Washington, DC, and Lanham, MD: The Roosevelt Center and University Press of America, 1986). My own contribution to this discussion may be found in *Latin America at the Crossroads: Debt, Development, and the Future* (Washington, DC, and Boulder, CO: Westview Press for the American Enterprise Institute for Public Policy Research, 1987).
2. Albert O. Hirshman, *A Bias for Hope: Essays on Economic Development in Latin America* (New Haven: Yale University Press, 1971).
3. See Howard J. Wiarda, "Can the Mice Roar? Small Countries and the Debt Crisis," in Robert Wesson (ed.), *Coping with the Latin American Debt* (New York and Stanford, CA: Praeger Publishers for the Hoover Institution, 1988) 119–36.
4. Charles E. Lindblom, *The Policy Making Process*. Englewood Cliffs, NJ: Prentice Hall, 1968).
5. This pessimistic prospect is further elaborated in Howard J. Wiarda, "The End of the Cold War: Superpower Cooperation in Conflict Management in Latin America," in Roger Kanet and Edward Kolodziej (eds.), *The Cold War as Cooperation* (Baltimore: Johns Hopkins University Press, 1991).

7. Opportunities and Obstacles to Superpower Conflict Resolution

1. See Roger Kanet and Edward Kolodziej (eds.), *The Cold War as Cooperation: Regional Patterns and Prospects* (Baltimore: Johns Hopkins University Press, 1991).

2. See my essay "Nueva Nicaragua," *World and I* 5 (April 1990): 122–25; chapter 11 in this book.

3. An influential statement in Frank Fukuyama, "The End of History?" *National Interest* (Summer 1989).

4. Elizabeth Kridl Valkenier, "New Soviet Thinking about the Third World," *World Policy Journal* 4 (Fall 1987): 651–74; Valkenier, *The Soviet Union and the Third World: An Economic Bind* (New York: Praeger, 1983); and Jerry F. Hough, "The End of Russia's 'Khomeini' Period," *World Policy Journal* 4 (Fall 1987): 583–604.

5. See the special issue of *World Affairs*, 150, no. 3 (Winter 1987–88) on "The Vulnerabilities of Communist Regimes," edited by Vladimir Tismaneanu and Howard J. Wiarda.

6. A recent statement of this position is Richard Pipes, "The Russians Are Still Coming," *New York Times*, 9 October 1989, 19; see also the papers collected in Jiri Valenta (ed.), *Gorbachev's "New Thinking" and Regional Conflicts in the Third World* (Boulder, CO: Westview Press, 1989).

7. For background see Cole Blasier, *The Giant's Rival: The U.S.S.R. and Latin America* (Pittsburgh, PA: University of Pittsburgh Press, 1983).

8. Jorge I. Domínguez and Rafael Hernández (eds.), *U.S.-Cuban Relations in the 1990s* (Boulder, CO: Westview Press, 1989).

9. Robert G. Kaiser, "The U.S.S.R. in Decline," *Foreign Affairs* 67 (Winter 1988–89): 97–113.

10. See Howard J. Wiarda and Mark Falcoff, *The Communist Challenge in the Caribbean and Central America* (Washington, DC: American Enterprise Institute for Public Policy Research, 1987).

11. Susan Kaufman Purcell, "Supporting the Sandinistas Still Pays Off for Gorbachev," *Newsday*, 18 April 1989, 5–9.

12. See, by the author, *In Search of Policy: The United States and Latin America* and *Finding Our Way: Toward Maturity in U.S.-Latin American Relations* (Washington, DC: American Enterprise Institute for Public Policy Research, 1984, 1987); and *The Democratic Revolution in Latin America: Implications for U.S. Policy* (New York: Holmes and Meier, A Twentieth-Century Fund Book, 1990).

13. The information here and in the preceding paragraphs is based on interviews with U.S. government officials.

14. Howard J. Wiarda, *Foreign Policy without Illusion: How Foreign Policy Works and Fails to Work in the United States* (Chicago: Little, Brown/Scott Foresman, 1990).

15. The logic here and in the following paragraph derives from S. Neil

MacFarlane, "Bush's Missing Link in Nicaragua," *New York Times,* 6 April 1989, and from Purcell, "Supporting the Sandinistas."

16. Jorge Domínguez, *To Make a World Safe for Revolution: Cuba's Foreign Policy* (Cambridge, MA: Harvard University Press, 1989).
17. Jiri Valenta and Herbert J. Ellison (eds.), *Grenada and Soviet/Cuban Policy* (Boulder, CO: Westview Press, 1986).
18. See the newspaper accounts in the *New York Times* and *Washington Post* for the first week of April 1989.
19. For background on the foreign policies of the individual countries see Harold Eugene Davis and Larman C. Wilson (eds.), *Latin American Foreign Policies: An Analysis* (Baltimore, MD: Johns Hopkins University Press, 1975).
20. Edward A. Kolodziej and Roger E. Kanet (eds.), *The Limits of Soviet Power in the Third World: Thermidor in the Revolutionary Struggle* (London: MacMillan, 1989).
21. See the comments of State Department spokesperson Margaret Tutwiler in *New York Times,* 19 September 1989.
22. See reports in *New York Times,* 5 April 1989, 1.
23. A good discussion is Richard C. Schroeder, "The Soviets' Central America Offer," *Times of the Americas,* 18 October 1989, 13.
24. *New York Times,* 6 April 1989, 1.
25. For some conjecture on what the deal was see *New York Times,* 7 May 1989, sec. 4, 2.
26. See Howard J. Wiarda, "U.S. Policy toward Latin America in the Bush Administration: Change, Continuity, and New Challenges," *Current History* (January 1990); chapter 2 in this book.
27. Robert Kurz, "U.S., Soviets Ambivalent on Nicaragua," *Miami Herald,* 6 August 1989.
28. Kanet and Kolodziej, Introduction and Conclusion to *The Cold War as Cooperation.*
29. Robert Kurz, "U.S., Soviets Ambivalent."
30. For elaboration see chapter 11.
31. See the arguments and recommendations in *Finding Our Way* and *Toward Maturity.*
32. For an analysis of Latin America's future see Howard J. Wiarda, "The United States and Latin America: Toward the 1990s," *Five College International Forum,* no. 2 (Fall 1988): 24–31.
33. On the reasons for such a gloomy prognosis see, by the author, "Sixteen Reasons to Be Pessimistic," *Times of the Americas* 33 (31 May 1989): 10; and "The End of the Cold War: Superpower Cooperation in Conflict Management in Latin America," in Kanet and Kolodziej, *The Cold War as Cooperation.*

8. State-Society Relations in Latin America

1. Gabriel A. Almond and James S. Coleman (eds.), Introduction to *The Politics of the Developing Areas* (Princeton, NJ: Princeton University Press, 1960).

2. See the special issue of *Daedalus* devoted to "The State," 108 (Fall 1979); Theda Skocpol, *States and Social Revolutions* (Cambridge: Cambridge University Press, 1979); the special issue of the *International Political Science Review* on "The Future of the State," 6, no. 1 (1985); and Joel S. Migdal, "Political Development Reconsidered: A Model of State-Society Relations," in Howard J. Wiarda (ed.), *New Directions in Comparative Politics* (Boulder, CO: Westview Press, 1985).

3. For extended discussion see Howard J. Wiarda and Harvey F. Kline, *Latin American Politics and Development*, rev. 2 ed. (Boulder, CO: Westview Press, 1985), chapter 5.

4. Theodore J. Lowi, "The Public Philosophy: Interest Group Liberalism," *American Political Science Review* (March 1967): 5–24.

5. David Easton, *A Systems Analysis of Political Life* (New York: Basic Books, 1969).

6. Ralph Milliband, *The State in Capitalist Society* (New York: Basic Books, 1969); and Nicos Poulantzas, *Classes in Contemporary Capitalism* (London: New Left Books, 1975).

7. Howard J. Wiarda, "Toward a Framework for the Study of Political Change in the Iberic-Latin Tradition: The Corporative Model," *World Politics* 25 (January 1973): 206–35; also Wiarda, *Corporatism and National Development in Latin America* (Boulder, CO: Westview Press, 1981).

8. Ronald Newton, "Natural Corporatism and the Passing of Populism in Latin America," in Fredrick B. Pike and Thomas Stritch (eds.), *The New Corporatism* (Notre Dame, IN: University of Notre Dame Press, 1974), 34–51.

9. That is the position of Alfred Stepan, *State and Society: Peru in Comparative Perspective* (Princeton, NJ: Princeton University Press, 1978).

10. That is Philippe Schmitter's position; see Schmitter and Gerhard Lehmbruch (eds.), *Trends toward Corporatist Intermediation* (London: Sage, 1979); but see also Lehmbruch, "Neocorporatism in Western Europe: A Reassessment of the Concept in Cross-National Perspective," Paper presented to the International Political Science Association Thirteenth World Congress, Paris, 15–19 July 1985.

11. My understanding of the "corporatist tradition" derives from classic social thought—Durkheim, Von Gierke, Weber—as well as more modern treatments: Matthew Elbow, *French Corporatist Theory, 1789–1948* (New York: Columbia University Press, 1948); Ralph Bowen, *German Theories of the Corporative State* (New York: McGraw Hill, 1947); Richard M. Morse, "The Heritage of Latin America," in Louis Hartz (ed.), *The Founding of New Societies* (New York: Harcourt, Brace, Jovanovich, 1964); and especially Antony Black, *Guilds and Civil Society in European Political Thought from the Twelfth Century to the Present* (Ithaca, NY: Cornell University Press, 1984).

12. For example, A. Arguedas, *Pueblo Inferno* (Barcelona: Tasso, 1910); J. Ortega y Gasset, *Invertebrate Spain* (New York: Norton, 1937); Claudio

Veliz, *The Centralist Tradition in Latin America* (Princeton, NJ: Princeton University Press, 1980).

13. Michael Crozier, *The Bureaucratic Phenomenon* (Chicago: University of Chicago Press, 1964).
14. H. H. Gerth and C. Wright Mills (eds.), *From Max Weber* (New York: Oxford University Press, 1958).
15. Charles W. Anderson, "Toward a Theory of Latin American Politics," Occasional Paper No. 2 (February 1964), Graduate Center for Latin American Studies, Vanderbilt University, Nashville, Tennessee.
16. Michael Novak, *Democracy and Mediating Structures* (Washington, DC: American Enterprise Institute, 1980).
17. For a reexamination of Oriental traditions using the same approach see Patricia Springborg, "The Contractual State: Reflections on Orientalism and Despotism," Paper presented to the International Political Science Association Thirteenth World Congress, Paris, 15–19 July 1985.
18. A first effort at applying this model is Howard F. Wiarda, *Politics in Iberia: The Political Systems of Spain and Portugal* (New York: Harper Collins, Little Brown Series in Comparative Politics, 1992).

9. Rethinking Political Development

1. For an earlier discussion of some of these themes see Howard J. Wiarda, ed., *New Directions in Comparative Politics* (Boulder, CO: Westview Press, 1985; revised edition, 1991).
2. Roy Macridis, *The Study of Comparative Government* (New York: Random House, 1955).
3. A useful but still incomplete effort is Irene I. Gendzier, *Managing Political Change; Social Scientists and the Third World* (Boulder, CO: Westview Press, 1985).
4. For some reflections on the "political culture" in which political development studies began and flourished see Gabriel A. Almond, *Political Development: Essays in Heuristic Theory* (Boston: Little Brown, 1970) Introduction.
5. W. W. Rostow, *The Stages of Economic Growth: A Non-Communist Manifesto* (Cambridge: Cambridge University Press, 1960).
6. Robert Heilbroner, *The Great Ascent* (New York: Harper and Row, 1963).
7. Karl W. Deutsch, "Social Mobilization and Political Development," *American Political Science Review,* 55 (September, 1961) 493–514.
8. Marion Levy, *The Structure of Society* (Princeton, NJ: Princeton University Press, 1952).
9. S. M. Lipset, "Some Social Requisites of Democracy: Economic Development and Political Legitimacy," *American Political Science Review,* 53 (March, 1959) 69–105.
10. Lucian W. Pye, *Aspects of Political Development* (Boston: Little Brown, 1966).

9. Rethinking Political Development **331**

11. David E. Apter, *The Politics of Modernization* (Chicago: University of Chicago Press, 1965).
12. Myron Weiner, ed., *Modernization* (New York: Basic Books, 1966).
13. Talcott Parsons, *The Social System* (Glencoe, IL: Free Press, 1951); Parsons and Edward A. Shils, eds., *Toward a General Theory of Action* (Cambridge, MA: Harvard University Press, 1951).
14. Gabriel A. Almond and James S. Coleman, eds., *The Politics of the Developing Areas* (Princeton, NJ: Princeton University Press, 1960).
15. For a brief history see Committee on Comparative Politics, *A Report on the Activities of the Committee, 1954–1970* (New York: Social Science Research Council, 1970) mimeo.
16. Social Science Research Council series, "Studies in Political Development": Almond and Coleman, *Politics of Developing Areas;* Lucian W. Pye, ed, *Communications and Political Development* (Princeton, NJ: Princeton University Press, 1963); Joseph LaPalombara, ed., *Bureaucracy and Political Development* (Princeton, NJ: Princeton University Press, 1963); Robert E. Ward and Dankwart A. Rustow, eds., *Political Modernization in Japan and Turkey* (Princeton, NJ: Princeton University Press, 1964); James S. Coleman, ed., *Education and Political Development* (Princeton, NJ: Princeton University Press, 1965); Lucian W. Pye and Sidney Verba, eds., *Political Culture and Political Development* (Princeton, NJ: Princeton University Press, 1965); Joseph LaPalombara and Myron Weiner, eds., *Political Parties and Political Development* (Princeton, NJ: Princeton University Press, 1966); Leonard Binder, James S. Coleman, Joseph LaPalombara, Lucian Pye, Sidney Verba, and Myron Weiner, eds., *Crisis and Sequences in Political Development* (Princeton, NJ: Princeton University Press, 1971); Charles Tilly, ed., *The Formation of the National States in Western Europe* (Princeton, NJ: Princeton University Press, 1975).
17. Almond, *Political Development,* Introduction.
18. For a twenty-year assessment and appreciation of this work see Myron Weiner and Samuel P. Huntington, eds., *Understanding Political Development* (Boston: Little Brown, 1987).
19. An especially brilliant collection was the inaugural (1968), Vol. 1. No. 1 issue of *Comparative Politics.*
20. Samuel P. Huntington, *Political Order in Changing Societies* (New Haven, CT: Yale University Press, 1968).
21. See, among others, Sidney Verba, "Some Dilemmas in Comparative Research," *World Politics,* 20 (October, 1967) 111–127; Mark Kesselman, "Order or Movement: The Literature of Political Development as Ideology," *World Politics,* 26 (October, 1973) 139–153; Philip H. Melanson and Lauriston R. King, "Theory in Comparative Politics: A Critical Appraisal," *Comparative Political Studies,* 4 (July, 1971) 205–231; Geoffrey K. Roberts, "Comparative Politics Today," *Government and Opposition,* 7 (Winter, 1972) 38–55; Sally A. Merrill, "On the Logic of Comparative Analysis,"

Comparative Political Studies, 3 (January, 1971) 489–500; Robert T. Holt and John E. Turner, "Crisis and Sequences in Collective Theory Development," *American Political Science Review,* 69 (September, 1975) 979–995; R. S. Milne, "The Overdeveloped Study of Political Development," *Canadian Journal of Political Science,* 5 (December, 1972) 560–68; Philip Coulter, "Political Development and Political Theory: Methodological and Technological Problems in the Comparative Study of Political Development," *Polity,* 5 (Winter, 1972) 233–42; Geoffrey K. Roberts, "Comparative Politics Today," *Government and Opposition,* 7 (Winter, 1972) 38–55; Ignacy Sachs, "The Logic of Development," *International Social Science Journal,* 24, no. 1 (1972) 37–43.

22. A. H. Somjee, *Parallels and Actuals of Political Development* (London: MacMillian, 1986); Howard J. Wiarda, *Ethonocentrism in Foreign Policy: Can We Understand the Third World?* (Washington, DC: American Enterprise Institute for Public Policy Research, 1985).

23. Reinhard Bendix, "Tradition and Modernity Reconsidered," *Comparative Studies in Society and History,* 9 (April, 1967) 292–346; S. N. Eisenstadt, *Post-Traditional Societies* (New York: Norton, 1974).

24. Fernando Enrique Cardoso and Enzo Faletto, *Dependency and Development in Latin America* (Berkeley: University of California Press, 1978).

25. See Lloyd I. Rudolph and Susanne Hoeber Rudolph, *The Modernity of Tradition* (Chicago: University of Chicago Press, 1967).

26. Somjee, *Parallels;* Wiarda, *Ethnocentrism.*

27. Max M. Millikan and W. W. Rostow, *A Proposal: Key to an Effective Foreign Policy* (New York: Harper, 1957); Gendzier, *Managing Political Change.*

28. This interpretation is quite different from that of the radical critics such as Noam Chomsky.

29. Huntington, *Political Order;* A. H. Somjee, *Political Capacity in Developing Societies* (New York: St. Martin's, 1982).

30. Cardoso and Faletto, *Dependency and Development.*

31. Among the better examples would be Theodore H. Moran, *Multinational Corporations and the Politics of Dependence* (Princeton, NJ: Princeton University Press, 1974).

32. See Andre Gunder Frank, *Capitalism and Underdevelopment in Latin America* (New York: Monthly Review Press, 1967).

33. Charles W. Anderson, Review in *American Political Science Review* (December, 1978) 1478; also Howard J. Wiarda, "Toward a Framework for the Study of Political Change in the Iberic-Latin Tradition: The Corporative Model," *World Politics,* 25 (January, 1973) 206–35.

34. Philippe C. Schmitter, "Still the Century of Corporatism?" *The Review of Politics,* 36 (January, 1974) 85–131.

35. Howard J. Wiarda, *Corporatism and National Developmental in Latin America* (Boulder, CO: Westview Press, 1981).

36. A solid, balanced treatment is Douglas Chalmers, "Corporatism and Comparative Politics," in Wiarda, ed., *New Directions.*
37. David Cameron, "The Expansion of the Public Economy: A Comparative Analysis," *American Political Science Review,* 72 (December, 1978) 1243–61; Douglas A. Hibbs and Heino Fassbender, eds., *Contemporary Political Economy* (Amsterdam and New York: North Holland Publishing, 1961).
38. Guillermo O'Donnell, *Modernization and Bureaucratic-Authoritarianism: Studies in South America Politics* (Berkeley: Institute of International Studies, University of California, 1973).
39. David Collier, *The New Authoritarianism in Latin America* (Princeton, NJ: Princeton University Press, 1979).
40. Among the better approaches is Ronald Chilcote, *Theories of Comparative Politics: The Search for a Paradigm* (Boulder, CO: Westview Press, 1981).
41. Wiarda, *New Directions,* Conclusion.
42. Rostow, *Stages of Economic Growth.*
43. Lipset, "Some Social Requisites"; Deutsch, "Social Mobilization."
44. Howard J. Wiarda, ed., *The Continuing Struggle for Democracy in Latin America* (Boulder, CO: Westview Press, 1979).
45. Enrique Baloyra, ed., *Comparing New Democracies* (Boulder, CO: Westview Press, 1987); Guillermo O'Donnell, Philippe Schmitter, and Laurence Whitehead, eds., *Transitions from Authoritarian Rule* (Baltimore: Johns Hopkins University Press, 1986); and Larry Diamond, Juan Linz, and S. M. Lipset, eds., *Democracy in Developing Countries* (Boulder, CO: Lynne Rienner Publishers, 1988).
46. See Peter Berger, *The Capitalist Revolution* (New York: Basic Books, 1986); also Howard J. Wiarda, *The Relations between Democracy, Development, and Security: Implications for Policy* (New York: Global Economic Action Institute, 1988).
47. Pye, *Aspects of Political Development.*
48. See the series of reports edited by Daniel Pipes and Adam Garfinkle, *Friendly Tyrants* (New York: St. Martin's, 1991).
49. Howard J. Wiarda, *The Democratic Revolution in Latin America: Implications for Policy* (New York: A Twentieth Century Fund book, Homes and Mier, 1990).
50. For a discussion of the discrediting and demise of the older more radical left and right wing models in Latin America, see the author's *Latin America at the Crossroads: Debt, Development, and the Future* (Boulder, CO: Westview Press for the Inter-American Development Bank, 1987).
51. Allan Bloom, *The Closing of the American Mind: How Higher Education Has Failed Democracy and Impoverished the Souls of Today's Students* (New York: Simon and Schuster, 1987).
52. Ronald Scheman, ed., *The Alliance for Progress—Twenty Five Years After* (New York: Praeger, 1988); also Howard J. Wiarda "Development and Democracy: Their Relationship to Peace and Security," Paper presented at

the Conference on "Regional Cooperation for Development and the Peaceful Settlement of Disputes in Latin America," International Peace Academy and the Peruvian Center for International Studies, Lima, October 27–29, 1986.
53. The outstanding study is Diamond, Linz, and Lipset, eds., *Democracy in Developing Countries.*
54. The most substantial report is Department of State, *Democracy in Latin America: The Promise and the Challenge* (Washington, DC: Bureau of Public Affairs, Dept. of State, Special Report #158, March, 1987).
55. Wiarda, *New Directions in Comparative Politics,* Conclusion.

10. Political Culture and National Development

1. S. M. Lipset, *Political Man: The Social Bases of Politics* (Garden City, NY: Doubleday, 1960); W. W. Rostow, *The Stages of Economic Growth* (Cambridge, England: Cambridge University Press, 1960).
2. Clifford Geertz, *The Interpretation of Cultures* (New York: Basic Books, 1973); Daniel Bell, *The Cultural Contradictions of Capitalism* (New York: Basic Books, 1976).
3. Lucian Pye, *The Mandarian and the Cadre: China's Political Cultures* (Ann Arbor: Center for Chinese Studies, University of Michigan, 1988); Samuel P. Huntington, *American Politics: The Promise of Disharmony* (Cambridge, MA: Harvard University Press, 1981); and Gabriel Almond and Sidney Verba (eds.), *The Civic Culture* (Princeton, NJ: Princeton University Press, 1963).
4. See the long interview with Bell in *The New York Times,* February 7, 1989, p. C13.
5. Howard J. Wiarda, "Toward a Theory of Development in the Iberic-Latin Tradition: The Corporative Model," *World Politics,* 25 (January 1973), 206–35; *Politics and Social Change in Latin America* (Amherst: University of Massachusetts Press, 1982); *Corporatism and Development: The Portuguese Experience* (Amherst: University of Massachusetts Press, 1977); and *Corporatism and National Development in Latin America* (Boulder, CO: Westview Press, 1981).
6. See the comments of Charles W. Anderson in *American Political Science Review* (December 1978), 1478.
7. P. Schmitter and G. Lehmbruch (eds.), *Patterns of Corporatist Policy-making* (Beverly Hills, CA: Sage Publications, 1982); but see also Antony Black, *Guilds and Civil Society in European Political Thought from the Twelfth Century to the Present* (Ithaca, NY: Cornell University Press, 1984).
8. For an attempt at an explanation of why corporatism evoked such strong feelings, see Mitchell A. Seligson, "Political Culture and Democratization in Latin America," in James Malloy and Eduardo Gamarra (eds.), *Latin American and Caribbean Contemporary Record,* Vol. 7 (New York: Holmes and Meier, 1989). My own attempt to wrestle with corporatism's receptivity as a theory is in "Interpreting Iberian-Latin American Relations: Paradigm

Consensus and Conflict," in Wiarda (ed.), *The Iberian-Latin American Connection* (Washington, DC: American Enterprise Institute for Public Policy Research, 1986).

9. E. Faletto, "Cultura política y conciencia democrática," *Revista de la CEPAL,* 35 (August 1988), 77–82.

10. Huntington, "Will More Countries Become Democratic?" *Political Science Quarterly,* 99 (1984), 193–218; Wildavsky, "Choosing Preferences by Constructing Institutions: A Cultural Theory of Preference Formation," *American Political Science Review,* 81 (March 1987); Harry Eckstein, "A Culturalist Theory of Political Change," *American Political Science Review,* 82 (September 1988), 789–804; and Pye, *The Mandarin and the Cadre.*

11. Inglehart, "The Renaissance of Political Culture," *American Political Science Review,* 82 (December 1988), 1203–30.

12. Geertz, *Negara: The Theatre State in Nineteenth Century Bali* (Princeton, NJ: Princeton University Press, 1980).

13. Barnett, *Social and Economic Development* (New York: Guilford Publications, 1989).

14. See the story in *The New York Times,* March 7, 1989, p. Clff.

15. Lechner, *Cultura política y democratizacón* (Santiago, Chile: CLACSO/FLACSO/ICL, 1987).

16 Harrison, *Underdevelopment Is a State of Mind: The Latin American Case* (Lanham, MD: University Press of America, 1985).

17. A similar critique of the Harrison book to the one offered here is Daniel H. Levine, "If Only They Could Be More Like Us!" *Caribbean Review,* 15 (Spring 1987), 19ff.

18. For amplification, see Howard J. Wiarda, "The Military and Democracy," *Harvard International Review,* 8 (May/June 1986), 4–9; this volume, chapter 4.

11. Turnaround in Nicaragua

1. This was the CIA assessment a month prior to the election.

2. For example, long-term Nicaragua scholars Thomas Walker and John Booth concede the regime's Marxism-Leninism at the highest levels.

3. Mark Falcoff, "Somoza, Sandino, and the United States: What the Past Teaches—and Doesn't," *This World* 6 (Fall 1983): 51–70.

4. My former research assistant was put in charge of distributing the funds to the opposition; her stories of the problems involved is worth another article.

12. Mexico

1. Among the better studies see Evelyn P. Stevens, "Mexico's PRI: The Institutionalization of Corporatism," in James M. Malloy (ed.), *Authoritarianism and Corporatism in Latin America* (Pittsburgh: University of Pittsburgh Press, 1977) 227–58.

2. José Luís Reyna and Richard S. Weinert (eds.), *Authoritarianism in Mexico* (Philadelphia: Institute for the Study of Human Issues, 1977).

3. An excellent statement is Jaime Sánchez Susarrey, "Corporativismo o Democracia?" *Vuelta*, 136 (March, 1988) 12–19. For further background see Howard J. Wiarda, *Corporatism and National Development in Latin America* (Boulder, CO: Westview Press, 1981). Sanchez Susarrey's essay won the prize for the best writing on "The Future of Democracy in Mexico."

4. Howard J. Wiarda, "Toward a Framework for the Study of Political Change in the Iberic-Latin World: The Corporative Model," *World Politics,* 25 (January, 1973) 206–35.

5. See the analysis, by the author, in *The Transition to Democracy in Spain and Portugal: Real or Wishful?* (Washington, DC: University Press of America, 1989).

6. Evelyn P. Stevens, *Protest and Response in Mexico* (Cambridge: MIT Press, 1974); Daniel Levy and Gabriel Székely, *Mexico: Paradoxes of Stability and Change* (Boulder, CO: Westview Press, 1983).

7. The analysis is based on figures compiled by the Inter-American Development Bank, *Social and Economic Progress in Latin America* (Washington, DC: IDB, yearly).

8. Based on field work in Mexico by the authors in 1985, 1986, 1987 and 1988.

9. Judith Gentleman, *The National Action Party and Political Change in Mexico* (forthcoming). Gentleman's study explores the historic weaknesses of *all* opposition groups in the face of the PRI's long monopoly.

10. On these issues see the companion books by the author, *In Search of Policy: The United States and Latin America* (Washington, DC: American Enterprise Institute for Public Policy Research, 1984), and *Finding Our Way? Toward Maturity in U.S.-Latin American Relations* (Washington, DC: AEI and University Press of America, 1987).

11. Alan Riding, *Distant Neighbors: A Portrait of the Mexicans* (New York: Knopf, 1985).

12. Michael Shuman, "Dateline Main Street: Local Foreign Policies," *Foreign Policy* (Winter, 1986) 154–74; Dan Pilcher, "The States and Mexico: An Experiment in Cooperation," *State Legislatures* (March, 1981) 18.

13. A good, balanced discussion is Richard B. Craig, "Illicit Drug Traffic: Implications for South American Source Countries," *Journal of Inter-American Studies,* 29 (Summer, 1987) 1–34.

14. Jorge G. Castaneda, "Don't Corner Mexico," *Foreign Policy,* 60 (Fall, 1985) 75–90; Wayne Cornelius, "México/EU: Las fuentes de pleito," *Nexos,* 118 (October, 1987) 25–35.

15. Howard J. Wiarda, *Latin America at the Crossroads: Debt, Development, and the Future* (Boulder, CO: Westview Press, 1987).

16. Snchez Sussarey, "Corporativismo o Democracia?", and Wiarda, "Toward a Framework," esp. pp. 229–35.

17. Merle Kling, "Violence and Politics in Latin America," in Paul Halmos (ed.), *The Sociological Review*, Latin American Sociological Monograph 11 (Keele: Staffordshire: University of Keele, 1967) 119–32.
18. See Howard J. Wiarda, "Can Democracy Be Exported? The Quest for Democracy in United States Latin America Policy," in Kevin Middlebrook and Carlos Rico (eds.), *The United States and Latin America in the 1980s* (Pittsburgh: University of Pittsburgh Press, 1986) 325–52; and more recently, by the author, *The Democratic Revolution in Latin America: History, Politics, and U.S. Policy* (New York: The Twentieth Century Fund, Holmes and Meier, 1990).
19. See the analysis in the volume emerging from the "Friendly Tyrants" project (New York: St Martins, 1991).
20. The analysis here is derived from several USIA surveys of Mexican political preferences; see also Ann L. Craig and Wayne Cornelius, "Political Culture in Mexico: Continuities and Revisionist Interpretations," in Gabriel A. Almond and Sidney Verba (eds.), *The Civic Culture Revisited* (Boston: Little Brown, 1980) 325–93.
21. Based on interview with Mexican government and PRI officials.
22. A listing of the types of successful projects these two agencies have carried out may be found in their annual reports.
23. As emphasized by Susan Kaufman Purcell in her chapter on Mexico in Robert Wesson (ed.), *The Latin American Debt* (New York: Frederick A. Praeger for the Hoover Institution, 1988).
24. Howard J. Wiarda, *Corporatism and Development: The Portuguese Experience* (Amherst: University of Massachusetts Press, 1977); by the same author, *Transcending Corporatism? The Portuguese Corporative System and the Revolution of 1974* (Columbia, SC: Institute of International Affairs, University of South Carolina, 1975).
25. Wiarda, "Toward a Framework."

13. The Dominican Republic

1. For some comparative perspectives that also put the Dominican Republic in context see Howard J. Wiarda and Harvey F. Kline, eds., *Latin American Politics and Development*, 2d rev. ed. (Boulder, CO: Westview Press, 1985).
2. See the preface to the volume from which this chapter is reprinted; and also Robert Dahl, *Polyarchy: Participation and Opposition* (New Haven, CT: Yale University Press, 1971).
3. Richard Morse, "The Heritage of Latin America." In *The Founding of New Societies,* ed. Louis Hartz (New York: Harcourt, Brace, Jovanovich, 1964).
4. Juan Linz, "An Authoritarian Regime: Spain." In *Mass Politics,* ed. E. Allardt and S. Rokkan (New York: Free Press, 1970), pp. 251–283.
5. For further discussion, see Howard J. Wiarda, *Corporatism and National Development in Latin America* (Boulder, CO: Westview Press, 1981).

6. Howard J. Wiarda, "The Struggle for Democracy and Human Rights in Latin America: Toward a New Conceptualization," *Orbis* 22 (Spring 1978): pp. 137–160.
7. Ian Bell, *The Dominican Republic* (Boulder, CO: Westview Press, 1981); Howard J. Wiarda and Michael J. Kryzanek, *The Dominican Republic: Caribbean Crucible* (Boulder, CO: Westview Press, 1981).
8. See the annual reports of the Inter-American Development Bank, *Economic and Social Progress in Latin America* (Washington, DC: IDB, yearly).
9. On the Indian background, see Samuel Hazard, *Santo Domingo, Past and Present* (New York: Harper and Row, 1873); and Frank Moya Pons, *Historia colonial de Santo Domingo* (Santiago: Universidad Católica Madre y Maestra, 1974).
10. Lewis Hanke, *The First Social Experiments in America* (Cambridge, MA: Harvard University Press, 1935).
11. The best study is Lyle N. McAlister, *Spain and Portugal in the New World, 1492–1570* (Minneapolis: University of Minnesota Press, 1984).
12. McAlister, *Spain and Portugal;* also Sidney Greenfield, "The Patrimonial State and Patron-Client Relations in Iberia and Latin America: Source of 'The System' in the Fifteenth Century Writings of the Infante D. Pedro of Portugal." Occasional Papers Series no. 1 (Amherst: Program in Latin American Studies, University of Massachusetts, 1976).
13. Hanke, *First Social Experiments.*
14. Donald Worcester, "The Spanish American Past: Enemy of Change," *Journal of Inter-American Studies* 11 (1969): pp. 66–75; Magali Sarfatti, *Spanish Bureaucratic-Patrimonialism in America* (Berkeley: Institute of International Studies, University of California, 1966).
15. Charles Gibson, *Spain in America* (New York: Harper and Row, 1966); C. H. Haring, *The Spanish Empire in America* (New York: Harcourt, Brace and World, 1963).
16. Moya Pons, *Historia colonial.*
17. A classic statement is Alfred Thayer Mahan, *The Interest of American Sea Power, Present and Future* (Boston: Little, Brown, 1898).
18. Rayford W. Logan, *Haiti and the Dominican Republic* (New York: Oxford University Press, 1968).
19. Franklin J. Franco, *Los negros, los mulatos y la nación dominicana* (Santo Domingo: Editora Nacional, 1969); Carlos Larrazabal Blanco, *Los negros y la esclavitud en Santo Domingo* (Santo Domingo: Postigo, 1967).
20. Antonio Sánchez Valverde, *Idea del valor de la Isla Española* (Santo Domingo: Editora Nacional, 1971); Miguel Angel Monclús, *El caudillismo en la República Dominicana* (Santo Domingo: Editora del Caribe, 1962).
21. Julio G. Campillo Pérez, *El grillo y el ruiseñor: Elecciones presidencialies dominicanas* (Santo Domingo: Editora del Caribe, 1966).
22. The same theme has been struck for other countries; see Raymond Carr, *Spain, 1808–1939* (Oxford: Clarendon Press, 1966); and Jacques Lambert,

Latin America: Social Structures and Political Institutions (Berkeley: University of California Press, 1967).

23. Glen Dealy, "Prolegomena on the Spanish American Political Tradition," *Hispanic American Historical Review* 48 (1968): pp. 37–58.

24. Sánchez Valverde, *Idea del valor;* Monclús, *El caudillismo.*

25. Selden Rodman, *Quisqueya: A History of the Dominican Republic* (Seattle: University of Washington Press, 1964); Sumner Welles, *Naboth's Vineyard: The Dominican Republic, 1844–1924,* 2 vols. (Washington, DC: Saville Books, 1966).

26. Miguel Jorrín and John Martz, *Latin American Political Thought and Ideology* (Chapel Hill: University of North Carolina Press, 1970).

27. Harry Hoetink, *The Dominican People, 1850–1900: Notes for a Historical Sociology* (Baltimore, MD: Johns Hopkins University Press, 1982).

28. Bruce J. Calder, *The Impact of Intervention: The Dominican Republic During the U.S. Occupation of 1916–1924* (Austin: University of Texas Press, 1984).

29. Welles, *Naboth's Vineyard.* Welles was the chief U.S. official involved in these events.

30. Howard J. Wiarda, *Dictatorship and Development: The Methods of Control in Trujillo's Dominican Republic* (Gainesville: University of Florida Press, 1968).

31. Jesús de Galíndez, *The Era of Trujillo* (Tucson: University of Arizona Press, 1973); Germán Ornes, *Trujillo: Little Ceasar of the Caribbean* (New York: Nelson, 1958).

32. Robert D. Crasswelder, *Trujillo: The Life and Times of a Caribbean Dictator* (New York: Macmillan, 1966).

33. Wiarda, *Dictatorship and Development,* ch. 9.

34. Lawrence E. Rothstein, "Aquinas and Revolution." Paper presented at the Annual Meeting of the American Political Science Association, Chicago, September 2–5, 1976.

35. Bernard Diederich, *Trujillo: The Death of the Goat* (Boston: Little, Brown, 1978).

36. Samuel P. Huntington, *Political Order in Changing Societies* (New Haven, CT: Yale University Press, 1968), p. 407.

37. For two contrasting views of these events, see John Bartlow Martin, *Overtaken by Events: The Dominican Crisis from the Fall of Trujillo to the Civil War* (New York: Doubleday, 1966); and Howard J. Wiarda, *Dictatorship, Development, and Disintegration: Politics and Social Change in the Dominican Republic* (Ann Arbor, MI: Xerox University Microfilms Monograph Series, 1975).

38. Quoted in Arthur M. Schlesigner, Jr., *A Thousand Days: John F. Kennedy in the White House* (Boston: Houghton Mifflin, 1965), pp. 769–770.

39. Martin, *Overtaken by Events;* Wiarda, *Dictatorship, Development, and Disintegration.*

40. Howard J. Wiarda, "Trujilloism without Trujillo," *The New Republic* 151 (September 19, 1964): pp. 5–6.
41. The best studies are Piero Gleijeses, *The Dominican Crisis* (Baltimore, MD: Johns Hopkins University Press, 1978); Abraham F. Lowenthal, *The Dominican Intervention* (Cambridge, MA: Harvard University Press, 1971); José Moreno, *Barrios in Arms* (Pittsburgh, PA: University of Pittsburgh Press, 1970); and Jerome Slater, *Intervention and Negotiation* (New York: Harper and Row, 1970). Revisionist interpretations include Howard J. Wiarda, "The United States and the Dominican Republic: Intervention, Dependency, and Tyrannicide," *Journal of Inter-American Studies* 22 (May 1980): pp. 247–260; and Michael J. Kryzanek, "The Dominican Intervention Revisited: An Attitudinal and Operational Analysis" (unpublished paper).
42. Michael J. Kryzanek, *Political Party Opposition in Latin America: The PRD, Joaquín Balaguer and Politics in the Dominican Republic, 1966–1973* (Ph.D. Diss., University of Massachusetts, Amherst, 1975); also Howard J. Wiarda and Michael J. Kryzanek, "Dominican Dictatorship Reconsidered: The Caudillo Tradition and the Regimes of Trujillo and Balaguer," *Revista/Review Interamericana* 7 (Fall 1977): pp. 417–435.
43. See G. Pope Atkins, *Arms and Politics in the Dominican Republic* (Boulder, CO: Westview Press, 1981).
44. Michael J. Kryzanek, "Diversion, Subversion, and Repression: The Strategies of Anti-Regime Politics in Balaguer's Dominican Republic," *Caribbean Studies* 1 (1977), and 2 (1977).
45. Michael J. Kryzanek, "The 1978 Election in the Dominican Republic: Opposition Politics, Intervention and the Carter Administration," *Caribbean Studies* 19 (1979).
46. Wiarda and Kryzanek, *Dominican Republic.*
47. Howard J. Wiarda, *Ethnocentrism in Foreign Policy: Can We Understand the Third World?* (Washington, DC: American Enterprise Institute for Public Policy Research, 1985).
48. Sánchez Valverde, *Idea del valor;* based also on interviews conducted by the author in the Dominican Republic in 1962, 1964–1965, 1966, 1969–1970, 1972, 1977, and 1978.
49. Interviews (see n. 48). For a report on some of these interview results see Howard J. Wiarda, *The Aftermath of the Trujillo Dictatorship: The Emergence of a Pluralist Political System in the Dominican Republic* (Ann Arbor, MI: Xerox University Microfilms, 1967).
50. See Juan Bosch, *Composición social dominicana* (Santo Domingo: Librería Nacional, 1970).
51. Howard J. Wiarda, "Constitutions and Constitutionalism in the Dominican Republic: The Basic Law within the Political Process," *Law and Society Review* 2 (June 1968): pp. 385–405.
52. Pedro Andres Pérez Cabral, *La comunidad mulata: El caso socio-político de la República Dominicana* (Caracas: Gráfica Americana, 1967).

53. Marvin Goldwert, *The Constabulary in the Dominican Republic: Progeny and Legacy of United States Intervention* (Gainesville: University of Florida Press, 1962).
54. Wiarda, *Dictatorship, Development, and Disintegration,* ch. 10.
55. Howard J. Wiarda, "The Development of the Labor Movement in the Dominican Republic," *Inter-American Economic Affairs* 20 (Summer 1966): pp. 41–63.
56. James A. Clark, *The Church and the Crisis in the Dominican Republic* (Westminster, MD: Newman Press, 1967).
57. Wiarda, *Dictatorship, Development, and Disintegration,* chs. 16–17.
58. *Ibid.*
59. Howard J. Wiarda, "The Politics of Civil-Military Relations in the Dominican Republic," *Journal of Inter-American Studies* 7 (October 1965): pp. 465–484.
60. Wiarda and Kryzanek, *Dominican Republic,* ch. 7.
61. Wiarda, *Dictatorship, Development, and Disintegration,* ch. 13.
62. *Ibid.,* ch. 14.
63. See the numerous comments in Martin, *Overtaken by Events.*
64. Wiarda, *Dictatorship, Development, and Disintegration,* ch. 16.
65. Jan Knippers Black, *The Dominican Republic: Politics and Development in an Unsovereign State* (Boston: Allen and Unwin, 1989).
66. G. Pope Atkins and Larman C. Wilson, *The United States and the Trujillo Regime* (New Brunswick, NJ: Rutgers University Press, 1972).
67. Michael J. Kryzanek, *U.S.-Latin American Relations* (New York: Praeger, 1985).
68. John J. Johnson, *Political Change in Latin America: The Emergence of the Middle Sectors* (Stanford, CA: Stanford University Press, 1958); W. W. Rostow, *The Stages of Economic Growth* (Cambridge: Cambridge University Press, 1960).
69. See the monograph-length report prepared by the author for the Inter-American Development Bank, *Latin America at the Crossroads: Debt, Development, and the Future* (Boulder, CO: Westview Press, 1985).
70. Howard J. Wiarda, ed., *The Continuing Struggle for Democracy in Latin America* (Boulder, CO: Westview Press, 1980); also *Corporatism and National Development.*
71. Howard J. Wiarda, "The Political Systems of Latin America: Developmental Models and a Typology of Regimes." *In Latin America,* ed. Jack W. Hopkins (New York: Holmes and Meier, 1985).
72. Richard M. Morse, "The Challenge of Ideology in Latin America," *Foreign Policy and Defense Review* 5 (1985): pp. 14–23.
73. See, for example, José Oviedo, *Las formas políticas del eterno retorno* (Santo Domingo: Instituto Tecnológico de Santo Domingo, 1985).
74. See especially Vicente Lecuna and Harold A. Bierck, eds., *The Selected Writings of Bolívar,* 2 vols. (New York: Colonial Press, 1951).

75. Howard J. Wiarda, "Updating United States Strategic Policy: Containment in the Caribbean Basin." Paper presented at a conference, Containment and the Future, National Defense University, Washington, DC, November 7–8, 1985.

14. Is Cuba Next?

1. Zbigniew Brzezinski, *The Grand Failure: The Birth and Death of Communism in the Twentieth Century* (New York: Scribner's, 1989).
2. The analysis is based on a review of the major literature as well as my two research trips to Cuba in 1987 and 1988. It is unusual for a serious scholar who is not a "true believer" in the Revolution to be admitted to Cuba as I was; moreover, while in Cuba, our group and some of us as individuals had remarkable access to high Cuban government and party officials. Access was particularly facilitated in my case by my affiliation at that time with the American Enterprise Institute for Public Policy Research in Washington and the assumption by Cuban officials that messages and positions conveyed to me would subsequently be relayed to Reagan and Bush administration officials. That assumption was not necessarily completely valid but it certainly gave me access to the highest levels of the Cuban regime. The two trips to Cuba were sponsored, respectively, by the Latin American Studies Association through a grant from the Ford Foundation and by the Center for International Affairs of Harvard University through a grant from the Heinz Foundation.
3. An early and preliminary report on a larger project dealing with the "Crises of Communist Regimes" is Vladimir Tismaneanu and Howard J. Wiarda, Introduction to Special Issue of *World Affairs* (Spring 1988).
4. The analysis was carried out by the State Department's legal office; see also Alan H. Luxenberg, "Did Eisenhower Push Castro into the Arms of the Soviets?" *Journal of Inter-American Studies and World Affairs* 30 (Spring 1988): 37–72.
5. On the decline of ideology in Marxist-Leninist regimes see Vladimir Tismaneanu, *The Crisis of Marxist Ideology in Eastern Europe: The Poverty of Utopia* (London: Routledge, 1988).
6. For a full-length discussion see Howard J. Wiarda, *The Democratic Revolution in Latin America: History, Politics, and U.S. Policy* (New York: A Twentieth Century Fund Book, Holmes and Meier, 1990).
7. The analysis here echoes that of Jorge Domínguez, Presentation on "Cuba in the 1990s," Annual Meeting of the New England Council on Latin American Studies, Durham, NH, 27 October 1990.
8. On Castro's leadership see Edward González, *Cuba under Castro: The Limits of Charisma* (Boston: Houghton Mifflin, 1974).
9. The literature on "ungovernability" may now be more relevant to Marxist-

Leninist regimes than to liberal-democratic ones; see Richard Rose and Guy Peters, *Can Governments Go Bankrupt?* (New York: Basic Books, 1978).

10. On this as well as the institutional changes see Jorge Domínguez, *Cuba: Order and Revolution* (Cambridge, MA: Belknap Press of Harvard University Press, 1978).

11. Lucian Pye and Sidney Verba (eds.), *Political Culture and Political Development* (Princeton, NJ: Princeton University Press, 1965).

12. Nick Eberstadt, *The Poverty of Communism* (New Brunswick, NJ: Transaction Press, 1988).

13. See the large, multiauthored study edited by Daniel Pipes and Adam Garfinkle, *Friendly Tyrants* (New York: St. Martin's Press, 1991).

14. For some comparisons see Howard J. Wiarda, *Politics in Iberia: The Political Systems of Spain and Portugal* (New York: Harper-Collins, 1992).

15. The best study is by Carmelo Mesa-Lago, *The Economy of Socialist Cuba* (Albuquerque: University of New Mexico Press, 1981).

16. Robert Packenham, "Capitalist Dependency and Socialist Dependency: The Case of Cuba," paper presented at the Annual Meeting of the American Political Science Association, New Orleans, 29 August–1 September 1985.

17. *New York Times,* 16 January 1989, D5.

18. For a more extended treatment see Howard J. Wiarda, "Cuba and U.S. Foreign Policy in Latin America: The Changing Realities," in Jorge Domínguez (ed.), *U.S.-Cuban Relations in the 1990s* (Boulder, CO: Westview Press, 1989).

19. Roger Kanet and Edward Kolodziej (eds.), *The Limits of Soviet Power in the Third World* (New York: MacMillan, 1989).

20. See Mikhail Gorbachev, *Perestroika: New Thinking for Our Country and the World* (New York: Harper and Row, 1987).

21. For a report on these activities see *Moscow-Miami Dialogue: The Mini Summit,* Occasional Paper Series Vol. 3, No. 1, Institute for Soviet and East European Studies, University of Miami, FL, 1990.

15. South American Domestic Politics and Foreign Policy

1. Statistics on this growth may be found in the annual *Social and Economic Progress in Latin America* (Washington, D.C.: Inter-American Development Bank, yearly).

2. Sanford J. Ungar, ed., *Estrangement: America and the World* (New York: Oxford University Press, 1985).

3. For an overall perspective on U.S. relations with Latin America, see Howard J. Wiarda, *In Search of Policy: The United States and Latin America* (Washington, D.C.: American Enterprise Institute, 1984); see also Frederick B. Pike, *The United States and the Andean Republics* (Cambridge: Harvard University Press, 1977). Good reviews of the foreign policies of the South American states may be found in Harold E. Davis and Larman C. Wilson,

344 *15. South American Domestic Politics*

eds., *Latin American Foreign Policies* (Baltimore: Johns Hopkins University Press, 1975); and Elizabeth G. Ferris and Jennie K. Lincoln, eds., *Latin American Foreign Policies: Global and Regional Dimensions* (Boulder: Westview Press, 1981).
  4. Howard J. Wiarda, *The Democratic Revolution in Latin America: History, Politics and U.S. Policy* (New York: Holmes and Meier, A Twentieth century Fund Book, 1990); see also Paul W. Drake and Eduardo Silva, eds., *Elections and Democratization in Latin America, 1980–1985* (La Jolla: University of California at San Diego, 1986).
  5. Guillermo O'Donnell, Philippe C. Schmitter, and Laurence Whitehead, eds., *Transitions from Authoritarian Rule: Prospects for Democracy* (Baltimore: Johns Hopkins University Press, 1986); an earlier survey is Howard J. Wiarda, ed., *The Continuing Struggle for Democracy in Latin America* (Boulder: Westview Press, 1980).
  6. See Kevin J. Middlebrook and Carlos Rico, eds., *The United States and Latin America in the 1980s* (Pittsburgh: University of Pittsburgh Press, 1986).
  7. For further elaboration, see by the author, *Finding Our Way? Toward Maturity in U.S.-Latin American Relations* (Washington, D.C.: University Press of America, 1987).
  8. See, for example, Wayne A. Selcher, *Brazil's Multilateral Relations: Between First and Third Worlds* (Boulder: Westview Press, 1978); also Teixiera Soares, *O Brasil no Conflito Ideológico Global* (Rio de Janeiro: Civilizaçao Brasileira, 1980).
  9. The materials in this section are based on observations made during extended research trips by the author to Latin America in 1985 and 1987.
 10. Raúl Alfonsín, "Address by the President of Argentina, Dr. Raul Alfonsín" (Amherst: University of Massachusetts, Mimeo., November 20, 1986).
 11. The apostle of this point of view is W. W. Rostow, *The Stages of Economic Growth* (Cambridge: Cambridge University Press, 1960).
 12. The analysis here reflects the conclusions of a major research project being carried out at the American Enterprise Institute under the author's direction entitled "Updating U.S. Strategic Policy in Latin America."
 13. Jack Child, *Geopolitics and Conflict in South America* (New York: Praeger, 1985).
 14. See the author's paper, "Interpreting Iberian-Latin American Interrelations: Paradigm Consensus and Conflict," Occasional Paper No. 10 (Washington, D.C.: Center for Hemispheric Studies, American Enterprise Institute, 1985); published also in Howard J. Wiarda, ed., *The Iberian-Latin American Connection: Implications for U.S. Foreign Policy* (Boulder: Westview Press and American Enterprise Institute, 1986).
 15. The information here is based on numerous United States Information Agency (USIA) surveys of various South American countries. See also *New York Times* (November 17, 1986), which reports on a major survey of Mexico; and Enrique J. Baloyra and John Martz, *Political Attitudes in Ven-*

ezuela: Societal Cleavages and Political Opinion (Austin: University of Texas Press, 1979).

16. See, by the author, *Latin America at the Crossroads: Debt, Development, and the Future* (Boulder: Westview Press and American Enterprise Institute, 1987); also Christine A. Bogdanowicz-Dindert, "The Debt Crisis—The Baker Plan Revisited," *Journal of Inter-American Studies and World Affairs* 28 (Fall 1986), pp. 33–46.

17. Howard J. Wiarda, "United States Relations with South America: Painful Readjustments," *Current History* (January 1987), pp. 1ff.

18. The Hemingway writings are *Death in the Afternoon, The Sun Also Rises,* and *The Fifth Column and Four Stories of the Spanish Civil War;* by García Marquez, see *One Hundred Years of Solitude.*

19. See Frederick Pike, *Hispanismo, 1898–1936: Spanish Conservatives and Liberals and Their Relations with Latin America* (Notre Dame: University of Notre Dame Press, 1971); also Mark Falcoff, "Spain and the Southern Cone," in Wiarda, ed., *Iberian-Latin American Connection.*

20. The author's own critiques of the Rostow thesis may be found in the essays "Misreading Latin America—Again," *Foreign Policy,* No. 65 (Winter 1986–87), pp. 135–153; and "Alternative Paradigms: The 'Conflict' and 'Consensus' Models," Chapter 5 in Howard J. Wiarda, *Corporatism and National Development in Latin America* (Boulder: Westview Press, 1981).

21. See the four-volume study by Larry Diamond, Juan Linz, and Seymour Martin Lipset, eds., *Democracy in Developing Nations* (Boulder: Lynne Rienner Publishers, 1989); one volume is devoted to Latin America.

22. Samuel P. Huntington, *Political Order in Changing Societies* (New Haven: Yale University Press, 1968).

23. John S. Fitch, *The Coup d'Etat as a Political Process: Ecuador, 1948–66* (Baltimore: Johns Hopkins University Press, 1977); see also the series of articles in the *Washington Post* (January 1987) reporting on the most recent Ecuadorian confrontations in this long process.

24. See Chapter 1 of *Latin America at the Crossroads;* also Howard J. Wiarda, "The Latin American Development Process and the New Developmental Alternatives: Military 'Nasserism' and 'Dictatorship with Popular Support,'" *Western Political Quarterly* 25 (September 1972), pp. 464–490.

25. Quoted in L. S. Rowe, *The Federal System of the Argentine Republic* (Washington, D.C.: The Carnegie Institution, 1921).

26. See the survey results reported in *New York Times* (November 17, 1986), p. 1.

27. By the author, "Interpreting Iberian—Latin American Relations."

28. See the discussion in Riordan Roett, *Brazil: Politics in a Patrimonialist Society* (Boston: Allyn and Bacon, 1984); also Wayne Selcher, ed., *Political Liberalization in Brazil: Dynamics, Dilemmas, and Future Prospects* (Boulder: Westview Press, 1986).

29. An excellent discussion of the issues is in Edward G. McGrath, ed., *Is American Democracy Exportable?* (Beverly Hills: Glencoe Press, 1968).

30. William R. Cline, *International Debt* (Washington, D.C.: Institute for International Economics, 1984); John H. Makin, *The Global Debt Crisis* (New York: Basic Books, 1984); M. S. Mendelsohn, *The Debt of Nations* (New York: Priority Press, 1984); Alfred J. Watkins, *Till Debt Do Us Part* (Washington, D.C.: University Press of America for the Roosevelt Center for American Policy Studies, 1986); and Thomas Scheetz, *Peru and the International Monetary Fund* (Pittsburgh: University of Pittsburgh Press, 1986).

31. *Latin America at the Crossroads;* based on the author's extensive research trip around South America, July–August 1985.

32. The analysis here is based on field research in South America in 1985 and 1987; see also John Mills, *The Underground Empire* (New York: Doubleday, 1986).

33. McGrath, *Is American Democracy Exportable?*

34. The analysis here is based on a variety of USIA surveys of Latin American democracy.

35. Natalio Botano, "New Trends in Argentine Politics," paper presented at the Seminar on the Southern Cone, The Argentine-American Forum, Washington, D.C., June 5–6, 1983; also Claudio Veliz, *The Centralist Tradition in Latin America* (Princeton: Princeton University Press, 1980).

36. Botana, "New Trends in Argentine Politics."

37. Richard M. Morse, "The Challenge of Ideology in Latin America," *Foreign Policy and Defense Review* 5, no. 3 (Winter 1985), pp. 14–23.

38. See especially Baloyra and Martz, *Political Attitudes*.

39. Based on USIA surveys; also *New York Times* (November 17, 1986), p. 1.

40. Falcoff, "Spain and the Southern Cone"; also Carlos Rangel, *The Latin Americans* (New Brunswick: Transaction Books, 1987).

41. For a more extended discussion of these differences, see Howard J. Wiarda, "Changing Realities and U.S. Policy in the Caribbean Basin: An Overview," in James R. Green and Brent Scowcroft, eds., *Western Interests and U.S. Policy Options in the Caribbean Basin* (Boston: Oelgeschlager, Gunn and Hain, 1984), pp. 55–98.

42. Mark Falcoff, "Arms and Politics Revisited: Latin America as a Military and Strategic Theater," in Howard J. Wiarda, ed., *The Crisis in Latin America* (Washington, D.C.: American Enterprise Institute, 1984), pp. 1–9.

43. Jeane Kirkpatrick, "The Hobbes Problem: Order, Authority, and Legitimacy in Central America," paper presented at the 1980 Public Policy Week of the American Enterprise Institute, Washington, D.C., December 1980; published in AEI's Public Policy Week *Proceedings* (1981).

44. See the analysis presented in *Finding Our Way*.

45. For example, Riordan Roett, "Democracy and Debt in South America," *Foreign Affairs* 62, no. 3 (1984), pp. 695–720.

46. Arthur P. Whitaker, *The Western Hemisphere Idea: Its Rise and Decline* (Ithaca: Cornell University Press, 1954).

16. Saving Latin America from the "Black Hole"

1. Rudiger Dornbusch, John J. Makin, and David Zlowe (eds.), *Alternative Solutions to Developing Country Debt Problems* (Washington, D.C.: AEI, 1989); Richard E. Feinberg and Valeriana Kallab (eds.), *Adjustment Crisis in the Third World* (Washington, D.C.: Overseas Development Council, 1984); John Williamson, *The Progress of Policy Reform in Latin America* (Washington, D.C.: Institute for International Economics, 1990).
2. Howard J. Wiarda, *The Democratic Revolution in Latin America* (New York: A Twentieth Century Fund Book, Holmes and Meier, 1990).
3. Roger Kanet and Edward Kolodziej (eds.), *The Cold War as Cooperation* (Baltimore: Johns Hopkins University Press, 1991).

17. The Democratic Breakthrough in Latin America

1. Howard J. Wiarda (ed.), *The Continuing Struggle for Democracy in Latin America* (Boulder, CO: Westview Press, 1980).
2. Howard J. Wiarda, *Corporatism and Development in Latin America* (Boulder, CO: Westview Press, 1981); Fernando Enrique Cardoso and Enzo Faletto, *Dependency and Development in Latin America* (Berkeley: University of California Press, 1979); and Guillermo O'Donnell, *Modernization and Bureaucratic-Authoritarianism* (Berkeley: Institute of International Studies, University of California, 1973).
3. The literature includes Enrique Baloyra (ed.), *Comparing New Democracies: Transition and Consolidation in Mediterranean Europe and the Southern Cone* (Boulder, CO: Westview Press, 1987); James M. Malloy and Mitchell A. Seligson (eds.), *Authoritarians and Democrats: Regime Transition in Latin America* (Pittsburgh, PA: University of Pittsburgh Press, 1987); Guillermo O'Donnell, et al. (eds.), *Transitions from Authoritarian Rule: Prospects for Democracy* (Baltimore, MD: Johns Hopkins University Press, 1986); and Howard J. Wiarda, *The Democratic Revolution in Latin America: History, Politics, and U.S. Policy* (New York: A Twentieth-Century Fund Book, Holmes and Meier, 1990).
4. Tad Szulc, *Twilight of the Tyrants* (New York: Holt, 1959).
5. The references are to S. M. Lipset, *Political Man* (New York: Doubleday, 1960); W. W. Rostow, *The Stages of Economic Growth* (Cambridge: Cambridge University Press, 1960); Gabriel A. Almond and James S. Coleman (eds.), *The Politics of the Developing Areas* (Princeton, NJ: Princeton University Press, 1960); C. E. Black, *The Dynamics of Modernization* (New York: Harper and Row, 1966); Robert Heilbroner, *The Great Ascent* (New York: Harper and Row, 1963).

6. Samuel P. Huntington, *Political Order in Changing Societies* (New Haven, CT: Yale University Press, 1968).
7. Based on extensive survey data and reported in Wiarda, *Democratic Revolution*.
8. Carl Friedrich and Zbigniew Brzezinski, *Totalitarian Dictatorship and Autocracy* (New York: Praeger, 1962).
9. The distinction is drawn clearly in Juan Linz, "An Authoritarian Regime: Spain," in E. Allardt and S. Rokkan (eds.), *Mass Politics* (New York: Free Press, 1970).
10. The shift is well documented in Tamar Jacoby, "The Reagan Turnaround on Human Rights," *Foreign Affairs* (Summer 1986): 1066–86.
11. The author's views have changed over time, from very skeptical to more supportive: see "Can Democracy Be Exported: The Quest for Democracy in U.S.-Latin American Policy," in Kevin Middlebrook and Carlos Rico (eds.), *The United States and Latin America in the 1980s* (Pittsburgh, PA: University of Pittsburgh Press, 1986), 325–52; as well as *Democratic Revolution*.

Selected Bibliography

Adelman, Alan, and Reid Reading, eds. *Confrontation in the Caribbean Basin.* Pittsburgh, PA: University Center for International Studies, 1984.

Arnson, Cynthia. *El Salvador: A Revolution Confronts the United States.* Washington, DC: Institute for Policy Studies, 1982.

Atkins, G. Pope. *South America into the 1990s: Evolving International Relationships in a New Era.* Boulder, CO: Westview Press, 1990.

Baloyra, Enrique. *El Salvador in Transition.* Chapel Hill: University of North Carolina Press, 1982.

Binnendijk, Hans, ed. *Authoritarian Regimes in Transition.* Washington, DC: Department of State, 1987.

Blachman, Morris, William LeoGrande, and Kenneth Sharpe. *Confronting Revolution: Security through Diplomacy in Central America.* New York: Pantheon Books, 1986.

Blasier, Cole. *The Giant's Rival: The U.S.S.R. and Latin America.* Pittsburgh, PA: University of Pittsburgh Press, 1983.

Boaz, David, ed. *Assessing the Reagan Years.* Washington, DC: CATO Institute, 1988.

Booth, John A. *The End and the Beginning: The Nicaraguan Revolution.* Boulder, CO: Westview Press, 1982.

Brzezinski, Zbigniew. *Power and Principle: Memoirs of the National Security Adviser, 1977–1981.* New York: Farrar, Strauss, Giroux, 1983.

Calvert, Peter. *The Central American Security System: North-South or East-West?* Cambridge: Cambridge University Press, 1988.

Cannon, Lou. *Reagan.* New York: Putnam's, 1982.

Cardoso, Fernando H., and Enzo Faletto. *Dependency and Development in Latin America.* Berkeley: University of California Press, 1978.

Carter, Jimmy. *Keeping Faith: Memoirs of a President.* New York: Bantam, 1983.

Child, John. *Unequal Alliance: The Inter-American Military System, 1938–1978.* Boulder, CO: Westview Press, 1980.

Christian, Shirley. *Nicaragua: Revolution in the Family.* New York: Random House, 1985.

Coleman, Kenneth M., and George C. Herring, eds. *The Central American Crisis.* Wilmington, DE: Scholarly Resources, 1985.

Collier, David, ed. *The New Authoritarianism in Latin America*. Princeton, NJ: Princeton University Press, 1979.

Committee of Santa Fe. *A New Inter-American Policy for the 1980s*. Washington, DC: Council for Inter-American Security, 1980.

Deibel, Terry, and John Lewis Gaddis, eds. *Containment: Concept and Policy*. Washington, DC: National Defense University Press, 1986.

Department of State. *Democracy in Latin America: The Promise and the Challenge*. Washington, DC: Bureau of Public Affairs, Dept. of State, Special Report #158, 1987.

Diamond, Larry, Seymour M. Lipset, and Juan Linz, eds. *Democracy in Developing Countries*. Boulder, CO: Lynne Rienner, 1990.

Domínguez, Jorge, and Rafael Hernández, eds. *U.S.-Cuban Relations in the 1990s*. Boulder, CO: Westview Press, 1989.

Durán, Esperanza. *European Interests in Latin America*. London: Routledge and Kegan Paul, 1985.

Erisman, H. Michael, and John D. Martz, eds. *Colossus Challenged: The Struggle for Caribbean Influence*. Boulder, CO: Westview Press, 1982.

Falcoff, Mark. *Small Countries, Big Issues*. Washington, DC: American Enterprise Institute for Public Policy Research, 1984.

Falcoff, Mark, and Robert Royal, eds. *Crisis and Opportunity: U.S. Policy in Central America and the Caribbean*. Washington, DC: Ethics and Public Policy Center, 1984.

Fauriol, Georges, ed. *Security in the Americas*. Washington, DC: National Defense University Press, 1989.

Feinberg, Richard E., ed. *Central America: International Dimensions of the Crisis*. New York: Holmes and Meier, 1982.

Garfinkle, Adam, and Daniel Pipes, eds. *Friendly Tyrants*. New York: St. Martin's Press, 1991.

Grabendorff, Wolf, and Heinrich Krumweide, eds. *Political Change in Central America: Internal and External Dimensions*. Boulder, CO: Westview Press, 1983.

Grabendorff, Wolf, and Riordan Roett, eds. *Latin America, Western Europe, and the United States: Reevaluating the Atlantic Triangle*. New York: Praeger, 1985.

Greene, James R., and Brent Scowcroft, eds. *Western Interests and U.S. Policy Options in the Caribbean Basin*. Boston: Oelgeschlager, Gunn, and Hain, 1984.

Gutman, Roy. *Banana Diplomacy: The Making of American Policy in Nicaragua, 1981–1987*. New York: Simon and Schuster, 1988.

Haig, Alexander. *Caveat: Realism, Reagan, and Foreign Policy*. New York: Macmillan, 1984.

Hayes, Margaret Daly. *Latin America and the U.S. National Interest: A Basis for U.S. Foreign Policy*. Boulder, CO: Westview Press, 1984.

Hodges, Donald. *Intellectual Foundations of the Nicaraguan Revolution*. Austin: University of Texas Press, 1986.

Inter-American Dialogue. *The Americas in a New World*. Queenstown, MD: Aspen Institute, 1990.

Jacoby, Tamar. "The Reagan Turnaround on Human Rights." *Foreign Affairs* (Summer 1986): 1066–86.

Kanet, Roger, and Edward Kolodziej, eds. *The Cold War as Cooperation*. Baltimore, MD: Johns Hopkins University Press, 1991.

Kirkpatrick, Jeane J. "Dictatorship and Double Standards." *Commentary* 68 (November 1979): 34–45.

Kolodziej, Edward J., and Roger Kanet, eds. *The Limits of Soviet Power in the Developing World*. New York: Macmillan, 1989.

Kryzanek, Michael J. *U.S.–Latin American Relations*. New York: Praeger, 1990.

Kymlicka, B. B., and Jean V. Matthews. *The Reagan Revolution*. Chicago: Dorsey, 1988.

LaFeber, Walter. *Inevitable Revolutions*. New York: Norton, 1984.

Lake, Anthony. *Somoza Falling: A Case Study in the Making of U.S. Foreign Policy*. Boston: Houghton Mifflin, 1989.

Langley, Lester. *Central America: The Real Stakes*. Chicago: Dorsey, 1985.

Leiken, Robert S., and Barry Rubin. *Central America Crisis Reader*. New York: Summit, 1987.

Leiken, Robert S., ed. *Central America: Anatomy of Conflict*. New York: Pergamon, 1984.

Lincoln, Jennie K., and Elizabeth G. Ferris, eds. *The Dynamics of Latin American Foreign Policies: Challenge for the 1980s*. Boulder, CO: Westview Press, 1984.

Lowenthal, Abraham F. *Partners in Conflict: The United States and Latin America*. Baltimore, MD: Johns Hopkins University Press, 1987.

———. "The United States and Latin America: Ending the Hegemonic Presumption." *Foreign Affairs* 55 (October 1976): 199–213.

Lowenthal, Abraham F., ed. *Exporting Democracy: The United States and Latin America*. Baltimore, MD: Johns Hopkins University Press, 1991.

Martz, John, ed. *United States Policy in Latin America: A Quarter-Century of Crisis and Challenge*. Lincoln: University of Nebraska Press, 1988.

Menges, Constantine C. *Inside the National Security Council*. New York: Simon and Schuster, 1988.

Middlebrook, Kevin, and Carlos Rico, eds. *The United States and Latin America in the 1980s*. Pittsburgh, PA: University of Pittsburgh Press, 1986.

Millett, Richard. *Guardians of the Dynasty: A History of the U.S.–Created Guardia Nacional de Nicaragua and the Somoza Family*. Maryknoll, NY: Maryknoll Press, 1977.

Molineau, Harold. *U.S. Policy toward Latin America*. Boulder, CO: Westview Press, 1986.

Montgomery, Tommie Sue. *Revolution in El Salvador: Origins and Evolution*. Boulder, CO: Westview Press, 1984.

Moreno, Dario. *U.S. Policy in Central America: The Endless Debate*. Miami: Florida International University Press, 1990.

Muravchik, Joshua. *The Uncertain Crusade: Jimmy Carter and the Dilemmas of Human Rights Policy.* Lanham, MD: Hamilton Press, 1986.

Newfarmer, Richard, ed. *From Gunboats to Diplomacy: New U.S. Policies for Latin America.* Baltimore, MD: Johns Hopkins University Press, 1984.

Nuccio, Richard A. *What's Wrong, Who's Right in Central America?* New York: Facts on File, 1986.

O'Donnell, Guillermo. *Modernization and Bureaucratic Authoritarianism.* Berkeley: Institute for International Studies, University of California, 1973.

O'Donnell, Guillermo, Philippe Schmitter, and Laurence Whitehead, eds. *Transitions from Authoritarian Rule.* Baltimore, MD: John Hopkins University Press, 1987.

Oye, Kenneth A., Robert J. Lieber, and Donald Rothchild, eds. *Eagle Resurgent: The Reagan Era in American Foreign Policy.* Boston: Little Brown, 1987.

Pastor, Robert. *Condemned to Repetition: The United States and Nicaragua.* Princeton, NJ: Princeton University Press, 1987.

Pierre, Andrew J., ed. *Central America as a European-American Issue.* New York: Council on Foreign Relations, 1985.

Poitras, Guy. *The Ordeal of Hegemony: The United States and Latin America.* Boulder, CO: Westview Press, 1990.

Report of the National Bipartisan Commission on Central America. New York: Macmillan, 1984.

Riding, Alan. *Distant Neighbors: A Portrait of the Mexicans.* New York: Knopf, 1985.

Ronfeldt, David. *Geopolitics, Security, and U.S. Strategy in the Caribbean Basin.* Santa Monica, CA: RAND Corporation, 1983.

Saunders, John, ed. *Population Growth in Latin America and U.S. National Security.* Boston: Allen and Unwin, 1986.

Scheman, L. Ronald, ed. *The Alliance for Progress: A Retrospective.* New York: Praeger, 1988.

Schulz, Donald E., and Douglas H. Graham, eds. *Revolution and Counterrevolution in Central America and the Caribbean.* Boulder, CO: Westview Press, 1984.

Smith, Hedrick. *The Power Game: How Washington Works.* New York: Random, 1988.

Stepan, Alfred. *Rethinking Military Politics.* Princeton, NJ: Princeton University Press, 1988.

Stockman, David. *The Triumph of Politics: The Inside Story of the Reagan Revolution.* New York: Harper and Row, 1986.

Ungar, Sanford J., ed. *Estrangement: America and the World.* New York: Oxford University Press, 1985.

Valenta, Jiri, and Frank Cibulka, eds. *Gorbachev's New Thinking and Third World Conflicts.* New Brunswick, NJ: Transaction Press, 1990.

Valenta, Jiri, and Experanza Duran, eds. *Conflict in Nicaragua: A Multidimensional Perspective.* Boston: Allen and Unwin, 1987.

Valenta, Jiri, and Herbert J. Ellison, eds. *Grenada and Soviet/Cuban Policy.* Boulder, CO: Westview Press, 1986.

Vance, Cyrus. *Hard Choices: Critical Years in American Foreign Policy.* New York: Simon and Schuster, 1983.

Walker, Thomas. *Nicaragua in Revolution.* New York: Praeger, 1981.

Wesson, Robert. *U.S. Influence in Latin America in the 1980s.* New York: Praeger, 1982.

Wesson, Robert, ed. *Communism in Central America and the Caribbean.* Stanford, CA: Hoover Institution, 1982.

———, ed. *Coping with the Latin American Debt.* New York: Praeger, 1988.

Wiarda, Howard J. *Corporatism and National Development in Latin America.* Boulder, CO: Westview Press, 1981.

———. *The Democratic Revolution in Latin America: History, Politics, and U.S. Policy.* New York: A Twentieth-Century Fund Book, Holmes and Meier, 1990.

———. *Ethnocentrism in Foreign Policy: Can We Understand the Third World?* Washington, DC: American Enterprise Institute for Public Policy Research, 1985.

———. *Finding Our Way: Toward Maturity in U.S.–Latin American Relations.* Washington, DC: University Press of America, 1987.

———. *Foreign Policy without Illusion: How Foreign Policy Works and Fails to Work in the United States.* New York: Scott Foresman/Harper Collins, 1990.

———. *Latin America at the Crossroads: Debt, Development, and the Future.* Boulder, CO: Westview Press, 1987.

———. *On the Agenda: Current Issues and Conflicts in U.S. Foreign Policy.* New York: Scott Foresman/Harper Collins, 1990.

———. *In Search of Policy: The United States and Latin America.* Washington, DC: American Enterprise Institute for Public Policy Research, 1984.

Wiarda, Howard J. ed. *The Crisis in Latin America.* Washington, DC: American Enterprise Institute for Public Policy Research, 1984.

———, ed. *Human Rights and U.S. Human Rights Policy.* Washington, DC: American Enterprise Institute for Public Policy Research, 1982.

———, ed. *The Iberian–Latin American Connection: Implications for U.S. Policy.* Boulder, CO: Westview Press, 1986.

———, ed. *Rift and Revolution: The Central American Imbroglio.* Washington, DC: American Enterprise Institute for Public Policy Research, 1982.

Wiarda, Howard J., and Mark Falcoff, eds. *The Communist Challenge in the Caribbean and Central America.* Washington, DC: American Enterprise Institute for Public Policy Research, 1987.

Wiarda, Howard J., and Harvey F. Kline, eds. *Latin American Politics and Development.* 3d ed. Boulder, CO: Westview Press, 1990.

Index